THE FATHERS
OF THE CHURCH

A NEW TRANSLATION

 VOLUME 108

THE FATHERS OF THE CHURCH

A NEW TRANSLATION

THEODORE OF MOPSUESTIA

COMMENTARY ON THE TWELVE PROPHETS

Translated by

ROBERT C. HILL
Australian Catholic University

THE CATHOLIC UNIVERSITY OF AMERICA PRESS
Washington, D.C.

Copyright © 2004
THE CATHOLIC UNIVERSITY OF AMERICA PRESS
All rights reserved
Printed in the United States of America

The paper used in this publication meets the minimum requirements of the
American National Standards for Information Science—Permanence of Paper
for Printed Library Materials, ANSI z39.48 - 1984.

LIBRARY OF CONGRESS CATALOGING-IN-PUBLICATION DATA
Theodore, Bishop of Mopsuestia, ca. 350–428 or 9.
[Commentary on the twelve minor prophets. English]
Commentary on the twelve prophets/ Theodore of Mopsuestia ; translated
by Robert C. Hill.
    p. cm. — (The fathers of the church ; v. 108)
Includes bibliographical references (p.   ) and indexes.
ISBN 0-8132-0108-X (pbk.)
    1. Bible. O.T. Minor Prophets—Commentaries. I. Hill, Robert C. (Robert
Charles), 1931– II. Title. III. Series.
    BR60.F3 T47
    [BS1560]
    270 s—dc21
    [224/.9
                    2003012928

To Robert Julian McDonald, AO,
of the Congregation of Christian Brothers,
Chancellor of the
Australian Catholic University

The righteous live by their faith (Hab 2:4)

CONTENTS

ABBREVIATIONS

Aug *Augustinianum*

Bib *Biblica*

CCG Corpus Christianorum Graecorum, Turnhout: Brepols

CCL Corpus Christianorum Latinorum, Turnhout: Brepols

CPG Clavis Patrum Graecorum III, ed. M. Geerard. Turnhout: Brepols, 1979

DS *Enchiridion Symbolorum, Definitionum et Declarationum*, 34th ed., edd. H. Denzinger, A. Schönmetzer. Freiburg: Herder, 1967

ETL *Ephemerides Theologicae Lovanienses*. Louvain: Peeters

FOTC Fathers of the Church, Washington DC: The Catholic University of America Press

GCS Die griechischen christlichen Schriftsteller (der ersten drei Jahrhunderte). Leipzig: J. C. Hinrichs, 1897–1949; Berlin: Akademie-Verlag, 1953–

GO Göttinger Orientforschungen, Wiesbaden: Otto Harrassowtiz

HeyJ *The Heythrop Journal*

ITQ *Irish Theological Quarterly*

JECS *Journal of Early Christian Studies*

LXX Septuagint

NJBC *New Jerome Biblical Commentary*, edd. R. E. Brown et al. Englewood Cliffs, NJ: Prentice Hall, 1990

NT New Testament

OCA Orientalia Christiana Analecta, Rome: Pontifical Oriental Institute

OT Old Testament

PG Patrologia Graeca, ed. J.-P. Migne, Paris, 1857–66

PL Patrologia Latina, ed. J.-P. Migne, Paris, 1878–90

RB	*Revue Biblique*
SC	Sources Chrétiennes, Paris: Du Cerf
StudP	*Studia Patristica*
TRE	*Theologische Realenzyklopädie*, Berlin: Walter de Gruyter
VTS	*Vetus Testamentum*, Supplement

SELECT BIBLIOGRAPHY

Barthélemy, D. *Les Devanciers d'Aquila*. *VTS* X. Leiden: Brill, 1963.

Bouyer, L. *The Spirituality of the New Testament and the Fathers*. Trans. M. Ryan. London: Burns & Oates, 1963.

Bruns, P. "Theodor von Mopsuestia." *TRE* 33:240–46.

Devreesse, R. *Le commentaire de Théodore de Mopsueste sur les psaumes (I–LXXX)*. Studi e Testi 93. Roma: Bibliotheca Apostolica Vaticana, 1939.

———. *Essai sur Théodore de Mopsueste*. Studi e Testi 141. Roma: Bibliotheca Apostolica Vaticana, 1948.

Drewery, B. "Antiochien." *TRE* 3:103–13.

Fernández Marcos, N. "Some reflections on the Antiochian text of the Septuagint." In *Studien zur Septuagint—Robert Hanhart zu Ehren*, 219–29. Göttingen: Vandenhoeck & Ruprecht, 1990.

———. *Scribes and Translators. Septuagint and Old Latin in the Books of Kings*. *VTS* LIV. Leiden: Brill, 1994.

———. *The Septuagint in Context: Introduction to the Greek Versions of the Bible*. Trans. W. Watson. Leiden: Brill, 2001.

Greer, R. A. *Theodore of Mopsuestia. Exegete and Theologian*. London: The Faith Press, 1961.

Greer, R. A. and J. L. Kugel, *Early Biblical Interpretation*. Library of Early Christianity. Philadelphia: Westminster, 1986.

Guinot, J.-N. "L'importance de la dette de Théodoret de Cyr à l'égard de l'exégèse de Théodore de Mopsueste," *Orpheus* 5 (1984): 68–109.

———. "La cristallisation d'un différend: Zorobabel dans l'exégèse de Théodore de Mopsueste et de Théodoret de Cyr." *Aug* 24 (1984): 527–47.

Hill, R. C. "*Akribeia:* a principle of Chrysostom's exegesis." *Colloquium* 14 (Oct. 1981): 32–36.

———. "Psalm 45: a *locus classicus* for patristic thinking on biblical inspiration." *StudP* 25 (1993): 95–100.

———. *St John Chrysostom. Commentary on the Psalms*. Brookline, MA: Holy Cross Orthodox Press, 1998.

———. *Theodoret of Cyrus. Commentary on the Psalms*. FOTC 101–2. 2000-1.

———. "Theodoret wrestling with Romans." *StudP* 34 (2001): 347–52.

———. "Theodore of Mopsuestia, interpreter of the prophets." *Sacris Eruditi* 40 (2001): 107–29.

———. "*Orientale Lumen:* Western biblical scholarship's unacknowledged debt." In *Orientale Lumen Australasia-Oceania 2000. Proceedings,* ed. L. Cross, 157–72. Melbourne: Australian Catholic University, 2001.

———. "*Sartor resartus:* Theodore under review by Theodoret." *Aug* 41 (2001): 465–76.

———. "Jonah in Antioch." *Pacifica* 14 (2001): 245–61.

———. "His Master's Voice: Theodore of Mopsuestia on the Psalms." *HeyJ* 45 (2004): 40–53.

Jellicoe, S. *The Septuagint and Modern Study.* Oxford: Clarendon, 1968.

Kahle, P. E. *The Cairo Genizah.* 2d ed., Oxford: Blackwell, 1959.

Kalantzis, G. "*Duo Filii* and the *Homo Assumptus* in the Christology of Theodore of Mopsuestia." *ETL* 78 (2002): 57–78.

Kelly, J. N. D. *Early Christian Doctrines.* 5th ed., New York: Harper & Row, 1978.

McNamara, K. "Theodore of Mopsuestia and the Nestorian heresy." *ITQ* 19 (1952): 254–78; 20 (1953): 172–91.

Nassif, B. "'Spiritual Exegesis' in the School of Antioch." In *New Perspectives in Biblical Theology,* ed. B. Nassif. Grand Rapids: Eerdmans, 1996.

Norris, R. A. *Manhood and Christ. A Study in the Christology of Theodore of Mopsuestia.* Oxford: Clarendon, 1963.

O'Keefe, J. J. "'A letter that killeth': Toward a reassessment of Antiochene exegesis, or Diodore, Theodore, and Theodoret on the Psalms." *JECS* 8 (2000): 83–104.

Pirot, L. *L'Oeuvre exégètique de Théodore de Mopsueste.* Roma: Pontificio Istituto Biblico, 1913.

Quasten, J. *Patrology* III. Westminster MD: Newman, 1960.

Schäublin, C. *Untersuchungen zu Methode und Herkunft der Antiochenischen Exegese.* Theophaneia: Beiträge zur Religions- und Kirchengeschichte des Altertums 23. Köln-Bonn: Peter Hanstein, 1974.

———. "Diodor von Tarsus." *TRE* 8:763–67.

Smith, R. L. *Micah–Malachi.* Word Biblical Commentary 32. Waco, TX: Word Books, 1984.

Sprenger, H. N. *Theodori Mopsuesteni Commentarius in XII Prophetas.* GO. Biblica et Patristica 1. 1977.

Stuart, D. *Hosea–Jonah,* Word Biblical Commentary 31. Waco, TX: Word Books, 1987.

Sullivan, F. A. *The Christology of Theodore of Mopsuestia.* Analecta Gregoriana 82. Roma: Gregorianum, 1956.

Ternant, Paul. "La θεωρία d'Antioche dans le cadre de sens de l'Écriture." *Bib* 34 (1953): 135–58, 354–83, 456–86.

Vaccari, A. "La θεωρία nella scuola esegetica di Antiochia." *Bib* 1 (1920): 3–36.

Vosté, J. M. "La chronologie de l'activité littéraire de Théodore de Mopsueste." *RB* 34 (1925): 54–81.

Wallace-Hadrill, D. S. *Christian Antioch. A Study of Early Christian Thought in the East.* Cambridge: Cambridge University Press, 1982.

Weitzman, M. P. *The Syriac Version of the Old Testament.* Cambridge: Cambridge University Press, 1999.

Wiles, M. F. "Theodore of Mopsuestia as a representative of the Antiochene school." In *The Cambridge History of the Bible* I, ed. P. R. Ackroyd and C. F. Evans. Cambridge: Cambridge University Press, 1970.

Young, F. M. *Biblical Exegesis and the Formation of Christian Culture.* Cambridge: Cambridge University Press, 1996.

Zaharopoulos, D. Z. *Theodore of Mopsuestia on the Bible. A Study of his Old Testament Exegesis.* New York: Paulist Press, 1989.

Zeigler, J. *Duodecim Prophetae.* Septuaginta 13. Göttingen: Vandenhoeck & Ruprecht, 1943.

INTRODUCTION

INTRODUCTION

1. Theodore, his life and works[1]

Theodore was born in Antioch about 350, brother of Poly-chronius, later bishop of Apamea, and biblical exegete. Along with his friends John (later, priest in Antioch and then bishop in Constantinople) and Maximus (later, bishop of Seleucia), he was a pupil of the noted sophist Libanius in philosophy and rhetoric. John persuaded both young men to join him in the school of spirituality, or ἀσκητήριον, under the direction of Diodore (later, bishop of Tarsus in Cilicia), who could arguably also be styled the founder of the Antiochene method of biblical exegesis.[2] The influence of that "wise father of ours" Theodore would repay in his own works with that sincerest form of flattery, imitation. After a brief return to the world, and summoned back by John's letter *Ad Theodorum lapsum*,[3] Theodore so gave himself to defense of the faith as to become celebrated

1. See Peter Bruns, "Theodor von Mopsuestia," 240–46; Robert Devreesse, *Essai sur Théodore de Mopsueste*, 1–53. The early Church historians who give an account of Theodore's life and work include Socrates, *Church History* 6.3 (PG 67.665–68), Sozomen, *Church History* 8.2 (PG 67.1516; GCS 50.351), and Theodoret of Cyrus, *Church History* 5.40 (PG 82.1277; GCS 5.347–48).

2. While Jean-Marie Olivier, *Diodori Tarsensis commentarii in Psalmos 1, Commentarii in Psalmos I–L*, CCG 6, ciii, awards the title "l'initiateur" of the method to Lucian, translator-priest-martyr of Antioch, for him it is Diodore who ranks as "le véritable fondateur." We may perhaps speak also of a "school" of Antioch in the sense of a fellowship of like-minded scholars joined by birth, geography, and scholarly principles, with some members exercising a magisterial role in regard to others. To this limited sense Johannes Quasten, *Patrology* 3:21–23, adds "a local habitation and a name," in the poet's words, by speaking of "the school of Antioch founded by Lucian" in opposition to the "school of Caesarea," Origen's refuge after his exile from Egypt.

3. The compliment to Diodore, that "wise father of ours," is John Chrysostom's in his *Laus Diodori* (PG 52.764). Devreesse, *Essai*, 3, argues on the basis of

1

as "a teacher of the whole Church in battle against every hereti-
cal column," especially those led by Arius, Eunomius, and Apollinaris,[4] and be appointed bishop of Mopsuestia in Cilicia,
where he died in 428.

The date is significant, not just for conclusion of forty-five
years of Theodore's own episcopate, but also for the accession
to the see of Constantinople by Nestorius, for whose formation
and controversial Christological teachings Theodore and Diodore were later held responsible.[5] As a result, all Theodore's
writings his enemies managed to have condemned at the fifth
general council held in Constantinople in 553[6] (though earlier
councils, in Ephesus in 431 and in Chalcedon in 451, had not
so resolved), and only his *Commentary on the Twelve Prophets* sur-
vives in its entirety in Greek, the bulk of his works perishing in
the consequent flames of prejudice. Yet when he died in his
late seventies, he had spent about sixty years at the task of commenting on the Old and New Testaments,[7] which later earned
him the sobriquet *Mephasqana*, "The Interpreter," from the Syrian church (as his friend John likewise earned posthumous
recognition as the golden-mouthed preacher).[8] On the length
of this exegetical career we have the evidence of one who
helped ensure that little of his work of biblical interpretation
would survive, namely, Leontius of Constantinople, who with

Sozomen's evidence for his classmate Theodore as the addressee of John's letter
(PG 47.277–316).

4. The complimentary reference to Theodore's work against heretics comes
from Theodoret, *Church History* 5.40 (PG 82.1277; GCS 5.348).

5. By Cyril of Alexandria, for example, in his *Contra Diodorum et Theodorum*
(PG 76.1437–52).

6. See DS 425–26, 433–37.

7. Commentary rather than exegesis is the term better applied to the work
of Theodore and his peers on the Bible—a reminder given us by Chrysostom's
biographer, John N. D. Kelly: "Neither John, nor any Christian teacher for centuries to come, was properly equipped to carry out exegesis as we have come to
understand it. He could not be expected to understand the nature of Old Testament writings" (*Golden Mouth. The Story of John Chrysostom, Ascetic, Preacher, Bishop*
[Ithaca, NY: Cornell University Press, 1995], 94).

8. Theodore's title appears in a text of a synod of the Eastern Syriac church-
es in 596 cited from J. B. Chabot, *Synodicon Orientale*, by Alphonse Mingana, *The
Commentary of Theodore of Mopsuestia on the Nicene Creed* (Woodbrooke Studies 5;
Cambridge: W. Heffer & Sons, 1932), 459.

undisguised malevolence relays to us a report that "the fellow was no more than eighteen when he took to subjecting the divine Scriptures to drunken abuse"[9]—an uncouth remark that reflects the spectrum of opinion, from adulation to opprobrium, regarding the bishop of Mopsuestia a century after his death.

Fortunately, a full account of Theodore's exegetical output was retained by his supporters, Syriac-speaking in particular, the Christians of eastern Syria adopting his literary heritage and preserving some works in their language,[10] including a *Commentary on the Gospel of John*, recently discovered; considering his unsympathetic remarks on Syriac scholars in the *Commentary on the Twelve Prophets*, there is an irony in this kindness. The Syriac documents list commentaries by Theodore on a wide range of other Old Testament books, including the major Prophets and the Psalms,[11] the latter work having been reconstituted in part in recent years; as seems to have been traditional,[12] the Psalter was the first biblical text on which he comment-

9. *Contra Nestor. et Eutych.* 8 (PG 86.1364). Marie-Josèphe Rondeau, *Les commentaires patristiques du Psautier (IIIe–Ve siècles)*, I. *Les travaux des pères grecs et latins sur le Psautier. Recherches et bilan*, OCA 219 (Roma: Pont. Inst. Stud. Orient., 1982), 102–3, believes that this remark is only "une exagération malveillante," ("a malicious exaggeration") and that the work reveals rather the hand of "un jeune savant audacieux" ("a bold young scholar").

10. For the Syriac catalogues, see Ebedjesus, *Catalogue des livres ecclésiastiques syriens*, in *Bibliotheca Orientalis* III, ed. J. S. Assemani (Rome: Typis S. C. de Propaganda Fide, 1926), 30–35.

11. That Theodore composed a commentary on the major prophets has been denied, largely on the grounds of silence by Greek and conciliar sources, by J. M. Vosté, "La chronologie de l'activité littéraire de Théodore de Mopsueste," 69–70. For the reconstituted text of the major portion of his *Commentary on the Psalms*, see R. Devreesse, *Le commentaire de Théodore de Mopsueste sur les psaumes (I–LXXX)*, Devreesse admitting of the text after Ps 81 that, "passé cet endroit, je n'ai rien retenu qui puisse être, en toute sécurité, attribué à Théodore de Mopsueste" (xxx).

12. Theodoret will say more than once in opening his *Commentary on the Psalms*, delayed because of popular demand for prior works on the Song of Songs, Daniel, Ezekiel, and the Twelve, that "I wanted to do a commentary on this piece of inspired composition first of all." For evidence of immaturity in the text of Chrysostom's Psalms homilies (incomplete and lacking a preface), see the introduction to my *St. John Chrysostom. Commentary on the Psalms* I, 4–5. For the *Commentary on the Psalms* being Theodore's first we have the word of Facundus of Hermianae, *Pro defensione trium capitulorum* 3.6 (PL 67.602).

ed. The internal evidence of the *Commentary on the Twelve Prophets* is that it immediately followed the Psalms; though he begins the work somewhat censoriously (an attitude that would irk Leontius all those years later) "as an indictment of those who presume to apply themselves to the prophetic utterances without due preparation," thus implying he himself comes to the task well prepared,[13] the overwhelming impression in a reader is that the part of the Scriptures he is especially, if not exclusively, familiar with is the Psalter. A further sign of Theodore's immaturity in the work is the intemperate language he frequently uses of his anonymous predecessors, probably in the main from Alexandria, like Origen[14] and Didymus,[15] a feature that also later riled Leontius: "In all his misinterpretation of the divine Scriptures that coarse fellow never ceased mocking and jeering at the efforts of the holy teachers who have worked on them."[16] We shall have to ask, therefore, why this piece of juvenilia in particular survived the flames and the heat of prejudice, unfamiliar as it has been to all later commentators and only now appearing in English.

2. *The text of the* Commentary; *Theodore's biblical text*

As good luck would have it, then, we do not have to depend on the Syriac church for survival in translation of this early work of Theodore's. It has come to us in direct tradition in manuscripts preserved in the Vatican library, on which no doubts are held of authenticity, and in particular ms Vat.gr.2204 of the tenth century;[17] it was edited by Cardinal Angelo Mai in 1832

13. Theodoret, the only other Antiochene to leave us a commentary on the Twelve, begins his work with an acknowledgement of indebtedness to his anonymous predecessors (including, doubtless, Theodore) and a typically modest claim to making some little contribution of his own (PG 81.1545–58). He was, however, no youngster when he did the work.

14. Eusebius of Caesarea, *Church History* 6.32.2 (SC 41.138–39), speaks of Origen's books on the Twelve, "of which we found only twenty-five."

15. See Didymus's *Commentary on Zechariah*: L. Doutreleau, *Didyme L'Aveugle. Sur Zacharie*, SC 83–85 (1962).

16. *Contra Nestor. et Eutych.* 11 (PG 86.1364).

17. See M. Geerard, CPG 3834.

with a lengthy preface, recast in 1854, and this text with both prefaces appears in cols. 124–632 of vol. 66 of Jean-Paul Migne's *Patrologia Graeca*. We also have a more recent critical edition from Hans Norbert Sprenger to help us assess the rather superlative claims that have been made for the Interpreter's exegetical skills.[18] Sprenger's text, followed here, and the relative brevity of his critical apparatus confirm the esteem accorded ms Vat.gr.2204 by Mai and Geerard.

Being unable and unlikely to access the Hebrew text of the Twelve, as we shall see, Theodore had available to him the local form of the Greek version in the Septuagint (if we are not to follow Paul Kahle in confining that term to a subsequent Alexandrian version).[19] Whatever be the origins of that Antioch text—whether a revision of an original translation accounted for in legendary fashion in the *Letter of Aristeas* or an independent version originating in Antioch—we can accept the terminology Antiochene or "Lucianic" employed both by modern scholars of the LXX and by Jerome, a contemporary of Theodore, who spoke of three forms of the LXX current in Alexandria, Constantinople-Antioch, and "the provinces in between," respectively, the second being "another version which Origen and Eusebius of Caesarea and all the Greek commentators call the popular text, and which by most is now called the Lucianic text,"[20] that is, a revision by the scholar priest Lucian of Antioch a century before, or (less likely) a version by him.[21] Theodore, who clearly accepted not only the legendary *Letter of*

18. *Theodori Mopsuesteni Commentarius in XII Prophetas.* Sprenger also includes some few Syriac fragments of Hosea, Joel, and Amos (432–53).

19. P. Kahle, *The Cairo Genizah*, 257, holds for a Greek translation made in Antioch, later revised by Lucian, that was "probably written before the text came into existence which we normally call the 'Septuagint,'" which was "fixed towards the end of the second century BC in Alexandria" (236). N. Fernández Marcos, *The Septuagint in Context*, does not accept Kahle's view of a process of translation occurring in the case of the LXX like that of the Aramaic Targums (57), though he does speak of the LXX as a "collection of translations" (ix, 23).

20. *Praef. in Paral.* (PL 28.1324–25), *Ep.* 106.2 (PL 22.838). The term "Lucianic" is acceptable to B. Drewery, "Antiochien," 106, and S. P. Brock, "Bibelübersetzungen I, 2," *TRE* 6:166–67. D. Barthélemy, *Les Devanciers d'Aquila*, 126–27, prefers "texte antiochien." Fernández Marcos speaks interchangeably of Lucian, Lucianic, and Antiochian recension.

21. S. Jellicoe, *The Septuagint and Modern Study*, 160–61, thinks there are no

Aristeas but also the current belief that the work of the Seventy translators of the third century BC included not just the Torah but the whole of the Hebrew Bible, had—perforce—great respect for the available LXX text, and—perforce—could not allow it to be seen in a bad light by comparison particularly with another version like the Peshitta. If he finds his predecessors citing this Syriac version of the prophets, which was in circulation and had attained authoritative status by about 170,[22] on first principles (an *a posteriori* approach beyond him) he spurns its claims by comparison with the esteem in which the LXX was held.

When, for instance, his text of Zep 1.5 reads "Milcom" (for "their king" of other forms of the LXX, as it happens), for which his predecessors with a knowledge of Syriac suggested that "king" is intended, Theodore lectures them on *a priori* grounds that they have no case.

They ought to realize this before everything else, that whereas the contents of the divine Scripture are composed in Hebrew, they were translated into Syriac by somebody or other (his identity is unknown to this day). The translation into Greek, on the other hand, was done by seventy men, elders of the people, possessing a precise knowledge of their own language and a knowledge of the divine Scriptures, approved of by the priest and all the Israelite people as particularly suited to translating. Their translation and publication the blessed apostles clearly seem to have accepted, and to the believers from the nations who formerly had no access at all to the contents of the Old Testament they passed on the divine Scriptures written in Greek in the translation of the Seventy. All of us, having come to faith in Christ the Lord from the nations, received the Scriptures from them and now enjoy them, reading them aloud in the churches and keeping them at home.

Theodore, necessarily committed to the high standing of the LXX, thus feels no need of further textual resources; unlike his earlier work on the Psalms, in this commentary he forfeits the opportunity to consult those other ancient versions associated

grounds for believing Lucian had enough Hebrew to produce an independent translation.

22. See M. P. Weitzman, *The Syriac Version of the Old Testament*, 253.

with the names of Aquila, Symmachus, and Theodotion, available in a copy of the Hexapla; he likewise has no familiarity with the Syriac. His resulting disadvantage compared, say, with his Antiochene successor, Theodoret, emerges in his approach to puzzling phrases in Mi 1.8–9, "lamenting like dragons," "her grief like daughters of sirens." He remarks,

He uses the phrase *like dragons and sirens* in terms of the fables spun by some people, meaning to convey that the accounts given by many people in the form of a fable they will endure in actual fact when the severe affliction is imposed on them by me, beginning with Samaria and traveling as far as Judah and touching on Jerusalem, since Babylonians later took it as well.

When, by contrast, Theodoret meets the phrase "daughters of sirens" in Jer 50.49 and Is 13.21–22, he goes to the trouble of consulting the alternative versions in the Hexapla and the Peshitta to come up with "ostrich" as a variant translation, claims that demons are thus being referred to, and concludes that the effect is one of general devastation.[23] Theodore, whose only response is to rationalize what is before him, shows typical reluctance to background his text.

Though he is unaware of it, the LXX text that Theodore (of necessity) esteems so highly often lands him in difficulties as a commentator because it is reading a form similar to but different from that found in our Hebrew text.[24] The LXX Jonah confides to the sailors in 1.9 that "I am a servant of the Lord," whereas his confession probably arises from reading *'ibdi* for *'ibri*, "I am a Hebrew." When the Lord in Am 1.6 threatens Gaza with punishment for taking into exile "entire communities" to hand them over to Edom, the LXX has him saying, "I shall not shun them because of their taking captive Solomon into captivity," evidently reading *shalma* as "Solomon" instead of "entire (captivity)" and leading Theodore to comment, "I shall no

23. PG 81.745; SC 295.80.
24. The relationship between the Masoretic Hebrew text available to modern scholars and the Hebrew text from which the LXX forms derive is unclear, of course, discouraging a presumption that versions like the LXX represent an inferior text.

longer put up with their committing many godless acts and persisting in their willful depravity; I shall punish them in particular for the fact that, after Solomon took captive the people
from Idumea and put them under the authority of the Israelites so that they remained for a long time in that condition,
the latter attacked, did away with that captivity by the norms of
war, and obliged them to go back again to Idumea."[25] He is, of
course, not to blame for the shortcomings of his version, but
neither is he capable of recognizing them.

As students of the Lucianic recension of the LXX remind us,
we know its nature principally from the text commented on by
the Antiochene Fathers;[26] hence the asset that the commentaries on the Twelve by Theodore and Theodoret constitute for
students of that text. It is therefore of interest to note that
Theodore's local text (in which, incidentally, the Twelve occur
in the order of the Hebrew Bible, not the LXX generally) differs in places from other forms, sometimes departing from
them to agree with our Hebrew, at other times being independent of both. In Hos 9.12b, for instance, Theodore is reading a
subordinate clause, "because I have left them," found in Hebrew but not in other LXX forms, like the phrase in Mi 7.12,
"from sea to sea, from mountain to mountain." In Hos 10.13
Theodore reads, "Because you trusted in your chariots," a plural noun that, while departing from Hebrew and LXX, makes
better sense in the view of editor Mai and modern commentators. Zechariah's vision of several horses of different colors on
different errands in 6.1–8 is inconsistent in Hebrew and Greek,
the Antiochene text making much better sense in matching
"horses" and "errands." And so on. The moral is that modern
commentators need to take account of *all* available ancient testimonies to the biblical text, not only to gather evidence beyond that of the Masoretic Hebrew, which may in places be de-

25. Further instances are noted in the text where they occur.
26. See Fernández Marcos, *Scribes and Translators*, 28: "One of the reasons
for the uncertainty concerning the Lucianic recension (of the Octateuch) was
the lack of critical editions of the Antiochene Fathers"; idem, *The Septuagint in
Context*, 228: "The Lucianic recension has been observed in all the prophetic
books."

ficient and inferior, but also to save themselves from delivering ill-founded comments like those found in Douglas Stuart and Ralph L. Smith—commendable though these particular scholars are for at least acknowledging the relevance of the versions—to the effect that a particular reading is "missing in the LXX."[27] "Septuagint/LXX" is not a univocal term: all its forms need scrutinizing, where available, even if this involves turning up a hoary edition of Theodore or Theodoret or any other ancient commentator.[28]

3. Theodore's approach to Scripture in general

The *Commentary on the Twelve Prophets*,[29] being Theodore's only exegetical work to survive in its entirety in Greek, provides us with a unique opportunity for estimating his skills in working with the biblical text, and for evaluating typically divergent judgments formed in ancient and modern times. For the partial Leontius, we saw, it was "drunken violence" with which he treated the sacred text; by contrast, other ancients entitled him the Interpreter. In our time Johannes Quasten has classed Theodore as "the most typical representative of the Antiochene school of exegesis";[30] he has also been called "the foremost exponent of Antiochene exegesis,"[31] and "not only the most original and radical biblical scholar in the Patristic age, but also in some respects a forerunner of the modern biblical scholar-

27. See Stuart, *Hosea–Jonah*, 362 (on Amos 6.8, 14), Smith, *Micah–Malachi*, 126 (on Zep 1.4), 193 (on Zec 1.18).

28. See my article, "*Orientale Lumen:* Western biblical scholarship's unacknowledged debt." Editions of biblical texts emanating from Göttingen, like Ziegler's, are therefore preferable to a text like that of A. Rahlfs, *Septuaginta*, 7th ed. (Stuttgart: Württembergische Bibelanstalt), 1962, because documenting more fully the Antiochene text.

29. Theodore would probably have been no more familiar with the somewhat pejorative term *prophetae minores* of Augustine, *De civitate Dei* 18.29 (CCL 48.619: "quia sermones eorum sunt breves"), than was Theodoret, who made the point at the beginning of his commentary (PG 81.1548–49) that the Twelve constitute one book for reasons only of length, the term "Twelve Prophets" being current at least since Ben Sira (Sir 49.10).

30. *Patrology* 3:402.

31. F. A. Sullivan, *The Christology of Theodore of Mopsuestia,* 1.

ship."[32] The editor of Theodore's *Commentary on the Psalms* may be pardoned for his endorsement of the accolade: "Théodore, le premier et vraisemblablement le seul des anciens commentateurs, fait intervenir la critique littéraire."[33] Another modern view is that "the Bible is allowed to speak in his commentaries (and in his theology) as it is in those of few, if any, of the patristic exegetes";[34] still another, "Sicher hat die Schule mit den Kommentaren des Bischofs von Mopsuestia ihre ἀκμή erreicht,"[35] and in the volumes of the *Ancient Christian Commentary on Scripture* beginning to appear it is not Diodore but Theodore who is listed as "founder of the Antiochene, or literalistic, school of exegesis."[36] Perhaps it is the fact that this unique work has not been available in a recent critical edition and in modern language translations that leads a reader of it to conclude that both ancient and modern assessments are overstating Theodore's strengths and weaknesses as a biblical commentator and his significance as an Antiochene.

We saw Theodore admitting above that his familiarity with the Old Testament, as in the case of others "who came to faith in Christ the Lord from the nations," depended on hearing the LXX text read aloud in the churches and keeping it at home. Like his friend John, he had benefited from an Antiochene formation in rhetoric from Libanius (and through him from classical rhetoricians) and in biblical science from mentors like Diodore of Tarsus, "his father and leader in vice and impiety," in the jaundiced view of Leontius.[37] He certainly accepted from Diodore rather uncritically that basic Antiochene principle of scriptural interpretation, "We far prefer τὸ ἱστορικόν to τὸ ἀλληγορικόν,"[38] even if Diodore could not impart to him other

32. D. Zaharapoulos, *Theodore of Mopsuestia on the Bible*, 50.

33. "Theodore was the first and arguably the only one of the ancient commentators to employ literary criticism." Devreesse, *Essai*, 58, in reference to Theodore's *Commentary on the Psalms*.

34. R. A. Greer, *Theodore of Mopsuestia*, 111.

35. "Unquestionably, with the Commentary of the Bishop of Mopsuestia the school had reached its zenith." C. Schäublin, *Untersuchungen zu Methode und Herkunft der antiochenischen Exegese*, 171.

36. Thomas F. Oden, ed. (Downers Grove, IL: InterVarsity Press, 2001).

37. *Contra Nestor. et Eutych.* 9 (PG 86.1364).

38. From a fragment of his work on the Octateuch; see Schäublin, "Diodor

skills necessary for conducting exegesis in the strict sense, such as a knowledge of the original languages (a deficiency he shares with his Antiochene peers and almost all the Fathers, of course).[39] As a young scholar he claims a grasp of Hebrew syntax he did not in fact possess (but which some of his commentators have mistakenly conceded);[40] he is not far into work on the Twelve before encountering a confusion of past and future tenses by his Septuagint version in Hosea 9.2, "They did not inhabit the Lord's land," which he corrects to read, "They will not inhabit," on the grounds that the Bible "expresses it as usual with a change in tense . . . as was pointed out on many occasions in blessed David's usage." He wrongly detects the same reversal of tenses in Hos 12.9, "which I sufficiently demonstrated in the case of the Psalms as well."[41] In other ways as well he shows his inability to appreciate the original. When he arrives in Amos 5.26 at the mention of two astral deities that his local text renders as Moloch and Remphan (Raiphan in other LXX forms), he admits his indebtedness to predecessors with more developed Semitic lore:

von Tarsus," 756. Schäublin, *Untersuchungen*, 84, points out that Diodore had not left any precise clarification of this principle: "Freilich, was heist in der Sprache der Antiochener 'historisch'? Ihre erhaltenen Schriften teilen keine Definition des ἱστορικόν mit, und einigen Bemerkungen Diodors vermag man blos eine sehr allgemeine Abgrenzung gegenüber der Allegorese zu entnehmen" ("What in fact did the Antiochenes' 'historical' mean in real terms? Their extant written remains contain no definition of 'historikon,' and any statement by Diodore only allows us to presume a very broad generalization opposing allegory").

39. Jerome is the generally acknowledged exception, owing his familiarity with Hebrew to time spent with a Jewish convert in Chalcis (J. N. D. Kelly, *Jerome. His Life, Writings and Controversies* [London: Duckworth, 1975], 50). Fernández Marcos, *The Septuagint in Context*, 204–6, assembles evidence on the degree of Origen's knowledge of Hebrew, beginning with the affirmative testimony of Eusebius and Jerome.

40. So Devreesse, *Le commentaire*, vi, in supporting his view of Theodore's "uncommon knowledge of the Bible," but without presenting evidence of the kind L. Pirot, *L'Oeuvre exégètique de Théodore de Mopsueste*, 96–100, painstakingly assembles to the opposite conclusion. R. A. Greer, *Theodore of Mopsuestia. Exegete and Theologian*, 100, thinks "Theodore probably knew some Hebrew. . . . He was not so proficient as Jerome." Theodore's editor Angelo Mai is unsure, thinking (on unconvincing grounds) that he did know Syriac (PG 66.121–22).

41. Further evidence of the close relationship of the two commentaries is noted in the text where it occurs.

By *Moloch* he refers to the idol worshiped by them, and by *tent of Moloch* he means, You frequent the idol's shrine and care for it, and you are also involved in worship of a star, giving it the name of a god (commentators claiming that in the language of the Hebrews the morning star is given this name).

As well as attributing confusion in tenses in his text to the Hebrew, and not to its translators, he is forever fastening on examples of synecdoche as illustrative of "Hebrew parlance" rather than general literary expression. When he notes a double focus in the prophecy of Habakkuk, he compares it to the LXX Ps 9, which he is aware appears in Hebrew as two psalms, but unaware that the alphabetic structure in the Hebrew confirms the judgment of the Seventy to maintain it as one piece. And so on.[42]

As an Antiochene commentator, one of his first principles would be expected to be that of ἀκρίβεια, the conviction that precision (not "accuracy," a common mistranslation: Antioch may be often inaccurate, never imprecise) in the biblical text requires a like precision in the commentator and the reader. Not as insistent on this principle as some of his peers,[43] he begins work on Hosea by noting that the names of the prophet's father and of King Jeroboam's are also supplied. He likewise commends Hosea for detailing the items used to pay for his wife; and he appreciates the chronological details supplied by Haggai, though unfortunately infringing "accuracy" by attempting to improve on them. On the other hand, his attachment to ἀκρίβεια can be inconsistent: he will use the term ἀκριβολογία to dismiss the attempts of his predecessors to bring precision to historical or topographical detail in the text, like the location of Tarshish in Jon 1.3, for which some commentators had suggested also Tarsus or Rhodes: "For my part, however, I consider this entire chase after detail to be irrelevant to the subject in hand in so far as the account by the prophet is just as equally beyond question, no matter which city you think it to be." Though such a peremptory attitude may seem to have

42. Further instances are noted in the text where they occur.
43. See my article, "*Akribeia:* a principle of Chrysostom's exegesis."

some merit in a commentator cutting to the chase, it frequently masks an inability or an unwillingness to take the trouble to investigate the background of his text, whether historical, geographical, topographical, and the like, that one appreciates finding in a more committed Antiochene like Theodoret. He cannot be bothered locating the home towns of prophets, like Micah's Moresheth and Nahum's Elkosh, or investigating why it is that Malachi is to transmit a word of the Lord to "Israel" long after the fall of that kingdom. We shall see him desperately trying to root the prophets in historical situations, even when the scenario is thoroughly apocalyptic, and yet impatient of historical detail; τὸ ἱστορικόν is a priority only when it suits.

Despite his reputation for a rationalistic approach to the canonicity of scriptural works that stems from the strictures of Leontius[44] and even of Theodoret (presuming that they are in fact commentaries by Theodore he has in his sights),[45] he has no difficulty conceding the divine inspiration of these prophets. The question of biblical inspiration he had been obliged to address, like many of the Fathers, in commenting on the opening to Ps 45, "My heart belched good news," the LXX verb ἐξερεύγομαι rendering a *hapax legomenon* in the Hebrew text, which the Greeks find an apt term for the irresistible activity of the Holy Spirit. When the psalmist proceeds, "My tongue the pen of a fluent scribe," Theodore comments, "The Spirit, just like a perfect writer, fills, as it were with ink, the human heart with the perceptions of revelation, and from there allows the tongue to speak loud and clear and to formulate the sayings in language and articulate them distinctly for those who are willing to receive the benefit that stems from them."[46] In

---

44. See *Contra Nestor. et Eutych.* 13–16 (PG 86.1366). Leontius claims that Theodore "excised the Song of Songs from the holy books."

45. See Theodoret's introduction to his *Commentary on the Song of Songs* (PG 81.29), taking issue with a predecessor's historical approach to the subject, although the Syriac catalogues do not confirm Theodore's composition of a commentary on the Song. The overly historical approach that Theodoret criticizes in the introduction to his *Commentary on the Psalms* (PG 80.857) is also usually taken to be that of Theodore (and Diodore).

46. See Devreesse, *Le commentaire*, 282. See also my article, "Psalm 45: a *locus classicus* for patristic thinking on biblical inspiration," 98–99.

this he is largely capitalizing on the thinking of his predecessors, especially Eusebius, though making a contribution of his own with the inclusion of the ink in the pen as the perceptions of revelation from the Spirit; and despite the involuntariness suggested by the LXX's "belching" he can perhaps be seen trying to maintain a balance between an instrumental notion of inspiration and Antioch's particular emphasis on authorial activity (Diodore having said on this verse, "I adjust my tongue to the extent possible to the movement of grace").[47]

Interestingly, when he comes to the prophets, with his focus on their historical situation Theodore does not accept an early cue for further comment on biblical and specifically prophetic inspiration even from a verse like Hos 12.10, "I spoke to the prophets, I multiplied visions and took on a likeness at the hands of the prophets." Before he concludes, however, he will admit in connection with the figure of the martyred shepherd of Zec 13.7 that the prophet (the one author being responsible for both chapters 1–8 and 9–14 of that book, in his view, of course) has been in receipt of many visions because "inspired," ἐνθοῦ, by the Spirit. That particular book, with its remarkable ἀποκαλύψεις of horses of many colors on various errands in 1.8–11, had led him with his focus on τὸ ἱστορικόν (already seriously challenged by the "novel and extraordinary things" of the book of Jonah) to account for them—perhaps with a touch of rationalism—as a different charism from other communications.

It is obvious, you see, that the whole revelation, and what was seen in it as well as question, answer, and suchlike, were all products of the imagination in the revelation, the result being that the prophet received instruction from it all, and he both personally gained a firm trust in the future events and also imparted the benefit to others.

---

47. *Commentarii in Psalmos I–L*, 269. Antiochene authors thus supply a necessary corrective to the generalization by Bruce Vawter on patristic thinking on inspiration as "the prevalence of a concept of divine authorship that could lead to a practical forgetting of the claims of human authorship" (*Biblical Inspiration* [London: Hutchinson, 1972], 38).

Where Theodore more markedly parts company with his Antiochene fellows such as Chrysostom, who will so allow for authorial contribution as to see inspired composition of every kind, προφητεία, as akin to the work of "a builder building a house, a shipwright making a ship,"[48] is where the term λῆμμα for "oracle" used at the opening of Nahum (also in Hab.1.1, Zec 9.1, Mal 1.1) he will relate to λαμβάνω to present ecstatic possession as the mode of inspiration for the prophets.

It was by ecstasy, therefore, that in all likelihood they all received the knowledge of things beyond description, since it was possible for them in their minds to be quite removed from their normal condition and thus capable of devoting themselves to the solitary contemplation of what was revealed.

Only in this way, with the prophet-historian reduced on these occasions to the insensate condition of pagan μάντεις, can τὸ ἱστορικόν in biblical composition be preserved, he obviously feels, at the cost of compromising his Antiochene principles.

4. Theodore's style of commentary

We are given no insight into the readers who are intended to benefit from Theodore's commentaries on the Twelve. If this is a work of his youth, as Leontius would have us believe, composed before his being ordained priest in his thirties and appointed bishop a decade later, he has not yet any pastoral responsibilities for a flock; certainly, no sense of such duty emerges from the text. Passages that are susceptible of parenesis and pastoral elaboration, like Hos 10.6 and Mi 6.8, Theodore at his desk passes over to keep the focus on the historical situation, and is never found moralizing in the manner of a preacher in his pulpit. The many celebrated passages in the Twelve on social justice, like Mi 3.1–3 and Zec 7.9–10, he does not develop, warming to the theme only briefly on Am 8.4–6. In Mal 2.13–16 he joins other Fathers in seeing a con-

48. PG 55.184.

demnation of divorce, and in unusual fashion elaborates on
the topic with associated proof texts as though rehearsing a
well-worn theme. His overall purpose is simply that of exposition—"by the grace of God to bring clarity" to the text, as he
says in introducing Haggai; it is a motto Theodoret will echo in
his aim of "leading obscurity to clarity" in the case of the Song
of Songs, and in fact none of his fellow Antiochenes could fault
him for keeping his focus on comprehension.[49]

He adopts the order of the Twelve found in his text, which is
that of the Hebrew Bible, not of the LXX generally. Commentary on some books is prefaced with opening remarks at considerable length,[50] setting out the book's theme, ὑπόθεσις, as in
the case of Amos, Obadiah, Jonah, Nahum, and Habakkuk, the
reason here being particular need of clarification of the historical situation or the nature of the material, like the "novel and
extraordinary things" found in Jonah that worry a commentator committed to adopting an historical interpretation. Each
commentary, and the series, closes without epilogue. These introductions can betray the writer's tendency to be prolix and
repetitive that earned the criticism of Photius of Constantinople in the ninth century, who also thought his style lacking
charm, unpleasing, and short on clarity;[51] and, to be sure, a
translator finds his periods more intractable than, say, Theodoret's. In commenting on the text, he is generally not inclined
to be expansive. We have noted that he is not interested in what
he describes pejoratively as ἀκριβολογία, chasing up details of
an historical, cultural, and geographical nature, though often
the reader could have done with them had the commentator

49. Maurice Wiles, "Theodore of Mopsuestia," 491, quotes his distinction
between the respective roles of exegete and preacher, given in the *Commentary
on the Gospel of John:* "I judge the exegete's task to be to explain words that most
people find difficult; it is the preacher's task to reflect also on words that are
perfectly clear and to speak about them." One would have to say that at this early stage in his career there are times when Theodore is seen shirking that former task.

50. There is no evidence from the mss surveyed in Sprenger's edition of the
Commentary of any general introduction to the work now lost. The preface to
Haggai quoted below also suggests that none such was composed.

51. *Bibliotheca* 38.177 (PG 103.69, 72, 517–18).

been prepared to go to the trouble of providing some background. Predecessors whom he finds providing such a service are faulted for their pains, as Leontius justifiably deplored. When in that remarkably universalist inclusion of Ethiopians, Philistines, and Syrians ("from Bothros" for the Hebrew *Kir*) in the divine *oikonomia* in Am 9.7, Theodore—ignoring the universalism—simply dismisses his peers for endeavoring to achieve precision: "While some commentators claimed the phrase *from Bothros* should be read as what is now called Kara and at one time Haran, I shall pass over this effort at precision on the place hereby indicated as a pointless exercise contributing nothing to the meaning, and treat of the sense in the present case." Likewise, when references to other parts of Scripture (beyond the Psalms) could throw light on a text, the reader is not thus enlightened, as in the case of the background to the antipathy between Israel and Edom mentioned in Am 1.11–12 and infringements of the Torah in 2.7–8.[52]

Though not to the degree evinced by Theodoret, as becomes a student of the renowned rhetorician, Libanius,[53] Theodore is sensitive to the imagery and figurative language of the prophets and to literary genres employed by them, provided these are consistent with prophecy as history; apocalyptic, we shall find, he is unable or unwilling to recognize, even in what Paul Hanson sees as "full-blown" apocalyptic in Deutero-Zechariah.[54] He has a particular eye for synecdoche, which he thinks a distinctively biblical figure, remarking on Hab 3.3, "Here too, note, he uses differentiation to imply commonality, a practice of the divine Scripture that we have illustrated on

---

52. From this work one would have difficulty endorsing the compliment that Devreesse, *Le commentaire*, vi, pays him for his "uncommon knowledge of the Bible."

53. It is the thesis of Schäublin that the approach of the Antiochenes, and of Diodore and Theodore in particular, derives from the grammarians who formed them (though Libanius gains little mention); see *Untersuchungen*, 158: "Theodor sein Rüstzeug als Interpret der paganen Grammatik verdankt" ("Theodore owed his formation as interpreter to pagan rhetoric").

54. P. D. Hanson, *The Dawn of Apocalyptic* (Philadelphia: Fortress, 1975), 369. All the Antiochenes suffer from this failing, which Theodoret's *Commentary on Daniel* illustrates in particular.

many previous occasions: he says that heaven and earth are opened by the excellence of God, implying the totality of things, and that praise of him for his works should be recited by everyone." When Nahum indulges in what modern commentators refer to as a taunt song in 2.11–13, Theodore empathizes with the prophet's satiric purpose and imagery: "*Where has the lion gone to gain entrance?* A very mocking remark: whereas they were ever doing battle and always making an assault on someone somewhere as though on prey of some kind, he asks, Where now has your leader gone? after what prey has he gone? He means, There is an end to your fighting, your former power and might is finished." He is prepared to subject his text to some degree of literary criticism when there is evidence of movement of thought that can lead his modern counterparts to doubt a work's literary integrity, an option not open to him. When Mi 4.1–4 reveals a verbatim identity with Is 2.2–5, which he does not acknowledge (not having composed, at least by that stage, a commentary on Isaiah), he does note the vacillation between gloom and optimism in the prophet, and finds biblical precedent for it.

After mentioning the disasters being inflicted on them to this point, however, he then mentions also what will happen to them after its capture, and the degree of change for the better that will ensue. This custom of the other prophets and blessed David we have often demonstrated, namely, the disclosure of pleasant things after the experience of harsh things and in turn mentioning baleful events in order that through both they might instruct them by the frequency of the disclosure, bringing them to their senses by the mention of baleful things and encouraging them by the brighter to hold fast to hope in God.

He is perceptive enough to note in his introduction to Habakkuk that the prayer in chapter 3 differentiates it from the book's first two chapters.

When Theodore turns to paraphrasing a passage in the text, a rare enough procedure,[55] it can mean he thinks its historical value is minimal, as with the apocalyptic material in the closing

55. Manlio Simonetti, *Biblical Interpretation in the Early Church. An historical in-*

chapters of Zechariah. By contrast and of necessity, rationalizing the meaning is a tactic to which he has frequent recourse (as do his fellow Antiochenes), his LXX text through its flawed transmission of the sense leaving no other option than admission of uncertainty, which this young commentator cannot entertain. When the Hebrew text of Mi 1.14 involves wordplay on the names of Micah's home town Moresheth-gath and Achzib, which escapes the LXX, resulting in a nonsense version, the commentator can only soldier on, he and the reader being none the wiser. Like Theodoret when faced with Pauline theology on the gratuity of divine mercy in Romans, a thesis unacceptable to an Antiochene,[56] Theodore is capable of rewriting his text if a prophet comes up with something of this kind, as the book of Jonah does in the case of Nineveh's prompt response to the prophet. With the LXX having lengthened the odds by allowing only "three days" for repentance instead of "forty" by dittography from the "three days walk" of the previous verse 3.3, the commentator just cannot accept that grace could strike so quickly, and so (at variance with the book's message, which this literalist never grasps) he has to rework the script, accusing the author of being economical with the facts.

The verse, *The men of Nineveh believed in God*, also brings out that he did not carelessly say only, *Three days more, and Nineveh will be destroyed:* they could never have believed in God on the basis of this remark alone, from a completely unknown foreigner threatening them with destruction and adding nothing further, not even letting the listeners know by whom he was sent. Rather, it is obvious he also mentioned God, the Lord of all, and said he had been sent by him; and he delivered the message of destruction, calling them to repentance.

If unsympathetic to the Ninevites, Theodore has been called *Ioudaiophron* for an historical accent that was taken to be typi-

---

troduction to patristic exegesis, Eng. trans. (Edinburgh: Clark, 1994), 69, takes no account of Photius's (justifiable) strictures on Theodore's prolixity in observing of him, "The tendency towards conciseness is such that, on occasion, parts of his commentaries are nothing more than paraphrases of the scriptural text itself." Paraphrase, of course, unlike précis, can be expansive and reach to gilding the lily.

56. See my article, "Theodoret wrestling with Romans," 347–52.

cally Jewish,[57] what Theodoret in an apparent reference to his predecessor's Psalms commentary saw as making "a case rather for Jews than for the household of the faith."[58] Admittedly, his repeated insistence that Zerubbabel (whom he mistakenly takes to be a king, owing to the LXX's misreading of Hg 1.1) has prior and superior claim to fulfilling messianic expectations to Christ could and did provoke Theodoret's rebuttal;[59] and we shall see he is obstinate in excluding an eschatological and specifically Christological interpretation of statements of the Twelve that are even cited in the New Testament. But along with an absence of any anti-Jewish polemic in his *Commentary*—appreciated in an Antiochene—there is as well in commentary on a passage like Mal 3.4 a refusal to see Temple worship retaining its validity after the coming of Christ, even if this is a rare extension of a deliberately foreshortened hermeneutical perspective.

5. *Theodore as interpreter of the prophets*

Theodore sees the prophets having a twofold mission: teaching and writing; as he says of Zechariah, at 11.4, "The prophet by divine revelation received knowledge of the essential elements of these events, and disclosed to the people what was to happen; and to their descendants he transmitted an account of them in writing." He is therefore in haste to situate each of the Twelve in his historical situation and to identify "what was to happen," and when. He loses no time at the opening of the work relating Hosea to the previous προφητεία of David, who had "foretold everything satisfactorily" for the intervening period until the Assyrian incursions made further predictions necessary; not without historical lapses,[60] he proceeds likewise with all the others. When he reaches Haggai, he reviews the sequence thus:

57. So Mai in his 1832 preface (PG 66.119–20).
58. PG 80.857.
59. See *Commentary on the Psalms* 89.38–39 (PG 80.1593), 118.22 (PG 80.1816).
60. For example, his listing of Assyrian kings to set the scene for the

The blessed prophets Hosea, Joel, Amos, and Micah directed their discourse in general to all the Israelite people, both those of the ten tribes ruled by Samaria and especially those of the tribe of Judah, who dwelt in Jerusalem. . . . Blessed Obadiah mentioned the punishment that would be imposed on the Idumeans at the time of the return. Blessed Jonah threatened the Ninevites with overthrow if they did not change their evil ways. Blessed Nahum clearly disclosed both the siege of Nineveh and the destruction of the whole kingdom of the Assyrians, which they were due to undergo at the hands of the Babylonians. After those in the ten tribes had already been deported by the Assyrians and had suffered total captivity and removal from their own place, the blessed prophets Habakkuk and Zephaniah charge those left behind, who were from the tribe of Judah and living in Jerusalem, with their acts of impiety and lawlessness.[61]

He thus envisages four eighth-century prophets, three others still prior to the fall of Samaria in 722, and two prior to the fall of Jerusalem in the early sixth century. Haggai and Zechariah are assigned to the restoration, and Malachi to a time when the Temple has been rebuilt and some apathy of the community has already set in (the LXX's not registering the Persian background of the term for "governor" in Mal 1.8 that suggests a later date for that book).

There is thus no need, in Theodore's limited perspective and limited conception of prophetic purpose, to look beyond those three centuries. He does concede at the outset that in his dealings with the prophets and people in those times God was "conducting affairs in their regard by way of preparation for the manifestation and coming of Christ the Lord": the whole of the divine oikonomia is the context, and the Incarnation (not a term he uses, preferring ἐπιφάνεια, παρουσία) its goal. Of

prophets omits Sargon II (not mentioned in the Bible) and Shalmaneser V, as happens also in Theodoret; Darius is "the fourth to reign over the Persians after Cyrus" (or is Theodore allowing for unnamed pretenders after the sudden death of Cambyses? or confusing Darius I with Darius II?).

61. Theodore is thus reflecting the purpose of the Masoretic text in ordering the Twelve in "actual or supposed" chronological order (the order also in the Antiochene text), whereas the LXX (for the first five) is guided rather by length; see O. Eissfeldt, *The Old Testament. An Introduction*, trans. P. Ackroyd (Oxford: Blackwell, 1965), 383.

Theodore we can to some extent say, as Frances Young says of the Antiochenes generally, that "what we have here is an important stress on the 'reality' of the overarching narrative from creation through fall to Incarnation and redemption,"[62] with a priority given to πράγματα, ἀλήθεια in prophetic statement taken as history. But the Interpreter has reduced the span of the arch to stretch only from David to Zerubbabel (or perhaps the Maccabees), the perspective effectively reduced to bracket out creation at one end and Incarnation and redemption at the other; there is really not a New Testament dimension to Theodore's hermeneutic.[63] Neither is a spiritual interpretation of prophecy required, the youthful commentator feeling no pastoral responsibility.[64] It is—perhaps predictably—a blinkered view of the minor prophets in an Antiochene neophyte drilled in (if not fully appreciating) the priority of τὸ ἱστορικόν, a hermeneutical principle that we saw master Diodore had not fully explicated.

Right from the outset, then, the task is "by the grace of God to bring clarity" to the historical sense of prophetic discourse and to establish the facts. Though modern commentators may debate the factuality of Hosea's marriage in chapter 1, it is beyond the realm of symbolism for Theodore: "The prophet obeys this command, and marries a prostitute, whose father's name he also mentions lest what was said should seem some tri-

---

62. *Biblical Exegesis and the Formation of Christian Culture*, 296.

63. This commitment to interpreting the Old Testament within the confines of the Old Testament Schäublin accounts for again by Theodore's rhetorical formation, and in particular the principle of Aristarchus, "to clarify Homer from Homer" (*Untersuchungen*, 84, 159). The approach he thus adopted (with Diodore's encouragement) "cut across opinions almost universally held in the ancient church," Greer tells us (*Early Biblical Interpretation*, 182).

64. To judge from his *Commentary on Galatians*, however, composed when he was a bishop (in Vosté's view, "La chronologie," 78), Theodore never thought much of spiritual interpretation. On Gal 4.24 (according to the fifth century Latin version edited by H. B. Swete, *Theodori Episcopi Mopsueteni in epistolas B. Pauli Commentarii* I [Cambridge: Cambridge University Press, 1880], 74–75), he commented, "When they turn to expounding divine Scripture 'spiritually'— spiritual interpretation is the name they would like their folly to be given—they claim Adam is not Adam, paradise is not paradise, the serpent is not the serpent. To these people I should say that if they distort *historia*, they will have no *historia* left."

fling fiction and not a true record of events." The next prophet
in Theodore's text is Joel, and likewise in his work what is to be
looked for is principally "facts" and "outcomes" as a guarantee
of their authenticity, or "truth."

The theme of his work, in general terms, is that also of all the
prophets, who were anxious to disclose what was going to happen in
regard to the people according to the grace of the Holy Spirit given to
them in regard to that. First place among them, as I said before, was
held by blessed David, who long ago—in fact, very long ago—and well
before the outcome of the events mentioned all that would happen in
regard to the people at different times. The same thing was done also
by the other prophets, who later mentioned what had long before
been said by him, and a little before the actual outcome of the events,
the purpose being both to remind everyone of what had been prophesied and, by saying what would shortly happen, to disclose the truth of
the prophecy.

In fact, with this perspective limited to "what would shortly happen," it is only Peter's quotation of Jl 2.28–32 in Acts 2 that
(perhaps because of its prominence in the liturgy of Pentecost)
wrings a concession out of Theodore that "the reality of the account was found to be realized in the time of Christ the Lord."

The shortcomings of this hermeneutical approach, where
Antioch's preference for τὸ ἱστορικόν is reduced to reading
texts at face value and seeing a proximate fulfillment, soon become evident.[65] Apocalyptic material in Joel and Zechariah goes
unacknowledged, even a banner like "Day of the Lord" passing
without comment. The mythological figure of Gog from Ezek
38–39 is repeatedly paraded as one of Israel's historical foes the
prophets have in their sights. Such an historical approach can,
of course, degenerate into literalist historicism. The satire of
prophetism in the book of Jonah is lost sight of in the commentator's overriding concern for the "novel and extraordinary
things" recounted there. The prophet cannot be allowed to appear as the ridiculous, disobedient, ill-tempered figure the author means to portray, nor as one who achieves the conversion

---

65. See Young, *Biblical Exegesis*, 168: "Whatever (the Antiochenes) meant by
'literal,' it was not exactly 'historical' in the modern critical sense."

of the Ninevites with but a few words; and as for his time in the sea monster's belly, we just have to throw up our hands.

It would, in fact, be a mark of extreme folly, after such extraordinary things happened to him, and most of all his salvation from the sea monster, to pry into the prophet's egress from the sea monster, and to think that one could grasp it by human reasoning and explain how it happened in our terms.

The challenge the book presents to this literalist is such that he accepts the lifeline the evangelists throw him in portraying Jonah as a type of Christ,[66] typology being a hermeneutic he will not generally adopt.[67] Allegory, unacceptable to an Antiochene, he only briefly dabbles with in connection with the prophecy of shepherds and their staffs in Zec 11, a prophecy that has been classed as one of the most enigmatic in the Old Testament, and then only with the encouragement of the psalmist.[68] Antioch's preferred hermeneutic, θεωρία, the discernment of a fuller sense in events and texts, Theodore does not invoke by name except in that passage at the opening of Nahum cited above, where the use of λῆμμα for "oracle" leads him to give an account of prophetic inspiration as ecstatic possession, which was not quite Diodore's sense in his work on the subject.[69]

In fact, it is θεωρία that is conspicuously missing from this

---

66. Mt 12.39–41, Lk 11.30. See my article, "Jonah in Antioch."

67. Though one can accept the statement of Young, *Biblical Exegesis*, 193, that "the word 'typology' is a modern coinage," it goes beyond the evidence to claim (152) that "ancient exegetes did not distinguish between typology and allegory, and it is often difficult to make the distinction." While Theodore is prepared to adopt typology with NT encouragement, he speaks of allegory (in that comment on Gal 4.24 quoted above in note 64) as "blatant absurdity." See Chrysostom's discussion of the two in his first homily on Is 6 *In Oziam* (SC 277.122), where he admits that his congregation would tolerate the former and disallow the latter. Working from Theodore's *Commentary on the Epistle to the Galatians*, D. S. Wallace-Hadrill, *Christian Antioch*, 36, concludes, "In short, typology based on historical fact is permitted, allegory is not."

68. See the summation of Theodore's approach in this work by Vosté, "La chronologie," 65, as "littéral et historique, pas d'allégorisation, nulle application morale" ("literal and historical, no allegorising, without any moral application").

69. Diodore is credited with a work on the difference between θεωρία and

young commentator's approach to the Twelve prophets, the blinkers one often notes in a serious neophyte that produce a narrow field of vision, and discourage a more flexible movement from one level of meaning to another. Though Theodore is prepared initially to set the prophets within the wide context of the *oikonomia*, with Christ at its endpoint (as he does at the beginning of the work), and to fall back on this wider interpretational framework when particular prophets challenge his historicist hermeneutic (as in introducing Jonah, Amos, and Haggai), he consistently refuses to recognize an eschatological and specifically New Testament or Christological sense in prophetic texts, even despite the encouragement of the New Testament itself. Texts such as the following are passed over without Christological comment or an acknowledgement of their New Testament echoes: "On the third day we shall arise" (Hos 6.2; see Lk 24.7); "They will say to the mountains, Cover us, and to the hills, Fall on us" (Hos 10.8; see Lk 23.30, Rv 6.6); "Son dishonors father, daughter rebels against her mother, daughter-in-law against her mother-in-law" (Mi 7.6; see Mt 10.35–36, Lk 12.53); "A sun of righteousness will arise" (Mal 4.2; see Lk 1.78, Jn 8.12, and the Advent liturgy). Not surprisingly in a commentator with the reputation Leontius perpetuates for demeaning the Theotokos,[70] Theodore does not find any Marian echoes in the clause, "Until the time the pregnant one will give birth" (Mi 5.4).

This exclusion stems partly (even from ignorance at times, one feels, but principally) from Theodore's insistence on recognizing Zerubbabel at the time of the restored community as the fulfillment of messianic expectations, with Christ coming a distant second, if placed anywhere. With a misjudgment that is at variance with other scriptural data and that will earn

---

ἀλληγορία; see Schäublin, "Diodor von Tarsus," 765. See also A. Vaccari, "La θεωρία nella scuola esegetica di Antiochia"; P. Ternant, "La θεωρία d'Antioche dans le cadre de sens de l'Écriture"; B. Nassif, "'Spiritual exegesis' in the school of Antioch." Theodoret, by contrast, right from the paradoxical account of Hosea's marriage (PG 81.1556–57) lectures on the need for θεωρία if the correct σκοπός of such scriptural texts is to be discerned.

70. *Contra Nestor. et Eutych.* 10 (PG 86.1364).

Theodoret's scorn,[71] he is encouraged to confer royal status on Zerubbabel from the LXX's reading Haggai's introduction of him as "son of Shealtiel, from the *tribe* of Judah," a passage where the Hebrew employs an unfamiliar term of Akkadian origins *paḥath*, "governor (of Judah)." From the outset, then, Zerubbabel becomes a king, successor of David, falling neatly within Theodore's self-imposed foreshortened time-frame, "what would shortly happen." As soon as the promise appears in Hos 3.5, "After this the sons of Israel will be converted and seek the Lord their God and David their king," the commentator brings his nominee into the picture: "He means that this will in fact happen after the return, when they were actually under one king, Zerubbabel, a descendant of David, and no longer held that attitude by which the ten tribes deserted the reign of the successors of blessed David and chose other kings." He is aware that his predecessors have taken many of these references Christologically, but with youthful temerity he dismisses their interpretation, as with the promise in Zec 9.9–10, "Lo, your king comes to you."

While, then, it is clear that here this refers to Zerubbabel, I am amazed at those adopting farfetched ideas, applying part to Zerubbabel and part to Christ the Lord, which results in nothing else than their dividing the prophecy between Zerubbabel and Christ the Lord. Now, this is the height of folly.

When pressed, however, he will make a concession (that gives the lie to the uncritical comment frequently heard that this work "contains nothing of Christological import"[72]) that a fuller realization comes in the person of Christ, as he does when faced with the familiar reference in Mi 5.2 to Bethlehem,

---

71. J.-N. Guinot, who speaks of the animus ("différend") in Theodoret's response to Theodore's treatment of Zerubbabel (in "La cristallisation d'un différend: Zorobabel dans l'exégèse de Théodore de Mopsueste et de Théodoret de Cyr"), catalogues the references by each Antiochene to Zerubbabel, noting Theodore's far greater insistence on historicizing the occurrences and Theodoret's proportionally greater willingness to see Zerubbabel as a figure of Christ. See also my article, "*Sartor resartus:* Theodore under review by Theodoret."

72. See n. 73, below.

from where "will come for me the one to be ruler in Israel." Zerubbabel is the automatic and obvious referent; but this is susceptible of qualification.

Now, he is referring to Zerubbabel: he was the one who at that time was reigning over the Israelites, a descendant of David, at the time of the return from Babylon and the attempted assault on Jerusalem by those of Gog's company. It is also clear, admittedly, that though, consistently with what has gone before, this refers to Zerubbabel, a successor of David, yet the true fulfillment of the words is achieved in Christ the Lord. While every promise made to David about his descendants reigning seems at first flush to indicate his successors in the kingdom of Israel, in reality it foretells Christ the Lord in the flesh, who as a successor of David exercises the true and abiding rule over all.

Gradually, then, this neophyte comes to see that taking texts "at first flush," κατὰ πρῶτον λόγον, is not an adequate hermeneutic if the "reality" and "true fulfillment" is to be discerned in a process of θεωρία. But as with youthful brashness he continues being utterly definitive in his interpretation of obscure prophecies even as he nears the close of the work in Zechariah, he has still to learn the lesson that some admission of uncertainty and acknowledgement of one's betters is not a fault in an interpreter.

6. Christological and Trinitarian theology of the Commentary

Despite Theodore's label as a *Ioudaiophron*, it seems clear that Christ is not bracketed out of the hermeneutical perspective of the *Commentary* on theological grounds. It is rather that if the commentator is to restrict his gaze to "what would shortly happen" (or, in Aristarchus's terms, "Clarify Homer from Homer"), a more proximate referent must be found for messianic prophecies—Zerubbabel in particular—and thus New Testament statement becomes irrelevant. In keeping with this foreshortened field of vision, he sees the Old Testament authors having no knowledge of, and making no reference to, the Trinity. So when he comes to the intriguing vision Zechariah has of horses of different colors sent on various errands, of a man riding a red horse and an angel speaking to him, he is typically dismissive of views by Hippolytus, Apollinaris, Eusebius, and Jerome that the rider is Christ.

Now, the statement of certain commentators, characterized by extreme error and stupidity, and not innocent of impiety, is to the effect that he saw the Son of God here, it being obvious that none of those who lived before the coming of Christ the Lord knew of Father and Son, none knew that God the Father was the father of God the Son, that God the Son was the son of God the Father, being what the Father is, in that he draws existence from him. While terminology for father and son is to be found in the Old Testament, since God is commonly called father for his care when people are shown attention from that source, and they are called sons in having something more on the basis of relationship with God, yet absolutely no one of those living at that time understood God the Father to be father of God the Son, as I said before, or God the Son to be son of God the Father. You see, the people before the coming of Christ the Lord in their religious knowledge were aware only of God and creation, identifying God as eternal in being and as cause of everything, and creation (to put it in a nutshell) as what was brought by him from nonbeing to being.

While the term ὁμοούσιος is not invoked, his thinking about God the Word is in accord with that of the creed of Constantinople (the *Commentary* probably composed prior to that council of 381). There is never any diminishment of the person of Christ; we saw the widely Christological context being set at the opening of commentary and invoked when particular prophets presented a hermeneutical challenge, like Jonah. And when a text cannot keep Christ from challenging Zerubbabel for perfect fulfillment, like the mention in Zec 9.9 of the humble figure that comes "riding upon a beast of burden, a colt," the admission is made that "the contents were seen to contain their irrefutable reality in the case of Christ the Lord." It is therefore a pity that formal studies of Theodore's Christology make little or no reference to this work, and that its silence on the topic is given as the principal reason for its surviving the flames of hostility.[73]

73. The verdict on this work by Sullivan, *Christology*, 1, that it contains

We find in him a similar resistance to recognizing in the Old Testament any reference to the Holy Spirit. When the Lord says in Jl 2.28, "I shall pour out my spirit on all flesh," Theodore hastens to comment, "The people in the time of the Old Testament did not understand the Holy Spirit to be a μοναδικόν ἐν ὑποστάσει distinct from the others, being both God and from God; by 'spirit of God,' 'holy spirit,' and every other such name at the time they referred to his grace, care, and affection." He is equally insistent in similar terms at another occurrence of "My spirit" in Hg 2.5:

The people of the Old Testament were unaware of a distinct hypostasis of a Holy Spirit identified as a person (πρόσωπον) in its own right in God, since everyone before the coming of Christ the Lord knew of God and creation but nothing further. The divine Scripture taught this to its readers at that time without having an insight into anything in invisible creation consisting of separate kinds, referring to all the invisible and ministering beings in general as angels and powers, which according to its teaching carried out the divine decisions. Consequently, they were not in a position to know of a Holy Spirit as a distinct hypostasis in God, being unable even to list separate kinds among the ministering beings or to associate with God what could be described as a distinct person (πρόσωπον), since they understood nothing of this sort.

And he proceeds to cite the need of Jesus to inform the disciples of this through the Trinitarian formula in Mt 28.19, "from which we learn of a distinct person (πρόσωπον) of a Father, a distinct person of a Son, and a distinct person of a Holy Spirit, believing each of them in similar fashion to be of a divine and eternal substance (οὐσία)," something communicated to later Christians (he says) by religious instruction and the baptismal liturgy.

"almost nothing of Christological import," is adopted verbatim by Quasten, *Patrology* 3:405, to account for its survival, and likewise by Zaharopoulos, *Theodore,* 32. Sullivan, citing the work only twice, declares no interest in Theodore's exegetical works on the *a priori* grounds that in them "Theodore would not be expected to develop his theology so fully in its more technical aspects" (32). It is likewise ignored by R. A. Norris, *Manhood and Christ. A Study in the Christology of Theodore of Mopsuestia,* and by K. McNamara, "Theodore of Mopsuestia and the Nestorian heresy."

Now, for Paul Galtier and others who have written on Theodore's terminology, the terms πρόσωπον and ὑπόστασις are not synonymous, the latter resembling φύσις in Cyril's usage and for Sullivan meaning "a real, substantial being."[74] Theodore brings the two terms together again in proceeding to comment on that verse from Haggai: "Now, the Old Testament, as I said, by way of distinction in God did not come to knowledge of a Holy Spirit as a distinct person and distinct hypostasis; by holy spirit, or spirit of God, it refers to his grace, his care, his attitude to something." The combination here of the two terms in the phrase "a distinct person and distinct hypostasis," which Sullivan (and Kelly after him) finds suspect in the Syriac version of Theodore's *De Incarnatione* as being "something for which we have no parallel in all the extant writings of Theodore,"[75] is admittedly here used in reference to the Spirit, though from Theodore's argument it is true of Father and Son as well. For them it has "a strongly Chalcedonian ring," and shows Theodore clearly subscribing to "the badge of orthodoxy" in the fourth century, the formula "one οὐσία, three ὑποστάσεις," and aligns him with the Cappadocians. Theodoret for one, not always his unequivocal supporter, and one partly responsible for convoking the council of Chalcedon, commended him for "being locked in battle with the forces of Arius and Eunomius and taking issue with the robber band of Apollinaris."[76]

74. P. Galtier, "L'*unio secundum hypostasim* chez saint Cyrille," *Gregorianum* 33 (1952): 382; Sullivan, *Christology*, 67.

75. Sullivan, *Christology*, 80; Kelly, *Early Christian Doctrines*, 306. Sullivan nonetheless concludes that we can agree with Cyril in classing Theodore as "the Father of Nestorianism" (284); likewise for McNamara, "Theodore," 172, in Theodore "we have the essential Nestorian position," the doctrine of the two sons. See Zaharopoulos, *Theodore*, 19: "Theodore's teaching on the two natures in Christ is not free from notable defects. It lacks an important theological feature which was strongly emphasised in the Chalcedonian fathers: the God-man who exists in two natures is one person and *one hypostasis*." George Kalantzis, "*Duo Filii*," shows that the extant Greek fragments of Theodore's *Commentary on the Gospel of John* confirm Theodore's Christological orthodoxy against Cyril's claims and the doctored text presented to the council of 553.

76. *Church History* 5.40 (PG 82.1277; GCS 5.347–48).

7. *Morality and spirituality of the* Commentary

External and internal evidence suggests that this work was composed in Theodore's youth, when he bore no pastoral responsibilities. We noted he studiously avoids adopting the moralizing manner of a preacher, with the exception of the lecture against divorce prompted by Mal 2.13–16 that seems lifted from a common stock; instead, he concentrates on cognitive aspects of the prophets, "by the grace of God bringing clarity" to them, as he says in introducing Haggai. He passes up the opportunity to develop a spiritual interpretation of the prophets' message, even when it almost demands it, as in the moving presentation by Hosea 1–2 of the Lord's uniting himself with his people in the intimate relationship of marriage, and in that distillation of refined Old Testament morality in Mi 6.6–8, with its hierarchy of cultic and moral obligations: "Has it been told you, mortal that you are, what is good, and what the Lord requires of you, other than doing justice, loving mercy, and being ready to walk behind the Lord your God?" If Louis Bouyer sees Antioch developing a spirituality that involves "asceticism without mysticism,"[77] Theodore sees it inappropriate for himself in his situation to dwell even on the former, let alone the latter; it is sufficient to leave the prophets to speak for themselves. To this extent Rowan Greer is right to conclude of Theodore that "the Bible is allowed to speak in his commentaries (and in his theology) as it is in those of few, if any, of the patristic exegetes."[78] Whether his readers appreciated this reticence is another matter.[79]

The slightest glimpse of Antiochene moral and spiritual principles is afforded—again—by Theodore's response to that challenging book of Jonah. He simply cannot accept that the

---

77. *The Spirituality of the New Testament and the Fathers*, 436.

78. Greer, *Theodore of Mopsuestia*, 111.

79. Pirot, *L'Oeuvre exégètique*, 280, one feels, does well to suggest that readers would find Theodore's work "si sec comparé aux homélies si vivantes, si intéressantes, si instructives de Saint Jean Chrysostome" ("so dry compared with St. John Chrysostom's homilies, which are so alive, so interesting, so instructive") (though, admittedly, a comparison with Chrysostom's homilies on the Psalms delivered to congregations in his διδασκαλεῖον is not quite fair).

repentance of the Ninevites resulted from a one-liner from the prophet; Jonah must have gone into much more detail if the remarkable moral response was to be commensurate with the effort invested—a first principle of Antiochene spirituality—and so we saw the commentator rewriting the script to supply for the lacuna. That word for a prophetic oracle, λῆμμα, that Theodoret encounters first at the opening of Nahum, also elicits a comment betraying Antiochene belief that a spiritual gift like ecstatic possession is granted only to those who earn it: "While this is the customary title of the prophetical books, there is need to clarify the sense of the word *oracle*. The Holy Spirit, you see, who to those thought worthy of such things provided the peculiar grace, was one," though his gifts are many. The role of human effort must be upheld to balance the gratuity of divine grace—a principle with implications also for scriptural interpretation, Christology and soteriology.

From a neophyte at his desk, however, free of any sense of pastoral responsibility, such insights into spiritual theology are few. If Photius thought Theodore an eastern Pelagius,[80] he could not have found much evidence of it in this early work. We saw that, in the commentator's blinkered perspective, creation and the Fall were excised as much as Incarnation and redemption, and so do not come in for comment.

8. Theodore's achievement in the Commentary

It could be argued that Theodore's principal achievement in his *Commentary on the Twelve Prophets* is his succeeding in having the work survive entirely in Greek as he wrote it, and thus providing later ages with an indubitable (and unique) reference for estimating his overall significance as exegete and inter-

---

80. *Bibliotheca* 177 (PG 103.513). Disallowing the charge, Kelly, *Early Christian Doctrines*, 373, believes "there are few, if any, traces of the alleged Pelagianizing strain in his authentic works, unless the Eastern attitude generally is to be dismissed as Pelagian." Norris in a chapter, "The Fall of Man: Theodore's 'Pelagianism,'" *Manhood and Christ*, 190, is probably siding with both in concluding that "he speaks (not unlike the semi-Pelagians) as though the divine grace presupposes some prior good intention on the part of man."

preter of the school of Antioch. His reputation in the meantime has veered so markedly, we saw, from outright condemnation and denunciation to superlative encomium and adulation
as to lead to doubts as to whether critics and supporters have
actually read his writing—hence the urgent need for its avail-
ability in English. One feels that claims, on the one hand, that
Theodore "subjected the Scriptures to drunken abuse," and on
the other that he deserves the accolade the Interpreter *par excellence* arise out of theological convictions, not exegetical, by
which he is taken either as the heresiarch or as the repository
of eastern orthodoxy,[81] and that such claims would be nuanced
by a close reading of the text.

The verdict arrived at in this study of the *Commentary on the
Twelve Prophets* (a biblical text on which we enjoy the advantage
of the survival also of another such work from Antioch, by
Theodoret) is that truth, as often, lies midway between the extremes. As a work of Theodore's youth, before pastoral responsibilities led—as often again—to balance and some humility, it
bears the marks of an intolerant novice prepared to sing treble
to the bass of his mentor Diodore alone,[82] an intolerance of alternative views that irked Leontius of Byzantium and that also
encouraged in the young commentator uncritical acceptance
of Antioch's accent on τὸ ἱστορικόν in interpretation. Certainly
at this stage he suffered from exegetical and hermeneutical
limitations he was loath to admit, such as ignorance of the original language, unwillingness to subject his local text to scrutiny,
and inability to recognize apocalyptic in Joel and Zechariah in
particular; he also showed less readiness to background his text
than his readers required and Theodoret would demonstrate,

81. Efforts have been made in recent times to rehabilitate Theodore as an
orthodox teacher and present the condemnation of 553 as a move orchestrated
by the emperor Justinian; see A. Stirnemann and G. Wilfinger, ed., *Syriac Dialogue. Third Non-official Consultation of Dialogue within the Syriac Tradition* (Vienna:
Pro Oriente, 1998), involving the Roman Catholic Church and the Syrian Orthodox Church of Antioch. Not all Orthodox communities hold this view.

82. See Guinot, "La cristallisation," 546: "Théodore paraît appliquer sans
grande souplesse les principes d'herméneutique hérités de Diodore de Tarse."
("Theodore gives the impression of applying without great flexibility the
hermeneutical principles inherited from Diodore of Tarsus.")

and to apply the prophets' message to readers' lives. Yet conversely we appreciate his setting himself the modest aim of exposition of the text of the Twelve, never encroaching on the role of a preacher by moralizing. In this task he shows the ability to respond to a prophet's imagery and other genres employed (apocalyptic excepted), if not measuring up to the claim made for him by Devreesse to be the first literary critic among the Fathers. The foreshortened hermeneutical perspective on these prophets that Theodore adopts, thanks to the maxims of Aristarchus mediated to him by Libanius, do "cut across opinions almost universally held in the ancient church," Rowan Greer reminds us;[83] but a reader detects immediately that he is prepared to allow an overall Christological context in which all the prophets are working—a fact that belies the verdict that the work owes its survival from the flames to its containing "nothing of Christological import,"[84] Sullivan's summation based on unfamiliarity with the text. If Christological reference in particular texts is rarely established, whereas a figure like Zerubbabel looms large, winning Theodore the pejorative title *Ioudaiophron*, at least this bias results in our finding here little of the anti-semitic tone not infrequently detectable in Antioch's composition.

If this is a qualified assessment of Theodore's achievement in his *Commentary on the Twelve Prophets*,[85] it is one based on a reading of the text, now available in English. It is also one that may be checked against his other at least partly-extant Old Testament work, the *Commentary on the Psalms*, which appears to have immediately preceded it. Together the two commentaries constitute an adequate basis for judgment on Theodore's exegetical and hermeneutical approach to the Old Testament at least, and a further contribution to our knowledge of the school of Antioch.

---

83. Greer, *Early Biblical Interpretation*, 182.

84. See n. 73.

85. For a similarly nuanced assessment, see Wallace-Hadrill, *Christian Antioch*, 33–38.

COMMENTARY ON THE TWELVE PROPHETS

COMMENTARY ON THE PROPHET HOSEA

S AN INDICTMENT of those who presume to apply themselves to the prophetic utterances without due preparation, and also by way of education of those coming after, let us come to the task of clarifying the prophetic books with God's assistance, making a start with Hosea, who happens to be the first in time of the other prophets.[1] Blessed David, remember, as I said before, had clearly addressed in psalms all the vicissitudes that would befall the people; but silence prevailed during the intervening time for the reason that he had foretold everything satisfactorily. The time came, however, for the ten tribes to begin their suffering, the Assyrians besieging them to the point where Sennacherib completely removed them from their own places and transported them to other places.[2] What had long been foretold by blessed David about the disasters that would befall the people had its beginning at that point,[3] namely, what happened in the time when Hezekiah reigned over Judah together with Benjamin, divine

1. As noted in the Introduction, Theodore comes to the Twelve Prophets as a young (and intolerant) commentator. If not earlier than Amos among the classical prophets, Hosea is about the same time (in the view of modern commentators; Amos occurs only third in the order of The Twelve in Theodore's text—in accord with Jewish practice; see his opening to *Comm Hg*).

2. Theodore, unlike Theodoret (who finds him too historically-minded), immediately sets Hosea in the historical situation of Israel in the late eighth century. But both Fathers have a blind spot about Sargon II, who (perhaps along with his predecessor Shalmaneser V) should be credited—not his successor Sennacherib—with the fall of Samaria and deportation of the population. (Sargon goes unmentioned in the Bible also; Shalmaneser and the deportation are mentioned in 2 Kgs 17.1–6—another blindspot? or did Antioch's text read "Sennacherib"?)

3. Judah being "the people" in question. What is extant of Theodore's *Commentary on the Psalms* shows him ready to see the psalmists' foretelling future historical developments (within the OT).

grace communicated to the prophets when the events were close at hand.

And before the others it communicated to Hosea, who was recounting what would befall them from God as though recalling what was said by David in the dim and distant past, [125][4] for him to show the Israelites to be responsible for the coming disasters, having, on the one hand, set aside the worship and appreciation of God, and, on the other, showered every attention on the idols and the demons. He was also to make clear that this was not happening by chance; rather, its occurrence has been told and foreseen well in advance by God, who understood these people's wickedness and clearly realized how he needed to conduct affairs in their regard by way of preparation for the manifestation and coming of Christ the Lord.[5] And so in fact to make clear to everyone that he has care for the people on account of the one expected to appear from their midst, on the one hand, he surrenders the ten tribes to captivity under the Assyrians, and, on the other, he keeps Judah alone in its place, since from it the Lord would appear as Christ according to the flesh. After it went into captivity at a later time for its sins, however, when Nebuchadnezzar was ruling the Babylonians, he caused it to return in marvelous fashion: though some few of each of the other tribes returned, the whole of Judah alone was brought back so that it might be obvious that God, had he wished, could have also brought back all the rest in a manner similar to it, but that he passed over the others and gave all his attention to it, from which the Lord was due to be revealed as Christ, who was coming for the salvation of all alike.

Now, by the same token the pronouncements of the prophets also proved to be necessary in showing that what had both been decreed of old by God and mentioned by blessed David

4. For readers' convenience, references are included in our text to the columns of PG 66.

5. Theodore thus maintains it is possible to have at the one time an historical and an eschatological viewpoint on biblical texts, God managing (οἰκονομεῖν) history with the Incarnation in mind—even if Theodore will proceed consistently to exclude a Christological interpretation of the work. (Theodore's documentation of the Israelites' "wickedness" follows 2 Kgs 17.7–18 closely.)

was now taking effect, God conducting everything to do with them in ineffable fashion.[6] In doing this, then, Hosea the prophet clearly announces what would happen in accord with the divine will to the people for their impious actions.

Chapter One

He begins this way, *The word of the Lord that came to Hosea son of Beeri in the days of Uzziah, Jotham, Ahaz, and Hezekiah, kings of Judah, and in the days of Jeroboam son of Joash, king of Israel* (v.1). This is a kind of title to the book summarizing its contents, indicating both the prophet to whom the words belong and the time he uttered them. By *word of the Lord* he means the divine force operating everywhere, like the verse, "By the word of the Lord the heavens were established,"[7] meaning they were formed by the divine force. Here, too, he means the divine force by which revelation of the future was made to the prophet: from it he had the ability both to speak and to disclose the future. Now, as a more precise indication he cites also the fathers' names.[8] He had to mention also the time he disclosed the future according to the revelation given him from God, saying it was at the time that Uzziah, Jotham, Ahaz, and Hezekiah reigned, from which you would get the idea that the prophet did not compose the book in one exercise; rather, he received at different times the revelations of the future, and made a disclosure of the future, [128] on many occasions recalling the same things by means of divine revelation, and actually telling them to the people as an indication of the future.[9]

6. Again God's management is behind human history: patterns can be discerned—though again this overarching pattern is not dwelt on in Theodore's commentary. See closing words to *Comm Mal.*

7. Ps 33.6. Scriptural verse references are given according to modern English versions. The Psalms, the subject of his previous work, will be seen to be the staple in Theodore's documentation of the text.

8. This detail, too, is of significance to an Antiochene, with his interest in the precision, ἀκρίβεια, of the text, requiring also precision in the commentator.

9. Theodore has a less sophisticated explanation for the repetition of oracles in a prophetic work than Theodoret, who in commenting on Is 51.9 allowed for the work of others who arranged a prophet's oracles at a later stage. Theodore

In just the same way blessed David also seems to have uttered many psalms on the same theme, each of which he composes under the revelation and recollection coming to him from the influence of the Spirit, and utters for the benefit of others. This prophet on many occasions received revelations about the same things and accordingly uttered them as often as he was vouchsafed the same revelations.

Now, after mentioning the kings of Judah at whatever time divine grace prompted Hosea to prophesy, he mentions also the one in Israel, that is, the Jeroboam who was ruling over the ten tribes at that time, the son of Joash, grandson of Joahaz, who was son of Jehu, whom at the time of the punishment of Ahab and all his house God promoted by the prophet Elisha; God promised his successors would be on the throne to the fourth generation,[10] the third of whom was Jeroboam, son of Joash and grandson of Joahaz. The fourth was Zechariah, son of Jeroboam, who died after reigning six months; in him the divine promise was fulfilled, the throne then passing from the line of Jehu to Shallum, who was not of the same descent. Jeroboam came to the throne of Israel, then, when Uzziah was reigning in Jerusalem; from that time the people of the ten tribes commenced behaving badly up to the time when the king of the Assyrians took them captive and deported them. So it was logical for Hosea to succeed to the office of prophecy at this time, recalling the predictions of blessed David and announcing that the words spoken about them in the past would be in the offing.

After this he says, *The beginning of the word of the Lord to Hosea* (v.2). It is clear that at this point God began the revelation to him: he bids him both marry a prostitute and have children of her.[11] He goes on to supply the reason, *Because in being unfaith-*

---

simply sees the prophet in receipt of the same message at different times, and presumably recording the oracles on receipt (the prophet's ministry thus being one of writing, συγγράφειν, rather than preaching). See n. 56, below.

10. 2 Kgs 9.1–10, 10.30. Theodore sees the mention of only one king, Jeroboam II, in Israel compared with four in Judah to be due simply to the length of the former's reign, thus making the two lines roughly contemporary, unlike a modern commentator like Dennis McCarthy, "Hosea," *NJBC,* 216, who believes "the compilers of the book of Hosea significantly ignore the miserable kinglets who followed Jeroboam."

11. Modern commentators point out that the Heb. does not actually say

ful the land will be unfaithful to the Lord. The fact that God had the prophets do a number of things that to the general run of people seemed unseemly, like ordering Isaiah to appear naked and barefoot in the midst of everyone,[12] clearly has the following explanation. Since we general run of people normally listen to words idly, but are startled at the novelty of what happens and comes to our attention, especially if it is at variance with the normal behavior of the one doing it, it made sense for God, with the Jews' disobedience in mind, to have the prophets frequently perform such things so that the people might in some fashion be converted by the novelty of what happened, and come to learn the reason and be instructed in their duty. Accordingly, he bade the prophet marry a prostitute: it would have been unusual for the prophet to choose such a woman to take into the marriage relationship—which is exactly what God ordered him to do. By the Law the prophet was allowed to take a woman into the marriage relationship, and on marrying her he probably brought her to chaste ways. In fact, while everyone could not but be surprised that a man [129] who was very conscious of propriety should pass over women who enjoyed a good reputation and choose to take a prostitute into the marriage relationship, the novelty of the event provided the prophet with the occasion of telling them their duty, and in addition of demonstrating the greater marvel of God's condescending to choose such ungrateful men for special attention by the powerful example—namely, the remarkable prophet's doing his duty by entering into association with a prostitute.[13]

"prostitute"; the LXX (which Theodore does not quote verbatim) says, like the Heb., "a wife of harlotry, infidelity." But Theodore thinks the distinction insignificant.

12. See Is 20.2–6. For evidence that Theodore composed a commentary on Isaiah, see the Introduction, section 4. He is clearly—and predictably—not disposed to treat the incident as mere allegorical fiction; like his modern counterparts, he relates it to other prophetic actions, citing the "brutal realism" of Isaiah's task. Theodoret, too, reacts strongly to such attempts to allegorize the account, probably by Alexandrian predecessors, and cites the prophetic actions of Isaiah plus Jeremiah and Ezekiel.

13. Theodore is committed to showing that the prophet's commission, odd though it may seem, is not out of keeping with a realistic interpretation.

I have been looking after the Israelites, he is saying, then, who have constantly behaved towards me in a faithless manner, and, day in day out, have exacerbated this attitude to this very time, and yet I have admitted them to familiarity with me beyond all other people. In a short time, however, they will be convicted of their attitude to me by the punishment inflicted on them by me when they are surrendered into captivity and completely banished from this land. When they lived in it and were vouchsafed my care, I bade them abide by my laws in the manner that women taken into the marriage relationship customarily abide by the marriage laws. In all this, however, they had no proper sense of what was happening, nor of what they were doing, nor of what they were deservedly suffering. For your part, prophet, by the novelty of what is happening, level an accusation at the impropriety being committed by them.

The prophet obeys this command, and marries a prostitute, whose father's name he also mentions lest what was said should seem some trifling fiction and not a true record of events.[14] He also has a son by her, whom God ordered to be called Jezreel. Now, that was the name of the place where Naboth was subjected to criminal slaughter, and in fact Jezabel was also slaughtered in payment of the penalty for the crime against him, Jehu by divine command doing away with her and the whole family of Ahab for that crime.[15] *In a little while I shall take vengeance on the house of Jehu for the blood of Jezreel, and shall bring to an end the kingdom of the house of Israel* (v.4), that is to say, appointed to the kingship by me, Jehu did away with the whole family of the house of Ahab for the impiety and the lawlessness that it committed against Naboth in the place predicted; but then he was not brought to his senses by this, nor did he limit his lawlessness to the other crimes he avenged. Instead, all those who ruled later over Israel imitated Ahab's attitude.[16] I shall shortly

14. Theodore, of course, looks in the Scriptures for this above all: ἱστορία, ἀλήθεια, πράγματα.

15. See 1 Kgs 21, 2 Kgs 9–10. Theodore—predictably in view of his lack of Hebrew—does not pick up the etymology of Jezreel, "God sows."

16. Perhaps recalling that Elisha in 2 Kgs 9 was responsible for telling Jehu of the Lord's direction to kill all Ahab's family, Theodore does not, in the words

bring the whole kingdom of Israel to an end since those experiencing captivity in future could not have their own king. *I shall also break the bow of Israel in the valley of Jezreel* (v.5), referring to their whole place by mention of a part, as if to say, I shall make all their power futile by subjecting it to the enemy, namely, the Assyrians.

He then says he had from the same woman a daughter, whom he ordered to be called *Not pitied* (v.6), giving a reminder by her very name that the Israelites would never attain mercy but would be surrendered to total captivity, by the power, not of the enemy but [132] of God clearly warring against them, the phrase *I shall completely oppose them* suggesting as much. As a clearer demonstration of my intention for this to happen to them, he is saying, I shall add the fate of Judah, on whom I shall have mercy when they are in danger of meeting the same fate from the Assyrians taking them captive. I shall save them by my power, not *by bow or sword or war* (v.7), nor when they are completely reliant on human assistance, but when escaping such danger by my power alone—which actually happened when an angel by night unexpectedly slew a hundred and eighty-five thousand with the result that the rest were put to flight and the inhabitants of Jerusalem indisputably gained their safety.[17] Another child, a son, was in turn born to him, whom as a confirmation of what was said he orders to be called *Not a people* (v.9), and he gives the reason, *You are not my people, and I am not yours:* You will eventually be alienated from my care, and I shall surrender you to impending troubles like foreigners. He then goes on, *Because the sons of Israel are as numerous as sand of the sea, and it will not be measured or numbered* (v.10): it was a greater wonder, providing also clear proof of God's wrath, to consign so many suddenly to captivity without any of such a multitude gaining any relief.

---

of Douglas Stuart, *Hosea-Jonah,* 68, proceed to "the conclusion that Hosea is condemning Jehu for fulfilling God's command. Instead, Yahweh now announces that he will turn the tables on Jehu because of the real issue, i.e., what has happened in the meantime." Theodore of all the Antiochenes looked in the Scriptures for "textual coherence" (in Frances Young's words).

17. See 2 Kgs 19.35–36, Is 37.36–37.

Then, as it is normal with the prophets and also with blessed David to mention good news in the very midst of bad, and a change for the better by way of consolation of those worse off, he says, *In the place where it was said to them, You are not my people, they will be called sons of the living God.* Blessed David also speaks in similar terms about the Assyrians, and goes on, "Who will give the salvation of Israel from Zion? When the Lord restores the captives of his people, Jacob will rejoice and Israel will be glad,"[18] showing that the time will come when God will utterly release them from captivity; in fact, he says the same thing here, too, where they were called "Not a people"—that is, rejected from my providence—here they will actually be called children of the living God, as if to say, Once again they will attain relationship with me. *In the place* was well put: he intended to return them to the same place from where he took them. So he goes on with greater clarity of expression, *The sons of Judah and the sons of Israel will be assembled in the same place, and will appoint for themselves a single authority, and they will go up from the land* (v.11). He means that after the captivity in Babylon a single liberation will occur for everyone from the tribe of Judah, that they will actually be under one rule, no longer divided as before but under one rule, with the tribe of Judah in command of all and those from that tribe exercising kingship and authority. Then he adds, *Because great will be the day of Jezreel.* You see, since he had said that they would pay the penalty for it, [133] he means that for those who had suffered badly for their former impiety that day would be awesome and glorious, when against all human expectation they would again return to their own.

Chapter Two

What proof is there? *Say to your brother, My people, and to your sister, Pitied* (v.1)—*Say* in the sense of "You will say," instructing

18. Ps 14.7. Theodore had a name for applying the Psalms to historical situations—here the blasphemy of Sennacherib recounted in 2 Kgs 18. It is notable that throughout this chapter he has not adopted a spiritual interpretation of any verse.

him to say that their names would be changed: facts are suggested by names; being called *People* and *Pity* will suit them (he means) insofar as they enjoyed close relationship and lovingkindness from me at that time. Then he takes occasion for remarks from the foregoing image, and says, *Pass sentence, pass sentence against your mother, because she is not my wife and I am not her husband* (v.2): whereas in terms of the foregoing image it is crystal clear that by *mother* he refers to the prostitute, and by *children* to those probably born of her, in this case he calls *mother* the assembly of the Jews, whom previously he had, as it were, betrothed and joined to himself and with an extraordinary degree of care led out from Egypt, and had also accorded them freedom and led them into the desert so as to instruct them in reverence and bring them to a better attitude to him, as blessed David also says, "Remember your assembly, which you acquired long ago, you redeemed to be the rod of your inheritance."[19] Its *children* he says are the people succeeding to it, the people of that time being called fathers of those coming later: "Your fathers ate manna in the desert and are dead,"[20] Scripture says, remember. Likewise its assembly could also be rightly called *mother*, since from it the body of the Jews was later formed. To reprove them for the depravity of their behavior, therefore, he expressed it well, You have been depraved from the beginning, and clearly related to your mother. If you were to compare their past and present behavior, then, you would clearly find a close relationship between them: despite the forebears' being granted so many wonderful benefits, they presumed to make a calf and say, "These are your gods, Israel, that brought you out of the land of Egypt";[21] on the basis of their likeness you forsook knowledge of me, who had always shown you such great care, and you turned to the worship of the idols, with the result that you are appropriately compared to the prostitute. With you so disposed it is not proper for you to be still called mine; on the evidence of the events themselves I present myself as alienated from you.

19. Ps 74.2. In using συναγωγή for "assembly," Theodore may intend as well the Jewish synagogue of his time.
20. Jn 6.49.   21. Ex 32.4.

And so? *I shall remove her prostitution from before me, and her adultery from between her breasts:* I shall put them far from me by captivity and by deportation to distant places so as no longer to behold her own prostitution practiced in my very sight, nor the adultery she is guilty of with great lewdness by giving herself totally to the idols. The phrase *from between her breasts*, in fact, says as much, since the [136] prostitutes offer their breasts in an excess of lewdness to their lovers. What follows is in keeping, *so as to strip her naked and restore her to her condition on the day of her birth* (v.3):[22] removing all the adornment in which I clad her in my providence, I shall reduce her to that condition in which she found herself originally in Egypt when she was in need, and hardship, and bitter slavery (by *birth* referring to that time, since that time was the beginning of the formation of the Jewish assembly). *I shall make her like a desert, and turn her into a waterless land,* thus being deprived of every good in the way the desert and waterless land are completely devoid of crops. *I shall kill her with thirst,* deprived of every good, longing for them, as you would expect, but getting none. *Her children I shall not pity because they are children of prostitution, because their mother prostituted herself, the one who bore them disgraced herself* (vv.4–5): on those proven guilty of such terrible evils I shall not have pity as I formerly did in Egypt, since they have adopted the same mentality as their own mother; by giving evidence of such an attitude to me long ago, she also covered the children born of her with shame insofar as they imitated the maternal wickedness. *Because she said, I shall go after my lovers, who give me my bread and my water, my garments and my linen, my oil and everything that belongs to me:* they have all devoted themselves to the worship of the demons, claiming to have from them all the good things they own, though obviously they have them from me, the maker of everything. He called the demons her *lovers* to make clear both the zeal they display in the ruination of human beings as well as their insane attitude to them in presuming to treat them as gods and as the cause of all good things.

22. Predictably, Theodore does not allude to the allegory of the abandoned waif in Ezek 16 at this point.

For this reason, lo, I fence in her path with thorns and shall block her tracks so that she may not even find her way (v.6): accordingly I shall invest them with inescapable troubles to this end, that just as someone hampered by blocked paths that are obstructed by many savage thorns has an impossible exit, so, too, caught up in the problem of the wars, the captivity and the pressures stemming from them they would find no escape from the troubles. *She will pursue her lovers and will not overtake them, she will seek them and will not find them* (v.7): at that time they will call upon the help of the demons they worshiped, but no good will come to them from that source. *She will say, I shall go and return to my former husband, because I was better off then than now:* at that time they will actually recognize their own error, and the fact that they would be better off keeping to worship of me than choosing the deception of the demons. *She did not know that it was I who gave her the grain, the wine, and the oil, and lavished silver and gold on her; instead, she used silver and* [137] *gold for the Baal* (v.8): they will learn that they were afflicted with some awful ignorance in attributing to them the influx of goods that in fact were clearly supplied in abundance by me, the creator of everything, who provided not only crops but also silver and gold, both at the exodus from Egypt and afterwards on other different occasions. Yet they did not hesitate to make from them idols for themselves, and on account of the abundance of the metals to regard as holy the worship of them.

Hence I shall have a change of heart and take away my grain in its time and my wine in its season (v.9): accordingly I shall cause extreme infertility among them; at the time when they have high hopes of enjoying them, I shall then suddenly deprive them of all the crops by a range of conditions that normally damage such crops—blight, for example, hail, and such things that often occur suddenly and cause the complete ruin of the emerging crop—so that by the onset of punishment and the removal of the gifts they may come to know clearly the one they did not know to be the source of these very benefits. *I shall take away my garments and my linen from concealing her shame:* every single thing supplied them by me that adorned them and showed them in a better light than other people who enjoyed them I shall take away, and make them more despicable than them all. *I shall now uncover her uncleanness in the sight of her lovers, and no one will rescue her out of my hand* (v.10) so that through my punishment the lawlessness they committed in leaving me and devoting themselves to the worship of the demons will become clearer to everyone, since they will patently be the victim of most oppressive punishment from me and fail to receive the slightest assistance from them, the force of any punishment inflicted on them by me outweighing it.

I shall cancel all her rejoicing, all her festivals, her new moon observances, her sabbaths and all her feasts (v.11): they will in fact no longer have occasion for feast and festival or any rejoicing, being surrendered to captivity and under pressure from the various demands of their captors. *I shall do away with her vine and her fig trees, All the payment, she said, that my lovers gave me:* I shall take away all the crops they assigned as a gift to the demons.[23] *I shall turn them to witness* so that their removal will be the most powerful witness of their former lawlessness in assigning to the demons what came under my control both in giving and in removing.[24] *The wild animals of the field devour them, and the birds of heaven and reptiles of the earth:* I shall make them a liability to everyone so that they will get no benefit from them (referring by *wild animals of the field, birds of heaven* and *reptiles of the earth* to the things likely to harm them, since the wild beast is equipped to do injury by its ferocity, the birds easily alight on whatever they please, and the serpents do harm by the severity of their bite).

I shall take vengeance on her for the days [140] *of the Baals when she offered sacrifice to them, put on her nose rings and her jewelry, and went after her lovers and forgot me, says the Lord* (v.13): they will suf-

---

23. Theodore's interest in the historical background to Hosea's prophecy does not extend to comment on the establishment of new moon and sabbath as festivals (see Is 1.13, 2 Kgs 4.23). Nor does he detect the play upon the similar Heb. words for "prostitute's fee" and "figtree," nor mention that the Law forbade use of such payments for Temple vows (Dt 23.18). The commentary is moving at a brisk pace, with no time or inclination for historical elaboration or scriptural documentation.

24. The LXX reads "witness" for Heb. "forest," evidently through metathesis. Theodore is not likely to detect such confusion.

fer this in retribution for their devotion to the idols, to whom they actually offered sacrifices, observing festivals in their honor, donning complete ornamentation, and observing festivals in the worship of the demons, while having no mind for me. He mentions, note, the *Baals*, that is, the idols,[25] by the part referring to the whole, and he customarily calls the demons *lovers*, as it is obvious that in the worship of the idols those worshiped by them were the demons. *Hence I shall seduce her, and put her in the wilderness, as it were* (v.14): I shall surrender her to captivity so that she will be deprived of every good and wander in the ways that formerly she did not know but now was forced by the calamities to travel. He next combines the sentence of punishment with the change for the better, as is the custom with the prophets, following the example in this of blessed David, who frequently in the Psalms both spoke of calamities and promised relief, as when he says in the Thirtieth Psalm, "Have mercy on me, O Lord, because I am in trouble, my eyes are disturbed with anger, my soul and my innards also, because my life is wasted with pain, and my years with groaning," and similarly what follows; then pressing ahead with his recital he says shortly after, "Blessed be the Lord, because he has marvelously shown his mercy in a fortified city," and similarly what follows.[26] You could find many such things in the Psalms, which the prophets necessarily imitated, providing much benefit for the listeners, the purpose being to raise hope though the promise of good things as to instil fear through words of calamity.

So what does he say? *I shall speak to her heart* (v.15): after this I shall encourage her, grown old in inconsolable troubles.[27] *And I shall give her from there her possessions:* I shall restore her once more to the enjoyment of former goods, plucking her from

25. As observed in n. 23, Theodore is not interested in filling his readers in on the precise character of Baalism.

26. Ps 31.9, 21. Theodore does not trouble to substantiate his claim that the prophets spoke in similar terms.

27. We would not expect Theodore to wax lyrical on a summons to a sojourn in the wilderness as an intensely spiritual experience, as do some modern commentators on this passage.

captivity. *And the valley of Achor to open her understanding,* so that whatever they experienced in that place might contribute to their improvement and correction of their former failings. They will probably perceive, in fact, from the change for the better that it was not because of neglect of mine that they experienced the troubles; instead, it was because they fell and had to sense the effects of their own sins. The phrase *valley of Achor* probably refers to the place where they sustained their worst reversal in war, with the result that captivity and the troubles stemming from it ensued (probably by the part referring in usual fashion to the whole place where they suffered innumerable disasters at the enemy's hands and were taken off into captivity by the enemy).[28] *There she will be humbled like the days of her infancy, and like the days of her coming up* [141] *out of Egypt.* Since apostasy and neglect of the divinity imply arrogance, by *humbling* he refers to the acknowledgement of what is due and to rightly fearing the Lord of all as both master and judge. She will attain this outcome in the time of calamity, he is saying, in a manner similar to what happened in Egypt, when they were distressed by the making of bricks and recognized where they should look for their release, and all cried out to God with the result that he assented to the requests of the petitioners, and with great marvels he provided them with his characteristic help. Their fortunes now, too, will in fact be similar when they likewise are brought to their senses by the calamity, recognize the source of the good things, beg help from there, and with great ease attain it.

On that day, says the Lord, she will call me My husband, and no longer call me Baals. I shall remove the names of the Baals from her mouth, and they shall mention their names no longer (vv.16–17): at that time they will recognize the one who cares for them, and abandoning all others they will be devoted to my worship, desisting from all worship of the idols so as to retain no further recollection of them or place any further store by them. The

28. Is Theodore guessing here? He seems to betray little knowledge of what really happened at "Trouble Valley" (the etymology of Achor also escaping him), not at the hands of an enemy but as punishment meted out for impiety, as recounted in Jos 7, captivity not being an issue.

phrase *she will no longer call me Baals* occurs because the one saying this is God: No longer, he means, will they apply my name
to the Baals, now that they are cut off from their deception and
know how to look to me in future as the true God. *I shall make
for you a covenant on that day with the wild beasts of the field, with the
birds of heaven and with the reptiles of the earth* (v.18): I shall cause
those formerly scheming against them and hostile to them to
opt for friendship with them. *I shall smash bow, and sword, and
war, from the face of the earth:* I shall relieve them of any experience of war. *I shall make them dwell in hope:* on the basis of the
goods accruing to them I shall cause them to have higher
hopes of what is to follow. *And I shall betroth you to me forever, and
I shall betroth you to me in righteousness, in judgment, in mercy, and
in compassion* (v.19): I shall bring you into close relationship
with me once more, and accord you familiarity with me, attending to righteousness, punishing those who wronged you at the
time of the captivity, judging everyone with righteousness, and
managing your affairs with mercy. *I shall betroth you to me in fidelity, and you will acknowledge the Lord* (v.20): I shall then admit to
intimacy those of you believing in me, as becomes God, and
those who acknowledge me as their Lord.[29]

　　*On that day, says the Lord, I shall hearken to heaven, and heaven
will hearken to earth, and earth will hearken to the grain, the wine,
and the oil, and they will hearken to Israel.[30] And I shall sow her for
myself in the earth, and shall have pity on Not pitied, and shall say to
Not my people, You are my people, and it will say, You are the Lord my
God* (vv.21–23): then you will have great abundance of crops as
well; [144] the sky will provide rain for the earth according to
my intention (by *heaven* referring to the sky, just as when he
speaks of *birds of heaven* he means those crossing the sky). Normally when the earth is watered, it will provide its crops in
abundance, and from these Israel will have enjoyment of the
good things of the earth. I shall cause them in turn to dwell in
their own land, whence they were previously removed, so that

29. Again, for lines that have been found to be redolent of spiritual intimacy, Theodore can manage but the barest of paraphrases.

30. Against Heb. and other forms of the LXX, which read "Jezreel" and proceed to play upon the term. But Theodore rationalizes his reading.

by living there they may practice worship of me. This, in fact, is the meaning of *I shall sow her for myself in the earth*, which means by analogy with the sowers, I shall once again scatter them over all their own land, and they will dwell in it securely and finally perform their duties to me. This will happen because as a result of my care your situation undergoes a change for the better, so that what was not pitied is pitied, and what was formerly not a people is a people. This benefit will come to them since they too will forsake their former error and acknowledge their duty, and with a clear voice they will say that he alone is truly their Lord and God, the maker and master of all things, who accorded his proper care to them from the beginning.

Chapter Three

The Lord said to me, Go again and love a woman in love with vice and adultery, just as God loves sons of Israel, though they have regard for foreign gods and are fond of raisin cakes (v.1). It is quite clear here, too, as we have often said, that the oracles of the prophets were not written in one form of composition uniformly, but were expressed at intervals according to the time of their revelation; at those moments they were necessarily impelled to communicate them to the people in fidelity to the divine revelations.[31] For instance, having mentioned the adoption of the prostitute and what was given as a reproof of the people on the basis of that image, it was proper for him here in turn to describe a different revelation, which he had received from God and could not but cite, the phrase *The Lord said to me* indicating as much, that the words were a revelation given to him from heaven with God himself speaking. So he means, He told me to have as my wife an adulteress guilty of all sorts of vices so that it might be a representation of the attitude I was anxious to preserve towards the sons of Israel, who lived a life of complete

31. See n. 9 on the nature of prophetic revelations, whether oral or written, and the process of composition of a work composed of them. Theodore, it would seem, presumes it is marriage to a second woman that is being commanded here, not remarriage to Gomer.

adultery and gave clear evidence of their own adultery in showing devotion to what were falsely considered gods by the nations in making much of the offer of worship accorded by
them. The phrase *raisin cakes* suggests as much, implying bread
variously prepared and mixed with raisins and dried fruits,
which according to a custom of those so disposed they offered
to the idols,[32] the phrase *fond of raisin cakes* meaning taking
pleasure in doing this out of respect for the idols. Now, what he
said previously was especially directed by way of reproof of the
ten tribes, who forsook God and attached themselves to the
idols, whereas this is by way of reproof of those [145] belonging to the kingdom of Judah, who, though having the Temple
in their midst and in fact giving evidence of some devotion for
festivals and sacrifices to the true God, in the manner of an
adulteress combined the worship of the idols with the display
of devotion for the divinity.

Then he says, *I bought her for myself for fifteen silver coins, an
omer of barley and a skin of wine* (v.2), employing precision of expression as proof of the truth of what happened.[33] There was
also need of the demonstration *I bought* since God had also attached the Jews to himself with great gifts as well as payments. *I
said to her, Stay with me for many days, and I with you; do not play the
prostitute or go with a man* (v.3). As if God also were minded to
have the Jews cleave to him not for a little while but for a long
time, and promised them his peculiar care, so he wanted them
not to drift off to the idols but to persevere in the right dispositions to him. Then he adds, *Because for many days the sons of Israel
will stay without a king, without a ruler, without sacrifice, without altar, without priesthood, without insignia* (v.4). In other words, just
as in the case of that woman not persevering in her agreement

32. Theodore may be guessing again, or at least suppressing scriptural examples of raisin cakes untainted by idolatry, such as their use in worship by
David in 2 Sm 6.19.

33. On an Antiochene such "precision of expression," ἀκριβολογία, would
not be lost nor its purpose passed over, viz., to establish historical veracity; once
again Theodore's view, as in ch 1, is that there is no mere figure being developed here (let alone any numerology at work). He does admit, nonetheless,
that the prophetic action conveys an obvious meaning.

and drifting off to other men in her unfaithful attitude, so he means here, With the Jews committing similar crimes against me, I shall impose on them a like punishment by consigning them to captivity for a sufficient time and causing them to be bereft of everything in their own place. The result is that they will be without their own king or ruler in being subject to another king whom they must serve as captives, their sacrifices and use of the altar will be removed along with all priestly worship on account of their being made captive and deported far from the places where service of God by Law was practiced, and they will be deprived of a solution of their problems by recourse to the prophets, which they had previously enjoyed in a variety of ways. *After this the sons of Israel will be converted and seek the Lord their God and David their king* (v.5): at that time they will be conscious of their own wicked deeds and change their attitude, participating zealously in the knowledge and worship of God, and will actually be glad to have as king the successor of David. He means this will in fact happen after the return, when they were actually under one king, Zerubbabel, a descendant of David, and no longer held that attitude by which the ten tribes deserted the reign of the successors of blessed David and chose other kings.[34] *They will be astonished at the Lord and at his good things in the last days:* all will be reduced to astonishment at the extraordinary marvel, reckoning up all the good things they came to enjoy through divine providence.

Chapter Four

After saying this against Judah by way of reproof, he then directs his attention to everyone, at one time the latter, at one time the former, and at another time reproving all in com-

---

34. This position, that Zerubbabel, presiding over the returned community of Judah, is the Davidic successor referred to, Theodoret—probably aware that Theodore has adopted it—will often (though in fact not at this point) resist on two grounds: first, that Zerubbabel is clearly not a king in the account in Ezra, and second, that Jesus is in fact the true successor of David. Theodore will predictably not look for such spiritual kingship, even avoiding reference to Luke's genealogy (3.27), which cites Zerubbabel as a Davidic ancestor of Jesus.

mon.³⁵ [148] Hence he says, *Listen to the word of the Lord, sons of Israel, because the Lord has a judgment against the inhabitants of the land, that there is no truth or mercy or knowledge of God in the land; cursing and falsehood, murder, and theft, and adultery are spread over the land, and blood is mingled with blood* (vv.1–2): listen to God coming to judgment with you on these matters and proving with how many awful evils you repaid his care.³⁶ None of you is interested in the truth, and there is not even a mention of lovingkindness amongst you. You have no concern for the knowledge of God; instead, deceit and utterly execrable behavior, murder, and theft, and adultery are committed everywhere in the land. You are so bent on slaying one another that the blood of one victim is mingled with the preceding one. *As a result the land will mourn, and will be diminished along with all its inhabitants* (v.3): all the land will be in mourning on account of the magnitude of what befalls them—for example, the enemy sweeping them away remorselessly so that the number of inhabitants surviving is reduced to a minimum, the meaning of *the land will be diminished along with its inhabitants. Together with the wild beasts of the field, the reptiles of the earth, and the birds of heaven.* In figurative manner, as is his wont,³⁷ he means that along with the rabble the mighty will perish, who prey upon weaker people like wild beasts, plunder the poor suddenly like winged creatures, and take pains to injure their neighbors just as much as reptiles. *And the fish of the sea will perish*—in a nutshell, all who fill the earth like the fish of the sea will suddenly perish.

To this he adds, *So that one will go to law and no one will be convicted* (v.4): such complete devastation will obtain that there will not even be anyone left to judge or anyone to correct the faults of others; all in similar fashion will fall victim to the same fate of captivity. *My people like a priest under attack*, falling from their

35. Modern commentators make similar observations about the prophet's changing focus; in Theodore's "reproof," ἔλεγχος, they distinguish different genres such as lawsuit and court speech. See n. 56, below.

36. Is it because he does not resonate with the echoes of the Decalogue that Theodore does not refer the reader to Ex 20 and Dt 5 for the source of this list of sins? or is he again abstaining from scriptural documentation?

37. Theodore is not insensitive to an author's imagery or use of literary genres.

former position with no semblance of any merit, like a priest falling victim to criticism, being deposed and losing the respect of everyone. *They will suffer infirmity by day* (v.5): for a long time they will be subject to infirmity from the evils besetting them. *And the prophet will suffer infirmity with you by night:* having formerly had recourse to false prophecies to deceive you, they themselves in great numbers will also suffer infirmity, being in the grip of the disaster as though enveloped in some nocturnal gloom and perceiving the involvement in deceit to be fruitless for themselves.[38]

By night I resembled your mother: thus they were forever caught up in ignorance and error. *My people gave the impression of possessing no knowledge* (v.6): you also resembled her, setting no store by knowledge of me.[39] *Because you also rejected knowledge, I too shall reject you from serving as my priest:* just as you gave no attention to knowledge of me, so I too [149] shall exclude you from my worship, by captivity putting you far from the holy places where it fell to you to serve as my priest. This is the meaning of *I shall reject you as serving as my priest:* since priesthood is a benefice held in common by all, as blessed Paul says,[40] hence the priest ought make offerings for the people's oversight as much as for his own; and so he was right to say that all were excluded from the priesthood when it came to an end, since when it was in force it provided a common benefice, and so when it ceased it involved a common loss. *You forgot the Law of your God; I in turn shall forget your children:* those defaulting on obligations of my Law I shall set at no account.

The more numerous they were, the more numerous their sins against me (v.7): since through my care their numbers grew and became incalculable, they should have acknowledged the one responsible for this gift to them; instead, they gave evidence of

---

38. Is it the obscurity of the LXX text that prevents Theodore from seeing the Jewish institutions of priesthood and (cultic) prophecy at the focus of Hosea's strictures? or is he predisposed in favor of such institutions?

39. Theodore is wise to hurry on in these cases where LXX and our Heb. read to different effect similar forms for "resemble" and "destroy," respectively.

40. See Heb 7.11. Again is Theodore reluctant to see priests (like himself?) particularly at fault? or is he egalitarian in recognizing a priestly people?

crimes against me commensurate with their great size, committing them in numbers beyond measure. What will happen, then? *I shall turn their glory into dishonor:* in place of their former prosperity I shall make them experience worse things. *They will feed on my people's sin* (v.8), that is to say, for having sinned this way against me, they will reap the results fitting their deeds, enjoying fruit of the same kind as the seeds they have sown, the phrase *They will feed on my people's sin* meaning, Those of my people will enjoy the kinds of things their sins involved. *In their sins others will take their souls:* for their sins against me they will pay the penalty through others, the enemy being on the verge of attacking them. *As with the people, so will it be with the priest as well* (v.9): in captivity they will find themselves in such confusion and calamity that there will be no single difference between the one exercising priesthood and the one subject to priesthood for the reason that there will be no one entitled to the divine priesthood at that time when all alike are caught up in the disaster of captivity. *I shall take vengeance on them for their ways and repay them for their plans:* I shall inflict on them punishments corresponding to the plans they devised and chose to enact. *They will eat and not be filled* (v.10): they will have an unceasing experience of troubles, later ones ever succeeding earlier, expressing it this way by analogy with those who eat without satisfaction and eat again, as if to say, they will experience troubles, and when the first lot passes, the second will take their place, and there will be no end to the process (saying *They will eat* here as above *They will eat my people's sins*, that is, They will experience).

They prostituted themselves and will lose their way: since they forsook me completely, nothing will turn out as it should for them. *Because they abandoned the Lord to practice prostitution, my people's heart tasted wine and intoxication* (vv.10–11): completely neglecting God, they gave full attention to devotion to the idols with the result that they were intoxicated with the vices and no longer had any sense of their own lawlessness. [152] *They sought an answer through omens, and announced it to him through his staff* (v.12): they followed the practice of pagans in seeking answers from the demons or their priests in their wish to learn through omens what they should do; their practice was to have recourse to their staff and deceitfully deliver an answer to the questions. *They were deceived by a spirit of prostitution, and they were unfaithful to their God:* adopting the attitude of a prostitute, they completely left God for error. *They sacrificed on the crests of the mountains, and made offerings on the hills under oak and poplar and shady tree because the cover is good* (v.13): they then betook themselves to the mountains and the hills, performing sacrifices there to the demons; choosing large and shady trees, they engaged in their peculiar error there, taking the extent of the shade of the trees to be something significant and solemn with the result that they they thought it even had a bearing on piety.[41]

For this reason your daughters will acts as prostitutes and your brides will commit adultery; I shall not call your daughters to account for acting as prostitutes, or your spouses for committing adultery, because the men themselves consorted with the prostitutes, and offered sacrifice with the initiates, and your people of understanding were involved with a prostitute (vv.13–14): you will pay penalties corresponding to your own faults, since the enemy will be in control of you and violate the daughters and spouses of your very selves. I shall make no account of it when it happens, since you are rightly subjected to it, having connived in the faithless error and made common purpose of abandoning me and taking up with the idols so as in many cases to perform rituals sanctioned by the pagans and offer sacrifices to them as though in return for some marvelous benefits.[42] To put it in a nutshell, the people that should, of all peoples, have known better and acknowledged their creator as God chose to throw in their lot with such people who performed this depraved and licentious prostitution by forsaking God and going over to the worship of demons.

As for you, Israel, do not be unaware, and Judah, do not enter into Gilgal, nor go up to the house of Aven, nor swear on the living Lord

41. Theodore is simply paraphrasing these verses without elaborating on the practices described there or documenting them from Scripture.
42. Theodore thinks the immorality involved is typical only of pagan rites, despite scriptural record of a long tradition of this deviant behavior in Israel (see Dt 23.17, 1 Kgs 14.23, Jer 2.20).

(v.15): do not all likewise suffer from the same dire ignorance so as to go up to Gilgal for worship of the idol ensconced there and pretend to reverence it as though the eternal and real God. You must realize it is impossible to treat them alike: there is a great difference between the eternal God and an idol built yesterday with human hands, as someone with belief in the eternal God would have to abstain from everything bearing this name fictitiously, like the idol Aven, whose house you enter and to whom you accord worship unbefitting to it.[43] *Because, like a stubborn heifer, Israel was stubborn* (v.16): like a heifer, [153] under the natural movement of desire for disorder, you abandoned my service and with your intemperate disposition you inclined towards the worship of the idols. *Now the Lord will feed them like a lamb in broad pasture:* accordingly I shall scatter them, leading them around hither and thither under the enemies' advance so that they are no different from a lamb roaming about a broad area and wandering in search of its mother (by "scattering" referring to the habit of those who graze and disperse their herds unremittingly). *Ephraim is involved with the idols* (v.17): they threw in their lot with the idols (by *Ephraim* referring frequently here and elsewhere to Israel as part to the whole, applying the name of the most powerful tribe to all ten, like "Children of Ephraim drawing and discharging bows").[44]

They set stumbling blocks for themselves: it gave thought to a turn for the worse for itself—how and in what fashion? *It opted for the Canaanites* (v.18) by emulating their impiety.[45] *They added*

43. Once again Theodore needs to unpack for his readers the nuances of the prophet's thought, namely, that Gilgal and Bethel had degenerated into northern centers of heterodox worship (see 1 Kgs 12.28–30); "house of Aven"—i.e., "house of trouble"—is but a case of "sarcastic metonymy" (Stuart) for "house of God," *Bethel,* where an oath "As the Lord lives," which implicitly abjured idolatry, was clearly inappropriate. All this is evoked by Am 5.5, which likewise escapes full comment by Theodore.

44. Ps 78.9. This is a helpful and observant remark on the synecdoche involved in the use of "Ephraim," occurring thirty-six times in Hosea, less frequently in the other prophets (Theodore citing the only psalm where the usage occurs).

45. The verse has textual problems in the Heb., which differs from the LXX, Theodore's being different in details again. He contents himself with brief paraphrase.

promiscuity to promiscuity: at this point they completely took a turn for the worse. *They loved dishonor from its wantonness:* showing awful stupidity and disdain of me, they chose worship of the idols, which will be a source of utter dishonor for them. *A wind storm will whistle about them in its wings* (v.19): as the bird flies by beating the wind in the sky with its wings and gains height by flying, so, when these people are caught in my wrath, they will become airborne, as it were, and be driven off with great force into captivity.[46] *They will be ashamed of their altars* so that they will then get a sense that the devotion they showed for the altars of the idols was futile and harmful.

Chapter Five

Hear this, you priests, and give heed, house of Israel, and house of the king, give ear (v.1). It is clear that here once again by a different revelation he commences the present discourse, addressing the priests, Israel, and all the royal household. *Because the judgment is against you:* I have come to subject you to my judgment, and to require an account of you for what you have committed. *Because you have proved a snare for the watchtower and like a net spread over Tabor, which the hunters set for their prey* (vv.1–2): you devised various schemes against my prophets, like the hunters spreading the nets for the prey, eager to ensnare them in various difficulties (calling the assembly of the prophets *watchtower,* like the phrase in Ezekiel, "I appointed you a watchman for the house of Israel").[47] *I am your chastizer:* since you resented what they told you would happen and hatched such plots against them, I personally shall inflict the punishment, chastizing you for what you have committed, and you will be completely subject to it against your will.

I know Ephraim, and Israel is not beyond me (v.3): I have a precise knowledge of what was done by them for the reason that I am everywhere. [156] *Because now Ephraim has prostituted herself*

---

46. Theodoret would have been proud of the effort to enter into the author's less than transparent image.

47. Ezek 3.17.

and Israel is defiled: I am therefore aware that they have completely forsaken me and are defiled with the worship of the idols. *They had no plans to return to their God, because a spirit of prostitution is in them, and they did not acknowledge the Lord* (v.4): they did not change and adopt an attitude of inclining towards me, since they had entirely taken a turn for the worse, preferring to set no store by me. *Israel's arrogance will be humbled before him* (v.5): for the insolence and arrogance that made them so reckless in forsaking me and devoting themselves to the idols, however, they will pay a fitting penalty by witnessing their own humiliation, to which they are reduced by my punishment. *Israel and Ephraim will become infirm through their iniquities, and Judah with them:* all sinned together, and all will suffer punishment together for acting at variance with knowledge of me. Blessed Paul also speaks in these terms, "Those suppressing the truth through iniquity,"[48] as if to say, Those wronging the truth by a turn for the worse. *With sheep and calves they will go to seek out the Lord, and they will not find him, for he has turned away from them because they abandoned the Lord* (vv.6–7): even if they offer sacrifices, thinking they will placate the divinity with them, they will gain nothing from it, since God is completely turned away from them because they forsook him and gave their complete obeisance to the idols. *Because they bore themselves illegitimate children:* mingling even with the nations in defiance of edict, they had children of illicit liaisons, blessed David also charging them with this in the words, "They mingled with the nations."[49] So here, too, their having children from them suggests their complete interrelationship with foreigners. *Now the blight will devour them and their farms,* as if to say, I shall surrender them and all their possessions to destruction like the blight.

Blow the trumpet on the hills, sound it on the heights, make a proclamation in the house of Aven (v.8): in all the places where you practiced your impiety by forsaking your traditional devotions, cry aloud all the more, highlighting the troubles that are due to befall you for them. What things? *Benjamin was aghast, Ephraim*

48. Rom 1.18.
49. Ps 106.35.

was laid waste in the days of censure (vv.8–9). By mention of *Ben-jamin* he refers to the kingdom of Judah, and by *Ephraim* he means the ten tribes. His meaning is not that one was aghast and the other was laid waste, but that both things would happen to each of them, that they would be aghast and would be laid waste; and by *in the days of censure* he means at the time of the enemy's assault, which he would inflict as obvious censure of their lawlessness. So his meaning is, They will be aghast and beside themselves at the sudden change in their situation, through which they will be completely laid waste when I inflict the enemy on them and [157] censure them for the lawlessness practiced by them. Now, implying a common fate by separate statement you would find frequently in blessed David as well— for instance, when he says, "By day I cried aloud, and by night before you,"[50] not meaning that he cried out in the daytime whereas by night he conversed with God, but as if to say, Day and night I cried out before you, thus implying the common action by separate statement. Likewise here, too, the expression *Benjamin is aghast, Ephraim is laid waste* is intended to mean that in common they were both aghast and laid waste. *Among the tribes of Israel I demonstrated faithfulness:* by inflicting this on them I shall establish the truth and reliability of my threats, which they did not believe would take effect despite the prophets, and they will learn from experience that all that was said was credible and reliable.

The rulers of Judah behaved like those who move boundary stones (v.10): as those who shift landmarks undermine the rights of ownership, so in your case, where there is a great difference between me and the idols, with the honor and title of God due to me and none to them, in many and varied ways you took it on yourself to abrogate irremovable rights, and invested those others with the title and honor due to me. *On them I shall let loose my*

50. Ps 88.1. Again Theodore has recourse to a scriptural locus to establish a point about biblical usage instead of giving an historical reference to a time when south and north were both involved, such as at the end of the Syro-Ephraimite war, when Judah attacked Israel, or an attack of Assyria against them both. He has lost interest in the historical context in which the prophet is working, highlighting instead religious and moral issues.

wrath like water: I shall direct my wrath against them for committing such crimes, inundating them with the vast number of the
enemy like water. *Ephraim dominated its adversary, trampled underfoot the judgment:* they had no respect for justice; each wronged
the other to the extent possible, trampling rights underfoot
and giving no importance to them, as the Lord also said in the
Gospels, "You abandoned love, justice, and mercy,"[51] as if to say,
You have no regard for love, righteousness, and lovingkindness.
And by *adversary* the Lord seems to be referring to the one who
has been wronged, like the saying, "Be on good terms quickly
with your adversary,"[52] recommending the wrongdoers to culti-
vate by every means those wronged by them. *Because he began to
take up idle pursuits:* they were guilty of this in choosing to devote their attention to the worship of the idols in still setting my
laws and their duty at naught. *I am like an alarm for Ephraim and
like a goad to the house of Judah* (v.12): I shall instil serious alarm
in them through the enemy, afflicting them with pains from it
like some harsh goad (it being obvious that he does not mean
Ephraim in one case and Judah in the other, but says he will
bring both the alarm and the goad on both together, as we
showed above as well).

   *Ephraim saw his sickness, and Judah his pain. Ephraim took him-
self off to the Assyrians and sent ambassadors to King Jarim, and he
could not rescue you* (v.13): at that time they will experience
[160] troubles (the meaning of *sickness* and *pain*) when
Ephraim is led off to the Assyrians, and though sending ambassadors to the king of the Egyptians he will get no help from that
source, either.[53] *Pain will not leave you, because I am like a panther
to Ephraim and like a lion to the house of Judah, I shall pillage and go
off, I shall take and there will be no one to recover* (vv.13–14): you will
continue in your unrelieved troubles, since I shall be to you

   51. Lk 11.42 loosely recalled. Evangelical references are rare, Theodore not
wishing to give the text an eschatological and specifically Christological dimension.
   52. Mt 5.25.
   53. Theodore is not helped to identify these historical developments by the
LXX's rendering an unusual Heb. form as a proper name, which he presumably
takes to refer to the appeal by King Hoshea of Israel to Egypt at a later date (see
2 Kgs 17.4).

like a panther and a lion, with great savagery pillaging and carrying you off through the enemy's attack, there being no one capable of ridding you of the evils besetting you. *I shall depart and return to my place until they disappear.* He went on in this vein in keeping with the figure employed: since it is typical of such beasts to pillage with great savagery and slaughter what falls in its path and take it off to its lair, where it eats and consumes its catch,[54] so he employed here as well the likeness to panther and lion, meaning, After pillaging you through the enemy and making you captive, I shall be with you, not interested in what is happening nor according you any help until you suffer complete ruin at the hands of your captors. *They will turn and seek my face:* then they too will be changed, and will beg my help. *In their distress they will rise to implore me, saying:*

Chapter Six

Let us go and return to the Lord our God, because it is he who has struck and will heal us, who will afflict and cure us, he will restore our health after two days, and on the third day we shall rise, we shall live in his sight and we shall know (vv.1–3): under the pressure of the tribulations besetting them they will charge towards me with great celerity, extremely confident that having afflicted them I shall also heal them completely and apply a cure to the wounds duly affecting them, improving their condition with great celerity and dexterity. This in fact is the meaning of *he will restore our health after two days, on the third day we shall rise:* he will heal us so promptly that in two days, or at the most three, he will restore us to our former prosperity, the phrase *and we shall know* meaning, We shall be in a position to enjoy better things, like the phrase "You made known to me the paths of life,"[55] that is, You

54. Again Theodore explicates the image well, without referring to similar passages where the Lord is depicted as a lion, like 13.7 below, Am 3.8, and Ps 5.22.

55. Ps 16.11. The echoes of this v.2 in resurrection statements in the NT like Lk 24.7 and 1 Cor 15.4, would have been so strong that it is almost perverse of Theodore not at least to advert to them, even without developing a Christological digression. The psalm echo is not nearly so deafening.

brought me to life. *We shall pursue the knowledge of the Lord:* we shall zealously show interest in knowing him. *We shall find him ready like the dawn:* we shall attain his help like dawn, as if our fortunes were changed from darkness to light. *He will come to us like early rain on the soil:* he will supply us with an abundant supply of good things, like crops yielded by the soil whenever it receives suitable rain at the right time.

What shall I do for you, Ephraim? what shall I do for you, Judah? Your mercy is like an early cloud, [161] *and like a morning mist that fades* (v.4). This, too, is the beginning of another discourse that the prophet delivered to the people, receiving it by revelation and making it the occasion of an address.[56] What is required to be done by me for you, he asks, now that you have been so committed to lawlessness? Though I want to have mercy on you, your crimes do not allow this to happen, inevitably attracting punishment to you; even if I wish to have mercy on you, my attitude to you necessarily remains unchanged, because your doings completely frustrate it, in the way a cloud or dew appearing in the morning is immediately dissipated. *For this reason I cut down your prophets, I killed them by a word of my mouth* (v.5): admittedly it was I who proved the cause of death even for my prophets, whom I sent for your benefit, since I bade them remind you of your duty; they tried to persuade you, but you had no respect either for what they said, or for me, who sent them, and you put them to death in various forms—hence *I cut them down* and *I killed them by a word of my mouth,* that is to say, I was responsible for it in giving them this order. He does not mean, note, that he personally by his own direction treated the prophets in that fashion, but as if to say, Through the orders I gave them for transmission to you, I myself came close to causing it. This resembles what is said also by blessed David, "You diverted our paths from your way,"[57] not that he personally divert-

56. Like modern scholars such as H. Gunkel and S. Mowinckel interested in literary genres, Theodore detects a movement in thought at this point, attributing it here as above to a separate oracle coming to the prophet, whereas the moderns retrospectively see vv.1–3 as the distinct unit, classing it as a penitential song. See nn. 9 and 35.

57. Ps 44.18 LXX (43.19). The LXX's version of the difficult v.5 in the Heb.

ed them, but that by allowing them to have experience of such evils, he attributes to himself the responsibility for what happened.

And my judgment will go forth like the light: but I shall not allow this lawlessness to go unavenged; instead, I shall exact penalties of you so that from the troubles you are about to endure light will be shed more clearly for everyone on the fact that, in judgment on the lawlessness committed against the prophets by you, I invested you with such calamities. And, to bring out that it is not without reason that he does this, *Because I prefer mercy to sacrifice, and knowledge of God to holocausts* (v.6): though proposing them, I sent the prophets to show the worthlessness of both sacrifices and holocausts, and to bring you to knowledge of me. Since, however, you responded to what was done by me by treating them in that fashion, you will pay a just penalty for your crimes; after all, it is also part of mercy to invest the wrongdoers with punishment for those who have been abused.

But they were like someone breaking an agreement, they scorned me there (v.7): you persisted in your transgression, showing no regard for the pact you made with me in the beginning, despising me completely to the point of killing those of the prophets who reminded you of this. *Gilgal is a city engaged in futility* (v.8): Gilgal is responsible for your doing this, the place where [164] you betray harmful and futile devotion to the idols, as he said above, *Do not enter into Gilgal*[58] and be engaged in futility, he means, hinting at what happens there. *Disturbing the water,* the work of those muddying the clarity and purity of the piety visible in knowledge of me by contaminating it with the idols. *Your force like that of a brigand* (v.9), which gives evidence of its peculiar power in the injury to those led astray in the manner characteristic of brigands' dedication to harming others and displaying their power in those people's ruin. *Priests concealed the way, they murdered at Shechem because they were guilty of lawlessness.*

---

leaves Theodore with some rationalizing to do, but he is up to it (that psalm verse offering Chrysostom and Theodoret similar problems).

58. 4.15. Theodore's text alone in v.8 reads Gilgal for Gilead, perhaps because Gilead was not known for any aberrations of the kind documented before in the case of Gilgal.

He intends by the comparison to demonstrate their wickedness: Your ancestors (he is saying, meaning Jacob's sons, Levi and Simeon) on seeing their sister subjected to indecent violence felt such indignation at the deed as to converse deceitfully and with guile with the Shechemites on pretence of friendship (the meaning of *concealed the way*), and took the opportunity to slay them all at the one time for the crime committed.[59]

In the house of Israel I saw terrifying things, Ephraim's prostitution there (v.10): while some things were done by them, I have now seen others fit to cause terror in the whole of Israel, prostitution on the part of all, involving, not the body but corruption of soul and desertion of God. *Israel is defiled, and Judah set aside its harvest* (vv.10–11): defiled with the cult of the idols, everyone set their sights on the one transgression; they all betrayed their own welfare as deficient and corrupt. In other words, just as when the sowing is finished and the crop requires harvesting, a farmer who prematurely sets his eyes on relaxation would lose what he has farmed and would render all his previous labor futile through his own idleness, so you enjoyed so many and such good things—escaping from Egypt, crossing the desert, being given the Law, taking possession of the promised land, getting a suitable place for worship. But when you should at that point have offered the fruits to God, then you showed all that was done for you to be useless through your own wickedness, *setting aside* the repayment to God of the fruit of so many and such great favors, and giving yourself idly in every case to a diversion in the wrong direction. Similar to this is the statement by Isaiah, "I waited for you to produce grapes, but you produced thorns."[60] *Begin harvesting for yourself when I reverse the captivity of my people, when I heal Israel* so that there is need of a new beginning on your part, which I shall provide out of my

---

59. See Gn 34. Though Shechem was an important religious center, where priests would be involved (even in brigandage), Theodore again prefers to exclude them from the guilty party, and instead comes up with the story of the violation of Dinah by Shechem and its vindication by Levi and Simeon.

60. Is 5.4. Theodore goes to unusual length to unpack the harvest image—if only to convince the reader that this is the prophet's meaning in a cryptic verse.

surpassing lovingkindness by bringing you back from captivity in defiance of all human expectation. Then finally you would agree to set your eyes on better things, needing a new beginning so that, should you eventually be embarrassed at the magnitude of the gifts and direct your attention to improvement in the future, then it will be possible for you to achieve it (the word *Begin* meaning, You will be able to make a beginning provided you are prepared to set your eyes on duty).

Chapter Seven

What is it in this case? [165] *The iniquity of Ephraim and the wickedness of Samaria in committing falsehood will be revealed* (v.1): the lawlessness you commit in forsaking me and setting your eyes on falsehood is obvious to everyone in the punishment you rightly endure for such lawlessness as you are guilty of. How, and in what way? *A thief will break in, a robber stealing in his path so that they have the one theme in their heart* (vv.1–2): like a chance meeting in the way with a thief or robber who robs those he meets, and goes into a house and takes its contents, so the enemy attack them and remove everything belonging to them inside the house and out, doing away with everything, so that you will all fall victim to the calamity and sing together songs with mourning as their theme, grieving at heart for what has happened, and lamenting with words of lament for the magnitude of the disasters befalling them.[61] *Now their schemes envelop them, they happened in my sight* (v.2): keeping in mind everything of theirs committed with great wickedness, I enveloped them in awful disasters commensurate with the plots they hatched with great disrespect in my sight.

They gladdened kings with their evil deeds and rulers with their lies (v.3) so that satisfaction was felt by the adversaries, whether kings or rulers, who will dominate them and take them captive for the evils they kept committing and because they dismissed

---

61. In a verse where the LXX departs considerably from our Heb., Theodore's text omits a clause, "I remember all their wickedness," though his following comment presumes it.

knowledge of me and involved themselves in the false and deceitful cult of the demons. *All committing adultery like a pan heated for cooking* (v.4): all are of one accord in forsaking knowledge of me and adopting an adulterous attitude, inclining to the worship of the demons and, like a pan heated for cooking, they sink into that licentiousness with a kind of ardent enthusiasm. *It will burn them with the flame:* they will instead be consumed by this very attitude. *From the kneading of the dough until it is all leavened, the days of your kings* (vv.4–5): as some dough left over and thrown into the flour leavens it and brings it all to completion, so when you set up this lawless kingdom by taking control from Jeroboam, you all similarly strayed to this attitude of wickedness.

Rulers began to seethe with wine: the rulers gave themselves to drunkenness and inebriation, giving way to intemperate anger against everyone as though from such indulgence. *They stretched out their hands with pests:* they had avarice in mind, choosing to associate with everyone of corrupt manners. *Because their hearts were heated like a pan by stirring them up all night* (v.6): they enkindled their mind like a pan with the drunkenness they pursued all night. *Ephraim was overcome with sleep:*[62] with such drunkenness, like people sunk in deep sleep, they paid no heed to duty. [168] *Morning came, and it was enkindled like a fiery flame; all were inflamed like a heated pan* (vv.6–7): when day broke, they set upon the same things again, inflamed like fire, as ardent as some pan and aroused for involvement in these unbecoming pursuits. *Fire consumed their judges:* so they endure an appropriate punishment, all of their number who succeeded to power being consigned to slaughter by the enemy as though by fire. *All their kings have fallen:* all will be consigned to ruin and slaughter. For what reason? *There was no one of their number to invoke me:* since they had the one attitude in common, completely unwilling to accord me any importance.

Ephraim mixed with the peoples (v.8). Blessed David also laid this blame on them in the words, "They mingled with the na-

---

62. The LXX reads Ephraim here for a similar Heb. form rendered "baker" by some modern commentators, "fury" by others.

tions."[63] Mingling with foreigners was completely forbidden them by the Law,[64] remember, so it was right for him to upbraid them for it here, too. *Ephraim was a pancake not turned over,* unchanged in its behavior, persisting in the same wickedness, just as that thing normally stays unmoved in the place it was put. *Foreigners devoured his strength* (v.9): so he is subjected to an appropriate punishment; having mingled illegally with foreigners, he will be completely destroyed by them. *He does not know; his hair has grown grey, and he does not know:* since he persisted in his ignorance of his duty, choosing even for a long time not to recognize his obligations, he will therefore suffer such things. *Israel's pride will be humbled to its face; they did not turn back to the Lord their God, and did not seek him in all these things* (v.10): for their acts of insolence against God in irreverently and unremittingly showing attention to the demons and putting devotion to them ahead of devotion to the true divinity, they will witness their own humiliation, to which they will rightfully be subjected, having shown no wish to turn towards God even when circumstances changed.

Ephraim has become like a dove, silly and lacking heart; they called upon Egypt, and they went to the Assyrians (v.11): like a dove that takes no notice of its own offspring, and when deprived of them is in the habit of building its own nest again in the same places without being at all worried by the loss of its offspring, exactly so did they behave as well, having no sense of their own destruction, and instead expecting help from the Egyptians but gaining none, for the reason that the Assyrians with great power took them off as captives to their own country. *As they go, I shall cast my net over them; I shall catch them like the birds of heaven* (v.12): they will be unable to escape captivity since I shall encircle them in my sentence like a net, I shall draw them into captivity like birds. *I shall correct them with the report of their tribulation:* I shall inflict such troubles upon them that the report of the troubles besetting them will in its gravity suffice for their correction. [169] He explains in turn what the cause of this was.

63. Ps 106.35.
64. See Lv 18.24, Neh 13.

Woe to them for straying from me. They are in a wretched state for their impious behavior to me, (v.13) for they will suffer this for their lawlessness to me. *I redeemed them, and they spoke lies against me:* from the beginning I treated them well, whereas they gave evidence of their characteristic ingratitude to me. I freed them from slavery to the Egyptians, whereas they uttered every blasphemy against me, at one time making a calf with the words, "These are your gods, O Israel, who brought you out of Egypt," at another time, "When he struck the rock, and water emerged, and torrents flowed out, 'Surely he will not be able to give bread or prepare a banquet for his people?'"[65]

Their hearts did not cry out to me (v.14): they did not give a thought to turning to me with a sincere mind and to looking to me for gifts. *Instead, they moaned on their beds, they cut themselves for grain and wine:* on the contrary, when they entered the land of promise, and gained enjoyment of the rest given them by me (referring to it as *their bed*), they paid me no attention and instead devoted themselves to the worship of the idols, moaning and cutting themselves according to their custom, which they performed while attributing to them the source of the good things given them by me. *They were corrected by me* (v.15): for the transgressions committed against me they will receive sufficient correction due to them from me. He brings out that in doing such things they were transgressing. *I strengthened their arms, and they devised evil plans against me:* because while it was I who provided them with all their strength against the enemy, they practiced everything absurd and full of impiety in their irreverence against me.

They turned aside to nothing (v.16): I made them appear, when they were transformed by my anger and punishment, as nothing. *They became an unstretched bow* with the result that they were no different from a bow with its string unstretched, useless to a fighter as long as it is in this condition; they will thus be ineffectual and weak against the enemy—the meaning of *They were corrected by me,* as if to say, Since they were not acknowledging the enjoyment of the things they received from me through their

65. Ex 32.4, Ps 78.20.

turn for the worse, I taught them their duty by providing them with a clear demonstration of their lawlessness. *Their leaders will fall by the sword because of their tongue's lack of discipline:* so, while they will therefore be weak, the enemy will have such power against them as even to destroy their rulers along with the others for what they uttered against me in an undisciplined way.

Chapter Eight

This is the grumbling in their throat in the land of Egypt, like a trackless land, like a trumpet, like an eagle on the house of the Lord (v.1):[66] they will suffer this when imitating the attitude of their ancestors, who in Egypt criticized the [172] gifts given them by God; they will be like a trackless waste, given over to utter devastation to which they will be reduced, the enemy trumpet sounding loudly against them and giving notice of the enemy's impending assault, which will befall them with great speed, like an eagle pouncing suddenly on its prey. In this very fashion the enemy will advance, wiping them out and torching the divine temple. Now, he added this as a proof of the extremity of his anger, namely, that he did not even spare his own house, surrendering it to the enemy for destruction along with the rest. Then, to indicate why this would happen, *In repayment for their breaking my covenant and failing to observe the Law:* since they had broken my covenant and completely failed to observe my Law, I considered it made no sense to spare the house they had defiled and polluted by their very entry.

They will cry out to me, O God, we know you (v.2): then, under the impact of events and the punishment inflicted on them, they will reluctantly acknowledge my power. *Because Israel spurned good things, they pursued a foe* (v.3): they will suffer such a fate for proving ungrateful for the gift of the good things from me, despite dominating their own enemies with great ease

66. The Heb. text is corrupt, and Theodore's version differs from other forms of the LXX without being itself transparent; but he soldiers on (at least as well as modern commentators, who afford themselves the luxury he could not—emending the text) to present a plausible explication.

when I provided them with my help. *They reigned as kings for themselves, did not rule through me, and did not bring it to my notice* (v.4): they so misled me as to set aside the king given by me and set up their own monarchy, giving no importance to my arrangements (the meaning of *they did not bring it to my notice*). *With their silver and their gold they made idols for themselves for their own destruction:* the kingship of mine and the observance of the Law they set aside, installing their own kingship (referring to the one appointed over the ten tribes, beginning with Jeroboam, who was also the first to make them the calves),[67] behaving in a fashion in keeping with the disorder of their choice of monarchy, and making many and various idols, some from gold and some from silver, from which they gained nothing but their own destruction.

And, since he reproached them for the innovation of kingship, whose first crime to be committed was that of the heifers, he logically proceeded, *Throw out your calf, Samaria, my anger against them has been provoked* (v.5): desist from the impiety involving the heifers; it is no idle wrath of mine against the lawlessness of what has been done. *How long will they fail to be cleansed in Israel? A craftsman made this thing, and it is not God* (vv.5–6): has not even length of time taught you your duty? did it not remove the stain of such awful impiety? do you instead hanker after idols made by human hand, whose claim to be properly regarded as gods is having such a cause of their existence? *Hence your calf is deceitful, Samaria:* are you unable to realize that the making of heifers proved the cause of your being led astray from God with the result that on this account you have good reason even to hate them? [173]

Because the wind has caused ruin, and their overthrow will be their lot; the sheaf has no power to produce flour but, if it did, foreigners would consume it (v.7): it is no different from those crops that are burnt up and spoilt by a scorching wind, and are completely useless as nourishment for human beings, ruin and loss being the result of it. It is useless for human beings, incapable as it is of producing flour suitable for nourishment; but if it

67. See 1 Kgs 12.26–29.

should actually be produced, it is thrown out as rubbish for feeding brute beasts. In other words, in the same way that the worship of the idols is harmful and brings no benefit with the result that, should something develop from a different quarter, it too would be of advantage to the enemy on account of the impiety innate in you. *Israel is overwhelmed; it has now been reduced to a useless vessel among the nations because they went up to the Assyrians* (vv.8–9): you will suffer complete annihilation for this, taken by the Assyrians; you will be like an utterly useless vessel among the foreigners, deserving no consideration. *It grew up for me of its own accord:* through my care they developed into a vast number, unwilling to set any store by me, the source of all their wonderful goods, and by their own volition they brazenly committed every crime (the meaning of *of its own accord*).[68] *Ephraim loved gifts:* not content with what they had, their eyes were bigger than their stomach.

For this reason they will be handed over to the nations (v.10): they will rightly be subject to their foes and feel the effects of their impiety to me and their wrongdoing. *I shall now admit them:* I shall await them in the region of the Assyrians, drawing them into it by captivity so that they will then experience the effects of their very own impious behavior. How and in what way? *They will shortly cease anointing king and leaders:* they will stop appointing these lawless kingships and governments, corrected by captivity and getting a sense of their own lawlessness. *Because Ephraim multiplied altars, they became on occasion of sin for him* (v.11): they rightly suffer for setting up that impious kingship; since they came up with that way of the manifold invention of the worship of the idols and setting up many and varied altars for themselves, on which they committed sin most of all, they will duly pay the penalty. *I shall write down for him a great number and his laws* (v.12): this great number of altars and new laws they devised regarding the cult of the idols I shall justly record

---

68. Modern commentators struggle to make sense of our Heb. text of these verses, again resorting to emendation, an option not available to Theodore. In this verse, to add to the difficulty of the thought, the LXX sees the verb "grow up" in a similar form appearing in our Heb. for "wild ass" or some such animal. But Theodore can rationalize the text before him.

as some kind of written accusation against them, delivering against them the sentence for such acts of lawlessness. *The beloved altars are counted as foreign:* the altars for which they displayed much love and zeal will also fall into the enemies' hands.

Hence, if they offer sacrifice and eat meat, the Lord will not accept it (v.13): even if they try to appease the divinity with sacrifices, sampling the meats in the sacrifices according to custom, no account of this [176] will be taken by God, nor will he accord them any forgiveness of these lawless acts. *Now he will remember their iniquities and take vengeance on their sins:* mindful of their acts of impiety, I shall not be propitious to them, but shall exact of them punishments commensurate with their lawless behavior. *They returned to Egypt, and will eat unclean food in Assyria:* in the midst of these disasters they will ask for help from Egypt,[69] but will gain not the slightest benefit from that quarter, being taken as captives to Assyria and experience the harshness of life in captivity. *Israel forgot the one who made him and built shrines; Judah multiplied fortified cities, and I shall despatch fire on his cities and their foundations will be consumed* (v.14): they did not want to take account of the one who made them, and built shrines for the worship of the idols; they then in addition tried to fortify the cities with walls, as if by this to find some relief from their problems—but it will be all to no avail for them, since by means of the enemy I shall inflict such an awful and so fearsome a punishment on them that it will spread over them like fire and all but destroy their every city from the foundations.

Chapter Nine

Do not rejoice, Israel, and do not be happy like the peoples, because you were unfaithful to the Lord your God (v.1): it is therefore not proper for you to be glad and rejoice like other people, since they did not receive instruction capable of leading them to

69. The LXX's misreading of Heb. tenses does not distract Theodore. See n. 71, below.

godliness, whereas, in your case, despite much instruction and knowledge of God, as a result of an adulterous attitude you were false to the knowledge supplied you, and turned to the worship of the idols. *You loved gifts on every threshing floor:* you actually offered firstfruits of every crop to the demons, judging them responsible for what was given. *Threshing floor and wine vat did not know them* (v.2): so you shall pay a just penalty, the loss of the crops.[70] *They did not inhabit the Lord's land:* you will not remain in the land given you (expressing it as usual with a change in tense, *They did not inhabit,* meaning, They will not inhabit, as was pointed out by us on many occasions in blessed David's usage).[71] *Ephraim inhabited Egypt, and will eat unclean food in Assyria:* after being fugitives to Egypt you will all be reluctantly transferred to captivity under the Assyrians.

They did not offer a libation of wine to the Lord, nor were they pleasing to him (v.4): in regard to offerings to the idols they displayed such zeal and prodigality as to give them firstfruits from every threshing floor, whereas to God, responsible for all good things, they preferred never to offer libations of wine or to do anything that could please him from the intention of the offerers; as blessed David says, "May my converse be pleasing to him,"[72] that is, May it seem pleasing and acceptable. Likewise his meaning here is, They were not [177] pleasing to him, that is, They chose never to do anything by way of favor to him. Then, to bring out that he is saying this to reproach them for their attitude, the divinity not being pleased with them, *Their*

70. Theodore does the best he can in a case where the LXX seems to have confused a Heb. form for "feed" with a similar form for "know."

71. As emerged in his comment on v.13 of the previous chapter (see n. 69 there), Theodore is aware of the habit of the LXX (though not understanding the morphology involved) of confusing future and past tenses of the Heb.—though "confuse" is not a term he is prepared to apply to the LXX. His further remark, that he has previously noted such usage on many occasions in commenting on David, confirms the view that his *Commentary on the Psalms* (immediately?) preceded this work on The Twelve and possibly was (in accordance with pious tradition?) his first exegetical work, as Theodoret had hoped it would have been his and possibly Chrysostom made it his, and as Facundus of Hermianae later maintained of Theodore. See Introduction for details, and n. 97, below.

72. Ps 104.34.

sacrifices will be like bread of mourning for them, everyone eating it will be defiled: he is so far from needing sacrifices or his honor being determined by them that even if they offered sacrifices, God would not accept them. Instead, it is as if you were to offer food to mourners: they would consider the sight of what seemed pleasing to everyone else unacceptable, pained by their sense of grief, and could not bring themselves to touch the food offered, and so whoever is obliged to partake of food in time of mourning does not touch it, as though regarding it as something defiled or harmful.[73] Just so would God regard the sacrifices offered to him if they actually chose to make such an offering: while gladly accepting them when offered by grateful people, he would by contrast consider unacceptable the sight of the present from the unworthy by the reminder of the impiety to which they are addicted and in which they appear to make the offering as a kind of irony.

Because their bread is for their own selves, they will not enter the house of the Lord: whatever present they make, therefore, will revert to themselves, being in no way acceptable to God (the meaning of *it will not enter the house of the Lord,* that is, it will not be acceptable to God, nor will he consider it presented to the Lord, putting it far from him as offered from an impious attitude). You see, just as God says to Cain, who made presents with a bad intention, "Its direction is towards you, and you will master it,"[74] that is, The offerings reverted to you, and you must be master of them, I have accepted absolutely nothing, so here he says, *Their bread is for their own selves,* that is, Whatever present they make will be for them, not being acceptable to God. Now, he called the offerings *bread* to refer to all offerings by mention of a single item, since they were accustomed to offer bread as

73. The pathos of the mourners' situation is well brought out; but modern commentators would see rather a reference here to the cultic uncleanness of anything touched by mourners who have been in contact with a dead body (see Nm 19.11–22). Theodore, we have seen, for all his insistence on the historical sense, is himself not familiar with aspects of the historical background.

74. Gn 4.7, the meaning of which, obscure also in the Heb., is disputed; Chrysostom in his nineteenth homily on Genesis lets his listeners choose between two interpretations, one of which approximates to Theodore's, though the preacher himself favors a different one.

well, as he also said above, "They are fond of raisin cakes" (3.1).

What will you do on the feastday, and on the day of the Lord's festival? (v.5): having been like this to God, what escape from the troubles will you find on that day when the feast and some kind of festival will be observed for God at your destruction for being his enemy and foe who are justly slaughtered? *For this reason, lo, they will proceed from the hardship of Egypt, Memphis will receive them, and Michmash will bury them; ruin will succeed even to their money, thorns in their tents* (v.6): in your case, after the great hardship you will endure, you will flee to Egypt in the hope of finding some relief, but will be rooted out by the Assyrians and taken off into captivity by them; you will pass through the cities of Egypt, a range of perils befalling you one after another—the meaning of *Memphis and Michmash*,[75] as if to say, You will pass through the cities of Egypt, [180] crushed and wiped out by the Assyrians, all your belongings will also be destroyed, such awful desolation will overtake your cities and regions that thorns will grow there in the absence of occupants.

The days of your punishment are coming, the days of your retribution are coming (v.7): you will endure this then when the time approaches for you to have to be punished for your impiety and to make due recompense for the acts of impiety of which you have been guilty. *Israel will be seated*[76] *like the prophet beside himself, the person who is vehicle of the spirit:* you will find yourself in such troubles as to be no different from a false prophet put into a deep trance under the influence of the evil spirit and lacking all sense of reality; in like manner will you be out of your mind at the magnitude of the troubles. Why? *Your madness is aggravated by the vast number of your iniquities:* since you lived a life of great iniquity, you have completely fallen victim to the madness about the idols. *Ephraim is a watchman with God, a prophet, a tangled snare on all his ways:* though you should have been a watchman

75. The identity of this city that goes unmentioned in our Heb. Theodore does not settle on, nor investigate why it and Memphis (known for its cemetery and pyramid tombs) rate a mention.

76. Theodore's text seems to have mistakenly copied the LXX to read "be seated" for "be abused." Theodoret, on the other hand, also presumably using the Antiochene text, reads the latter.

for the good for others, and with God have taught the others their duty insofar as you learnt it from him, yet on the contrary you proved to be for everyone a path in the wrong direction, with the result that you are no different from a harsh snare enveloping its victims in danger; thus you proved a norm of impiety for everyone. *You established madness in the house of God himself:* you filled all the land of promise with idolatry (by *house of God* referring to the land of promise, in that it is dwelt in by God). *They were corrupted according to the days of a hill* (v.9): you changed everyone from better to worse, taking on a corrupt mentality that was no different from those who once committed sacrilege in the wilderness by building a calf and saying, "These are your gods, Israel, who led you out of the land of Egypt"[77] (referring by *days of the hill* to that time). So it follows that you were corrupted by them, that is to say, You contracted the same affliction as theirs. *He will remember their iniquity, he will avenge their sins:* so it follows that he will recall your acts of impiety and exact of you penalties appropriate to your sins against him.

Like a bunch of grapes in the wilderness I found Israel, and like an early fig on a fig tree I saw their fathers (v.10): I gave evidence of as much benevolence to their ancestors as if you were to find a bunch of grapes in the wilderness and see it in defiance of all expectation, or a fig appearing on the tree before due time. *But they entered Baal-peor and practiced idolatry to their shame, and they became objects of detestation:* taking the false path of adoration of the idols,[78] they opted for alienation from me, proving themselves to be deserving of nothing else than utter shame for switching from God, who had been the source of so many good things for them, to an idol, from whom they had received nothing—hence their becoming objects of detestation, falling to their very enemies.

77. Ex 32.4, a favorite text of Theodore's, who proceeds to invite the reader to trust his assurance that the desert period is referred to in an obscure phrase in which the LXX has taken "Gibeah" (notorious for its depravity in Judg 20–21) as (the identical form for) "hill." But he himself shows his uncertainty by returning to the phrase further on.

78. See Nm 25.1–5, ἀλλοτρίωσις, "estrangement," taking the particular sense of "polytheism, idolatry" here, which Theodoret also gives the term in his comment on Ps 81.

After saying this about them he goes on, [181] *Ephraim was spread out like a bird's wings* (v.11), in his wish to establish the meaning of that verse, *They were corrupted according to the days of the hill.* So he fittingly says, Despite such wonderful care that they enjoyed from me, like their ancestors they forsook my counsel like a bird. *Their glory from births, pregnancies and conceptions:* then when they commit such acts of impiety, they consider themselves blessed to have large families (the meaning of *from births, pregnancies, and conceptions,* since the newborn issues from conception, pregnancy, and birth). *Hence even if they suckle their children, they will have no one left as a child* (v.12): they give no thought to the fact that even if the newborn reach the height of maturity, no good will come of it for them, for they will be reduced to childlessness by the slaughter of war. *Hence, woe to them because I have left them:* when I have cut them off from my care, ruin and destruction await them.[79] *My flesh from them:* admittedly, my feeling for them was formerly so great that I considered myself one of them, and had such an attitude towards them as those people normally have who have received their being from someone. *Ephraim, as I saw him, presented his children as prey, and Ephraim brought out his children for slaughter* (v.13): but despite my having such affection for them previously, since I saw the complete turn for the worse they took, their fate will be the opposite of before, and they will be given into the enemies' hands like prey; tortured and wounded by them, they will all be done away with. *Give them, Lord, what will you give them? Give them a childless womb and dry breasts* (v.14): they suffer this just and appropriate punishment, affected with childlessness and incapable of rearing the newborn, to the point where utter ruin takes them in this condition.[80]

Then, after mentioning what had justly been inflicted on them by God, he proceeds to add the following: *All their troubles began in Gilgal, because it was there I hated them for the wickedness of their pursuits* (v.15): there they practiced every form of impiety,

79. The subordinate clause, represented in our Heb., is not found in other forms of the LXX.
80. The pathos of the passage leaves Theodore unmoved, contenting himself with paraphrase aimed at clarity of exposition, his primary goal.

and as a result of that I justly hated them for committing such crimes. *I shall drive them out of my house:* I shall drive them out of the land of promise (by *house* referring to the whole land, as though he chose to live in it). *I shall no longer continue to love them; all their leaders are disobedient:* I continue to have a steadfast hatred towards them, since they all took the path of disobedience; but those thought to be leaders among them are most of all their guides in wickedness. *Ephraim was in difficulties, his roots dried up; he would no longer bear fruit* (v.16). By analogy with trees, he said that they would wholly perish like the trees that dry up completely when the root rots, no longer being in a position to bear fruit. *Hence, even if they have children, I shall kill the desires of their belly:* I shall do away with all who come from them. *God will reject them because they did not hearken to him, and they will be wanderers among the nations* (v.17): he will make them all alienated from his [184] care, since they were unwilling to listen to him and have an eye to repentance; as a result of this they will be taken and will be held captive amongst the foreigners, forced to be led hither and thither and roam about under the pressure of extreme need.

Chapter Ten

Israel is a flourishing vine (v.1): Israel is no different in its vast numbers from a luxuriant vine with numerous and large branches. *Its fruit abounding:* they daily grew in size, their offspring being numerous on account of the prosperity accruing to them. *It increased altars according to the increase in its fruits:* the abundance in which they found themselves owing to God's blessing they repaid with a great extension of impiety, erecting altars in honor of the idols to match their own numbers. *It built pillars according to the good things of its land:* enjoying many good things from the land, in return for them they erected pillars for worship of the idols. *They divided their hearts* (v.2): their frenzied devotion to the idols was such as to divide their attention in their cult of the idols, some being devout to these ones, others to other ones. *Now they will be done away with:* they will justly be subjected to destruction for this. *He will overturn their altars:* neglected by them, God will personally bring about the overthrow of all the altars they impiously erected for the worship of the idols. *Their pillars will wear out:* they will totter and fall.

Hence they will now say, We have no king because we did not fear God. What would a king do for us? Speaking words as a pretext, he would make a covenant (vv.3–4): now they will feel the effects of their own folly in choosing a king in opposition to God's wishes, and because they did not fear God and consecrated some futile and lawless kingship in opposition to David's line ruling by divine promise, their kingship has been done away with and they all have been surrendered to captivity. No gain came to them from the king; on the contrary, by using deceitful words, he made some depraved covenant with them to forsake God and to adore the heifers made by him. *Judgment will spring up like fodder in a barren field:* God will judge their lawless exploit, inflicting on them such awful punishment as retribution that God's judgment delivered against them will burst forth and appear dreadful and fearsome, just as if fodder springing up suddenly in barren ground were to produce its growth in abundance.

The inhabitants of Samaria will dwell near the calf of the house of Aven (v.5): when troubles befall them, they will all take themselves off to the heifers worshiped by them in the hope of gaining some assistance from that quarter. *Because its people mourned for it:* it will obtain no benefit from that source; on the contrary, they will mourn the heifers themselves, witnessing some fearsome destruction of them at the hands of the enemy. [185] *As they provoked it, they will rejoice at its glory:* the enemy will heap much dishonor on the idols, and they will be filled with deep satisfaction to see their glory removed, which previously they wrongly enjoyed from those devoted to their worship. Just as blessed David says, "Do not let my enemies rejoice over me,"[81] that is, let them not take satisfaction from observing what they think has befallen me, so here the clause *they will rejoice at its glo-*

---

81. Ps 38.16. Theodore is wise to pass over the subordinate clause, where the LXX seems to have confused similar Heb. forms for "priests (will mourn)" and "provoked."

ry means, They will be pleased to see them deprived of their own glory. *Because they left it:* they witness the removal of the glory that they had wrongly enjoyed in the past. *After binding it and taking it to the Assyrians, they offered gifts to King Jarim* (v.6): when those who previously seemed to worship them see the Assyrians advancing, they will smash the heifers, made of gold as they were, and wrap them up with the intention of presenting them as though ordinary gold, and will offer them as a gift to the king of the Egyptians in the expectation of finding some assistance from that quarter. The prophet, remember, in many places seems to reproach them for this, their futile expectation of help from the Egyptians.

What will happen, however? *Ephraim will get shame in return for the gift:* for the offer of the gift and the present Ephraim will be shamed by gaining no benefit, instead displaying this interest to no avail. *For its plan Israel will be shamed:* it will predictably fail to realize its expectation. *Samaria will cast off its king like a stick on the surface of the water* (v.7): they will gain no benefit from that stratagem and that endeavor; they will all be held in custody, the king also captured, who will be seized by the Assyrians and taken off to a foreign country like wood carried along on water, led wherever his captors please. *The altars of Aven will be carried off, the sins of Israel* (v.8): the worship of the idols, the cause of Israel's sinning against God, will cease. *Thorns and thistles will grow up on their altars:* there will be such desolation that no one will set foot there, and thorns and thistles will grow in the place of the altars. *They will say to the mountains, Cover us, and to the hills, Fall on us:* they will long to suffer a rapid destruction by falling under these things rather than putting up with punishments one by one.[82]

Israel sinned from the time of the mountains (v.9): it was from this point that the zeal for sinning began, from the time they forsook God and showed interest in the hills and attention to the idols.[83] *There they stayed.* But in fact their lawlessness will be

82. Theodore is resolute in ignoring any NT echoes of the text, reminiscent though this verse would be of Lk 23.30 and Rv 6.6 to his readers.
83. See n. 77 on the confusion of "Gibeah" with "hills"—though a modern

brought to a stop by punishment. *It will not grip them on the hill:* captivity will rid them of their fascination with the hills, with the result that they will not be found worshiping in the hills, but will be occupied with the troubles of captivity. *War came to the children of iniquity:* this will happen as a response to their iniquity and impiety, war befalling them at the hands of the Assyrian enemy. [188] *I shall correct them according to my desire* (v.10): I shall therefore inflict upon them evils capable of correcting them sufficiently, and when corrected by them they will sense their own evil. *Peoples will be assembled against them when they are corrected for their two wrongs:* I shall gather a vast number of enemy against them, I shall correct them for both their neglect of me and their attention to the idols.

Ephraim is a heifer trained to be fond of opposition (v.11): like a heifer bucking and wanting to get the better of the handlers, so it forsook God and resisted the yoke of slavery. *I shall harness the beauty of her neck:* I shall remove all her comeliness of which she is so proud. *I shall harness Ephraim:* with all my strength I shall harness her like a feisty heifer. *I shall pass over Judah in silence:* I shall ignore Judah, tested with troubles, not according him the slightest assistance, as is said in blessed David, "Do not pass me over in silence,"[84] that is, Do not ignore my situation, tested as I am by harsh developments. *Jacob will gain strength for himself:* I shall give evidence of my strength to the whole of Israel. It is quite obvious, of course, that by *Jacob* and *Israel* he is referring to the whole nation of the Jews, called by both the names of their ancestor, who was called Jacob first, and Israel after the vision, as also in blessed David, "He chose David his servant, and brought him up from the flocks of sheep, from behind the nursing ewes he promoted him to shepherd his servant, Jacob and his inheritance, Israel,"[85] clearly referring to the Jewish nation by both the names.

---

commentator like Stuart feels Hosea himself may be playing upon the formal similarity in the second half of the verse.

84. Ps 28.1. The relatively frequent, almost exclusive, reference to "the blessed David" is accounted for by Theodore's (perhaps immediately) previous work on the Psalter.

85. Ps 78.70–71. His modern counterpart Stuart makes the same point as

Sow for yourselves righteousness, and harvest a crop of life (v.12):
put into practice what belongs to complete righteousness,
then, for from such seeds it is possible to reap a crop of life.[86]
Shed on yourselves a light of knowledge while there is time: share in
the knowledge of truth, repenting before the time of punishment to the extent possible to avoid experiencing troubles. *Seek
the Lord as long as the fruits of righteousness come to you:* give every
attention to what pleases God so that it may be your lot to reap
righteousness. *Why did you pass over impiety in silence, reap its fruit,
and eat a false crop?* (v.13): stop doing the sorts of things you did
before, dismissing and hushing up the occurrence of such
impiety, when there are grounds for anger at your harvesting a
crop full of deceit and harm. *Because you trusted in your chariots,[87]
in the vast number of your forces. Ruin will develop* [189] *for your people, and all your fortresses will be demolished* (vv.13–14): you believed your own power was sufficient for the war against your
adversaries, but everything turned out to the contrary, ruin taking hold of all the people to the destruction even of fortified
cities. *Just as Shalman was wiped out in the house of Arbel in times of
war, when they flung mother on children, so shall I do to you, house of
Israel, at the sight of your wickedness* (vv.14–15): the slaughter they
suffered when horrendous slaughter and warfare happened to
them, parents being exterminated along with their children,
you too will now endure, children of Israel, receiving a punishment commensurate with your wickedness. He is probably
mentioning something of awful savagery that happened to
them at that time,[88] which he naturally reminded them of as a
familiar event, as if to say, For what you did at that time out of

---

Theodore, "Ephraim and Judah are Yahweh's people, not his 'peoples.'" If his
grasp of the author's thought seems sound, he seems less secure, on the other
hand, in accounting for Jacob's second name bestowed in the incident in Gn
32.28–30: "Israel"—at least in the popular etymology of the text—refers to his
"striving with God," not the vision of God suggested by Jacob's naming the place
Peniel, "the face of God." Theodoret interprets the name in exactly the same
way in commenting on Ps 125.5.

86. The passage is generally parenetic and susceptible of pastoral elaboration; but Theodore is too focused to apply it to the lives of his readers.

87. Stuart prefers this reading to our Heb. and other Grk. readings.

88. Theodore anticipates modern commentators in putting this gloss on an
undocumented act of barbarism.

an excess of wickedness, you will now rightly suffer a similar fate. *At dawn they were cast out:* they will fall with great speed. *Like the dawn, the king of Israel was cast out:* like the dawn, that appears for a brief time and then comes to an end, their king will fall.

Chapter Eleven

Because Israel was an infant, and I loved him, I called his children to leave Egypt; just as I called them, thus they departed from my sight; they sacrificed to the Baals and offered incense to the carved images (vv.1–2). He refers to Israel as *an infant* on the basis of the time in Egypt, when they began to take shape as a people and to experience the divine attention. I displayed great providence to them from the very outset when they began to take shape, he is saying, so as even to snatch them from Egypt, but they gave evidence of their own wickedness in proportion to the love and care shown them, immediately forsaking me, taking a turn for the worse and actually directing to the idols all the devotion that was due to me. *I bound Ephraim together* (v.3): though they were scattered by the troubles in Egypt, I gathered them together in my care. *I took him up in my arms:* I accorded him care in keeping with my power. *They did not know that I heal them:* they were not ready to acknowledge the one ridding them of such awful troubles. *I drew them in their human corruption with bonds of my love* (v.4): despite the fact that by human standards they were due to perish, I snatched them away, ineffably clutching them to me in my love. *I shall be like someone striking a person on their cheek:* the blows and punishments I shall inflict for their folly will be as severe as it is painful to receive blows delivered to the face. *I shall bend down to him and prevail with him:* I shall give myself wholly to punishing him so that at least by this he will come to know my power.[89]

89. The pathos of the expression of God's parental love in this chapter, which has attracted from modern commentators such encomiums as "Das Hohelied der Liebe Gottes" ("The canticle of God's love"), "Divine passion in Hosea," "One of the high points of the OT revelation of God's nature," leaves

Ephraim dwelt in Egypt, and Assyria was their king (v.5): they will go off as fugitives to Egypt, thinking to avoid the Assyrians' attack, but they will gain no advantage, since by my decision they will gain complete control of them. [192] Why will they suffer this? *Because they were not willing to turn back:* because they obstinately persisted in their wickedness, refusing to show any signs of conversion. *He was weakened by the sword in his cities, and met his end at his hands* (v.6): so they will not prevail in fighting with the enemy, nor secure any salvation for their own cities, since all their weapons and their complete military equipment will prove to be unserviceable and useless, with me resisting them on account of their wickedness and inflicting the Assyrians on them as punishment. *They will feed off their schemes:* they will be repaid for their own stratagems, subjected to due punishment. *His people dependent on its dwelling* (v.7): they will not remain in their own dwelling place, nor have a secure habitation in the same place, since the Assyrian will suddenly seize them and take them all off into captivity as though suspended and lacking the slightest support. *God will be angry at his privileges and will not exalt him:* whatever seems precious to him and worth special attention God will abolish in his anger, bringing them all to extreme abjection.

How am I to treat you, Ephraim? Am I to protect you, Israel? (v.8) What action should I take towards you for such numerous acts of wickedness? Why should I help you when convicted of the height of wickedness? *How am I to treat you, Ephraim? Shall I treat you like Admah and Zeboiim?* I find you do not deserve protection; on the contrary, I find the punishment inflicted on you would match your crimes if you were to endure the disaster that happened to Sodom and Gomorrah, Admah and Zeboiim.[90] *My heart underwent change, I was moved to repentance by this; I shall not act in accord with my wrath and anger, I shall not abandon*

Theodore unmoved. (Admittedly, he is not helped by the LXX's habitual difficulty with Heb. verb tenses in v.4, which this time he does not recognize, unlike v.5.) Nor does he acknowledge Matthew's explicit quotation of 11.1 in his narrative of Jesus infancy at 2.15 that lends it also a Christological dimension.

90. See Dt 29.23. Theodore does not elaborate on the disaster that overtook those cities.

Ephraim to destruction (vv.8–9): though I find you deserving of this punishment, my attitude to you is changed, and disturbed by the sight of your calamity I am moved to repentance to the extent of desisting from being angry with you any longer, and cannot bring myself to let you be surrendered to complete destruction.[91] *Because I am God and not anyone of your number:* I am God, who made everything and cares for everything as my own works, not at all like the way you live, and those with whom you associate. *I am holy, and I shall not enter the city:* I am unaffected by all human events and superior to them; I do not live in cities by human norms, nor am I in the habit of spending time there with you, hence having nothing in common with your attitude and the wicked way of life to which you are devoted. On the contrary, in my surpassing mercy I am moved to free those due to become subject to due punishment and suffering from it.

They will follow behind the Lord (v.10). The prophet supplies this sequel, as it were, to God's previous remark,[92] meaning something like this, [193] You should in future follow such a God and do everything in accord with the wishes of a God who is so mild and loving towards you. *He will roar like a lion, and children of the waters will be astonished:* if we were to present ourselves this way, he would, like a lion that is frightening to cattle, raise his voice against all those who advanced against you in their great numbers like water, and would reduce them to astonishment with the fear he instils.[93] *They will come like a bird from Egypt and like a dove from the land of the Assyrians, and I shall restore them to their own homes, says the Lord* (v.11). In other words, God promises to lead them back from all directions after freeing them from the grip of captivity, and to restore both the captives in Assyria and the fugitives in Egypt like birds to their own

91. In addition to the pathos of the verses, there is also here the notion of divine repentance, which normally an Antiochene—sensitive to the suggestion of mutability in God—would pause to clarify and mitigate. But Theodore continues to hurry on, unaffected.

92. Some modern commentators also see the thought taking a different turn here, as does Theodore, though naturally he is not prepared to see it as an insertion.

93. Theodore succeeds in explicating the references to the Lord as a lion and to "water" (the "sea" probably meaning the west).

homes. *Ephraim surrounded me with lies, and the house of Israel and Judah with impiety; now God knows them, and it will be called God's holy people* (v.12): since formerly they all lived in impiety, degenerating into falsehood and the worship of the idols and paying no heed to me, I necessarily invested them in those awful troubles; but now that they have repented and have turned their eyes to better things, I shall make them my own (the meaning of *he knows them*), and by dint of experience they will appear as mine in being worthy of so many wonderful good things thanks to my help, since I am ready to provide them with such goods from me.

Chapter Twelve

What, then? *Ephraim an evil spirit* (v.1), as if to say, a depraved will, by *spirit* Scripture referring in many places to free will, as for example, "They were led astray by a spirit of infidelity," and "Restore an upright spirit in my innards," and of Caleb, son of Jephunneh and Joshua, son of Nun, "A different spirit is in him."[94] *He pursued heat all day long:* he was constantly involved in things that are like heat in being damaging to crops and that can automatically bring destruction on them. *They multiplied idle and futile actions:* they set up a vast number of idols, that are completely destructive and the source of great harm. *He made a treaty with the Assyrians, and oil was transported to Egypt:* then, falling foul of troubles for this, they hoped to gain some good, at one time through the Assyrians, at another time through the Egyptians; with the former they agreed to make a treaty of friendship, and from the latter they begged aid, but no benefit came from either of them.

The Lord has a judgment against Judah to take vengeance on Jacob (v.2): God comes personally in actual events to deliver judgment against them and avenge what was done improperly by them (by *Jacob* here referring to the nation of the Jews, which were called both Jacob and Israel from the names of their an-

---

94. Hos 4.12, Ps 51.12, Nm 14.24. See also Nm 27.18.

cestor, as we indicated above).[95] He goes on from here, *according to his ways,* [196] *and repay him according to his pursuits,* as if to say, I shall exact a penalty of them commensurate with their failings. Then also by a comparison with their ancestor he charges them with their wickedness: *In the womb he supplanted his brother* (v.3): even before birth one by a gesture betrayed his deceit in intending to supplant the rights of the firstborn. *And in his struggles he strove against God:* though undergoing much effort and deceit, he could not bring himself to withdraw from God's favor. *He struggled with an angel and prevailed* (v.4): suspecting a plot on the part of his brother, he was accorded a vision of an angel, with whom he was seen to wrestle and emerged superior.[96]

While that is what happened to him, then, what happened to his descendants? *They wept and begged me:* all are weeping and begging, asking for release from the troubles in which they find themselves for their own impiety. Of what kind was this? *They found me in the house of Aven:* they gave themselves to the worship of the idols, honoring with my name those who had no right to it—in other words, honoring me as though present in that place when I was not present. So the clause *They found me in the house of Aven* means, As they found me present there, the one who should have been honored by them as God, so they applied to the idol both the name and the honor due to God. *There he spoke with them:* in that place they received the just sentence for their impiety. *The Lord God almighty will be his memorial* (v.5): he will encounter such troubles as will be the cause of his acknowledging the true God and forever having an efficacious remembrance of him who made them, was their benefactor in every situation, even when they were guilty of impiety, and by

95. Theodore has in fact already established the identical reference of both names (in comment on 10.11), but the issue at this point for modern commentators is rather the relevance of the mention of Judah.

96. Theodore touches on the events in Jacob's life in Gn 25 and 32, mention of a vision entering either from reference to Peniel in the latter or from conflation with the account in Gn 28 of the vision at the place Jacob calls Bethel. The LXX proceeds to speak of "the house of Aven" instead of Bethel, so that Theodore thinks Jacob is no longer in focus.

correcting them brought them to a better frame of mind in his characteristic power. *Turn back to your God, practice mercy and justice, and always keep close to your God* (v.6): give evidence, then, of genuine conversion to God, and give attention to lovingkindness and justice; be zealous for always being in God's company and holding fast to worship of him, which duly proves to be a source of benefit, and completely abstain from devotion to the idols.

Canaan, scales of injustice in his hands, he loved to oppress (v.7). Having summoned them to conversion in these words, he reproaches them in turn with their wickedness at this point, saying, You were shown to be no better than the Canaanites, whom God expelled from the land on account of their extreme impiety and wickedness and replaced with you; in similar fashion you turned to injustice and with great dedication you persecuted the weak in the power you had acquired.[97] *Ephraim said, But I have become wealthy, I have found relief for myself* (v.8): he then amasses riches from unjust dealings, takes satisfaction in his wealth, and finds enjoyment of it satisfying. *None of his efforts will be found to benefit him on account of the injustices he committed:* he should have reasoned that everything he amassed with lawless effort [197] would all perish through the injustice with which he amassed it, since God intended to call them to account for the crimes they had continued to be involved in. *I, the Lord your God, brought you out of Egypt* (v.9): you should have desisted from injustice against the needy on the grounds that I expelled you from Egypt when you were reduced to harsh servitude. *I shall make you dwell in tents as on the feastday:* I provided you with habitation—that is to say, enjoyment of the land of promise—supplying you with the means of celebrating the enjoyment of your assets. The phrase *I shall make you dwell*, note, means, I made you dwell, employing the customary change in tense, which I sufficiently demonstrated in the case of the Psalms as well, as for example, "I cried to God, and the Lord

---

97. Theodore is not quite responding to Hosea's mocking use of a nickname for Ephraim, like Israel for Jacob, and the sense of merchant given to "Canaanite" in places like Prv 31.24 and Ezek 17.4.

heard me," to which he adds, "Evening, morning, and midday I shall recount and report, and he will hear my voice,"[98] where "heard" is not consistent with "will hear": if it had happened, why ask for it to happen? The former statement, however, "And the Lord heard me," means, He will hear. In short, many cases of the Hebrew usage are found scattered throughout the Psalms, and likewise in the prophets you could probably find the same thing, as when it says, "He was led like a sheep to the slaughter," in the sense, He will be led.

I spoke to the prophets, I multiplied visions and took on a likeness at the hands of the prophets (v.10): at that time I consecrated prophets and vouchsafed the people of that time very many visions, manifesting myself in various ways to righteous people of that time, like Moses, Joshua son of Nun, and their contemporaries.[99] I chose gladly to do all these things, and they should have been mindful and content with what was given, and not unjustly snatched other people's possessions. *If not in Gilead, there was surely falsehood in Gilgal* (v.11). He means, If you got something from Gilead and Gilgal—that is, from the idols— you would have some excuse for what you have now done; but if you got nothing from Gilead nor from Gilgal—that is, if no benefit came to you from the idols—how was it not obvious to you that you had become involved in falsehood? As it was, you abandoned the truth, forsook your benefactor, and turned to those who were of no benefit to you; then you offered sacrifices

---

98. Ps 55.16–17. As observed in n. 71, Theodore has been alerted to the LXX's practice of confusing past and future tenses. He thinks he sees it operating in this v.9, apparently on the basis of logic, and suggests we read the LXX's future as past—wrongly, in fact (see also n. 20 on ch 2 of *Comm Jl*). As before, he supports his suggestion by reference to his recent work on the Psalms, again using logic and not morphology to document the same "Hebrew usage"—precariously again, though comparison with modern commentators (like Dahood) and versions (like NRSV) of those psalm verses reveals that even on the basis of morphology the experts can differ. But he would find no one (Theodoret excepted) to support him in proceeding to give a future sense to Is 53.

99. One might have thought that, for a commentator on prophets, such a text would prove fertile soil for developing a study of the charism of prophecy. But Theodore, with his focus exclusively—if inadequately—on the historical situation (he is only now identifying Gilead and Gilgal as centers of idol worship), hurries on. See n. 43.

to them along with your leaders (by *Gilead* and *Gilgal* meaning the idols). As he said above, "Do not go into Gilgal,"[100] as if to say, Do not become involved with the idols, by the place referring to the rites celebrated for them, so here too he makes mention of Gilead and Gilgal, where extensive worship of the idols took place, by the places indicating the worship of the idols, his meaning being, So much accrued to you from me, but nothing from the demons and the idols, that it was surely by deception and under the influence of falsehood that you have forsaken me and involve yourselves in their sacrifices. *Their altars* [200] *like turtle in a dry countryside:* devotion to them will be of no good to you, since God will utterly destroy them all by means of the enemy; in other words, because a *turtle* normally lives in water and would be completely destroyed when taken on dry land, he meant by the example to suggest the destruction of the altars.[101]

Once more by means of a comparison with the ancestors he portrays them as guilty of impiety. *Jacob withdrew to the country-side of Syria, Israel entered service for a wife and kept guard for a wife* (v.12): it was for the sake of virtue and the blessing of the forebears that he made his choice, opting to become a fugitive from his own family, to make for Syria, endure servitude under Laban, with great difficulty enter into marriage to avoid marrying a Canaanite in defiance of his father's wishes,[102] endure such hardship and marry a wife in observance of the parental norms and God's wishes, as his brother had defied the wishes of God and his parents by marrying a Canaanite. *By a prophet the Lord brought Israel up from Egypt, and by a prophet it was protected* (v.13): after he went down into Egypt following those events, he showed such care for his descendants as to bring them all up from Egypt by the ministry of the prophet Moses and protect them with his characteristic care in the desert until they entered the land of promise. *Ephraim enraged and provoked me*

100. 4.15.
101. Theodore makes an honest attempt to unpack the figure involved—though he has probably not taken the intended sense of "turtle," χελῶναι, a pile (of stones, or of soldiers' shields in the case of a siege).
102. Gn 28.1.

(v.14): *though sprung from such good forebears* and enjoying from me such great goods on their account, they reduced me to an awful rage by proving ungrateful to me for the great favors I had done them and by taking to the worship of the idols, from whom they drew no benefit. *His blood will be poured out upon him:* so the punishment will revert to him for his crimes. *And the Lord will repay him for his insults according to the word of Ephraim:* for the calumny he directed in his impiety against God he will require just penalties to match what he said against him.[103]

Chapter Thirteen

He also received ordinances in Israel, he assigned them to the Baal and died (v.1): though he personally received the directions from the Law of Moses for doing as he was obliged, he transferred them all to the Baal, applying to it the worship due by Law to me; this led to his death. *Now they continued to sin, and made for themselves an object molded from their gold and silver in the form of idols, works made for them by craftsmen* (v.2): they have persevered in impiety, preparing some idols out of gold, others out of silver, made by human hands. They then give evidence of such devotion to these things—and the result? *They say, Sacrifice human beings: calves have proved inadequate:* and so, despite many sacrifices, which they offered with brute beasts, they were not content with the great number of those victims, and went so far as to transfer the ritual of sacrifice to human beings. [201] Blessed David also says in these terms, "They sacrificed their sons and their daughters to the demons."[104] *Hence they will be like an early cloud, and like a dew at dawn that disappears, like a spider web blown away by a tempest from a threshing floor, and like a haze from locusts* (v.3): as some cloud or mist that dissipates and completely disappears, and a spider web set down on a threshing floor by a blast of wind, and even a light haze appearing for a

103. The final phrase of the text occurs as an opening to 13.1 in Heb. and modern versions.
104. Ps 106.37. The final part of v.2 in the Heb. is obscure.

short time from the flight of locusts,[105] so they will all suddenly disappear in the face of my wrath.

I am the Lord your God, establishing heaven and creating earth, whose hands created all the hosts of heaven; I did not present them to you for you to follow after them. It was I who brought you up[106] from the land of Egypt; you will know no God but me, there is none to save you but me (v.4): he shall inflict the impending punishment on you justly because you went off to idols, abandoning me, who am creator of all things, those in heaven and those on earth, at the time I brought you from the land of Egypt, with the number and the magnitude of those marvels. I freed you from the slavery in which you were held, and to teach you to recognize my might, I ordered you clearly to accord the name of God to no other being on earth or other heavenly body, but me alone to confess and know as God, who alone am able to save and free you from impending evils, since I am Lord of all. I provided you also with a precise demonstration of this lest you believe that my laws are only words and phrases, since they rightly combine truth and fact.[107] *It was I who fed you in the wilderness, in an uninhabited land in their pastures* (v.5): bringing you out of Egypt, I also conducted you with my own care through the desert in an uninhabited land, in which there were pastures for wild beasts and reptiles, allowing no one to lack necessities.

They were filled to satiety, their hearts were lifted up, and for this reason they forgot me (v.6). Then they entered the land of promise, and enjoyed so many good things in defiance of all human expectation, emerging as mighty compared with all people throughout the world on account of what was done for them by me; and yet they no longer retained the memory of the one

105. Theodore simply restates the metaphors in the text without elaboration, perhaps puzzled by the mention of spiders and locusts, which seem to have crept into his version by confusion of similar Heb. forms.

106. The text from "establishing" to this point occurs only in the LXX. Stuart thinks it may be original, though lacking in our Heb., and Theodore finds it grist to his mill, expatiating on salvation history at unusual length.

107. This is Antioch's, and particularly Theodore's, first principle about all the Scriptures, that they contain ἀλήθεια and πράγματα, not just σκιά and ὀνόματα (or, as Theodore says here, λόγοι and ῥήματα), as Eustathius had claimed of Origen's position.

who gave them the abundance of such good things. *I shall be like a panther and like a leopard to them on the way of the Assyrians* (v.7): so like a panther and a leopard I shall crush them with great ferocity and destroy them, and shall take them all into the captivity of the Assyrians. *I shall come upon them like a bear bereft of her cubs* (v.8): like a bear deprived of her own offspring and in her loss doing harm to all she meets, I shall wreak havoc on as many of them as possible. *I shall tear open the covering of their heart:* all their innermost thoughts by which they [204] commit impiety with complete devotion I shall prove to be vain and idle through the punishment inflicted on them. *The cubs of the forest will eat them there, and wild beasts of the field will tear them to pieces:* in this way the enemy will consume them in a manifold slaughter, like lions from the forest or some other wild beasts like them, suddenly falling upon them and tearing them to pieces with their teeth.

In your corruption, Israel, who will help you? (v.9) Corrupted and destroyed by so many evils, whom would you find as an ally? *Where is this king of yours? Let him save you in all your cities; let your judge be the one of whom you said, Give me a king and ruler, and in my rage I gave you a king* (vv.10–11): he will not provide any benefit from either royal care or military might, not being geared up for helping when it is I who am in opposition. After all, my decision that a just man Samuel would rule you and with complete virtue administer both priesthood and government of the people you utterly disallowed, claiming that like the other nations you had to have a king to be a defence for you in time of war with the foreigners.[108] The time has come, however, for you to feel the effects of your own folly: those who seem to be king for you will provide you with no benefit, all your cities meeting the same fate. None of them, accordingly, will judge you to be the victim of an invasion by the enemy, considering it insignificant, or will provide any help against them, though it is the custom for monarchs to do this for their own people, come to their aid against wrongdoers. Now to the extent possible, on

108. See 1 Sm 8.4–7.

the contrary, the enemy are more powerful than those who play king in your midst. When, however, you asked for rule by a king in the expectation of gaining some good, though angry at the wickedness of your attitude I nevertheless agreed to your getting a king so as not to seem opposed to your doing the best for yourselves. *I put up with it in my anger:* angry now both at that act and at your subsequent lawlessness, I took away my support from you, and I allowed you to learn though experience itself how much better for your salvation it would have been for you to be conducted everywhere under protection from me than to entrust yourselves to a king's power.

The core of Ephraim's iniquity is in his hidden sin; there will come for him pangs like those of woman in labor (vv.12–13): since in every case you demonstrate (by *Ephraim* referring as usual to the whole from the part) some deep core, nourishing the intention of committing impiety and sinfulness against me in various ways, while your mind is bent on committing sin (meaning by this a hidden sin, the soul's scheming not being obvious on the outside), for this you will be invested with such awful punishments that like a woman in labor you will be affected by the pains of the troubles besetting you. *Has this son of yours any sense?* Is there any wisdom to these deeds of yours—you who fail to distinguish the difference between being content with me and falling under my patronage [205] and going over to the idols and what is opposed to my wishes? *Hence now he will not survive the crushing of his children:* despite all your schemes, then, you will not manage to sustain your own ruin.

Then, after promising troubles, he proceeds, as is his custom, to speak of relief. *I shall rescue them from the hand of Hades, and ransom them from death* (v.14): having given you all these lessons through punishment, however, I shall save you all at the very moment of death in defiance of all human expectation. *Death, where is your punishment? Hades, where is your goad?* And so it is possible for you to utter these words when you espy that manifold death of those inflicting punishment on you, namely, the Assyrians. *Consolation is hidden from your eyes:* amidst such awful troubles you will attain consolation, which for the time being is not obvious to you, but you will see it then from experience itself.[109]

Hence he will distinguish between brothers (v.15). It was the view of some that while it had taken the ten tribes of the Israelites off into captivity, it had left those in Judah. This, however, was not the intention of the Assyrian, who had in mind to dispose of Jerusalem and those in Judah similarly, but was prevented by the divine power and the angel's intervention;[110] so as far as he was concerned he made no distinction. The prophet, however, wanted to mention the magnitude of the troubles in which those taken by the Assyrians were caught up as an example of what God would bring upon them, intending as he did that they would later be punished. The Assyrian, then, captured them and scattered them hither and thither by settling them in various places so that they would not be able to offer one another any assistance or together plot any further release from there. Blessed David also says likewise, "He will gather those of Israel who are scattered," as if to say, he shall bring back against all hope those scattered hither and thither; and elsewhere, "Let it be said by those redeemed by the Lord, those he redeemed from the hand of the foe and assembled from the east and west, north and south,"[111] implying they were scattered everywhere. So this is what he means here, He who has taken you captive and led you off to a foreign land has scattered you to places

109. Though Hosea seems, at least in our Heb. and modern versions, to be continuing the theme of retribution, different readings by the LXX encourage Theodore to see a change of heart on the Lord's part, something that soon involves him in hermeneutical gymnastics. (Stuart comments: "Grk normally translates Hosea clause by clause, as literally as possible, without much regard for the sweep of the logic"—and Theodore is not in a position to improve on that procedure.) Paul in 1 Cor 15.55 naturally takes this version of v.14 for his theme of resurrection (though reading "victory," νίκη, for "punishment," δίκη)—but Theodore ignores this NT citation. Theodoret, by contrast, will see both historical and eschatological fulfillment of the Hosean words.

110. 2 Kgs 19.35–36. As a result of a different reading of similar forms, the LXX has come up with a version that, together with his finding good news in v.14, leads Theodore off on an atypically long explication of the respective fates of north and south and the scattering of the people.

111. Pss 147.2, 57.2–3, the Psalms again the basic source of documentation for Theodore.

many and varied lest you seem to enjoy some consolation from being gathered together, whereas he would intensify your troubles by having you scattered to different places.

After saying this by way of demonstration of both the power and the savagery the Assyrians employed against them, he goes on, *The Lord will inflict a hot wind from the desert on them, will dry up his veins and exhaust his springs, and all his desirable possessions:* he will inflict an enemy on him. He means the king of the Babylonians, who as though advancing suddenly like a hot wind from some far distant region will completely devastate him, transforming his prosperity and the abundance of the good things in his possession into a desert; he [208] will also completely destroy all his possessions and valuables. To the verse *Death, where is your punishment? Hades, where is your goad?* is added *Hence he will distinguish between brothers* and what follows, so that in the middle comes the phrase *Consolation is hidden from your eyes,* implying, What is for the time being unclear to you will come to pass. Then, after mentioning their change for the better,[112] he refers in turn to the punishment now on the point of affecting them. *Samaria will be wiped out because it rebelled against God; they will fall by the sword, their babes will be dashed to the ground, and those with children in the womb will be torn open* (v.16):[113] while at that time he will against all hope provide these things to those made captive, before then destruction of the harshest kind will overtake them for what they chose to do in opposition to God; they will be made to experience a most bitter conflict of the kind where enemies have no mercy even on children at the breast, or even on pregnant women.

Chapter Fourteen

Since he had sufficiently brought them to their senses with the reminder of the troubles due to overtake them, he follows

112. The implications of his positive (mis)reading of v.14 are now becoming clear to Theodore, who notes the resulting lack of consistency in thought.

113. Modern versions number as 13.16 the verse that appears as 14.1 in Heb. and LXX.

on the promise he had made above by mentioning the relief from their distress that would reach them, adding, *Return, Israel, to the Lord your God, because you have grown weak through your iniquities* (v.1): now turn to God and what pleases him, giving consideration to the extent of the weakness to which you have been reduced for your acts of impiety; unexpectedly receiving relief from the troubles befalling you, be zealous in attending to your duty in future. *Take words with you and return to the Lord your God; say to him, You can remove our sin, so that you may not take up iniquity but may take up good* (v.2): use some such words to one another as will enable you to turn to God wholeheartedly and have unwavering faith that God can fully wipe away all your sins if he sees you repenting in the midst of the troubles befalling you, so that you may never again turn to impiety, and thus enjoy an abundant supply of good things from God. "And we shall in return offer the fruit of our lips": Exhort one another constantly, all of you, to repay him with hymns and acts of thanksgiving for the goods you possess.

Assyria will not save us, we shall not ride on horses, no longer did we say Our gods to the works of our hands (v.3): we no longer need help from Assyria, rendered superior to it, thanks to divine care, nor by recourse to horses shall we take to flight.[114] For God has come to help, and we are now far removed also from that error of calling things made by us gods. *Because in you it will have mercy on an orphan:* devote yourself to God with ardor and fellow-feeling for the needy.

I shall heal their dwellings, I shall love them openly, because my wrath has turned from them (v.4): if you do such things, you will hear God [209] promising and doing this in your regard, and the news that he will restore to you the ancient dwelling with the same authority;[115] he will give evidence of a similar love in

114. Hosea's mention of horses has reference, not to the possibility of flight, it seems, but to the covenantal veto on acquiring more wealth through them, as laid down in Dt 17.16, and touched on by Is 31.3, 36.8. But, we have noted, Theodore is not attuned to echoes of other parts of the OT except the Psalms (unless perhaps he has got the notion of flight on horseback from Is 30.16).

115. The LXX version of the verse's opening clause ("dwellings" for "apostasy") is unlikely—"though not entirely impossible," concedes Stuart. Theodore has no alternative but to wrestle with it, or at least paraphrase it.

equal quantity to all in so far as he dismisses all anger against you. *I shall be like a dew to Israel* (v.5), nourishing him with care from me in the way the dew is in the habit of nourishing the crops. *He will blossom like a lily:* he will be more glorious than all. *He will strike his root like Lebanon:* he will put forth luxuriant growth like that place packed with cedars. *His branches will develop* (v.6): his offspring will be extended to the limit of prosperity. *He will be like a fruitful olive tree, and his smell like Lebanon:* thanks to my care he will be loaded with fruit, and like frankincense pleasant to those hearing good things of him. *They will return and take their place beneath his shade, they will live and gain strength from grain* (v.7): when they come back, they will enjoy their own possessions, and will continue to have an abundant supply of crops, thanks to my care. *His memorial will blossom like a vine, like a wine of Lebanon:* it will be pleasant and welcome to the onlookers as a flowering vine, and as wine that customarily grows on the mountain of Lebanon.

Ephraim, what does he still have in common with idols? I humbled him, and I shall empower him (v.8): you should no longer have anything in common with idols, since you will not need anything from them, either. I humbled you, remember, for your devotion to them, and when you repented I returned you to your former prosperity. *Like a dense cypress your fruit will be found to come from me.* Since this tree is evergreen, he means, Just as it always has foliage on its branches, so will they constantly enjoy an abundance of good things, enjoyment of which accrues to them from my care.

Logically the prophet added to all this, *Who is wise and will understand this? or has understanding and will know this? The Lord's ways are right, and good people will walk in them* (v.10).[116] You could really demonstrate that a wise and understanding person

116. Theodore's text does not contain the final clause, which the LXX renders, "but the impious will grow weak in them," though his commentary suggests he read it. He classes it a logical codicil, in line with those modern commentators who also see it as Hosea's work; and he proceeds to elaborate on it morally (its morality rather pedestrian), without showing by way of a conclusion that it picks up the prophet's thought on Israel's course in history. Hosea's message is rather more potent. Nor does he note its similarity to the conclusion of Ps 107.

is the one with knowledge of what has been said and with zeal for the things by which it is possible for people who avoid evil and zealously practise good to be established in freedom from lower things and in enjoyment of higher. This is because everything done by God is marked by great correctness, with which he also applies punishment to the fallen and knows how to achieve their salvation when they repent. You could also demonstrate that the righteous are those of their number who also know how to profit from each category, and who develop greater self-control from the punishments, on the one hand, while taking the enjoyment of the good things stemming from repentance as a stimulus to virtue, on the other. You could also demonstrate that the impious are those who deserve troubles in every way and of very kind, gaining nothing from them, stuck fast in a downward direction, and as a result not able to understand anything of their duty. [212]

COMMENTARY ON THE PROPHET JOEL

HE TASK NOW BEFORE US is to begin clarifying blessed Joel the prophet.[1] The theme of his work, in general terms, is that also of all the prophets, who were anxious to disclose what was going to happen in regard to the people according to the grace of the Holy Spirit given to them in regard to that. First place among them, as I said before, was held by blessed David, who long ago—in fact, very long ago—and well before the outcome of the events mentioned all that would happen in regard to the people at different times.[2] The same thing was done also by the other prophets, who later mentioned what had long before been said by him, and a little before the actual outcome of the events, the purpose being both to remind everyone of what had been prophesied and, by saying what would shortly happen, to disclose the truth of the prophecy.[3] Since the events that we said were mentioned previously by blessed David were varied and occurred at various times, for the most part each of the prophets necessarily emerged to mention events whose outcome was shown to be close at hand. They were led to it by a certain logic and made the connection with some of the events

1. In the codex of Theodore's text (one of two located in the Vatican) edited by Mai as complete and more ancient, unlike other forms of the LXX (where the order varies), Joel follows Hosea and precedes Amos, in accord with Jewish tradition. Theodore confirms this order in opening the *Comm Hg.*

2. Theodore's previous work on the Psalms provides him with his principal source of scriptural documentation, we noted. All OT composers are προφῆται, including David and the Latter Prophets (the term not being applied to NT composers, though this is not to deny their inspiration).

3. While what Antioch generally looks for in Scripture is primarily truth/reality/events, Theodore it is who in particular would like to remain at this historical level of meaning, not admitting an eschatological sense. He will have to give ground, however, when he acknowledges Peter's quotation of 2.28–32 on the day of Pentecost.

due to happen later, namely, the very things mentioned also by blessed David. Blessed Hosea, for example, tells what will happen later in regard to the people at the hands of the Assyrians and Babylonians in an effort to bring them to their senses. Joel, on the other hand, while mentioning the same things in his own case for the reason that he lived at the same time as Hosea[4] and was entrusted in a spiritual revelation with the task of speaking about the same things, included as well what happened to them immediately after the return from Babylon. It was when the Scythian nation attacked them under Gog's men, bent on destroying them all; the Jews, however, proved to be superior to them by divine assistance, as was mentioned also by blessed David in the Psalms.[5]

Chapter One

The word of the Lord that came to Joel, son of Bethuel (v.1). As a kind of title, this is also similar to Hosea, indicating that from some revelation made to him he was moved by God to tell us what follows, directed to the benefit of the people.[6] *Hear this, you elders, and give ear to it, all you inhabitants of the land, to determine whether such things happened in your time* (v.2). As though they show indifference for what is being said, he tries to stir

4. While it is admitted today that Joel is the most difficult of the prophets to pinpoint chronologically, most modern commentators place the book in the post-exilic period, referring back to invaders and exile, and silent on Israel, Samaria, and monarchy as if past history. Theodore, for his part, has no difficulty locating him in the eighth century with Hosea, and as a seer—one aspect of a prophet's role—looking forward. The order in which The Twelve occur in his text, which is that of the Hebrew Bible rather than the LXX generally, would also influence him.

5. Apocalyptic material looms large in Joel, and it is not out of character for the figure of Gog, appearing in the allegory in Ezek 38–39, to be detected by Theodore, who thinks the Psalms—possibly a passage like Ps 18.7–15 redolent of Canaanite mythology—also treat of the subject.

6. While confining himself to the level of history, Theodore is not always willing or able to investigate historical issues raised in the text, such as the identity of the prophet and his father. Bethuel, incidentally, the father's name in its LXX form (Pethuel in our Heb.), already occurs at Gn 22.3 (Rebekah's father), Jos 19.4, and 1 Chr 4.30.

them up with fear of what is mentioned, with the result that the very beginning to his words is a threat. [213] I am directing this word of promise, he says, to all the inhabitants, and ahead of the others to the elders among you, who owing to their length of life ought know better whether something like this has happened before, either in your time or your fathers', of the kind God will now do to you. While for a long time he put up with you, he is doing so no longer, since he sees you gain no benefit from his longsuffering, and on the contrary you take a turn for the worse. *Tell your own children about it, your children to their children, and their children to the next generation* (v.3): the magnitude of the troubles coming upon you now is so awful that you must transmit it through your own successors to following generations so that the novelty of the events may succeed in bringing them as well to their senses by report of it.

What was left by the cutting locust, the locust consumed, and what was left by the locust, the young locust consumed, and what was left by the young locust, the blight consumed (v.4). In a figurative manner he wants to convey to them the impending troubles; as always, the earlier ones are surpassed by those coming later. Tiglath-pileser, king of the Assyrians, came like a cutting locust, he is saying, and laid waste no small proportion of your possessions; after him Shalmaneser, like some kind of locust further ravaging your goods; after them Sennacherib, like a young locust wreaking general destruction on the twelve tribes of Israel; like some kind of blight in addition to these came the attack of the Babylonian, who took the people of Judah as well and inflicted the evil of captivity on all in common.[7]

The next question, what is the purpose of mentioning them? *Sober up, you drunkards, from your drinking, and lament, all you who drink wine to excess, because gladness and joy have gone from your*

---

7. As observed in n. 4, Theodore sees Joel speaking figuratively, τροπικῶς, in referring to a locust plague as the invaders, unlike most modern commentators, who prefer to find a real locust plague described. Perhaps because the Bible itself is silent on Sargon II, here as in introducing Hosea, he mentions only Tiglath-pileser III, Shalmaneser V, and Sennacherib, thus omitting the Assyrian king responsible (perhaps along with Shalmaneser) for the fall of Samaria, Sargon's reign spanning the years 721–705. (Theodoret has a similar blindspot.)

mouth (v.5): set aside the drunkenness in which you are now gripped in your downward slide, unwilling as you are to recognize your duty; take to tears and dirges instead, in the hope of expunging the former drunkenness. After all, since the impending disasters permit you to rejoice and be glad no longer, it is better to employ lamentation and tears for repentance so that you may gain some alleviation of the troubles. Then, to mention their cause, he says, *Because a nation has invaded my land, strong and beyond counting; its teeth a lion's teeth, its fangs like its cub's* (v.6): many powerful enemies have attacked my country, no different from lions, with their teeth and their fangs slaughtering and consuming the cattle they chance upon, thus destroying and subduing with their weapons. *It has reduced my vine to ruin, and my figs to smithereens* (v.7): the whole of Israel, which I tended like a vine and beautified with my care, it ravaged and completely destroyed along with the figs in the middle, smashing them completely. He means to hint at those of their number eminent for wealth and power, since the vine plant is thought to be pre-eminent among such trees. [216] *It stripped it bare and cast it aside, it left its branches white:* it encircled it, tore it up, and took it off into captivity in such a manner that it was in no way different from all the branches left white and completely dried out after the uprooting of a vine.

It will address laments to me more than a bride clad in sackcloth for the husband of her virginity (v.8): at that time they will feel the effects of their own lawlessness, and will turn to me in deep mourning, lamenting the troubles affecting them, no less than a wife who is recently married and then suddenly loses her husband, and to whom the suddenness of the loss imparts extreme suffering. *Sacrifice and libation are canceled in the house of the Lord* (v.9). Here he makes clear reference to the troubles about to befall them at the hands of the Babylonians, since the cult performed in God's Temple came to an end at that time when the Babylonian burnt the Temple and took captive all those in the city.[8] *Mourn, you priests ministering at the altar, because the country-*

---

8. As if to confirm his view that Joel wants the invaders to be understood as the Babylonians, Theodore sees reference here to the destruction of the Tem-

side languishes. Let the land mourn, because grain crops languish, wine has dried up, oil has diminished, farmers are dismayed. Lament, produce, for wheat and barley, because the harvest has disappeared from the field, the vine has dried up and figs are in short supply, mulberry, palm, apple, and all the trees of the field are dried up (vv.9–12): a dirge is appropriate for those serving at the altar because utter sterility grips the fields, from which those in receipt of first-fruits and tithes used have an abundance of the necessities of life; and a dirge is no less appropriate for the land completely bereft of its crops. The result is that dismay overwhelms those farming the land for this reason, that they have labored in vain, and likewise for the produce of the land, because it is impossible to see, as normally happens, anything growing from the land or anything harvested from the produce of the trees. *Because people stifled joy,* as if to say, no one had the occasion to rejoice, ashamed to be grieving at so many overwhelming troubles. In all this he portrays the land of the Israelites[9] in the grip of extreme infertility such that the trouble was two-fold, an enemy at its most hostile and the land bereft of the produce of crops.

So what is the response to this? *Gird yourselves and beat your breasts, you priests, lament, you ministers at the altar, go in, pass the night in sackcloth as you serve God, because sacrifice and libation have departed from the house of your God* (v.13): of all people it behoves you in particular in discharging your priesthood to don sackcloth, not removing it even when lying down or actually performing the divine liturgy, and to give yourselves to weeping and wailing for the fact that all the worship duly devoted to God has come to an end. *Sanctify a fast* (v.14): since what is exclusive and unavailable to the general run of people is called holy, *Sanctify a fast* means, Organize yourselves for it, set apart and completely removed from everyone as you are, devote and arrange yourselves for observing it. *Proclaim worship:* [217] remind everyone to desist from human affairs and attend to the

---

ple and cessation of the cult (not proceeding, as do some moderns, to class Joel as a cultic prophet).

9. As observed in n. 4, Joel is in fact silent on Israel, dwelling on the fate of Judah and Jerusalem.

worship of the divinity. *Gather elders, all the inhabitants of the land, to the house of your God, and cry aloud to the Lord at great length, Alas, alas, alas for the day, because the day of the Lord is near* (vv.14–15): as it is right for you to lead the others, encourage everyone in your land to enter in common into the house of God as long as it is safe for you to enter; lift up cries with much groaning—the meaning of *Alas, alas, alas*—praying not to have experience of that day,[10] which according to the divine threat is not far off.

It will come like one hardship after another: it is going to come upon you with no interruption to the troubles. *Because your food has dried up before your eyes, and happiness and joy from the house of your God* (v.16): so that you will not be eyewitnesses of these troubles, because there will be a severe—even extreme—lack of crops; worst of all, all worship that is fitting and due to God will be abolished from the house of God, which could have been a source of extreme happiness and joy to those witnessing proper ritual. *Heifers leaped in their stalls* (v.17): under the pressure of the hunger gripping them, they turn to leaping and being alarmed, naturally looking for nourishment, and in the absence of what nourishes them they are moved to disorderly leaping. *The granary became moldy from their anointing:* since it was the custom to grease the grain bins for safety's sake, and since they were empty of contents, the one greasing them used mud for grease on account of there being nothing at all to deposit.[11] *Storehouses have been destroyed:* every place that usually receives crops will be useless, with nothing ready to lodge. *Wine vats have been overthrown:* they will seem useless, with nothing to store. *With the grain dried out, what will they put in them?* By individual mention of the grain he intended to refer to all crops, wanting to cite this in confirmation of what had been said because, with

10. After helpfully glossing the term "sanctify" from the meaning of "holy" in biblical terms, Theodore has nothing to say on that other key biblical notion, the Day of the Lord, a hallmark of Joel's thought, which features also in other minor and major prophets.

11. In a verse that is notorious, as Stuart says, for "the vast and sometimes hilarious differences among ancient and modern translations," Theodore's local text includes a rogue clause about moldy granaries (possibly derived from confusion of similar Heb. forms) that prompts him to offer a comment that probably only a farmer of the time could confirm or (hilariously?) deny.

the crops completely destroyed, every place that usually takes crops will be useless, nothing due to be deposited. *Herds of oxen wept because there was no fodder for them, the flocks of sheep have disappeared* (v.18): the cattle's usual feed in the place has been destroyed.

To you, O Lord, I shall cry out, because fire destroyed the charming things of the wilderness, flame consumed all the trees of the field (v.19): with the troubles gripping us, we shall all in common beg from you relief from such awful troubles, because like fire all the place is devastated along with the trees in it (by *charming things of the wilderness* referring to the places in the mountains that were ready for the sowing of seed and are normally called in common parlance "mountain country"), as if to say, every place and every tree has been destroyed as though scorched by some fire. *The cattle of the countryside looked to you, because* [220] *outlets of water were dried up* (v.20): the cattle are dying of thirst, with the springs no longer able to discharge water owing to the severe drought.[12]

Chapter Two

Then, to suggest the vast number of troubles by his expansive treatment, he continues in a similar vein to what preceded. *Sound a trumpet in Zion, proclaim on my holy mountain, and let all the land's inhabitants be assembled, for the day of the Lord has come, because the day of darkness and gloom is nigh, a day of cloud and mist* (vv.1–2): using the trumpet as signal according to the custom in law,[13] assemble everyone on Mount Zion, where it is customary to render me worship, in the same place begging the divine mercy, since it is not far from coming to pass that the day threatened by God will be with us, capable of filling everyone with darkness and gloom so that it is impossible to see everything, once shrouded in cloud and mist. Now, he was right to summon everyone to Mount Zion, on which according to Mo-

12. For fairly obvious reasons Theodore's text does not contain the final clause of the verse, "Fire consumed the charming things of the wilderness."

13. See Lv 23.24.

saic practice arrangements were made for the divinity to be worshiped,[14] for the reason that, when those from the ten tribes desisted from worship of the divinity in that place, they offered it instead to the heifers on advice from Jeroboam.[15] Now, at any rate, he urges them to desist from their folly and look to Mount Zion and the Lord of all whom they were ordered to worship there so as to secure an escape for themselves from the expected disasters, which in fact you would easily find actually happening to those living around that place in the time of Sennacherib when Zedekiah was king of Judah.[16]

Like dawn, a numerous and strong people will pour over the mountains; its like has not been from of old, nor will it be again after it for generations of generations of years: like dawn spreading over all the land at its own time, a people beyond counting will come covering all the mountains, the like of which never happened before, and will not easily happen again. *Fire devouring what is in front of them, and flame igniting what is behind them* (v.3): in its very advance it destroys everything round about, like fire. *As a garden of delight the land before it, and behind it a countryside of destruction:* the places it has not yet attacked you would see as no different from a garden in the number of its inhabitants and the beauty of its buildings, whereas once it has arrived it is possible to see all that charm suddenly removed. *There is no one safe from it:* it is difficult for anyone to escape its assault.

Like a vision of horses is their vision, and like a horse so will they pursue; like the noise of chariots they will leap on the crests of the mountains, and like the sound of a fiery flame consuming stubble, and like a numerous and strong people deployed for war (vv.4–5). The particle he uses not for comparison but for narrative, as in the case of the verse, "How good is God to Israel,"[17] meaning good, [221]

---

14. Mosaic determination of Mount Zion as the locus of divine worship may not have been as easy for Theodore to document as Davidic, even a psalm like Ps 2.6 tracing its nomination as "my holy hill" back to the Lord himself.

15. See 1 Kgs 12.26–29.

16. Theodore is probably referring again to the slaughter of the Assyrians in 2 Kgs 19.35.

17. Ps 73.1. It is the particle ὡς that Theodore is referring to, which can mean "as, like" (a relative adverb in classical grammar), and also "how" (an emphatic exclamation). Theodore feels (against the opinion of his editor Mai)

and so is the meaning here, too—namely, it is possible to see the numerous cavalry at his disposal. There are some mounted on horses who are fearsome as they charge their adversaries; his many chariots are employed in attack to the very heights; they are no different from fire feeding on stubble, and in this way they attack all the places they want, being numerous and very bold, ready for war more than anything.

Before him people are crushed, every face like the blackness of a cauldron (v.6): in all likelihood they will destroy a great number in their assault so that to him all the fallen seem to resemble a cauldron blackened by fire. He continues the description in the same vein so as to instil greater fear in the listeners. *Like fighters they charge, and like men of war they scale the walls* (v.7): with great speed they charge into the fray, and with great boldness they also climb the walls of the cities, not expecting any injury from it. *Each travels by his own way, not straying from his own path or leaving the side of his brother* (vv.7–8): in battle order they deploy their attack, no one ever deviating left or right, each instead keeping to the way determined and planned, all conducting the assault with complete unanimity in fighting. *Though weighed down with their armor they go forward, they will fall under their spears but are not finished:* this is the best proof of their readiness for battle, that they are never parted from their own weapons—in other words, they do not jettison their weapons even while marching, gladly putting up with the weight in preference to appearing unarmed to their foe, nor are they parted from their weapons even if they turn off for a rest. He said *they will fall* to mean they will flag and lie down, intending to convey that they both march and lie down with their weapons—hence his excellent further remark, *but are not finished,* that is, they know no end to the battle, ever being involved with weapons and fighting.

They will attack the city, charge onto its walls, climb up on its hous-

---

that the context requires the latter usage for narrative purposes, though his comment seems to accept the comparisons with natural and military phenomena. In deference to his wishes, perhaps we should retranslate the verses thus: "How striking they are to behold and how quick in pursuit! How awesome the noise they make as they climb mountain tops and advance inexorably, how numerous and well-equipped for war."

es and enter through the windows like thieves (v.9): with great power they gain control of the cities, not shrinking from running up to the walls with their weapons, continuing to enter every city so as to enter every house through doors and through windows with the purpose of removing all the contents, the phrase *like thieves* meaning, to remove and steal everything. *Before it the land will be troubled and heaven shaken, the sun and the moon will be darkened, and the stars lose their light* (v.10). The prophet is in the habit of saying many things by way of hyperbole for greater impact on the listeners, since, no matter what the words are, they pale before the events.[18] It is clear in this case, too, that he is not describing the elements being troubled and changed; instead, since it is typical of people caught up in troubles to adjust in many cases their ways of thought to their present state of need, so here he means, They will be filled with confusion when he comes [224] on earth; it seems to those suffering such things at his hands that heaven moves and the sun, moon, and stars no longer shine, since the severity of the troubles robs the sufferers of the sense of light. *The Lord will raise his voice before his host, because his force is very numerous, because powerful is the effect of his words. For great is the day of the Lord, great and exceedingly splendid—who can cope with it?* (v.11) God will also have his say in what happens, since it is by his will that you will suffer this for your own wickedness, and so you will then recognize all this as his arrangement, by whose will it has been put into effect. And you will recognize as well the force of his words, who formerly told you when you did not believe what he said, and later brought it to pass and proved that every word of his is a powerful force, and that the day of the evils befalling you will be so great and splendid. Then, in keeping with the divine will, it will happen that no one will be capable of sustaining the magnitude of the troubles then occurring.

18. As he showed above a reluctance to admit the full force of the prophet's imagery, so here in encountering further features of Joel's apocalyptic genre Theodore is anxious to demythologize it in case his readers take it in literalist fashion. Perhaps as well as decoding the apocalyptic landscape he might have explained further its purpose as a prophetic device; robbing the material of its emotive force undercuts the prophetic message.

After describing the oppression by the enemy in these words, he goes on, *The Lord our God now says, Turn back to me with all your heart, with fasting, with weeping and with lamenting; rend your hearts, turn back to the Lord your God, because he is merciful and compassionate, longsuffering and rich in mercy, ready to repent of your troubles* (vv.12–13): since this is the way things are, come now, let us all change our thinking from worse to better, let us all turn to God with our whole mind, having recourse to fasting, weeping, and lamenting, not rending our garments (your custom that often does not come from the heart), but opening our hearts and presenting them undisguised to God so as to set aside the former wickedness and be seen to cling to your attitude to him. It is in fact not out of the question that, since he is loving and shows great patience with sinners, he will think better of the troubles he intended to inflict on you. *Who knows if he will turn and relent and leave behind him a blessing, sacrifice, and libation to the Lord your God?* (v.14) Even if it is not clear to all of you that this happened to you when your own conscience was affected, at least you should be very aware that if we repent and intend to turn towards him, he in turn will repent of what he did to us, and he will grant us in time to come an abundance of his own good things (referring to this as *blessing*). The first token of this will be participating in the ritual of the customary offering of sacrifices and libations. It is clear, after all, that God is said to bless when he bestows his characteristic gifts—hence reference to such a gift as *blessing.*[19]

He then goes on, *Sound a trumpet in Zion, sanctify a feast, announce worship, gather* [225] *the people, sanctify the assembly, select elders, gather together infants at the breast. Let the bridegroom leave his alcove, and the bride her chamber* (vv.15–16): with God adopting such a loving attitude, let this be done by us: summon everyone to Mount Zion with signals from the trumpets, determine and announce a fast in worship of God, gather all the people so that when gathered in assembly they may examine themselves in re-

19. The connection between God's blessing and the people's offering is not made clear in a verse that, in Stuart's words, is "somewhat laconic in phrasing"; but Theodore, as an Antiochene not ignoring the ellipsis, succeeds in explicating it as human participation due to divine liberality.

penting of their attitude, with the older people present and even the infants present, including babes in arms, and even newly-marrieds leaving married bliss for the sake of attending to repentance—in short, everyone of every age and situation participating in repentance, everything else left aside. *Between the step and the altar the priests serving the Lord will weep, and they will say, Spare your people, O Lord, and do not make a reproach of your inheritance lest nations get the better of them and lest they say among the nations, Where is their God?* (v.17) Let all standing before the altar who have been assigned to the office of priesthood and allotted divine service beg with tears for reconciliation with God so that he would then spare his people and not surrender them completely to the power of the nations nor abandon them to be mocked by the nations on the score that it is vain for us to take pride in our relationship with God.

To this he adds, *The Lord became jealous for his land, and spared his people* (v.18). He does not mention this as if already done, but says it is something in the future: he will be jealous and spare you if he sees you repentant and doing what was prescribed; the tense has been changed according to the Hebrew usage, employing *spared* to mean will spare, as we showed also in other cases from the Psalms. You see, the fact that he is not mentioning what happened is clear from the troubles that came upon them after this reference.[20] *The Lord said in reply to his people, Lo, I shall send you grain, wine, and oil, and you will be filled with them, and I shall no longer make you an object of reproach for the nations. I shall chase away from you the enemy from the north, and shall chase him into waterless land, I shall drive off his front into the first sea and his rear into the last sea, his putrid smell will rise up and repulsiveness will rise up* (vv.19–20). The phrase *The Lord said in reply* means, The Lord will say in reply, the tense being

20. Already in commentary on Hosea (see nn. 71 and 98 there) Theodore has informed the reader that he is aware that verb tenses in the LXX do not always reflect the Hebrew, blaming this on Hebrew usage rather than a misreading by the LXX, and citing his comments on his former work on the Psalms. Here, too, the Hebrew tense (the prophetic perfect) is said to be misleading because Joel in Theodore's view is looking ahead to Judah's fall, and so the Lord cannot be referring to the past (see n. 4 to the preface to Joel); again ἀκολουθία, not morphology, is the criterion.

changed here, too; he means to say, He will definitely give an abundance of crops to you when you repent, and he will put your enemies to flight, as God therefore did after the return, just as blessed David in foretelling the people's return first said, "A hymn in Zion becomes you, O God, and a prayer will be rendered to you in Jerusalem. . . . Your holy Temple, remarkable in your righteousness,"[21] to show that they will return to [228] their own land and they will once again render to God the customary worship in the Temple. After this he goes on, "You visited the earth, intoxicated it, and filled it to enrich it," and so on, mentioning the abundance that would accrue to them at that time. In the same way here he mentions the restoration of fertility, saying, I shall no longer let you be subject to the nations, the meaning of *I shall no longer make you an object of reproach for the nations;* instead, I shall exact penalties of those attacking you, consigning them to devastation and complete destruction. First, I shall punish the Assyrians through the Babylonians; after that I shall utterly destroy the Babylonians through the Persians, and I shall wreak such ruin upon them that their smell and stench will be like dead bodies and corpses and will escape no one, the meaning of *putrid smell and repulsiveness* like those already dead and stretched out as corpses. The term *will rise up* means Will be audible to all. The reason for all this? *Because he has magnified his works:* God will demonstrate the magnitude of his works in punishing them.

He continues the same theme, *Have confidence, earth, rejoice and be glad, because the Lord had been magnanimous in creating. Have confidence, cattle of the countryside, because the countryside in the wilderness has blossomed, because a tree bore its fruit, vine and fig tree showed their vigor* (vv.21–22): the earth will enjoy happiness at the magnitude of the things done by God, receiving the yield

21. Ps 65.1, 4, 9, the logic being that David could speak of the return as future because living in the past; so Joel. (The grounds for seeing the psalm referring to return from exile probably come from its title in the Antioch text, which, according to Theodoret, reads, "A song of Jeremiah and Ezekiel and of the people in exile when they were on the point of returning.") Was Theodore aware of the view of Joel's living later than the exile and return, and hence was obliged to counter it?

of its crops, and no less the cattle of the countryside enjoying the fodder in generous measure, and in addition to them the fact that the fruit of the trees is provided generously to those in need. *Children of Zion, be glad and rejoice in the Lord your God because he has given you food for righteousness, and he will send you early and late rain as before, the threshing floors will be filled with grain, and the vats of wine and oil overflowing* (vv.23–24). What he said above would be done away with he now says will be restored. Everyone assembled around Mount Zion, he is saying, and performing the worship due to God would be right to rejoice in receiving the abundance of the crops, which God provided to them for rightly repenting of their sins, and in the fact that he will meet their need for timely and adequate rain, the result being that germination of seeds in the soil and fruit on the trees will come into their possession in great abundance.

I shall repay you for the years that the locust, young locust, blight, and cutting locust consumed, my great force that I sent against you. You shall eat in plenty and be filled, and you will praise the name of the Lord your God, because he worked marvels in your midst. My people will not be confounded in future, they will acknowledge that I am in the midst of Israel; I am your God, and there is no God but me. My people will not be confounded in future (vv.25–27): all the necessities that [229] the enemy in attacking laid waste in many and various ways (obviously referring to them by *locust, young locust, blight,* and *cutting locust*)[22] I shall restore to you so that you will have abundant enjoyment of what is given and be obliged to render hymns to God for the mighty and marvelous things he has done for you, the result being that you will no longer be ashamed of remaining without assistance from me and falling foul of such awful troubles, and instead will be in a position to gain from experience itself the knowledge that I am among you, being both your Lord and your sole carer.

It will happen after this that I shall pour out my spirit on all flesh, your sons and daughters will prophesy, your elders will dream dreams,

22. Theodore is only being consistent here, feeling no need to debate further the identity of the invaders. Stuart notes that the Targum here renders the four terms as "peoples, language groups, powers and kingdoms"—perhaps an element of Jewish tradition familiar to Theodore.

your young people will see visions. Even on my[23] *slaves and on my fe-*
male slaves I shall pour out my spirit in those days, and they will proph-
esy. I shall provide portents in heaven and on earth, blood and fire and
clouds of smoke. The sun will revert to darkness and the moon to blood
before the great and striking day of the Lord comes. It will happen that
everyone who calls on the name of the Lord will be saved, because on
Mount Zion and in Jerusalem they will be saved, as the Lord said; good
news will come to those whom the Lord has called (vv.28–32): I shall
provide my wealth and care to all—the meaning of *I shall pour*
out my spirit. The people in the time of the Old Testament did
not understand the Holy Spirit to be a unit as a person distinct
from the others,[24] being both God and from God; by "spirit of
God," "holy spirit," and every other such name at the time they
referred to his grace, care, and affection, as in applying to God
also "soul": "My soul hates your new moons and your sabbaths,"
meaning the affection by which he hated the festivals. A similar
example is "Your good spirit will guide me on level ground,"
meaning, out of care for me you will provide this on account of
great goodness." A similar example is "Take not your holy spirit
from me,"[25] as if to say, Do not remove your care for me—and
so on, not to provide scriptural texts beyond need. Here, too,
he is saying something of the kind, In this way I shall provide
you with my care so that you may be accorded all visions and be
in a position to disclose something of the future. I shall work
marvels in heaven and on earth for everyone, great slaughter of
my adversaries and punishment of them, as well as clouds of
smoke betraying the divine wrath; the sun will be changed into
darkness and the moon into blood in the perception of the onlookers, which they will experience owing to the magnitude of
the problems befalling them.[26] This will happen before that

23. The pronoun does not appear in all other forms of the LXX, though it
does appear in the citation of the verse at Acts 2.17. (In the Heb. text these verses are now numbered 3.1–5.)

24. Theodore's term here for personhood of the Spirit is μοναδικόν ἐν
ὑποστάσει.

25. Is 1.14; Pss 143.10, 51.11. Theodore implies he could document the usage *ad nauseam*, though we have noted he is parsimonious in scriptural documentation, the Psalms excepted.

26. Again (see n. 5) Theodore gives the impression of being out of sympathy

day, which he will render *striking* by the [232] punishment of
the adversaries. In the midst of them, all those who call upon
the divine name will attain salvation, and those who will go up
to Mount Zion and Jerusalem will be saved, since God promised this and allowed all those whom he summoned to this return to hear the good news.

While this is in fact the obvious sense of the passage, blessed
Peter at any rate used it in speaking to Jews on the occasion of
the descent of the Holy Spirit. And rightly so, since the Law
contained a shadow of all things to come,[27] whereas the people
were vouchsafed care owing to the expectation of what would
appear at the coming of Christ the Lord. What happened in
their time was all insignificant and like a shadow so that the account was given with use of hyperbole rather than containing
facts, whereas the reality of the account was found to be realized in the time of Christ the Lord, when everything was important and awesome, novel and really baffling, surpassing what
had happened under the Law to the greatest extent imagina-
ble.[28] So whereas what happened in the time of the Old Testament had the function of a puzzle, the magnitude of what happened in the time of Christ the Lord was in the order of reality.
Blessed David likewise says about the people, "Its soul was not

with apocalyptic, of which this is a conspicuous exemplar. He demystifies it
rather than helps his readers experience the impact the author intended it to
achieve. The visionaries on "that day" are simply having hallucinations, he tells
them.

27. For the first time in this commentary, Theodore is acknowledging an NT
realization of an OT prophecy, whose surface meaning has already been carefully established; he admits there is a promise-fulfillment, shadow-reality relationship between the testaments. And he begins by elliptically adverting to the
character of the feast of Pentecost at which Peter's address is given, in which
Joel and Ps 16 are quoted—namely, its commemorating the giving of the Law.
This character, however, additional to the feast's original character as celebrating the giving of the land, was applied to it only by rabbis in the second century—known to Theodore (and to his readers without prompting?), therefore,
but not to Luke.

28. Theodore is going to lay out for the readers his Antiochene hermeneutical principles (rehearsed decades later in identical terms by Theodoret in his
Commentary on Isaiah). Some (particularly the prophetical) passages of the OT
are a kind of shadow, σκιά, or a puzzle, αἴνιγμα, whereas the NT in recording
their fulfillment provides the facts, πράγματα, or reality, ἀλήθεια.

abandoned to Hades, nor did its flesh see corruption,"[29] which cannot be understood at the level of fact; rather, by the use of hyperbole or metaphor he says it was rescued from danger or corruption. The factual reality of the text, on the other hand, is demonstrated by Christ the Lord, when it happened that neither was his soul abandoned to Hades, being restored to the body in resurrection, nor did his body suffer any corruption, so that not only did it remain with its own appearance in which it actually died but it was also transformed into an immortal and incorruptible nature. So, while the former situation was a puzzle, the latter was reality. Hence blessed Peter used the passage as something expressed metaphorically at a particular time for a particular reason, but now having an outcome in reality at the time of the facts themselves. The moral is that we should have faith in the events of this time to a much greater extent than they felt wonderment at that event in the past.[30]

Now, since there are many instances of this kind in the divine Scripture, the present one is obviously also of much the same character. You see, while the Lord God in speaking to Jews in the manner then customary promised to provide them generously with his care, and so on in the way we have interpreted, everything turned out in reality in the time of Christ the Lord—the sun was actually darkened and the moon with it, great portents occurred in heaven and many on earth, the saving blood of Christ the Lord appeared, as well as fire, in keeping with the particular action of the Spirit's visit, preceded by

29. Ps 16.10, which along with vv.8–11 (significantly adapted by Luke at Acts 2.16–21) is cited together with the whole Joel passage by Peter on Pentecost day. While Theodoret would admit the whole psalm was Christological, dealing with the passion and resurrection, as Peter implies, Theodore characteristically sees the people as its originally intended recipients, his text of v.10 accordingly cited in a form that neither Theodoret nor the LXX generally represent. So Theodore's approach to interpretation of OT texts that are later used by the NT is: first establish the original meaning in its context, shadow though this may be; then look for the reality as demonstrated by NT authors and figures. Some Antiochenes would speak of this process of discerning a text's fuller meaning as θεωρία.

30. Apart from a particular accent or two of his own, this hermeneutical treatment by Theodore embodies a breadth of perspective with which he was—and is—not always credited.

clouds of smoke, to suggest by way of proof the punishment wreaked on those guilty of the crucifixion.[31] At that time also everyone received a share [233] of the grace of the Holy Spirit in being vouchsafed many and varied charisms, with which some foretold the future, others worked a great number of marvels as confirmation of the greatness of what had happened and as proof of the glory concerning Christ the Lord. The result is that what had formerly been said through the prophet as metaphor or hyperbole had its demonstration in reality with the promise being superseded by the fulfillment; such could reasonably be thought to be the reason why the blessed apostles applied either this passage or the others as well as everything else said by the prophets on different subjects to the Incarnation of Christ the Lord. As a result, the story of events at that time does not have the appearance of being concocted, and the magnitude of events today is more clearly established by comparison with them, and through them all there is more precise proof that there is a certain relationship between former and latter, and that the previous events are surpassed by the present to the extent that shadow is surpassed by reality, even if it seems to be related to it.

Chapter Three[32]

Since at any rate the prophet revealed in the prophecies the return from Babylon and the good things that would accrue to them at that time in various ways, he adds the following in keeping with it. *Because, lo, in those days and at that time when I cancel the captivity of Judah and Jerusalem, I shall assemble all the nations and lead them down into the valley of Jehoshaphat. I shall take issue with them there over my people and my inheritance, Israel, who were scattered among the nations; they divided my land, cast lots for my peo-*

31. For an argument of this kind, it is helpful if Theodore can find some NT event fulfilling the promise; he seems to refer to Matthew's account of phenomena accompanying the crucifixion at 27.45–54 and Luke's description of Pentecost day at Acts 2.1–4.
32. Now numbered ch 4 in the Heb.

ple, gave boys for prostitutes, and sold girls for wine, and drank (vv. 1–3). He makes a disclosure of what happened amongst them after the return and the incursion of Gog's men,[33] which they would conduct in great numbers by making a raid on Jerusalem, and the destruction they would suffer for this rash exploit. After I bring you back to Jerusalem, he is saying, many nations will advance in concert against you from all directions (by *I shall assemble all the nations* meaning, not that he would lead them, but because he allowed them to give effect to his own intention). He punished those who committed themselves to an assault on the Israelites: far from achieving what they had planned against the Jews, they suffered a fearsome and unexpected punishment by an intervention of God—hence his mention of *assembling all the nations*, meaning, I allowed them to exercise their depraved purposes and lead an attack against Jerusalem, so as thereby to call them to account and provide everyone with a demonstration of my care for the people and of my own power. After saying, *I shall assemble all the nations*, therefore, he went on, *and lead them down into* [236] *into the valley of Jehoshaphat*—in other words, There I shall lead them to Jerusalem, and in the same place I shall punish them deservedly by inflicting on them a kind of vengeance for my people for what they have committed against them in their wish to scatter them in all directions and divide up the land in which they dwelt against my will, and also to divide them up by lot. In addition to all that, they went to the extent of selling both their boys and girls so as to satisfy their own lusts and have an abundance of strong drink.

After saying this about Gog's men, he goes on, *What are you to me, Tyre and Sidon, and the whole of Galilee of foreigners? Surely you*

---

33. It is perhaps the apocalyptic character of the prophecy that again invites a brief mention of the figure of Gog from the allegory in Ezek 38–39, as at the opening of this commentary (see n. 5 there); that also absolves Theodore from being precise about historical details. On the other hand, he shows no interest in explaining the significance and location of the valley of Jehoshaphat or the play upon words involved (perhaps "valley of judgment" or "Yahweh has judged"), nor does he see a reference to the eschatological judgment of the nations, insisting this chapter is still "in keeping with" the return from Babylon.

are not visiting retribution on me, or nourishing a grievance against me? Swiftly and promptly I shall return your retribution at your heads for your taking my silver and, for your introducing choice things of beauty into your temples, for selling the sons of Judah and the sons of Jerusalem to the sons of the Greeks so as to remove them from their borders. Lo, I am stirring them up from the place where you sold them, I shall return your retribution upon your heads, I shall sell your sons and your daughters into the hands of the sons of Judah, and they will sell them into slavery to a far distant nation, because the Lord has spoken (vv.4–8): since they saw Gog's men attacking Jerusalem, the people of Tyre and Sidon, and all the foreigners[34] round about thought they had an opportunity to destroy the Israelites completely, nourishing a grudge against them for the wars they had often conducted and the victories they had won against them through God's intervention. So the meaning is, What grudge are you nourishing, finding an opportunity to enact your designs, and committing such crimes against those belonging to me? After all, you know that I shall swiftly inflict punishment for this attitude in return for your taking all their belongings and introducing them into your temples; furthermore, you sold their sons in the hope of expelling them all from their borders. So for this I shall exact penalties of you, freeing them of their pressing condition of need. I shall now render them superior to their enemies so as also to repay you for what you have perpetrated against them, and shall have your sons and daughters taken captive and sold off in foreign parts whence it will be impossible for you to recover them again.

After communicating this to the people of Tyre and Sidon, and all their neighbors, who at that time were endeavoring to band together with Gog's men in bringing destruction on the Jews, he resumes his theme in the words, *Proclaim this among the nations: Sanctify a war, rouse up the fighters, draw near and ascend, all you men of war, hammer your ploughs into swords and your prun-*

---

34. Theodore may feel uneasy about a reference in the LXX v.4 to "Galilee," arising out of a misreading of a form meaning "districts, coastal regions," which would encourage a translation "Philistines" for ἀλλόφυλοι instead of simply "foreigners." So, though unable to account for the error, he wisely avoids associating Tyre and Sidon with Galilee.

ing hooks into spears. Let the weakling say, I am up to it. Assemble and advance, [237] *all you nations round about, and gather here. Let the gentle person turn fighter* (vv.9–11). As he said above, I shall assemble them for the aforementioned reason, so he does here as well to urge them on in person: Assemble with great ardor, all who have this hostile attitude to those belonging to me, wage war together against them, and even turn farming implements into use as weapons so as to have weapons enough for the vast number of attackers. With greater numbers it will be easy for you to bring ruin on all the Israelites as you intended. Then, to rouse them up to war, he states the reason, *Arise and ascend, all you nations, to the valley of Jehoshaphat, because it is there I shall sit in judgment on all the nations round about* (v.12): all of you intending to gather together against the inhabitants of Jerusalem I urge to do so in order that I may exact penalties of you in that place for this presumption and audacity by destroying all with many forms of death.[35]

What, then? *Apply pruning hooks, because it is time for harvest; go in, tread it down, because the wine vat is full, the vessel overflows, because their wickedness abounds* (v.13): so extensive will be their slaughter and so complete the fall of all those armed against one another that you inhabitants of Judah will not be required to fight; instead, you will think it is time for a harvest of some kind, in which there is need of pruning hooks and people to tread the wine vat for wine to be pressed down to overflowing. This in fact is exactly what happens now, too: since war is conducted by my power and everyone falls victim to slaughter, you ought to be on hand to witness them falling to indiscriminate slaughter like branches cut off at harvest, as it were, and the blood of the victims overflowing in the manner of a wine vat be-

35. Because Theodore does not seem clear about the prophet's foretelling the eschatological judgment of the nations in the valley of Jehoshaphat, he is ambiguous about the object of the assault, whether Judah/Israel or the nations. Having been definite at the outset that Joel is a contemporary of Hosea, though vague about the enemy involved (turning to the Scythians under Gog), he is now not in a position to be precise about an historical reference for this apocalyptic scenario. Recalling similar imagery in Is 2.4 and Mi 4.3 would have assisted him to recognize the nature of the material, which is eluding him or he is reluctant to acknowledge.

ing trampled down. This will be the way their wickedness will abound, and so extensive will be their slaughter, not yours in battle, but theirs as they turn their hands on one another in response to my decision.

He then states what follows in the same vein. *Sounds rang out in the valley of judgment, The Day of the Lord is nigh in the valley of judgment* (v.14): certain fearsome sounds from the great number of the slain will be heard in this valley, in which I shall require an account of them for their audacity against you (by *valley of judgment* referring to the valley of Jehoshaphat from the impending infliction of punishment on them there by God). *The sun and the moon will be darkened, and the stars will lose their brightness* (v.15). In consequence he said that there would be no light for the slain; to explain how this will happen, he goes on, *The Lord will cry aloud from Zion, he will cry aloud and from Jerusalem he will utter his voice, and heaven and earth will be shaken. The Lord will spare his people, the Lord will empower the sons of Israel, and you will know that I am your Lord, dwelling in Zion on my holy mountain* (vv.16–17): he is the God who arranged for worship of himself according to the Law to be introduced to Zion, [240] and it is he who raises this loud voice against them, at which heaven and earth will almost seem to shake on account of the startling character of the events and the awful slaughter so remarkably accomplished. God will be responsible for it, sparing his own and showing them to be superior to their adversaries, the result being that it is clear to everyone that he really is God of all and the Lord who is customarily worshiped on Mount Zion.

Jerusalem will be holy, and aliens will nevermore pass through it. On that day the mountains will drip with sweetness and the hills flow with milk, all the springs of Judah will flow with water, a fount will issue from the house of the Lord and will water the torrent of ropes (vv.17–18): Jerusalem will be shown to be holy from the events themselves, no foreigner ever again presuming to attack it. There will be an abundance of good things for all the Jews dwelling in the land of promise, with the result that the mountains and the hills will produce for them crops many and varied, the springs will give a plentiful supply of their waters in customary fashion,[36] and the abundant wealth of good things will flow for those entering there, anxious to discharge their debt to God (saying this *fount will issue from the house of the Lord;* it will be so abundant as to extend its prodigality even to those far distant).[37] Then, after saying, *Egypt will be wiped out and Idumea with it for what they have done to you and the great numbers of you they wrongly destroyed* (v.19), he goes on, *But Judah in the strength of its prosperity will be inhabited in Jerusalem by its own people* (v.20). To this he adds, *I shall demand an account of their blood, and I shall not leave it unpunished, and the Lord will dwell in Zion* (v.21), as if to say, Those perpetrating anything against them I shall continue to invest with extreme punishment, and I shall continue to make myself known among them in future through my ineffable care, with which I shall proceed to supply them abundantly in the future.[38] [241]

36. At this point in the text a reader has inserted a rogue phrase, "the usual gifts will be supplied from the divine Temple," Mai notes.

37. The final phrase in v.18, reading in our Heb. "the torrent of thorns," rendered in the NRSV as "the Wadi Shittim" and of indefinite location, Theodore reasonably takes to represent a distant place.

38. Opting at the outset for Joel's place in history at the time of Hosea, and not responding to the apocalyptic character of the prophecy despite repeated references to the Day of the Lord and the sweeping scenario of universal judgment, Theodore has refused to make any reference to NT times or similar NT eschatological passages like 1 Thes 5.2–8; Rv 21.1–2, 22.1–2; he is not inclined to Stuart's view that "Joel 3 (4) is also Christian eschatology." His acknowledgement of Peter's lengthy citation of 2.28–32, prompting a rare explication of his hermeneutical principles, was forced upon him, possibly by reading of Acts 2.16–21 in the liturgy. As with Hosea, he closes the book of Joel without any formal conclusion.

COMMENTARY ON THE PROPHET AMOS

T IS QUITE OBVIOUS, on the one hand, that the blessed prophet Amos, on whom with the grace of God it is now our task to comment, speaks in almost all his prophecy of the fate that would befall the people. Thus he reveals the ten tribes would suffer first at the hands of the Assyrians, and what was due to affect Jerusalem, and the tribe of Judah, and then the rest of that kingdom at the hands of the Babylonians. On the other hand, it was not without purpose[1] that reference to this was made by the prophets; it was because God devoted complete attention to the people with a view to the manifestation of Christ the Lord, which would occur at a time of his choosing for the common salvation of all human beings.[2] The reason, in fact, that he also marked them off from the nations, gave them in circumcision a mark of distinction, caused them to have a country of their own, and instructed them in provisions of the Law to conduct worship of him in isolation on Mount Zion was that when Christ the Lord came, he would make clear on the basis of such events, in keeping with the prophetic revelations and in addition to them the above provisions made for the people, the fact that God was not at some late stage making a new arrangement for the salvation of all people. Instead, at the outset and from the far distant past, he had of his own accord predetermined this, according to blessed Paul,[3] and had chosen Abraham, established a race de-

---

1. After only brief introductions to the books of Hosea and Joel, Theodore is about to launch into a lengthy introduction to Amos. With typical Antiochene ἀκρίβεια, he declines to let pass as of no consequence certain features of the text, nothing in Scripture being "without purpose."

2. We shall have to see whether in commenting on this prophet, unlike the others, Theodore is prepared to apply this eschatological perspective consistently.

3. See Rom 8.29–30, Eph 1.11.

scending from him, and has bestowed attention on it in the manner of which we have spoken, so that in coming later in this line according to the flesh for the salvation of all people Christ the Lord should obviously be seen to have come in accord with the original determination of the divine plan.[4]

For their sake he caused the whole people to be deported in the captivity, and he brought back again those of them he intended, the tribe of Judah alone leading them, all of whom were allowed to return, for the reason that from them according to the flesh Christ the Lord was due to appear; of the other tribes, in fact, only a few from each came back in their wake. The purpose was that from the manner in which the captivity took place and the return was effected God's designs in caring for the people might become clear in respect of the one who would descend from them and achieve everything to do with the salvation of all human beings. And so, in case they be reduced to complete despair and by suffering that captivity be mingled with the nations, and no longer have a land of their own to return to nor be kept apart from the other nations, [244] from the outset through the prophets he disclosed both the captivity and return from it so that, clinging to these hopes, they might after the occurrence of captivity look forward to the return, which then happened in the way we described and for the reason we gave.[5]

This is the reason that, while in olden times and well in advance this was said by blessed David in many of the Psalms,[6] when the time for its realization came close divine grace raised up the prophets: at one time, they disclosed the imminent troubles from the Assyrians, at another, they hinted at those coming upon them from the Babylonians, and in addition to all of these they mentioned the return and every other detail they were supposed to disclose of what happened at that time. With

4. As mentioned above, Theodore does not always set a particular biblical work or passage within the whole divine plan, οἰκονομία, as Antiochenes liked to do. See also n. 70, below.

5. Reading this preface as Theodore develops it gives color to Photius's criticism of his long drawn-out periods, something that taxes a translator.

6. We recall that Theodore had completed a commentary on the Psalms, perhaps immediately before this, as his first exegetical work.

the outcome of past events happening in accordance with the prophecies, there was confidence that what was prophesied afterwards would probably also take place according to prophecy.[7] Hence they all mention what was done by the Babylonians, since even if it happened that these attacks differed, with Assyrians invading first and Babylonians later and a period intervening, nevertheless there was one overall captivity, beginning with the Assyrians in respect of the ten tribes and moving on to the others, who belonged to the kingdom of Judah, with the siege of the Babylonians.

For this reason, then, the other prophets for their part disclose these events and direct the full force of their treatment to them, apart from including in their discourse a few details slightly irrelevant to them. For his part the present prophet does something of the kind, clearly directing his entire prophetic discourse to what would happen both to Israel and to Judah at the hands both of Assyrians and of Babylonians. By way of introduction, however, he briefly mentions also the great damage that was due to be inflicted on the Israelites in the same period by the neighboring peoples so as to make clear that it was not out of some lack of compassion, or attention, or through a change of heart, that he gave the people over to calamities at the hands of both the Assyrians and the Babylonians, but in his wish to correct their ungodly behavior, since at the same time he punished as well those of their neighbors who sinned against them. He would not have called the latter to account for this if he had not set greater store by the former; rather, by punishing their wrongdoers he demonstrated greater care for them, whereas in bringing troubles also on them he was shown to be acting not out of pitilessness, contempt, or hatred, but from a desire to bring them to their senses, correct them, and lead them on to higher things. Such is the book's theme.[8]

---

7. With the interest in τὸ ἱστορικόν inherited from Diodore, Theodore predictably envisages prophets as seers (of the future) rather than spokesmen; commentators (on the present and past), like a prophet with religious and social concerns, as in the case of Amos.

8. It has been an unusually lengthy summary of this prophet's ὑπόθεσις as well as of every prophet's purpose.

Having thus said everything in regard to the people, the prophet also mentions briefly what was due to happen in connection with those near the city at that time and especially at the hands of the Babylonians on account of their sins against them, for the reason I gave. Now, he delivers the prophecy, not in Jerusalem but in the locality of the nations close to Israel in the sanctuary of Bethel, where some Israelites offered sacrifices to the idols. [245] Had he prophesied in Israel, you see, it would not have been clear either to Israel or to the other nations what he had in mind in their regard, since none of the latter could bear to go up to Jerusalem. By delivering his prophecy in the aforementioned places, however, he could not fail to be obvious both to Israel and at least to those nations nearby, who often mingled with one another in the course of worshiping the idols. The result was that everyone who was the object of his preaching both knew what was said about them, and by receiving the prophecy before the event and seeing its outcome at close quarters had greater faith in divine grace working in the prophets.

What is claimed by some commentators, however, that the prophets did not upbraid Uzziah for aspiring to the role of priesthood and for that failing they all ceased prophesying, strikes me, on the contrary, as being altogether in the realm of fantasy.[9] The book of Hosea in fact puts it this way, "The word of the Lord, which came to Hosea, son of Beeri, in the time of Uzziah" and so on; in Isaiah the prophet it says this, "A vision that Isaiah, son of Amoz, saw, that he received in criticism of Judah and of Jerusalem in the reign of Uzziah"[10] and so on; and in the present prophet it says this, *Words of Amos, which came in*

9. Where he found this version of events (possibly in Eusebius of Caesarea, a source for the *Commentary on Isaiah* of Theodoret, who relays it without being discouraged by his earlier fellow Antiochene) is not clear; Chrysostom, Theodore's contemporary, also has it in his six homilies on Isaiah 6, but they are probably later than this comment. Editor Mai attributes it also to Jerome and Procopius. Theodore is correct: the effrontery of King Uzziah is described in 2 Chr 16.16–21, but someone has joined to it the punishment for the misbehavior of the priest Eli and his rascally sons reported in 1 Sm 3.1. His rebuttal proceeds, however, rather on logical grounds.

10. See Hos 1.1, Is 1.1.

Kirjath-jearim in Tekoa, which he saw in Jerusalem in the days of Uzziah, king of Judah.[11] How, then, could it be that in the days of Uzziah prophetic speech against his contemporaries came to an end, when Hosea, Isaiah, and Amos in the titles to their books are shown to be exercising prophecy in the days of Uzziah? In addition to that, it is also obvious that the prophets were not bidden by spiritual revelation to upbraid Uzziah and hesitated to do so, since they put greater credence in the divine revelations than the respect they showed for the wayward king. If they were not granted a revelation to this effect, let no one fairly blame them for failing to take on a task not conveyed to them by divine revelation, especially since they were in the habit of responding to spiritual revelations to speak or not to speak in keeping with them, and on the contrary never to speak or to keep silent in defiance of them, nor choose to say anything in defiance of them. This opinion, then, arrived at by many commentators—how, I know not—which in my view is quite contrary to the biblical text, I thought it not proper to pass over in silence. The text of the whole prophecy is devoted to Israel and Judah, and to what happened to former and latter, first at the hands of the Assyrians and later at the hands of the Babylonians, with some brief mention in the introduction to the troubles befalling their neighbors. The reason for what happened to the people we claimed to be, as mentioned previously,[12] that God accorded it all his special care with a view to the one due to appear from their midst [248] according to the flesh, Christ the Lord coming for the salvation of everyone. The fate of the neighboring peoples is put ahead of the rest by way of proof that God was not under the influence of pitilessness against his people, since he calls the others to account for their crimes against them.

---

11. The LXX misreads a Heb. form for "shepherds, sheep breeders" as a place name, different from the place name Kirjath-jearim in Theodore's text.

12. Yes, Theodore has in fact told us this above. Photius faults him also for his repetitiveness.

Chapter One

It is time now, however, to begin the book, which goes as follows, *Words of Amos, which came in Kirjath-jearim in Tekoa, which he saw in Jerusalem in the days of Uzziah, king of Judah, and in the days of Jeroboam, son of Joash, king of Israel two years before the earthquake* (v.1). As we remarked also in the case of the other prophets, this has the function of a kind of title, indicating what the book means, by whom and about whom it is composed, and when. Now, there is nothing remarkable in his saying *Words, which he saw in Jerusalem:* admittedly he is about to say everything in regard to Israel—that is, the ten tribes—and no less in regard to the neighboring peoples; but he believed that outranking everything else was the fate of Jerusalem—in other words, his own people, this being the tribe of Judah, as we said in what preceded—other things as a consequence being said and done on its account.[13] Thus the reason for his prophesying he indicated from the most important item, beginning his prophecy with these words, *The Lord made utterance from Zion, and from Jerusalem he gave voice, the pastures of the shepherds have languished and the summit of Carmel has dried up* (v.2). It is quite remarkable that he began the discourse with this: since he was not in Jerusalem but spoke in those places that belonged to the nations and the kingdom of Israel, he logically included the information, *he made utterance from Zion, and from Jerusalem he gave voice,* so that the listeners would not attribute what was said to the demons worshiped in that place, but that all would know that he said this by the will of God, who is creator and Lord of everything. He ordered the worship due to him to be performed on Mount Zion according to the provisions of the Law, and gave this to the prophet to say at this time, and at the right moment put into effect what was disclosed. *The pastures of the shepherds have languished, and the summit of Carmel has dried up,* as

13. The book's title is obviously significant, and—ignoring that solecism Kirjath-jearim, the location of Tekoa (unlike Theodoret, he is no geographer), and the earthquake—Theodore seizes on one item, the unaccountable inclusion of Jerusalem in the LXX text where our Heb. has Israel, which he proceeds to rationalize.

if to say, By this sentence all the neighboring peoples along with their leaders have been made to languish, and indeed those of Israel with them, whom he called *the summit of Carmel* for dwelling in that region and putting their eminent position to no proper use.

He next divides his discourse into separate items, speaking of each of the neighboring peoples. *The Lord said, For three godless acts of Damascus and for four I shall not shun it in return for their sawing with iron saws the pregnant women in Gilead. I shall send fire on the house of Hazael, and it will consume the foundations of the son of Ader. I shall smash the gate bars of Damascus, and destroy inhabitants from the countryside of* [249] *Aven. I shall cut down the tribe from the men of Haran, and the people called Syria will be taken captive, says the Lord* (vv.3–5). The phrase *for three and for four* means very many: since the number after one and two suggests plurality, *for three* means many, and *for four* an increase in plurality.[14] He means that he overlooked many godless acts of Damascus, but since they continued to take their godlessness to extremes, it was impossible any longer for him not to shun and hate them. He then passes over their other crimes and mentions what had been done by them to the Israelites so as to bring out that amidst their many godless acts he would punish them most of all on behalf of those to whom he was concerned to show great care. The term *Gilead*, therefore, means Israel by reference to one part of it, Gilead being a part of Israel. So since they had taken their crimes to such extremes, he is saying, as to cut with iron saws their pregnant women (probably citing this an index of their savagery, by which they spared not even the pregnant women, actually cutting them open with saws or with swords, the practice in war, which he calls *iron saws* for greater

14. A modern commentator like Stuart explicates no better than Theodore the semitic usage of numerical synonymous parallelism in remarking, "It cannot be taken literally to indicate a precise number of crimes, but it does connote multiplicity." Theodore is less familiar, however, with the local political developments involving the coalition of Aramean cities dominated by Hazael of Damascus, whose son took the name Ben-Hadad (a name obscured by the LXX's reading Hadad as Ader, despite 2 Kgs 8), all to be overthrown by the Lord. If not a geographer, he is also vulnerable as an historian.

effect),[15] for their sakes I shall inflict on them destroyers so that even their palaces will be laid low (the meaning of *foundations of the son of Ader*) and all the power of their mother city will be destroyed (the sense of *I shall smash the gate bars of Damascus*). And I shall actually destroy all of them so as to destroy even their neighbors from Haran, who were expected to provide them with much assistance from their own resources. In a word, I shall completely surrender to captivity all from that kingdom who bear the name of Syria as a title.

Thus says the Lord, For three acts of godlessness of Gaza and for four I shall not shun them because of their taking captive Solomon into captivity to confine them to Idumea (v.6). Here it has the same meaning, I shall no longer put up with their committing many godless acts and persisting in their wilful depravity; I shall punish them in particular for the fact that, after Solomon took captive the people from Idumea and put them under the authority of the Israelites so that they remained for a long time in that condition, the latter attacked, did away with that captivity by the norms of war, and obliged them to go back again to Idumea (referring here, too, to the wrong they did to the Israelites).[16] What response, then? *I shall send fire on the walls of Gaza and it will consume its foundations, and I shall destroy the inhabitants of Ashdod, and the tribe from Ashkelon will be eliminated, I shall put my hand on Ekron, and the remnant of the Philistines will perish, says the Lord* (vv.7–8): I shall inflict the same punishment on them as well, he is saying (by *fire* referring here as well to war in that it feeds on them in that way: [252] it will remove the walls of Gaza, root up the whole city, wipe out those inhabiting it along with those dwelling in Ashdod and Ashkelon). Nor can I put up with those in Ekron. Gaza is given a mention, in fact, as head-

15. Stuart, like Theodore, feels the expression is exaggerated for effect: "The reference to threshing pregnant women appears to be a hyperbole, the intention of which is to summarize all sorts of gruesome treatment inflicted on the Gileadites by invading Aramean soldiers." Theodore might have referred his readers to 2 Kgs 8.12 to document this practice.

16. The scenario Theodore sketches here arises from the misreading by the LXX of the Heb. for "entire [captivity]," *shalma*, as "Solomon." None the wiser, he comes up with this account.

ing the provinces among the Philistines; but in general he is referring to the punishment that will befall all the Philistines—
hence his adding, *the remnant of the Philistines will perish, says the
Lord,* as if to say, In short I shall destroy all the Philistines, just as
above he said that all the people who were called Syria would
be enslaved.

*Thus says the Lord, For three godless acts of Tyre and for four I shall
not shun it for confining the captivity of Solomon to Idumea and not remembering the covenant of brethren. I shall send fire upon the walls of
Tyre, and it will consume its foundations* (vv.9–10): though I put up
with them for a long time, I shall no longer put up with the godlessness that they take to extremes, and most of all the fact that
they were responsible for the captivity of Solomon in Idumea,
having this lawlessness in common with the Philistines. They in
particular should have refrained from committing any such
crime by recalling the treaty that Solomon and their king made
with each other out of friendship;[17] but they set no store by it,
and have now perpetrated such crimes. For this the enemy will
attack in accord with my decree, remove the walls, and destroy
the whole city.

*Thus says the Lord, For three godless acts of Idumea and for four I
shall not shun it for pursuing its brother with a sword, bringing a
womb in dishonor to the ground, snatching its horror as evidence, and
maintaining its attack as a victory* (v.11): having borne their extreme godlessness, I shall no longer put up with their godless
behavior, and especially their waging war against the Israelites,
unashamed by their kinship with them and the fact that they
were brothers one of the other, one people descended from
Esau and the other from Jacob (the meaning of *his brother*). The
phrase *bringing a womb in dishonor to the ground* means,[18] They

17. Once again Theodore has to deal with the same misreading by the LXX
(see n. 16); and he also addresses the true reference to the "covenant of
brethren," which he might have documented from Solomon's relations with
King Hiram of Tyre mentioned in 1 Kgs 5 (as would Theodoret).

18. Again the LXX text by its independent reading of Heb. forms, especially
in rendering them "womb" and "evidence," has left Theodore with the need to
conduct some creative commentary that, if striking us as far-fetched, does not
betray any sense of difficulty.

slew them all and brought them to the ground, a mark of people sinning against the womb that bore them. In other words, since he spoke of brothers borne from brothers, he spoke of the slaughter of brothers as *dishonoring a womb* in that they were dishonoring in this way the mother they shared. They have also done horrible things to them, he is saying, such that they provide the onlookers with a greater example of their own savagery; and they actually directed against them a really fierce attack, giving evidence of the same attitude of hatred towards them to the very end (the meaning of *maintaining as a victory*). What is the response to them? *I shall send fire on Teman, and it will consume the foundations* [253] *of its walls* (v.12). Teman was the celebrated city of the Idumeans. I shall therefore inflict war on them, he is saying, which will completely destroy their biggest and most royal city, uprooting it along with its walls.[19]

For three godless acts of the sons of Ammon and for four I shall not shun them for cutting open the pregnant women of Gilead so as to extend their own boundaries. I shall endkindle fire on the walls of Rabbah, and it will consume its foundations with shouting on the day of battle, it will be shaken on the day it is consumed, and Milcom will go off in captivity, their very priests and leaders at the same time, says the Lord (vv.13–15). After making the same accusations about these people as well, he says he is particularly angry with them for cutting open the pregnant women of Israel in a manner resembling the savagery of the men of Damascus with the expectation of destroying the whole nation by this vicious act against the pregnant women so as to get possession of their country and thus extend their own occupation. For this the enemy will attack them, he is saying, demolishing all the walls of Rabbah, which was their capital, uprooting the city and enkindling such

19. Theodore does not bother to document the antipathy between Israel and Edom celebrated in OT passages like Ps 137 and the doublets occurring in Obadiah and Jer 49. In v.15 the Antiochene text reads "Milcom" where the other forms of the LXX read "its kings," which Stuart classes as "an inexplicable corruption." See J. Gray, *I & II Kings*, 3d ed., Old Testament Library (London: SCM, 1977), 291, on the "Milcom" in 1 Kgs 11.33: "Greek, probably nearer the truth, reads 'their king', preserving a trace of the use of the word as a title of the god of Ammon, which the orthodox Jewish scribes deliberately perverted to *milkôm*, with the vowels of *siqqûs* ('abomination')."

an awful war against it as to raise unbearable laments in the victims at the events occurring. It will suffer utter ruin, therefore; their idol, bearing that name *Milcom,* will also be taken off into captivity along with all those acting as priests and leaders of the people.

Chapter Two

The Lord says this, For three godless acts of Moab and for four I shall not shun it for burning to ashes the bones of the king of Idumea (v.1). It is clear that in all the rest he cites the nations' crimes that they perpetrated against Israel. Here, too, he does not deviate from the theme of the preceding sections, saying that he moves on to vindication of the king of Idumea, who seemed above to fall under the same threats as the Idumeans. But since the king of the Idumeans at one time wanted to move in the direction of peace and friendship with the Israelites, the Moabites were angry with them and made war on the Idumeans out of hostility to the Israelites, and after defeating them they offered the execution of the king of Idumea to their own idols as a kind of triumphal sacrifice, even burning him in the course of sacrifice. This, then, is the meaning of the phrase *they burnt to ashes the bones of the king of Idumea,* referring to the offering and the execution in which they turned his bones to ashes as though making them a whole burnt offering.[20] So he says he is enraged with the Moabites on the score that they displayed such terrible wrath towards the king of Idumea out of hostility to the Israelites. What is the response to this? *I shall send fire on Moab, and it will consume the foundations of its cities; Moab will die from impotence where it stands, with noise and with sound of a trumpet. From its midst I shall destroy judges,* [256] *and kill all its leaders with it, says the Lord* (vv.2–3): the enemy will attack, laying waste all their cities, reduced to extreme weakness as they are and incapable of sustaining the magnitude of the troubles befalling

20. Theodore investigates the significance of the Moabites' action; Stuart explains it as an attempt to prevent the person participating in resurrection, claiming support from the passage on the dry bones in Ezek 37.

them, meeting their death with a mighty noise and sound of the enemies' trumpets. In short, their overthrow will be so complete that not even any judge or leader will survive, absolutely all of them perishing.

Having thus spoken of what would befall the neighboring peoples for their crimes against the Israelites, the prophet now turns to the fate of the people, bringing out that while the former were due to be punished for the wrong done them on the grounds that they were doing injury to the people that happened to belong to God, the latter also would not escape punishment for being ungrateful to God. He first mentions the tribe of Judah as particularly deserving of punishment for being no less impious despite living close to the divine Temple, putting it this way, *The Lord says this, For three godless acts of the sons of Judah and for four I shall not shun them* (v.4), meaning he also hated them for being frequently godless, especially since they persisted in their godlessness. Then he cites the reason for the punishment, *For rejecting the Law of the Lord and not keeping his commandments. They were led astray by the futile things they made, which their ancestors had adopted:* they were minded to set no store by my laws and commandments, and instead gave themselves up to the worship of the idols, committing sins in keeping with their own ancestors. So what follows? *I shall send fire on Judah, and it will consume the foundations of Jerusalem* (v.5): I shall destroy all the people of that kingdom by means of the enemy, and Jerusalem along with them. Now, it is quite clear that in this he refers to the Babylonians:[21] they reduced Jerusalem to ruins and took captive the people of the tribe of Judah; and yet in what follows he discloses the troubles befalling Israel—that is, the ten tribes—and probably refers to the Assyrians, who took them captive and departed. So it is clear that he considers

21. Some modern commentators have doubts about the authenticity of this oracle against Judah. Theodore, of course, would not entertain such doubts, nor does he have difficulty with this eighth century prophet in Israel foretelling sixth century disasters for Judah; the deuteronomic language and the oracle's brevity do not worry him, either. He simply feels the prophet does not distinguish between the different times, different foes, and different fates; but since all tribes constitute one people, the reader should have no real problem seeing one captivity referred to.

as one the captivity affecting the people at the hands of both
Assyrians and the Babylonians, even if they were different foes
who in the one case captured the ten tribes—Assyrians, I
mean—and in the other case Babylonians who took the people
of the tribe of Judah. As well, some time intervened, since it
happened that the captivity of the whole people was effected
this way, beginning with the ten and completed with those from
the tribe of Judah. Hence also the prophets in announcing
what would happen to the people mention at one time the former and at another the latter, since both constitute the people
and were in common taken off to one captivity, as it were, even
if it happened to them at different times.

*The Lord says this, For three godless acts of Israel and for four I shall
not shun them* (v.6). Then after saying that for their extended
godlessness he is justified in shunning them, he goes on to
mention as well the great number of their actual faults. [257]
For selling the righteous for money. By *the righteous* he refers now,
not to the person of virtue but to the one with whom right lies
in matters under dispute, as if to say, for money they betrayed
people with right on their side. And he extends his comment,
and the needy for sandals trampling the dust of the earth (vv.6–7):
they so multiplied their ill-gotten gains as to betray the rights of
the needy for the basest profit (the meaning of the phrase *sandals trampling the dust of the earth,* which was clear proof of their
setting no store by justice, especially as they easily did so for
base profit). *They pummeled the heads of the poor.* Of the same people he says that they not only failed to vindicate their claim on
justice but they even belabored them without risk—hence his
going on, *and strayed from the path of the lowly:* though their behavior was correct, they changed the verdict to a negative one,
scorning them for their lowliness. *A son and his father went into
the same girl, so that the name of their God is profaned. Binding their
garments with ropes, they made curtains for the altar; and they drank
wine from false accusations in the house of their God* (vv.7–8): in
an extraordinary degree of licentiousness they set no store by
the laws of nature, both father and son freely associating with
the same women, proving guilty of such awful blasphemy of the
God they seemed to invoke. They built tents out of garments

near the altar, showing no regard for the nearness of holy places, and practiced this kind of debauchery. From the abuse of the needy whom they wronged in manifold ways, they celebrated a festival by being drunk in the house of God.[22]

But I destroyed the Amorite before them, whose height was like the height of a cedar and who was as strong as an oak; I destroyed his fruit above him, and his roots below him. I brought you up from the land of Egypt, and conducted you through the wilderness for forty years to inherit the land of the Amorites. I took some of your sons as prophets, and some of your youths for consecration (vv.9–11): you committed these crimes without recalling my favors, neither my completely destroying the Amorite, who was so great and powerful, leaving no vestige of him on the earth, nor my bringing you up from Egypt when enslaved, nor my nourishing you in various ways for forty years in the wilderness, so as to put you in possession of the land of the Amorites that in no way belonged to you. In addition to all this I gave to some of you a share in the grace of prophecy for the common good, and I also selected some of your number to devote themselves to a more observant and better life, thus bringing adornment to everyone else.[23] And since this was obvious to all, he says in similar fashion, *Surely this is so, sons of Israel? says the Lord:* It is impossible for you to deny the truth of this. [260] Consonant with the above he adds, *You made the consecrated ones drink wine, and you gave the prophets this instruction, Do not prophesy* (v.12): you clearly persisted in openly abusing my grace, obliging those set apart for a more observant life to partake of wine and all the other things they had been anxious to abstain from by their own promise, and openly preventing the prophets from discharging their particular role.

22. Though the LXX version somewhat blurs the references, some provisions of the Law are cited by Amos as infringed by the Israelites: the veto on interchange of sexual partners (see Dt 22.30), restitution by night of garments surrendered as collateral by day (Ex 22.25–27), perhaps the symbolic sandal-transfer of property and persons (Dt 25.9–10). Theodore as usual, however, does not document these provisions.

23. Theodore somewhat improves on Amos in this exaltation of consecrated life, and in the travesty of it—something he had personal experience of in his earlier life, entering monastic life and temporarily abandoning it.

What is the response to this? *For this reason, lo, I shall roll under you in the way the cart full of straw is rolled. The runner will be deprived of flight, the strong man will not exercise his strength, the warrior will not save his life, the archer will not stand firm, the speedster will not be saved by his feet, the rider will not save his life, and the strong man will not find courage among the mighty* (vv.13–16): I shall inflict such awful punishments on you that, like a heavily laden cart that gives out a squeak from the weight of the burden it is carrying, you are weighed down with troubles and give vent to wailing and groaning from the extreme effort. The result is that flight will be impossible even for the one trained to run, no advantage will come to the strong man from his great strength, no possibility of finding salvation for the man prepared for fighting and warfare, the task overwhelming for the skilled archer, the fleet of foot unable to find any salvation, and, instead, those able to ride a horse and those boasting of their great strength will find no means of exercising the resources left to them. After saying this as indication of the magnitude of the troubles, he goes on, *The naked will flee on that day, says the Lord,* as if to say, only the most needy and of no importance among the rest on account of the degree of their lack of resources and status will find salvation at that time, since the enemy will not be interested in their capture on account of their unimportance.

Chapter Three

He then makes a connection with what has been said. *Hear this word that the Lord has directed at you, house of Israel, and against the whole tribe that I brought up from Egypt, saying, But of all the tribes of the earth it is you I have known; hence I shall take vengeance on you for all your sins* (vv.1–2): do not make nonsense of what has been declared about you by God, since it is the one who freed you all from slavery in Egypt and at that time gave evidence of his special care for you beyond all other people who has now also declared this about you in threatening just retribution for your being ungrateful in this way to such a wonderful benefactor. *Will two people go together without their knowing each other?* (v.3) As confirmation of what has been said, and as proof of the words not being spoken by chance, he goes on in this vein meaning something like this, If it is possible for two people to make a short journey together while all the time hiding from each other the reason for the journey and not communicating [261] with each other about it, and engaging in travel with a common purpose, it will be possible also for the enemy to come against you in defiance of God's will. *Will a lion roar from the forest when it has no prey? Will a cub utter a cry at all if it has not caught anything?* (v.4): is it possible for a lion to cry out from its den when it has no expectation of prey, and for it to see something without catching it (by *cub* referring again to the lion, as if to say, "What is a human being, and the son of a human being?")?[24] So if this is possible, he is saying, it is possible also for your enemy to engage in an attack on you without capturing you like some kind of prey. *Will a bird fall to earth without a fowler? will a snare open its mouth on the earth without catching something?* (v.5) As birds are normally caught by fowlers, and snares fall at the time they are about to catch something, so too you must expect some sort of trouble, with the enemy attacking and capturing in defiance of God's will, and even taking you off into captivity. *Will a trumpet sound in a city without a populace taking fright?* (v.6) If it is possible for a trumpet to be suddenly blown in a city without fright affecting everyone from the uncertainty of what is happening, it will be possible also for you to hear the enemy's trumpet without fear or harm. *Can trouble happen in a city without the Lord's causing it?* As it is impossible for it not to happen in the way mentioned, so it is impossible for the troubles affecting your city to occur without God bringing them on you. *Hence surely the Lord God will do nothing without revealing his teaching to his servants, the prophets* (v.7): far from our

24. Ps 8.5. Stuart labels the passage "A list of inseparables," which is not a transparent index of the prophet's drift. Theodoret, too, takes some time to plumb the meaning of the rhetorical questions, which through natural examples convey the sense of both inevitability and communication; only by vv.6b–7 does he discern both these meanings, though on v.8 Amos would have been disappointed that he omitted to highlight the prophet's ineluctable role.

uttering anything to no purpose, therefore, God has given us everything to say; his wish is before the event to disclose through us the future and what he intends to inflict for your correction so that you may be aware of the reason for the troubles coming upon you, and by whom, and for what reason it is due to be inflicted. *The lion will roar, and who will not be afraid? The Lord God has spoken, and who will not prophesy?* (v.8) In other words, when a lion utters a loud roar, it is impossible that the cattle will not be seized with fear, and when God makes a declaration, it is impossible for us not to comply with his wishes in dread.

Announce to the regions in Assyria and to the regions in the land of Egypt; say, Assemble on the mountains of Samaria, and behold many marvels in its midst and oppression in it. It does not know what will be in opposition to it, says the Lord (vv.9–10). As though entrusted with disclosing the future to them by God's will, he says, Assyrians and Egyptians, come to Samaria, beholding the power they exercise against those who are weaker, not reckoning what they will suffer for their sins, with God enraged against them; know that he will inflict such awful punishment on them for their actions. When the Assyrians besieged them, remember, they dragged back from there those who had fled from them to Egypt, [264] and they punished Egypt itself, as it says in Hosea, "They will proceed from the hardship of Egypt, Memphis will receive them and Michmash will bury them."[25] For this reason he says to them that they should learn the reason for their punishment. *Those storing up injustice and hardship in their regions:* they wrought deep and unrestrained injustice against the needy, in particular plying them with abuse. *For this reason the Lord God says this, Tyre and your land round about will be devastated, and it will bring you down from your position of strength, and your regions will be pillaged* (v.11): for this crime God will inflict on you Assyria, who will render desolate Tyre[26] and all the country bordering you—that is to say, all your neighbors—so that no hope

25. Hos 9.6. Theodore does not venture for scriptural documentation beyond works on which he has recently commented.
26. Tyre unexpectedly rates a mention in the LXX text only because of confusion of similar Heb. forms; but Theodore goes on to rationalize its inclusion.

of salvation will be left you when under siege from such a powerful enemy; after wiping out all the possessions of your neighbors, he will subject your whole country as well to rapine so that nothing thought to be of any value to you will be left.

Then, to suggest the severity of the ruin to which they will be subjected, *The Lord says this, In the way the shepherd pulls from the mouth of a lion two legs or an earlobe, so will the sons of Israel dwelling in Samaria be pulled out in the face of the tribe of Damascus* (v.12): such awful ruin will occur that very few will survive, and it will be no different from the situation of a sheep taken by a lion and consumed to the point where the shepherd can recover the merest limb falling from its mouth of such a kind as to be passed over as fleshless and unfit for food (the meaning of *two legs or an earlobe*). Similarly, a few insignificant people will survive the war out of the inhabitants of Samaria in the face of the people of Damascus, just as they will see them destroyed by the enemy like themselves. He made mention first of Tyre and now of Damascus, note, as an index of the magnitude of the troubles, showing that there was not the possibility for any of the neighbors to escape in the event of the Assyrians' attack; what he had said when indicating the ruin of them all in his introduction took effect.

Priests, hear and testify against the house of Jacob, says the Lord God almighty, because on the day when I take vengeance on Israel for its godlessness, I shall also take vengeance on the altars of Bethel; the horns of its altar will be overthrown and fall to the ground. I shall smash and strike the winged house on the summer house, and the ivory houses will perish, and all the others will be done away with, says the Lord (vv.13–15): let those who perform the unholy priesthood for the idols hear this most of all so as to learn from it that when God calls the people to account for impiety, all the altars of the idols will also be overthrown, being put to use in war.[27]

---

27. The mention of priests has evidently occurred as a result of a transliteration of the unusual Heb. word for "couch," *heres*, at the end of v.12 (not an unusual procedure in a text prepared by Jews for Jews, as Kahle maintains of our Antiochene text) as *hieres*, which was then copied by a Christian as ἱερεῖς. Again Theodore (naturally unaware of this solecism) does not bother documenting Bethel's being the centre of idolatry for Israel (see 1 Kgs 12.28–30), nor the ivory houses as a sign of affluence under Ahab (1 Kgs 22.39).

He used *Bethel*, in fact, to mean all idols from mention of one example, and the phrase *the horns of the altar will be overthrown and fall to the ground* to mean that all of their magnitude and all the splendor they enjoyed [265] from the devotion of those worshiping them impiously would be completely done away with. I shall destroy their houses, he is saying, from the foundations (by *winged* house meaning winter house in that it is covered in on all sides on account of the onset of the cold). His meaning is, I shall totally destroy all the houses so that neither summer nor winter parts will be left in them, and the more pretentious houses among them I shall do away with (this being the meaning of *ivory* ones, which will fall along with the others for the reason that one sentence has been passed against all by God).

Chapter Four

Hear this word, cows of Bashan, who are on Mount Samaria, who oppress the poor, trample on the needy, and say to their lords, Bring us something to drink (v.1). At this point he directs his attention to the women, who turned to a useless and arrogant way of living and did wrong to the needy from their great influence; acting in this manner and actually dominating their own husbands, they adopted unseemly practices for their own ends. This was shown to be the case with Jezebel, when Ahab was deterred by the opposition of Naboth, justified as it was; acting in a vile, outrageous, and murderous way, on the contrary, she had no qualms about doing away with Naboth so as to get control of his vineyard, which he had good grounds for refusing to sell.[28]

---

28. This reference to the froward women of Samaria prompts Theodore, whom we have seen generally reluctant to document his commentary from the Scriptures, to wax eloquent on their uncontrolled ways as exemplified in Jezebel's conduct in 1 Kgs 21. Having explained the mention of Bashan, he could likewise have documented it from Dt 32.14, Ezek 39.18, or Ps 22.12, and perhaps also have reminded his readers of the strictures of the mother of King Lemuel in Prv 31.4–5 against immoderate use of wine; instead, he returns to his usual reticence, the failings of women perhaps the spark that momentarily ignited him.

Now, he calls them *cows of Bashan* for the reason that cows raised in that place were particularly wild and fierce; and after mentioning their injustice to the needy, he went on, *who say to their lords, Bring us something to drink,* as if to say that their own husbands, whom they should have respected as their leaders by the disposition of nature, they had no qualms about abusing to suit their licentiousness; they all but commanded them to do everything that would promote their licentiousness.

What is the response, then? *The Lord swears by his holy ones, The days are coming upon you and will take you with weapons; those who are with you they will throw into boiling kettles, and you will be cast out naked, a wife and her husband against each other, and you will be hurled on to the mountain of Harmon, says the Lord* (vv.2–3): God made a declaration that could not be altered (the sense of *swears*), namely, The time is at hand for you to pay for this; enemies will attack you, taking you captive and casting you into unbearable disasters such that you will now all together be deprived of your possessions—both the wives guilty of such crimes and the husbands pandering to their awful crimes—and will be led off as captives to the land of the Assyrians (by *Harmon* referring to the Armenian mountain, which at that time was in the hands of the Assyrian monarchy).[29]

Go into Bethel and commit sin, into Gilgal and extend your godless behavior, offer your sacrifices in the morning, and your tithes every three days. In public they read a law aloud, and made open profession (vv.4–5). Here, too, he upbraids them for devotion to the idols, the meaning of *Go into Bethel and into Gilgal,* [268] a normal reference to the worship of the idols: You practiced godlessness with great enthusiasm, you also offered sacrifices with devotion (the phrase *every three days* or "on three days" to be taken as proof of their constant making of offerings, or the way in which they performed the sacrifices to the idols at that time). In the same place you offered tithes, and read out some law of your own choosing, making covenants with the idols in it. In short,

29. The LXX has difficulties with the Heb. of these verses, obscure enough themselves, and Theodore's text differs again, as in the mention of wives and husbands. He makes his own attempt to locate Harmon, as do modern commentators in various ways.

everything you should by the divine Law have done for God in
Jerusalem you did in the aforementioned places for the idols in
imitation of what I commanded. From this he properly continues, *Announce that the sons of Israel loved this, says the Lord God:*
let their devotion for these things be known to everyone so that
it may also be obvious to everyone why they are being penal-
ized.

What penalty, in fact? *I shall give you grinding of teeth in all your
cities, and lack of bread in all your places, and you will not turn back
to me, says the Lord* (v.6): I shall also cause you great distress and
inflict on you lack of necessities; you will not come to your senses over this and turn towards me (by *grinding of teeth* referring
to the extreme distress, as also in the verse in blessed David,
"God will break the teeth in their mouth, the Lord smashed the
lions' fangs,"[30] which refers to extreme distress, as if it will extend even to grinding of teeth. *I withheld rain from you for three
months before the harvest; I shall send rain; on one part there will be
rain, and another on which there will be no rain will dry up. Two or
three cities will gather at one city to drink water and will not be filled,
and you did not turn back to me, says the Lord* (vv.7–8): I kept rain
from you for you to be affected by utter loss of crops (the
phrase *for three months before the harvest* meaning this, since a
drought occurring at that time without relief causes the complete loss of crops, living things being unable to be fed or grow
fat; it also prevents feed from the soil being given to the cattle).
What follows he also takes from normal experience: Since in severe droughts it often happens that a small storm comes out of
the sky, and some insignificant rain falls on different places,
which is of no benefit to the growth of the crops, likewise you
will be given a supply of rain insufficient for your needs, only a
little falling in parts, so that while one part may seem to have
had rain, another will be completely dry, no good coming to
the crops from the brief fall. In particular he used the drought
to mean that two [269] and often three cities will go off together to the place where they hear water is to be found, not satisfy-

---

30. Ps 58.6. The LXX in these verses confuses Heb. tenses in many cases, not
remarked on by Theodore.

ing their need by so doing, but enjoying some slight comfort from it. Yet you will not improve as a consequence of this, he says.

I struck you with mildew and with blight, and you extended your godless behavior (v.9): I afflicted you with various pests, but you aggravated your godlessness. *Your gardens, your vineyards, your fig trees, and your olive trees you multiplied, but the locust consumed them, yet even so you did not turn back to me, says the Lord:* I wiped out all your gardens with the locust, but even so you remained the same as ever. *I sent death upon you in the way of Egypt, and I killed with the sword your young men with the capture of your horses; in my wrath I put your camps to the torch, yet even so you did not turn back to me, says the Lord* (v.10): as you were fleeing to Egypt in the hope of salvation, I inflicted on you in the same place death and slaughter; those of your number who still survived along with all their possessions I took off into captivity, consuming with fire all your vast numbers through the punishment inflicted on you by the enemy, yet you did not repent even then. *I overthrew you as God overthrew Sodom and Gomorrah, and you became like a brand snatched from the fire, and you still did not turn back to me, says the Lord* (v.11): I inflicted on you the ultimate devastation, as in the case of Sodom and Gomorrah, with the result that you were set alight like a burning brand and invested with the troubles besetting you; but you were still incapable of recovering any sense from it.

After citing all the kinds of things inflicted on them without their becoming any better, he goes on, *Hence I shall treat you this way, Israel; but because I shall treat you this way, prepare to call upon your God, Israel, because, lo, it is I who create a thunderbolt and make a wind, and announce to people their anointed, producing dawn and cloud, and proceeding on the heights of the land—the Lord God, the Almighty is his name* (vv.12–13): but even if you are like this towards me, I nonetheless after the experience of those troubles plan to change your situation for the better in the hope of your coming to your senses as a result of such troubles and being willing to turn to me. The wind in the sky, remember, though gentle and scattered, insubstantial and light, is capable of being worked up to such a state that the crash of thunder developing

from it is intolerable to those on earth, while I myself bring
about the greatest change in you, revealing to you complete salvation at impossible odds.[31] I bring to your notice Cyrus, king of
the Persians, who will be appointed by me to this end, to gain
control over the most powerful, relieve the troubles affecting
you, and bid them return to their own place. I am the one, remember, who brings dawn from darkness, allows clouds to develop and dissolves them with the rising of the sun, and am situated on the heights and above everything; I am he who will
solve your problems like darkness of some kind, [272] I shall
cause satisfaction to burst forth on the good like the day. By removing all the oppression bedeviling you, I shall through my
care for you clearly prove myself to be superior to all things, being Lord and maker of everything. Through everything made
by him he guaranteed the continuity of all things existing. Now,
it is not surprising that he called Cyrus *anointed* since he is accustomed to refer by this term not only to those anointed with
oil but those selected at some time, as in the verse, "Lay no
hand on my anointed, and do not behave badly to my prophets,"[32] here using "anointed," not of those of Abraham's number anointed with oil, but only of those chosen.

Chapter Five

*Hear this word,[33] which I raise over you in lament: the house of Is-
rael has fallen, no more to rise; the virgin of Israel has collapsed on its
own soil, with no one to raise her up* (vv.1–2). After having in the
foregoing disclosed relief from the troubles, once again as usual he threatens retribution, by the latter inspiring fear and a re-

31. Theodore develops to good effect the reference in the LXX text to the
thunderbolt, though our Heb. does not contain it.

32. Ps 105.15 (the psalm speaking earlier of Abraham, Isaac, and Jacob).
Again our Heb. text provides no basis for mention of an anointed, χριστός,
which to Theodore suggests Cyrus (not Jesus, significantly); to Stuart the occurrence of the term "reflects an already corrupt Heb. text."

33. Other forms of the LXX read "this word of the Lord," leading Stuart to
believe it "might well represent the original wording"; but Theodore's text
(though, interestingly, not Theodoret's) stays with our Heb.

turn to good sense, and by the former inviting her to repentance. Your situation calls for lament, he is saying: you have sustained a great fall through your own lawlessness, and it is impossible to hope for relief from it on account of the magnitude of the disaster. *Hence the Lord says this, Of the city that marched out a thousand strong a hundred will be left, and of the one that marched out a hundred strong ten will be left to it in the house of Israel* (v.3): the slaughter coming to you from the enemy is so awful that scarcely a hundred from a thousand and ten from a hundred will be able to be found in any one city. *Hence the Lord says this to the house of Israel, Seek me out and you will live. Do not seek out Bethel, do not go off to Gilgal, and do not go up to the well of the oath, because Gilgal will surely be captured and Bethel will be nonexistent* (vv.4–5): my advice to you, then, is to look towards me, and turn away from Bethel, Gilgal, and the well of the oath, whither you now direct your steps, worshiping idols and demons in those places, knowing full well that all these things along with you will be reduced to a wilderness.[34] *Seek out the Lord and you will live, lest the house of Israel catch fire, as it were, and it will consume it, and there will be no one to quench the house of Israel* (v.6): give up these things and be devoted to God lest punishment from God incinerate you all like fire, for should God dispatch this upon you, there will be no finding anyone to defend you.

He who puts judgment on high and brings righteousness down to earth (v.7): you should not disbelieve anything threatened or promised by God, since it is he who puts judgment and righteousness on high and brings them down to earth, as if to say, He it is who is able to give judgment in your favor when he is wronged by the enemy, and, on the one hand, to punish [273] those who brought such awful troubles on you, and, on the other hand, to demonstrate righteousness and justice, which he does for you who live on earth—something that is wonderful and marked by marvels of every kind. As confirmation of these very things he adds in turn, *He who makes and transforms everything* (v.8): he is easily able to make everything that exists and

34. The LXX breaks down Beer-sheba into its parts and turns it "well of the oath," which evokes no explanatory comment from Theodore.

transform what is made to what he wishes. *Who turns the darkness of death into morning, and darkens day to become night:* he is capable of transforming dangers involving death into joy unalloyed and enjoyable;[35] those apparently enjoying serenity he is easily able to envelop in the gloom of disasters. He intends here, too, you see, to establish the general principle that he is capable of transforming their situation as he wishes, at one time bringing them from disaster to prosperity, at another time reducing them from prosperity to disaster. *Who summons the water of the sea and pours it out on the surface of the earth. Lord God almighty is his name:* he who raises the water of the sea by means of the clouds, and pours it out across the whole earth, is capable now also of pouring out on you in his wrath the army of the Assyrians, which resembles the size of the sea, being Lord of all as he is and capable of doing what he pleases. *Who keeps destruction apart from strength, and brings trouble upon fortification* (v.9): he it is who relieves distress when it befalls, and makes strong even those weakened by troubles, whereas those seeming especially able to do great things he all at once besets with difficulties. This is he who, having willed it, transformed your situation from the better to the worse, and in turn having willed it, he will easily transform it from the worse to the better.

They hated the one reproving in the gates, and they abhorred a holy word (v.10). He now begins at this point to unfold their acts of lawlessness. For one thing, they hated the prophets who had the commission to charge them with acts of lawlessness by way of correction, and, for another, they abhorred whatever they said to them in advising them to take leave of their vices and opt for better things. This is the meaning of *in the gates,* it being the custom in olden times for city folk to make arrangements for urgent business at the gates, at that spot to make a reply to enemy ambassadors on some question, and in fact to hold more important cases there so that the proceedings might be obvious to everyone entering the city and leaving it. Hence blessed David says, "They will not be ashamed when they speak to their enemies in the gates," since it was there that they gave

---

35. Again Theodore is not tempted to give the verse an eschatological sense.

their response to those from foreign parts; and "Those sitting at the gate gossiped about me," their custom being to hold most gatherings there.[36] Here in the same fashion he mentions those *reproving in the gates* for the reason that the prophets made it their business to proclaim to them what concerned the divine will in the place where what was said was obvious to everybody, [276] not only to the residents but also to any foreigners who came to the city.

Then in what follows as well he mentions their acts of lawlessness, which he had also mentioned before. *Hence in return for your buffeting the poor and taking from them chosen gifts, you built houses of polished stone and will not dwell in them, you planted desirable vineyards and will not drink their wine* (v.11): since you inflicted troubles on the poor, making your own their best possessions by robbing from them, and you built handsome houses from the unjust proceeds, and farmed fields with great assiduity, be well aware that you will not enjoy what has thus accrued to you through injustice, for you will not continue in those houses, nor have anything to show of crops from those fields. *Because I know your many ungodly acts, and your sins are grave, trampling on justice, taking bribes, and pushing aside the needy at the gates* (v.12): the great number and magnitude of your ungodly acts and sins have not escaped me, nor the fact that you substituted money for justice, and once you got it from the wrongdoers you perverted justice in contradiction of the truth (including here as well the phrase *at the gates* in the sense we explained before). *Hence the sensible person will keep silent at that time, because the time is evil* (v.13): once the threatened punishment is inflicted, therefore, everyone who can understand what is to be done will allow silence to prevail, being struck, as it were, with the magnitude of the disasters, and suspecting that the time has come in which he said above that these things would happen.

Seek after good and not evil, so that you may live, and the Lord God

36. Theodore's relatively lengthy comment on the mention of proceedings at city gates perhaps derives from his recent *Commentary on the Psalms* (126.5 and 69.12 cited here); the more celebrated examples of business at the gates, such as Ru 4 and Dt 25.7, are passed over.

almighty will thus be with you for the claim you made, We hated evil and loved good. Restore justice at the gates, so that the Lord God almighty may have mercy on the remnant of Joseph (vv.14–15): in the time available I urge you all to forsake the worse and choose the better; in this way you will gain the enjoyment of good things, with God providing his characteristic care. As a response to this, choose good things and turn away from worse things; provided you change your former attitude and are ready to deliver right judgments at the gates in the customary way, you will attain the divine lovingkindness that rescues most of you from ruin. Now, by *Joseph* here he refers to the ten tribes by mention of the leader among them, namely, Ephraim, who was the son of Joseph.[37]

Hence the Lord God almighty says this, In all the streets wailing and on all the roads lamentation will be raised, Alas, alas (v.16): since you give no attention to this, every city and every town will be full of lamentation and wailing at the extent of the slaughter committed by the enemy. *Farmers will be summoned to grieving and to wailing and to those versed in lamentation, and on all the roads there will be wailing, for I shall pass through the midst of you, says the Lord* (vv.16–17): farmers will leave their work on the land and be occupied in wailing, and grief, and various kinds of lamentation, lamenting the slaughter by the enemy and at the same time the land's barren condition. [277] They will suffer this when God passes among them in the person of the enemy and envelops them in so many awful disasters. *Alas for those longing for the day of the Lord! Why do you want the day of the Lord? It is darkness and not light* (v.18): since many had altogether taken a turn for the worse and, as though the prophets were wrong in what they disclosed, they dared to say, Let the disasters come that you foretell and disclose, if there really is some truth in your words, he means, You are most to be pitied in wishing for that day, you will not believe it when you come to it, you will learn

---

37. Theodore gives a reasonable explanation of the reference to Joseph, though Stuart finds in it and in the phrase "house of Joseph" in v.6 a way of including both Ephraim and Manasseh and thus covering both heterodox sanctuaries, Bethel and Gilgal.

from experience the gloom of the darkness affecting you from the multitude of the disasters.

He then confirms his words also with an example. *Just as if someone fled from a lion and chanced upon a bear, and burst into the house and rested his hands on the wall and a snake bit him. Is not the day of the Lord darkness and not light, gloom with no brightness in it?* (vv.19–20). He wanted to bring out through an example the harshness of the day: just as if someone along the way hears the approach of a lion, runs away in the direction of the city but chances upon a bear that causes injury to those happening to be near the city, bursts into his own home in the hope of finding some relief from his troubles, then for some reason or other puts his hand on the wall and is suddenly bitten by a snake, would it not be inevitable that to such a person after such experience of calamities and such awful bad luck in falling foul of the inescapable wound from the snake what seemed day to others would be darkness? and that an onlooker would fail to discern what was happening before his very eyes?[38] In your case likewise, he is saying, when you hear on all sides the enemy's advance, you will make for the city; but alarmed by the uproar in it, which necessarily affects it when the enemy attacks, you will go into your own homes, but that will be of no benefit to you, the enemy dragging you off to captivity from the innermost recesses of the house. For those experiencing this, how could that time fail to be darkness?

Then he adduces proof of their depravity. *I hate, I reject your feasts, and I get no fragrance from your festivals* (v.21): on account of the depravity of your behavior I have hatred for the festivals that you think you observe in my honor, and I do not accept them. *Hence even if you bring me your burnt offerings and sacrifices, I shall not accept them, and I shall have no regard for the show meant for your benefit* (v.22): even if you offer sacrifices or burnt offerings, hoping to gain from them benefit from my manifestation, I shall not accept them, nor shall I pay any attention at all to

38. While it is Theodore's text that encourages him to see one continuing story of bad luck in these verses, the long coordinated structure recalls Photius's criticism of his style.

what is done. What, then? *Take away from me the sound of your songs, I shall not listen to your playing of instruments* (v.23): stop performing for me the songs from that playing, since I take no account of it. [280] *Judgment will flow like water, and righteousness like a torrent that cannot be crossed* (v.24): when I look at your way of life and on that basis I deliver my judgment on your situation, I see the punishment that will be inflicted on you to be most just, one that I shall inflict on you all, exactly like a torrent that cannot be forded on account of its size.

Surely you did not offer me victims and offerings in the forty years in the wilderness, house of Israel? (v.25): for proof that I take no account of sacrifices, you should have learnt in particular from the fact that for the forty years in the wilderness I required nothing of the sort from your ancestors, yet I continued to pay them due attention. *You adopted the tent of Moloch and the star of your God Remphan, the images you made for yourselves; I shall deport you beyond Damascus, says the Lord God, almighty is his name* (vv.26–27): though unwilling to reason as you should, you expect to appease me with sacrifices, men who make no account of me, committed to devotion to the idols; by *Moloch* he refers to the idol worshiped by them, and by *tent of Moloch* he means, You frequent the idol's shrine and care for it, and you are also involved in worship of a star, giving it the name of a god (commentators claiming that in the language of the Hebrews the morning star is given this name),[39] and in fact you give all your devotion to these figures that you made with your own hands. While giving no importance to my worship, you expect to appease me with sacrifices that will be of no benefit to you, for you will be taken off into captivity to places far removed from places nearby. This, in fact, is the force of *Damascus,* suggesting by a detail the people deported far away; blessed Stephen, at any rate, in the Acts of the holy apostles employs this testimony

39. The LXX has come up with "tent of Moloch" and "Raiphan" (for Theodore's Remphan) from reading different forms in the Heb. (and Stephen, whom Theodore goes on to quote, thus cites the verses in Acts). Theodore recognizes that the latter name has to do with worship of astral deities, assisted by commentators with some knowledge of Hebrew, an exegetical skill that he (like most of the Fathers) lacked—though today's commentators suggest it should read Kaiphan, from the Akkadian name for Saturn.

against Jews, "I shall deport you beyond Babylon,"[40] making clearer reference to the places foretold here.

Chapter Six

Since they had abandoned God and were devoted to these things, he goes on, *Woe to those setting Zion at naught and those who trust in Mount Samaria* (v.1): most of all to be pitied are you who dismiss Mount Zion and the God worshiped on it and display devotion to Samaria and the idols set up there. *They made a selection of the firstfruits of the nations, and went in to them, the house of Israel:* you gave no thought to all that was provided to you by God, who bade all worship be directed to him on Mount Zion, nor to the fact that he cut down and totally destroyed all the many nations and their rulers, and provided you with an entry into those places and with a dwelling. [281] To bring out the great extent of the divine bounty, *Cross over, all of you, and look into Calneh, pass though from there into Hamath the great, go down from there to the land of the Philistines, the most powerful of all these kingdoms, and see if their territories are more extensive than your territories* (v.2): travel about the country of the Philistines and all the neighboring people, and by taking note of the biggest of the cities among them, estimate the length and breadth of your country and theirs so as to realize by comparison the extent of the land he gave you as a dwelling better than all theirs for living in it with great comfort.

He then in turn upbraids their inappropriate behavior. *Those who are moving to an evil day, who are approaching and laying hold of false sabbaths, who recline on ivory beds and behave wantonly on their couches, who eat kids from flocks and sucking calves from the midst of herds, who clap their hands to the tune of instruments and think things are permanent and not ephemeral, who drink strained wine and anoint themselves with the best oils, and were not affected by the oppression of Joseph* (vv.3–6): you will come to have experience of that day that will inflict on you a mighty flood of troubles, pretending to

40. Acts 7.42–43, citing these vv.25–27 with the replacement of "Damascus" by "Babylon" in the light of past history, as Theodore suggests.

observe the sabbaths, not out of piety but to devote the leisure to lawlessness. You make a display of great wealth and lewdness even to the point of beds and the lounging on them, and by robbing the needy you slaughter kids, and oxen, and animals of all kinds, employing instruments for songs and handclapping. You provide strained wine so as to imbibe as much as possible, and anoint yourself with choice unguents. You do this in the expectation that your enjoyment will last and never fail you, giving no thought to the degree of punishment you will sustain for it (by the *oppression of Joseph* here making a general statement from one particular, as if to say, You do not give a thought to the current oppression that you will sustain for these vices).[41]

For this reason they will now be taken captive under the rule of the powerful, and horses' neighing will be removed from Ephraim, because the Lord has sworn by himself in the words, the Lord God of hosts,[42] *I loathe all the wantonness of Jacob, I have hated all his regions, and I shall annihilate the city along with all its inhabitants* (vv.7–8): since you give no importance to the threats, you will learn from experience itself the truth of the disclosures, all of you being taken off into captivity by rulers invested with great might, with the result that the panoply of war will be completely wrested from you along with the horses. Since God, you see, abhors all your lawlessness, which you have no qualms about committing as an insult to him to the extent of filling your cities and your regions with this impiety, it will be right for him to annihilate all your cities along with the regions and their inhabitants.

Then as proof of the extent of the devastation, he says, *If ten men are left in one house, they will die;* [284] *if the survivors remain and their kin lay hold of them and make efforts to carry their bones out of the house, he will say to those in charge of the house, Is there anyone still left with you? he will reply, No more, and he will say, Be careful about mentioning the name of the Lord* (vv.9–10). The passage in-

---

41. The LXX departs significantly from our Heb. in these verses. It is unlikely that Theodore would have noticed any departures.

42. Stuart observes that the Greek omits this second mention of the Lord in v.8, leading him to conclude it is secondary. As with so many modern western commentators, he needs to advert to the Antiochene form of the LXX to avoid reaching any ill-founded conclusions about the text.

volves deep obscurity from the viewpoint of commentary. It resembles the part in the creation story where there is mention of the treaty that Laban and Jacob made with each other about ownership of the offspring of the sheep, one man owning some, the other owning others,[43] since while that too is obscure in its expression, the sense gains clarity in the course of comment. Now, it is necessary to expound the sense of this passage as well, whose meaning is not clearly expressed. His intention, in fact, is to cite a proof of the devastation affecting them in that it was very extreme, saying, In many cases scarcely ten will be left from a large household of many members, the rest being done away with in various ways through the war—as he said above that of a hundred only ten will survive, and of a thousand only a hundred.[44] Then, he goes on, when the others die, the survivors will make great efforts to bring out all the bodies of the dead lying inside and consign them to the grave, meaning that war causes manifold forms of slaughter, and the slain are lying in different ways in different parts of the house, with the result that in such a situation some parts of the house collapse and fall on the bodies—hence his using the term *they make efforts* to emphasize that they will try something involving effort and difficulty in wanting to consign all the bodies to the grave. He next says, Exhausted by the great number of the corpses carried out, they will direct some remarks to one another in disagreement as to whether all the bodies have been carried out or there are still some lying unburied; he says that even of those in charge of the households ten will survive from the whole number, as if to imply they are saying this to one another. You see, once it has somehow proved possible for them to remove all the bodies and give them burial, they will know that there are no more corpses, perceiving the silence gripping the house from the devastation evident in the great number of the dead and the annihilation of the occupants, there being very few sur-

43. See Gn 30.25–34, not quite a parallel case of obscurity, Jacob displaying rather ingenuity (Theodore referring to the book as Κτίσις, different from Diodore's Κοσμοποιία and the LXX's Γένεσις for the Heb. *Bereshith*). He goes on at some length to bring out the accent in the text on complete devastation.
44. See 5.3.

vivors of such a large household and great number of its occupants. Reduced to silence in the grip of so many awful troubles,
and all but losing their voice on account of the gravity of the
evils befalling them, they will at that time ponder the cause of
the occurrence of so many awful troubles, and the fact that for
the neglect they showed for worship of the divinity, for rejection of appeal to the Lord of all,[45] and for devotion to idols,
these troubles beset them—captivity, overthrow of houses, vast
numbers of slain, and annihilation of occupants.

By way of confirmation of what was said, then, he goes on,
*Because, lo, the Lord gives commands, and he will strike the big house
with blows, and the small house with cracks* (v.11). As though referring to the cause of there being such trouble in bringing out
and burying the bodies of the dead, [285] he says, God gave orders, and thus will consign every house, big and small, to particular damage (suggesting as much by *cracks* whereas by *blows* he
makes the point generally). It means, not that he strikes the big
with blows and the small with cracks, but that neither the big
nor the little house will escape punishment, but in different
ways, some partly sustaining damage, some totally affected by it,
as naturally happens in war and prolonged siege. And, to bring
out the incontrovertibility of what was said, he goes on, *Will
horses pursue on rocks?* (v.12) No one would ride horses on rocks,
but where the surface happens to assist the movement of the
horses; nor would this have happened to us if we ourselves had
not provided the cause of our suffering such things. *Will they
keep silence among mares?* Nor would horses that are amongst
mares not remain peaceable when those are present who are in
a position to deal with their frowardness; so neither is it possible for the enemy to remain peaceable in your regard when
through your iniquity you provide the occasion for such things
to be done to you by them.[46] *Because you have changed judgment
into anger, and the fruit of righteousness into bitterness:* as it is, you

45. Other commentators would see the omission of mention of the divine
name as due to respect, not negligence.

46. The LXX departs from our Heb. and modern versions of this clause to
such a degree that Stuart describes the Grk. as "idiosyncratic to say the least";
but Theodore rationalizes it.

will suffer this for what you have committed, provoking God to anger so as to pass judgment against you and, since he knows you are liable to just punishment, to inflict on you such awful bitterness in the troubles. He goes on to mention also what was done improperly by them, for which the aforesaid troubles will beset them. *You who rejoice in no good word, saying, Do we not have horns from our own strength?* (v.13) You are not prepared to heed the counsels of the prophets reminding you of your sins and recalling you to your duty; you attribute to your own might your complete conquest of all the enemies, and set no store by the gravity of the threats, as though you are capable even now of resisting the enemy.[47]

What is the response, then? *Because, lo, I am raising up against you, house of Israel, says the Lord God of hosts, a nation, and they will oppress you so as to prevent your entering Hamath and as far as the torrent of the west* (v.14): for this attitude of yours, the Lord of all the powers everywhere will raise up against you the enemy to inflict an awful experience of troubles, so that the trouble will extend from Hamath (referring to a place situated on the boundaries belonging to them) to the end of your territory. He thus refers to the reign of Jeroboam, son of Joash, when this prophet himself lived: "He restored the border of Israel from the entrance to Hamath as far as the sea to the west."[48] So it is clear that the extremities of the Israelite territories are indicated in these terms, the meaning being, Beginning from there, the trouble will come upon you all so that no one will be able to escape the hands of the enemy, and you will learn by experience from the events themselves that in the past you had no success against the enemy [288] without divine intervention, and now you are reduced to such awful experience of troubles since you are bereft of his help.

47. Theodore's readers might have expected some light on the phrase "we have horns" (arising from a literal rendering of a place name, Karnaim, a city whose capture by Jeroboam II becomes a claim to invincible power—as "no good word" represents Lo-debar, also captured). But he is content to paraphrase.

48. See 2 Kgs 14.23–25.

Chapter Seven

To this the prophet adds a revelation he had in confirmation of what was said. *This is what the Lord showed me: lo, a horde of locusts coming early, and, lo, one young locust, King Gog. It was possible that it would end up eating the grass of the soil. I said, Lord, Lord, be merciful. Who will raise up Jacob, because he is tiny? Relent, Lord, in this. Let it not happen, says the Lord* (vv.1–3). He says he had a vision of a vast number of locusts and young locusts, the former of whom he suggested was the Assyrian and the latter the Babylonian, in that they would attack and wipe out everything, like a locust and a young locust. But, he says, after I saw the vast number sufficient to wipe out all the fruit yielded by the earth, I fell to my knees and begged for pardon to be given for our faults, seeing, on one side, the vast number of the lost, and seeing, on the other, the small number of the survivors. Then, in the belief that the salvation of the survivors was beyond hope unless God proved to have mercy on our sins and changed things for the better, he said, God did not accept my petition, since he considered the great number of their sins too great for pardon.[49] Now, one should not be surprised if he said *King Gog*, since first to the Assyrians and after that to the Babylonians many also from the Scythian nations were allied in war, their king being Gog,[50] whom he referred to, not as leader in the war at that time but as ally of the leaders. It is well known, in fact, that the Assyrian was in control of many nations at first, and afterwards the Babylonian, all of whom together with their own satraps or the king's were probably present as their allies in war.

Then in turn he mentions a different revelation. *This is what the Lord God showed me. Lo, the Lord God summoned justice by fire, and it consumed the deep abyss, and consumed the part. I said, Lord, Lord, cease: who will raise up Jacob, because he is tiny? Relent, Lord, in this. This will not happen, says the Lord God* (vv.4–6): I had a fur-

---

49. Theodore takes God's reply to be a negative response rather than relenting, as with the other visions.

50. Though we have seen Theodore inclined to give the figure of Gog from Ezekiel's allegory historical value (as in *Comm Jl* 3), his appearance here seems due to confusion with the similar Heb. form for "mowing."

ther vision of God calling for justice as he is accustomed to judge all people, being in the habit of managing their affairs with great precision and close scrutiny. He *summoned by fire* since he considered the deeds worthy of such awful punishment; in it, he says, I saw the multitude of the Israelites resembling an abyss being consumed, and once again I cried aloud begging for some mitigation; but God indicated it would happen. He mentions also a third revelation. *This is what the Lord showed me. Lo, a man stood on an iron wall, and in his hand was iron. The Lord said to me, What do you see, Amos? And I replied, Iron.* [289] *The Lord said to me, I am imposing iron on my people Israel; I shall never again pass them by. The altars of laughter will be destroyed, the initiations of Israel will be left desolate, and I shall rise up against the house of Jeroboam with the sword* (vv.7–9): he showed me someone standing on a wall of iron, with iron in his hand; these were signs of the delivery of an inflexible and ineluctable sentence by God against the Israelites, since iron surpasses everything else in inflexibility. So, he is saying, with complete inflexibility I shall inflict troubles on the people, no longer prepared to bypass their crimes; all the altars will be done away with on which they took satisfaction in worship of the idols;[51] and in short everything performed by them in honor of the demons will be given over to devastation, and all the power of Jeroboam now reigning over you I shall destroy in war. Now, in this he seems by *the house of Jeroboam* to be referring to the monarchy as a whole, by the ruler indicating the whole race, as it is clear that in the time after Jeroboam the invasion of the Assyrians took place against Israel.[52]

When the prophet had disclosed that such things would happen to the race of Israel for their various acts of impiety and lawlessness, Amaziah, who was serving as priest at Bethel and took a leading role among all the people in such awful impiety,

51. The LXX has obviously stopped short at the roots of the name Isaac in the Heb. text (given in Gn 7.17, where it is derived from the verb "to be amused"). Not recognizing this confusion, Theodore endeavors to get some mileage or at least satisfaction from the notion of laughter.

52. This is a useful historical clarification about a king who was well dead before the Assyrian invasion occurred later in the eighth century.

realized that further such statements by the prophet would cause most people to be less zealous for the worship of the idol for the reason of their being gripped by fear at the disclosures of the prophet. He tries to rouse the anger of King Jeroboam against the prophet for saying so many things against him and all his kingdom, and by the fact that not even the report of the magnitude of the threats could be tolerated, foretelling, as he was, the king's death and the captivity of the whole people.[53] Now, the reference to the king was manifestly false, since nothing of the sort had been said by the prophet; but he still intertwined it with the sentence on the people so as by this to provoke the king further. Amaziah did not succeed, however, in convincing the king, who was afraid of doing anything to the prophet on account of his knowledge of what had in the past been foretold and performed by Elijah and Elisha, and especially since he was aware that on the initiative of Elisha his forefather, Jehu, had, through taking vengeance on Jezebel and Ahab, succeeded to the throne, which was also passed on to him through the promises made to his ancestor by God.[54]

So Amaziah by his own insolence then personally said to Amos, *On your way, seer, off with you to the land of Judah, live there and prophesy there, but continue prophesying no further in Bethel, because it is a king's sanctuary and a temple of a kingdom* (vv.12–13). He said *seer* ironically, this being the name they used to give to the [292] prophets as special people who had visions by revelation, thanks to divine activity, as it says in the books of Kings, "The people gave the name prophet to the one previously called the seer."[55] So it was with irony that he said, *Seer*—that is, you who make these promises—leave here for the land of Judah, a country where you will be free to say this. But leave these parts where everything belongs to the kingdom of Israel, and where you, being from the tribe of Judah, have no right to stay and speak your mind and thus upset the kingdom that belongs to us.

53. 9.10–11.
54. See 2 Kgs 9.
55. 1 Sm 9.9, Samuel being the prophet in question.

To this the prophet by divine revelation made the following reply, *I was neither a prophet nor the son of a prophet* (v.14): I have not learnt any such skill, nor did I receive it from my father as an inheritance, since it is an effect of divine grace and comes to those whom God wishes to acquire it. *Instead, I was a goatherd and a cutter of mulberries*, as if to say, I was occupied in pasturing goats and farming land to the extent possible (by *mulberries* meaning figs, as blessed David also says, "He destroyed their vine with hail and their mulberry trees with frost,"[56] it being obvious that he indicated that along with the vines there perished not mulberries but figs); and the term *cutting* means hoeing and tending. Now, by the particular mention of the mulberries his meaning is, I was always involved in pasturing goats and farming; but God snatched me *from the sheep* (so it is clear that *goatherd* means tending both goats and sheep at the same time) and bade me prophesy and disclose to everyone what would happen to the people at his hands—something not for me to know, only for one taught by God as proof of the truth of the message.

Hear your own fate: while you in your own case bid me desist from prophesying here lest I assemble the populace to listen to such teachings, be sure that everything said by me will happen: the enemy will attack, and besides the many other crimes that they will commit they will abuse your wife in the middle of the city and violate her,[57] they will slaughter all your children along

56. Ps 78.47, Theodore—fresh from comment on the Psalms—perhaps recalling a precision made there that frost affects not tree but fruit, and also interpreting mulberries (συκάμινα) as figs (σῦκα) (an association similar to that noted by Theodoret in his comment on that psalm's alternative versions, to which Theodore does not bother to refer in this work). The first half of v.14, on the other hand, perhaps the most discussed verse in Amos, he has no difficulty with, not seeing any reference to a prophetic guild, and with the LXX simply taking the words of Amos as a denial of a prophetic charism. As an Antiochene, he is concerned rather with the prophet's precision about his agricultural occupation—whether with goats only or also with sheep (v.15), and whether with trees or their fruit—though he does not succeed in being quite so precise as Theodoret, who cites a Palestinian agriculturalist to the effect that mulberries require slitting to ripen, the job Amos refers to as his.

57. Theodore (whom we saw not mincing words about the fate of another woman, Jezebel: see n. 28) likewise embroiders the description in v.17 of the fate of Amaziah's wife.

with many others, and the land belonging to you will be measured up and handed over to others who are on the point of taking possession of what is here. *And you will meet your end in an unclean land* (v.17): you yourself will meet your end among foreign and lawless people (the meaning of *unclean*), to whom with all the rest you will be taken off in captivity.

Chapter Eight

After saying these things, he goes on with the revelation given him in addition to them. *The Lord showed me something: lo, a fowler's basket. And the Lord said to me,*[58] *What do you see, Amos? I replied, A fowler's basket* (vv.1–2). The vision meant that all Israel, like a bird snared by a fowler's skill, would be taken and led away captive, with no one able to rescue them from the captors: just as the sparrow caught by the snare cannot get away, so since the power of the attackers is stronger than any snare, [293] it will hold them and lead them off into captivity. At any rate he goes on, *The Lord said to me, The end has come upon my people Israel. I shall no longer pass by them; the ceilings of the Temple will lament* (vv.2–3). He was referring to the force of the visions: The time will come when all will be consigned to punishment, he is saying, and their freedom and power will come to an end, and along with them impiety and the attention paid to impiety and lawlessness. No longer, you see, can I bear to pass over their vices and let such awful things go unavenged; in fact, trouble will lay hold even of the Temple, since with the ruin of everything even it will be consigned to flames. Now, it is clear, as I have often remarked, that in recalling their vices, even if he is speaking of Israel, he nevertheless combines it also with what is due to befall the tribe of Judah under the Babylonians, when it will actually happen that Jerusalem will be taken and the Temple burnt.[59] *On that day, says the Lord, the fallen will be many;*

58. Stuart remarks that the phrase "to me" occurs in the Syriac whereas the LXX "supports MT"—an argument weakened by Theodore's testimony.

59. An apparently legitimate response to a possible anachronism for the benefit of his readers—though Theodore might also have recalled that Amazi-

in every place I shall cast silence: at that time in every place death will take many, and there will be no counting the slaughter of the fallen, some slain, some taken captive; silence will seize everything at the extreme devastation.

He next makes mention in turn of the lawless acts they perpetrated. *Hear this, you who oppress the poor in the morning, and withdraw the rights of the poor to the land, who say, When will the moon pass and we shall engage in commerce? and when will the sabbath come and we shall open the stores so as to set the measure short, increase the weight, make the balance unfair so as to get ownership of the poor with silver and the lowly for a pair of sandals, and trade by every kind of sale?* (vv.4–6) Consider that this most of all is directed to you, he is saying, you who constantly employ unfair influence to the detriment of the poor, waiting for each moon to wane so as to amass the lawless profits from your loans.[60] You wait also for the sabbaths, not to observe them in God's honor, but to engage in more lavish trading, abusing the festal occasion; you also amass unjust treasures for yourselves, setting measures and weights small and heavy so as to trade with each in your own favor. You amass money from injustice to the poor, with no qualms about even the most shameless profiteering (the meaning of *for a pair of sandals*), and with an eye in every transaction to what is in it for you (the meaning of *we shall trade by every kind of sale*).

On this arrogance of yours (he calls the injustice to the needy *arrogance*, note, which they practise by not heeding God's justice) God delivered a severe and irreversible verdict, the phrase *The Lord swears* (v.7) indicating that he will by no means consign to oblivion the crimes committed by them, but, as it were, shaking the whole earth and investing them with such aw-

---

ah seemed to be referring rather to the Bethel temple in 7.13. He is wise to pass over the idea of ceilings ("songs" in our Heb.) lamenting.

60. Theodore to some extent (one thinks of the preacher Chrysostom's philippics) warms to this celebrated theme of social injustice in Amos, though not troubling to clarify for his readers the covenant violations involved; here it is not so much the expiration of a monthly period of a loan that is at issue but the observance of the New Moon festival on which no work was permitted (Lv 23.24; Nm 10.10, 28.11), and likewise the sabbath (Ex 20.8–11).

ful troubles through the invasion of the enemy that everyone will be affected by grief at the magnitude of the disaster befalling them; like the river flooding Egypt and [296] in turn receding, the enemy will attack you and destroy all of you, taking you captive and hauling you off to their own land. At that time, he says, the sun will seem to lose its light in the middle of the day in the eyes of those affected by the distress; darkness will seem to grip everyone on the earth on account of the magnitude of the troubles. Abandoning your lawless festivals, you will fall to grieving; in place of your former melodies you will have recourse to deep lamentation; in place of your luxurious finery you will don sackcloth in mourning for your current disasters; neglecting your former coiffure you will go shorn in recognition of your awful troubles; and, in short, as though mourning a beloved only-begotten son,[61] you will spend your days in the grip of pangs, lamenting the magnitude of the evils besetting you.

Further troubles pending in addition to these, the prophet brings out as more grievous: The days will come, he says, when you will not only be affected by lack of food and drink, but will also suffer a severe deprivation, being granted not even a single divine message that customarily comes through prophets for the encouragement of those caught up in calamities. His meaning is that found also in the blessed prophet Hosea, "The sons of Israel will stay without a king, without a ruler, without sacrifice, without altar, without priesthood, without insignia," by which he suggests the loss of all these advantages of theirs after the captivity in Babylon.[62] In this case, too, the prophet conveys the same meaning: You will be given over to the troubles; at that time you will look for the prophets whom you now ignore, longing to find out if your situation will take some turn for the

---

61. The apocalyptic description of the retribution in vv.7–10 Theodore is content to paraphrase, at this point including a phrase "only-begotten son" (found in our Heb. but not in other forms of the LXX) which with "beloved" would have prompted some Christological comment in any other commentator.

62. Hos 3.4, though here as in commentary on that passage Theodore seems in two minds as to whether it is the fate of Israel or of Judah that is in Hosea's mind.

better. For he says, *The waters will be shaken from sea to sea, and from north to east they will run about in search of the word of the Lord, and will not find it* (v.12), as if to say, all that boundless population of Israel will in various ways be scattered in all directions, trying to find where some prophet appears by God's will to disclose the future to them, whom they will therefore never reach.

Next, he says, everything that now seems most beautiful to you and worthy of attention will completely disappear: the girls brought up with great care as virgins in your midst will perish, and the boys most admired for youthful vigor will perish. Why will you suffer this? *Those swearing by the mercy of Samaria in the words, As your God lives, Dan, and As your God lives, Beer-sheba, will fall, never to rise again* (v.14): because they forsook God, the Lord of all, and were zealous in serving the idols in Samaria and called them gods,[63] for this they will experience a completely irreversible fall.

Chapter Nine

Then he goes on to mention a further revelation. *I saw the Lord standing at the altar; he said, Strike the mercy seat and the gates will be shaken, break it on the heads of everyone, and those of them who are left I shall kill with the sword. None of them will escape, and none of them will manage* [297] *to be saved* (v.1): I had a vision of God standing before the altar—namely, the one in Jerusalem[64]—telling me to strike the mercy seat, that is to say, the altar (referring to it as *mercy seat* because offerings were made on it to win mercy). The fact that he was bidden to strike it is an indication of its really being hit and brought down. At any rate he goes on, *and the gates will be shaken*, to suggest by reference to one part that the whole Temple would be rocked by this blow, since the whole building would necessarily share in the damage to the al-

63. Theodore is wise not to attempt an explanation of "the mercy" of Samaria, a phrase on which commentators on the Heb. text are not agreed.

64. Once again Theodore does not entertain the possibility of a temple or an altar in the north, such as at Bethel, a decision involving him in the presumption of a different audience for Amos (see n. 62).

tar. Put some signs on the heads of everyone, he is saying, as indications of everyone's thereby being sealed in the sense of consigned to destruction, since no one is going to escape that fate. In other words, just as in the land of Egypt he gave a sign of the blood on the doorposts to separate the lost from the saved,[65] likewise here he bids him put some sign on everyone's head in keeping with the divine revelation as an indicator that all were consigned to death.

He adds by way of confirmation of this, Even if they are brought down to Hades, I shall draw them up from there; even if they ascend to heaven, I shall bring them down from there; even if they hide in the caves of Carmel (in other words, the mountains, using a part for the whole), I shall track them down and consign them to captivity; even if they go off to the depths of the sea, I shall destroy them there by means of the wild creatures; and following the vast number of troubles they will all encounter in being taken off into captivity, there by my command they will rightfully perish.[66] From here he goes on, *I shall set my eyes on troubles and not on blessings*, that is to say, I shall continue to take note of them, not to give them a share in some blessing, but to oblige them to experience every kind of trouble, since they rendered themselves liable to such things by their own actions.

God is, in fact, both creator and Lord of everything, who is capable of shaking the whole earth by his mere touch; this very thing he will do also to this land, shaking the whole of it with his verdict and reducing it to great devastation so that all its inhabitants will be seized with grief, since like the river in Egypt the enemy will attack them and do away with many, and the rest he will carry away and lead off into captivity. Then by way of confirmation of what was said, *He who builds his ascension into heaven, and his promise on the foundations of earth* (v.6): he is the

---

65. Biblical realities like "mercy seat" and "passover" Theodore allows himself to document only from the OT (in this case Ex 12.21–27), studiously eschewing any NT or Christological application. (His LXX text comes up with "mercy seat" through confusion of similar Heb. forms.)

66. The content and rhythm of these vv.2–4 resemble Ps 139, but evoke no such comment in Theodore.

one who makes himself visible everywhere in heaven, whither he ever ascends and lives, positioned over all and confirming everything he promises without fail to do on earth.[67] He is the one who takes the water of the sea and pours it out over the whole earth; he is now doing the very same thing in bringing upon your land the Assyrian, who in his vast numbers resembles the sea. These, in fact, are the works of God, who is both Lord and creator of all.

Then, in his wish to give evidence of their ingratitude on the basis of God's attitude to them, he goes on, [300] *Are you not like sons of Ethiopians to me, sons of Israel? says the Lord* (v.7): did I not make you for myself like Ethiopians? At least I seem to have made no special provision for them. *Did I not bring Israel up from Egypt?* Nor was I seen to do on their behalf anything like my taking you from Egypt, freeing you from that harsh slavery and appointing you masters of such a large and marvelous land that did not belong to you. *And the Philistines from Cappadocia and the Syrians from Bothros?* While some commentators claimed the phrase *from Bothros* should be read as what is now called Kara and at one time Haran, I shall pass over this effort at precision on the place hereby indicated as a pointless exercise contributing nothing to the meaning, and treat of the sense in the present case.[68] The meaning here is, you see, *I brought the Philistines up from Cappadocia and the Syrians from Bothros,* wishing to bring out the opposite, in fact, that he provided the others with no

67. The LXX tests the commentator to the fullest by making heavy weather of "upper chamber" ("ascension") and "storeroom" (which by a confusion of similar Heb. forms comes out as "promise"); so rationalizing is the last resort.

68. Theodore, who here launches into an uniquely extensive comment on v.7, is correct in claiming that the thrust of the verse does not depend on geographical precision (the Heb. speaking rather of Caphtor—possibly Crete—and Kir, an unknown locality), despite his predecessors. What prompts him to lengthy and quite ardent debate is the issue that intrigues modern commentators as well, the unity and sequence of thought in this chapter. Unable to entertain any fragmentary hypothesis, he is equally unable to admit that the prophet has switched from a theme of Israel's ingratitude to a universalist statement embracing other nations on the same basis of election and exodus. So he twists the obvious sense of the verse to mean what he takes to be the prophet's overall drift. Theodoret, reading all this, also settles for a simple message of the Jews' ingratitude.

such advantage as he did them, and so an even more intense gratitude should be maintained towards him by them beyond all others. The obverse is clear, at any rate, that if he had brought the others up as well in a manner similar to them, he would have mentioned also that some providence had been shown them, and the purpose of that providence would also have been familiar to everyone, since it was not without reason that he brought Israel up from Egypt, but with the purpose of guiding it with great care and rendering it suitable for the manifestation of the salvation of all from its ranks, Christ the Lord.[69]

What, then, is he saying? Many migrations occurred from place to place, such as happened in the case of Terah, father of blessed Abraham, who left the land of the Chaldeans, arrived at Haran, then died there. It also happened that Abraham later migrated from there to Palestine. It is well known also that blessed Jacob with all his family migrated to Egypt.[70] Something quite similar probably happened to others; some people set out from Cappadocia, migrated to the lands of the Philistines, intermarried with them and became part of them; likewise from Bothros others in turn migrated to the Syrians, stayed with them, and underwent assimilation with them. Accordingly, in his wish that such gifts not be bestowed on anyone as he had bestowed them on them, God said, I did not class you with Ethiopians (referring to all nations from mention of one), and that he has never been seen regaling anyone with the same gifts. In fact, it was you alone, he is saying, whom I brought up from Egypt with many marvels and to the surprise of a great number; I also led you into such large and wonderful land, of which I made you masters though it did not belong to you. You did not enter it as did the Philistines of mixed race from Cap-

69. While Theodore is not in the habit, as we have seen, of acknowledging any eschatological sense to the text, at the outset he did situate the prophet's oracles within the oikonomia as preparing for the coming of Christ. And here too, pushed to account for what might seem to some a change of heart by Amos, he has recourse to the wider perspective of prophetic statement.

70. See Gn 11.31, 12.4–5, 46.5–7. Again, Theodore's general reluctance to document his commentary from Scripture (apart from the Psalms) yields to his present need to establish his unlikely interpretation.

padocia, or the Syrians from Bothros: [301] they experienced some migrations, with no surprises, or anything to show my special care of them, not to mention the fact that they lived as sojourners among the people there. In your case, on the contrary, it is clear with how many marvels I rescued you, how I led you through the wilderness, how I brought you into the promised land, of what kind of land I made you masters by destroying everyone who was in it previously, how much care I continued to lavish upon you beyond all other people. Though heavily obligated to show me respect for this, you give the impression of evincing no regard for what has been done by me for you.

What follows, therefore? *Lo, the eyes of the Lord God are upon this sinful kingdom, and I shall remove it from the face of the earth, except that I shall not finally remove the house of Jacob, says the Lord* (v.8): for all this ingratitude, then, I shall remove you from the land and take off into captivity the kingdom that is so wicked. I cannot allow your complete annihilation, mindful of my decision to accord you such care. *Because, lo, I shall give the command, and I shall scatter the house of Israel among all the nations in the way grain is scattered with a winnowing fan, and no fragment will fall to the ground* (v.9): like those winnowing in the granary and separating husk from grain, I shall consign you as captives to the nations, but I shall not bring about your complete annihilation, keeping alive those whom I judge worthy of attaining this salvation. *All the sinners of my people will die by the sword, those who say, Troubles will not approach or come upon us* (v.10): I shall destroy in war those who take a turn for the worse and do not take the advice of the prophets that any distress will come to them.

Having thus disclosed in every way the troubles that would come upon the people in the impending fate of the ten tribes at the hands of the Assyrians, and later of the others at the hands of the Babylonians, he adverts also to their turn for the better afterwards, saying, *On that day I shall raise up the tent of David that is fallen and rebuild what has collapsed, I shall raise up its ruin and rebuild it as in the days of yore, so that the remnant of people may seek me out, along with all the nations on whom my name has been invoked, says the Lord who does all these things* (vv.11–12): after the experience of distress, however, I shall change everything for the better, I shall raise up the fallen kingdom of David, and from it I shall in turn give a leader for all the people, so that not only the survivors from their number but also many of their adversaries, astonished at the events, will profess belief in God the maker and Lord of everything, since it is clearly God who brings these things to fulfillment. At this point, then, he is referring to the events of the return from Babylon, saying that all who returned to their own place would have Zerubbabel as a king in the line of David.[71] Blessed James in the Acts [304] of the holy apostles, on the other hand, seems to have applied this verse to Christ the Lord on the grounds that it had its realization at the time when the fallen kingdom of David was really raised up and attained maturity by casting off all decadence. At that time also the kingdom that succeeded to David received its confirmation, akin to *the days of yore*, in so far as it then gained its continuing existence; as well, the fact that the knowledge of God spread to the rest of humankind and to all the nations the truth of the facts themselves are seen to testify. The result is that, whereas at that time the passage was meant by the prophet to disclose the coming events of the return, the firm and unshakable truth of the words is revealed and established in the person of Christ the Lord and the application of the passage takes its true force from blessed James.

He next reveals in general the troubles about to beset them at that time, and in a manner similar to the other prophets he mentions their benefiting from an abundance of crops to such

71. In these final verses, which many modern commentators take as an editorial conclusion, Theodore sees an immediate reference to the restoration of the community of Judah under Zerubbabel after the exile as outlined in Ezra, and then a fuller sense (by a process of θεωρία—a term he does not invoke—with NT support: Acts 15.15–17, where James cites this text to approve the mission to the Gentiles) in the coming of Christ to erect a mature, incorrupt, universal, and permanent kingdom. While we may admire his willingness here to acknowledge an eschatological sense to the text (under pressure from the NT), his readiness to see a reference to Zerubbabel was dismissed by Theodoret in his commentary, who elsewhere berated those with Jewish proclivities prepared to see Zerubbabel as successor to David, especially as he was no king. Editor Mai, by contrast, takes this passage as less indicative of such proclivities as others that won Theodore the sobriquet of *Ioudaiophrón*.

an overwhelming extent that the harvest followed upon the crops collected from the threshing floor, only ripe fruit being produced, hills and mountains yielding them a great abundance and bearing as good a return as possible. I shall cancel the captivity of my people, he says, so that they will enjoy tranquillity, live amongst their own, restore their houses to their former condition, work the land and gather crops from it.[72] I shall also settle them permanently in their own land (the meaning of *I shall plant them in their own land*), and not allow them to be any longer outside their own country, which I put under their control (the meaning of *they will never again be plucked up from the land I gave them*), as if to say, they will not be far from it and thus held back by captivity as if by a kind of veil and unable to see their own land. This, he says, is the verdict and the work of God, who is both maker and Lord of all.

72. Theodore is content to paraphrase the concluding vv.13–15.

COMMENTARY ON THE PROPHET OBADIAH

DUMEANS WERE HOSTILE to the Israelites from old-en times, giving high priority to their destruction and taking satisfaction in the disasters befalling them, to the extent that they even conspired [305] in every scheme with those attacking them at times when by divine permission they were reduced to experiencing troubles. Israelites were descended from Jacob, you see, and Idumeans from Esau, and these men were brothers, sons of Isaac: when by divine decision the privileges of the firstborn passed to Jacob, Esau felt hatred for his brother and intended to do away with him when opportunity offered, so his mother had Jacob go off to Haran in order that in his absence Esau's rage might abate; vouchsafed divine providence, Jacob altogether escaped injury from his brother.[1] Still, the enmity passed down to their descendants: the Idumeans, taking their descent from Esau, continued to be hostile to the descendants of Jacob, as I have already remarked. Accordingly, in giving evidence in various ways to their hostility against them, they betrayed much the same attitude also at the same time as Assyrians happened to be attacking Israelites and Babylonians were later attacking Jerusalem and those of the tribe of Judah so as to assist the Babylonians to the greatest degree possible in the destruction of the Jews.[2]

Hence blessed David in his inspired composition says against Babylon, on the one hand, "By the rivers of Babylon there we sat and wept" and so on, in which he brought out the troubles that had befallen them in that captivity; but since, on the other

1. Gn 27–28.
2. Of the history of Edomite hostility and treachery Theodore rightly selects the assistance given to the Babylonians to raze Jerusalem in 586, as also highlighted by Ezek 25.12–14 and in the even more celebrated Ps 137, which he begins to cite. Edom briefly surfaces again in a list of enemies in *Comm Mi* 7.

174

hand, he meant to advert also to their change in fortunes, he
went on, "Remember, O Lord, the sons of Edom, who on the
day of Jerusalem said, Ruin it, ruin it, down to its foundations."
By *sons of Edom*, of course, it is clear he means the Idumeans,
who were called by both these names, as you can discover in
many places in the divine Scripture, and especially in the
records of the Kings, where it says in the fourth record that
Amaziah made a strike on Edom in war, then sent to the king of
Israel inviting him, but he arrogantly replied to him, saying in
addition to other things, "You really made a strike on Idumea,
and you are carried away with your violent disposition,"[3] the author here calling Idumeans the ones he referred to before as
Edom.

His meaning therefore is, Remember all that the Idumeans
did against us, who made the time of our difficulties an occasion of their own malice so as to cooperate with those attacking
us in the hope of bringing down the whole city, and not leaving
any relic of it still standing. He goes on, "Wretched daughter of
Babylon, blessed is the one who gives you your recompense for
what you did to us,"[4] bringing out that God will inflict punishment also on the Idumeans for that attitude at the time when
he brings down the power of the Babylonians, handing over
their royal city along with its king and all its inhabitants to the
Persians for them in turn to suffer at their hands what they had
already done to Jerusalem, whereas he freed Israelites from the
captivity oppressing them and led them back finally to their
own country. [308]

God had often mentioned through the prophets, then, the
troubles that would befall the Israelites, first from Assyrians and
after that from Babylonians, namely, that the whole of Israel
would be taken off into captivity in this fashion. The Idumeans
lent their willing cooperation on those occasions, as I remarked, thinking they had found a suitable occasion for the total ruin of those of Israelite descent. In this they were clearly at
odds with God, who it was that had accorded Jacob the blessing

---

3. The reply to Amaziah by King Jehoash of Israel in 2 Kgs 14.10.
4. Ps 137.8.

of the firstborn and continued bestowing generous and particular care on everyone descended from him. The Israelites had every right to be displeased with this on the grounds that it was by divine decision that descendants won the blessing of the firstborn and yet suffered such things at the hands of those who had lost the divine blessing in the person of their particular ancestor. So of necessity God prompted the blessed prophet Obadiah to this task, to disclose in his whole prophecy the retribution due to befall the Idumeans at a time when God would see fit to change the fortunes of the Israelites to the better, bringing them back from captivity and restoring them once again to their own land so that they might rebuild Jerusalem, erect the Temple in it, in which they had a special obligation to assemble and perform there the worship prescribed by divine arrangement. At the time, in fact, the disclosure of these events brought no little consolation to the wronged; and after the fulfillment of the disclosures they believed even further that this had been said of old by the will of God and had later come into effect, both representing proof of God's care for them.[5] So it was obvious that he had made this disclosure out of care for the people, to whose salvation God directed great attention, as I have often remarked.[6]

Vision of Obadiah (v.1). This differs not at all in its import from the phrase "word of the Lord": Scripture calls God's activity "word of the Lord" in reference to the spiritual grace by which the prophets received the revelations of the future, and in the same way by *vision* he refers to the divine revelation by which in fact they received the knowledge of the unknown.

---

5. Theodore is entering the much-discussed issue of the time of Obadiah's prophecy, whether (as he suggests) in advance of Edom's own misfortune, at the time of the Babylonian's sacking of Jerusalem, or later in fifth and fourth centuries when the Nabateans overran Edom, in which case it would be prophecy *ex eventu*—an option Theodore would not entertain. He has not ventured to explore the prophet's own background, for the good reason of lack of internal evidence.

6. It has been an unnecessarily lengthy introduction; perhaps Theodore felt that the shortest book in the Bible needed some padding. His sympathies are totally with the Jews, there being no suggestion that they rather than the Edomites had it coming—despite the message of Amos.

Since, you see, they received also some insights in ineffable fashion through spiritual activity in their own soul, and in response to the activity occurring within them from the Holy Spirit they obeyed the instruction in what was said as though from someone speaking, consequently Scripture calls it both *vision* and "word of the Lord," and probably also "report," in that they receive knowledge as though by a report of some kind. Hence the blessed prophet Isaiah also says, "Lord, who has believed our report?"[7] as if to say, by the knowledge of what was shown to us and in which we were instructed from on high. In the same vein blessed Paul also included this verse in divine fashion, "Faith comes through reporting, to be sure, and reporting through the word of God,"[8] bringing out that it would not be easily possible for [309] such a report to come to the prophets other than through the activity of the Holy Spirit. Blessed David also says, "I shall bend my ear to a proverb, I shall unfold my proposition to the music of a harp,"[9] as if to say, Making my hearing available and receiving knowledge from on high, I shall transmit the instruction on their duty to human beings. In this case also, therefore, it said *Vision of Obadiah*, which in a similar fashion to the others was a kind of title for the book that contains an explication of what was said and how he received the ability to say such things.

He therefore begins the words of the prophecy thus, *The Lord God says this to Idumea*, to indicate with what the prophecy deals. *I heard a report from the Lord*: as to the fate of Idumea, which was unclear to human beings but due to occur a long time later, I received instruction from God. Next, what report? *He sent a confinement to the nations*. By *confinement* he means what circumscribes something, like a wall or something of the kind,

---

7. Is 53.1. Did Theodore not advert to the occurrence of "vision," ὅρασις, also in Isaiah (1.1), not to mention Ezek 7.26, Na 1.1, Hab 2.2? When he reaches that opening to Nahum, he will supply some cross-referencing.

8. Rom 10.17, ἀκοή being the term in question, which the NRSV well turns here "[Faith comes from] what is heard" rather than the familiar "hearing," the word being susceptible of either meaning, both suggesting a communication (from the Spirit).

9. Ps 49.4.

as is said in the verse, "Who will bring me to a city of confinement?"[10] as if to say, to a fortified city, that is, surrounded with the wall. So his meaning is, I heard this report, that God sent to the nations his own command like a kind of confinement, assembling them all together in a circle around Idumea. *Rise up, and let us take our position against it in war.*

Implicitly the word "saying" is to be understood so as to give the sense, *He sent a confinement to the nations, saying, Rise up and let us take our position against it in war,* as if God were speaking and commanding this, assembling the nations from all sides against it and actually ready to act as general in the wars against Idumea. This somewhat resembles what blessed David also said, "Who will bring me to a city of confinement? Who will lead me to Idumea? Are not you the God who rejected us?" as if to say, God will act as my general in the wars against Idumea. You could find this expression also in blessed David when "he is saying" or "they are saying" is intended, as in the verse, "Why did nations rage and peoples ponder vain things? The kings of the earth and the rulers assembled as one against the Lord and against his anointed, saying, 'Let us burst their bonds, and cast off their yoke from us,'"[11] where in this case also "saying" is to be understood by way of clarification of the intention with which they perpetrated their lawless exploit. Of the same kind is the verse, "In my distress I cried aloud to the Lord, and he hearkened to me: 'Lord, rescue my soul from unjust lips and from a deceptive tongue,'"[12] the word "saying" being intended implicitly here too, as if to mean, In my distress I cried to the Lord, saying, Lord rescue my soul from unjust lips and from a deceptive tongue, the phrase "he hearkened to me" being put

---

10. Ps 108.10. Where our Heb. reads "messenger," the LXX reads this puzzling term, probably through confusion of similar forms; so Theodore has to rationalize his way out of it.

11. Ps 2.1–3. We have noted Theodore's readiness to cite the Psalms as his previous subject of commentary, and his familiarity with them relative to other parts of the Bible.

12. Ps 120.1–2. Though the LXX text seems to be creating unnecessary problems for Theodore by its rendition of a phrase that the NRSV turns thus, "that he may answer me," which would no longer require the insertion of "saying," Dahood translates the Heb. as does the LXX.

in the middle of the whole by way of response. Likewise [312] here too, then, he means, God assembled the nations, rousing them by his own command, as if by word of mouth, to war against Idumea.

Then, as though having specified the war,[13] he goes on to address Idumea. *Lo, I made you least among the nations; you are quite without honor* (v.2): having caused your grievous slaughter at the hands of the enemy, I shall now reduce your nation to small numbers, so that you will be the least of all and brought into deep dishonor, under siege by great numbers and invested with countless troubles. Next, what was the cause? *The arrogance of your heart lifted you up, inhabiting as you do the clefts of the rocks, elevating its dwelling, saying in its heart, Who will bring me down to earth?* (v.3) Since the Idumeans inhabited mountain country, he means something like this: You excessively exalted your thinking, living as you do in recesses of rocks, and in your own estimation you made a splendid and spacious dwelling. You also had the idea that there would never be anyone capable of removing you from your current prosperity. For this you will suffer what has been said so as to gain a realization that it was vain for you to think yourself something when divine counsel is working against you. *Even if you are exalted like an eagle, and set your nest among the stars, I shall bring you down from there, says the Lord* (v.4): and so even if you are lifted up on high like an eagle, which naturally flies above the mountains, and in your excessive splendor set yourself among the stars, you will not match my power when I decide to pull you down.

If thieves came into you and robbers by night, where would you be cast out? Would they not have taken as much they needed? And if grape pickers came into you, would they not leave behind gleanings? How Esau has been found out and his hidden things seized (vv.5–6). If some thieves, accustomed as they are to rob furtively by night, entered your house, they would take a few things and perhaps leave, whereas you would not be cast out of the house, because those who by robbery remove what they chance upon cannot

13. What this combined assault on Edom was, the Bible itself does not specify.

deprive you of your dwelling. And if some people got into the vineyard with eyes on the harvest, they would in all likelihood leave some of the fruit on the vines.[14] What is now about to befall you, on the contrary, will not be like that: there will come upon you enemies who will so dominate you that they will search out all your possessions and not leave anything unharmed; thus everything of yours will fall into their hands, and they will go off taking everything they choose. Then, as proof of the extent of the disaster, *All the men allied to you despatched you to the very borders, they opposed you, they prevailed over you* (v.7): those who formerly were connected with you by treaty, friendship, and alliance will on perceiving the magnitude of your calamity take the part of your adversaries so as in league with them to expel you from all your borders, driving you into captivity as a favor to the enemy. They will oppose you, and by conspiring with your enemies they will prevail. He says the same thing again in a different way. *Men of peace who ate with you set a trap for* [313] *you; there is no understanding in it:* those who accepted you in friendship and shared a repast with you are the ones who devise traps for you, plotting your downfall, since on account of your overweening folly you do not know how to distinguish real friends from enemies.

On that day, says the Lord, I shall wipe out wise people from Idumea, and understanding from Mount Esau; your warriors from Teman will be terrified with the result that people from Mount Esau will be eliminated on account of the slaughter and disloyalty towards your brother Jacob. Shame will cover you, and you will be annihilated forever (vv.8–10): all of your number who boast of having skills in warfare and of being powerful will perish, along with those in Teman priding themselves on martial arts,[15] or the city that seems

14. The close resemblance between vv.1–5 and Jer 49.14–16, 9, which has led commentators to conclude that both passages derive from a similar source, escapes Theodore, confirming the view that his work on the major prophets (not extant, but testified to by his medieval Nestorian Syriac sympathisers) came later.

15. The Edomites' reputation for wisdom, confirmed also in that Jer passage and by the mention of Eliphaz the Temanite in Jb 2.11, also passes without comment by Theodore, who sees here a reference only to martial arts.

to be your greatest; overcome by fear at the troubles ensuing, they will be reduced to terror and dread. The destruction of your people will be as drastic as this for what you yourselves did in giving over to lawless slaughter your own brothers descended from Jacob, who was the brother of your forebear; for this, shame will overwhelm you, and you will suffer total ruin. *From the day you turned adversary, on the day when foreigners reduced his might to captivity, strangers entered his gates, cast lots for Jerusalem, and you were like one of them* (v.11): you brought on yourself the sentence of the troubles that would befall you in perpetrating such crimes at that time against your own brothers when strangers took them captive, while you adopted the role of adversary, as if to say, You took the part of a foe; foreigners entered their remaining cities, and Jerusalem besides the others, dividing up their contents by lot, while you joined in with those committing such crimes.

Do not despise the day of your brother on the day of foreigners, do not gloat over the sons of Judah on the day of their destruction, do not glory in the day of their tribulation, do not enter the gates of peoples on the day of their misfortunes, do not despise their assembly on the day of their overthrow, do not join in attacking their might on the day of their ruin, do not position yourselves at their exits to cut off those of their number escaping, and do not imprison their fugitives on the day of distress (vv.12–14). By the phrase *Do not despise* he means, Do not take satisfaction. Be careful not to do this, he is saying, meaning to continue in the same vein as above: You will pay the penalty for this and suffer the predicted punishment, since you gloated over the calamities of your brother at the time they suffered destruction at the hands of the foreigners. When they were subjected to hardship, you expressed yourself in a way typical of someone taking satisfaction in their ruin (the meaning of *glory in*); when they were in trouble, you personally also entered the city with the others to add to the troubles besetting them. If some of them somehow managed to escape, [316] looking forward to gaining their salvation, you made efforts to destroy them, picking off the fugitives from their number and giving them over to punishment—which is the meaning of *Do not position yourselves at their exits to cut off those of their number escaping, and do not imprison their fugitives on the day of distress,* in all this conveying the sense, For taking satisfaction in the ruin of the Israelites, who were really your brothers, conspiring with the enemy against them, taking satisfaction in their troubles, and inflicting various troubles upon them yourself to the extent of your power, you will suffer the retribution to come.

Hence he goes on, *Because the day of the Lord is near for all the nations. As you have done, so it will be with you; your response will come back upon your own head* (v.15): the time has come when God will bring retribution upon all who at any time acted against them, and on you most of all he will inflict severe punishment, bringing on you a disaster similar to what you caused them. *Because in the way you drank on my holy mountain, all the nations will drink wine; they will drink and ascend, and will be as though they do not exist* (v.16): because you committed these awful crimes against those who dwelt on my mountain, despite being on it yourself, you will be punished, and those who participated with you in this attitude and these exploits will as expected share in the punishment, being given over to utter destruction, and differing in no way from what does not exist. The phrases *you drank* and *they will drink,* you see, indicate the punishment to be inflicted on them and on the rest, like the verse, "In the hand of the Lord a cup full of unmixed wine, and he moved it from one to another, but its dregs will not be emptied; all sinners on earth will drink it."[16] The phrase *on my holy mountain* means, Because you committed these awful crimes against those who dwelt on my mountain, despite being on it yourself, you will be punished, and those who participated with you in this attitude and these exploits will as expected share in the punishment, being given over to utter destruction.[17]

But on Mount Zion there will be salvation, it will be holy, and the house of Jacob will take possession of those possessing them (v.17): to

16. Ps 75.8.

17. This, of course, is but a repetition of the paraphrase already given of v.16. Theodore is filling out this brief prophetic piece, substituting repetition for clarification of obscure items in the text, like "they will ascend" ("descend" in other forms of the LXX), which probably occurs as a result of the rarity of the Heb. verb "gulp down."

you and those who shared this attitude with you these things will happen; they will be saved and will be beyond every hardship on Mount Zion after being under attack previously, with the result that it really will appear holy through their assistance, since the successors of Jacob, whom you from that time attacked along with the others, will have as subjects all who previously controlled them. *The house of Jacob will be a fire, and the house of Joseph a flame, whereas the house of Esau will act as stubble; they will burn it and consume it* (v.18): thus the Israelites will get the better of all the Idumeans so as to do away with them all by force of war like fire consuming stubble. *There will be no firebearer for the house of Esau, because the Lord has spoken.* Because he said Israel would be a fire for Esau, as though [317] due to consume them all in war, accordingly there will be no firebearer for the house of Esau[18]—in other words, There will be no one among them capable of bringing trouble on the Israelites; instead, far from their experiencing at their hands a chance fate, they will once and for all be unable to avenge themselves or do any harm to them.

All of this would actually happen since God is the one who declares it would happen; and since he said above that *the house of Israel will take possession of those possessing them*, in his wish to go into further detail he says that the Israelites in the Negeb will gain possession of the places belonging to Esau, those in the Shephelah the regions of the Philistines, and will probably gain also their own country, those of Ephraim the plain of Samaria, Benjamin Gilead, and those in exile their own land, beginning with the region of Zarephath and finally Ephrathah. He means that they will occupy all the Canaanites' places in the middle, which they previously had; thus, in short, all of them who are close to Mount Zion and perform the worship due to God will receive all their own cities in the Negeb. They are the ones who will attain salvation and will inflict on the successors of Esau very heavy reprisals for what they suffered from them. To all

18. Theodore has an obscure term "firebearer" to explicate here—or rather to rationalize—because of a further confusion with a similar Heb. form for "survivor."

this he added a verse to conclude the prophecy, *And the kingdom will be the Lord's* (v.21), as if to say, Through all the good experiences of the Israelites and the sufferings in payment of the penalty on the part of those who sinned against them, God emerges as true king, Lord and maker of all, doing with authority what he pleases in regard to his own and those seeming to be foreigners.

COMMENTARY ON THE PROPHET JONAH

HE GOD OF BOTH the Old and the New covenant is one, the Lord and maker of all things, who with one end in view made dispositions for both the former and the latter.[1] While of old he had determined with himself the manifestation of the future condition of things, whose commencement he brought to light in the Incarnation of Christ the Lord, he nevertheless judged it necessary for us first, to take on this condition—I mean our present one—and later, to be transformed into the other through the resurrection from the dead so that we might realize by comparison the greatness of the goods revealed. Then, for the purpose of making it clear and to prevent it being thought novel that he had at a later stage made plans and decisions in our regard, he conveyed to human beings through other means as well the coming of Christ the Lord so that all Jews might look forward to it from a distance. [320] This he achieved in particular through the promises he made to Abraham and David, in the former case, that through his offspring all the nations would be blessed, and, in the latter, that he would guarantee the monarchy in perpetuity to his descendants.[2] So though in popular belief these things suggested the person in whom they were due to be fulfilled, the reality of the events was seen to take effect in the Incarnation of Christ the Lord, in whom the nations proved to be truly blessed and the monarchy guaranteed in perpetuity to his descendants.[3] Hence God's providence for the people

1. Theodore speaks of the Old and New διαθήκη, probably with each covenant in mind rather than exclusively its literary record, as would be suggested by "testament." He also speaks of God's dispositions within that context as οἰκονομία, the preeminent exemplar being the Incarnation.

2. See Gn 12.3, 2 Sm 7.13–16.

3. While Theodore in the course of commentary on the text of each prophet focuses narrowly on the historical events involved, in the introductions to each

proved to be considerable, since everyone kept in mind the promises given and looked forward to the expected coming of Christ the Lord. This was the reason why he made a great number of dispositions in the Old covenant in such a way that the happenings both provided the people of the time with the greatest benefit and also contained a revelation of the developments that would emerge later, as well as the fact that the excellence of these latter would be seen to surpass the former.

In this way the events in olden times were found to be a kind of type of what came later, containing some outline of them as well as meeting needs at the time, while suggesting by the events themselves how far they were inferior to the later ones. Thus God brought Israel out of Egypt and freed them from that harsh slavery; by causing the death of the firstborn, he thus completely secured the salvation of the Israelites. By a sign he determined that they would not experience the same fate as the Egyptians, this being the marking of the doorposts with blood.[4] Now, while these events at that time provided the Israelites with great benefit in that they were enabled to enjoy them, in some fashion they also prefigured by way of a type the fact that Christ the Lord would similarly rescue us, not from the slavery of Egypt but from that of death and sin. This he secured for us with the anointing of his own blood: by shedding it for all and undergoing death for us, he effected the resurrection of the dead and provided us all, freed as we are from all slavery thereby, with the expectation of enjoying immortality, incorruption, and sinlessness. We shall not dwell in the promised land like them, but we shall be in the kingdom of heaven. It becomes obvious to everyone from experience itself how great the difference is between the two, as well as the fact that, whereas they had the advantage of those things for a short

---

he adopts a wider perspective that is eschatological and even Christological. And, as an Antiochene, at these times he evinces a concern for the overarching context in which particular oracles and events occur, the whole divine oikonomia leading up to the Incarnation, which is the ἀλήθεια ("fulfillment") of past events, these being also but a type of things to come. This wider hermeneutical pattern does not often emerge in the course of his commentary, but should be acknowledged.

4. Ex 12.21–27.

time, the benefit of these really great and wonderful things comes to their recipients forever.

Likewise, in the wilderness he inflicted punishments on the wayward Israelites so as to instruct us by certain types to dread sin for being sufficient to bring us to a worse condition.[5] This is what Paul suggests in his words, "Now, all these things happened to them as types, and they were written down as instruction for us, on whom the ends of the ages have come."[6] [321] Likewise through the provisions of the Law he gave directions so that people's recourse to brute beasts as blood offerings might be beneficial, and that we might gain a stronger faith through comparison with the fact that we shall attain to greater goods through the blood of Christ the Lord. Hence blessed Paul says, "For if the blood of bulls and goats with the sprinkling of the ashes of a heifer sanctifies the unclean so as to purify their flesh, how much more will the blood of Christ, who through the eternal Spirit offered himself to God, purify our conscience from dead works?"[7] In other words, through the difference of Christ the Lord from brute beasts he left us in no doubt that we ought believe far more in these things than the people of that time had faith in those. When the Israelites in the wilderness through unbelief perished from snake bites, God bade blessed Moses make a bronze serpent so that those bitten might look on it and gain a simple cure from the injury of the assailants; God was capable of delivering them completely from the attack, or at least causing them to find some other remedy for the bite, and he wanted them to gain a cure from the injury of the assailants by way of an example in case we should marvel greatly at God's giving a cure from death through the death of Christ the Lord, and providing us with immortal life through the resurrection. Hence the Lord also says, "As Moses lifted up the serpent in the desert, so must the Son of man be lifted up, so that everyone believing in him may

5. Theodore is not in the habit of employing typology as a hermeneutical strategy, as is true of the Antiochenes generally; they would normally cite NT support for recognizing it, and Theodore proceeds to do likewise.

6. 1 Cor 10.11.

7. Heb 9.13.

not perish but may have eternal life,"[8] bringing out that as at that time a replica healed the injury from the bite of the assailants, in the same way now as well death spread among people, but in happening to Christ the Lord it will provide the cure for death not only to him but also to all people.

What happened in the case of blessed Jonah, the prophet, was similar: when Jews were unbelieving and reluctant to heed his prophecies, God had him go instead to the nations. Then, after remarkably keeping him safe inside the sea monster for three days and nights, he brought him to the city that was full of countless vices, and caused him to preach repentance, and become a source of salvation for all in that place, so that from the comparison we might not lack faith in Christ the Lord's being kept incorrupt for the same number of days, rising from the dead and providing all nations in general with salvation by way of repentance and enjoying immortal life. Hence the Lord also said at one time, "As Jonah spent three days and three nights in the belly of the sea monster, so must the Son of Man spend three days and three nights in the heart of the earth," and at another time, "Men of Nineveh will rise up and condemn this generation, because they responded to the preaching of Jonah and, lo, a greater one than Jonah is here."[9] [324]

It is clear that, while there is a certain similarity in events, there is a great difference between the latter and the former, and that, whereas these people persisted in unbelief like the Jews of that time, the nations will gain salvation from preaching. It was to do with them that the case of blessed Jonah was cleverly proposed: the prophet would not have persisted in his disobedience of God to the point of refusing to do what was told him, sent as he was for the salvation of so many people, nor would it have been at all necessary for him in his disobedience to experience the troubles on sea so as to be thrown into the sea monster, kept safe in it beyond belief, and still more remarkably enjoy a return from there. God was capable of prompting the reluctant and disobedient prophet to his duty in

8. Nm 21.6–9, Jn 3.14.

9. Mt 12.40–41, the latter saying recalled loosely and attributed to a different occasion.

other ways, just as we are aware of his acting in the case of Moses, who was reluctant about the ministry on which he was sent, and in the case of Jeremiah, who likewise tried to avoid the magnitude of his ministry.[10] Instead, it is obvious from the facts that he chose to employ blessed Jonah and do novel and extraordinary things, for the reason that he intended to present him as a type of the life of Christ the Lord, and so for this reason he was led on by such incredible novelty and proved worthy of belief, displaying in his own person a type of such a great reality.[11]

While you might say, then, that this was the principal reason for the marvels that happened in that way to blessed Jonah, the other reason also follows on and takes its lead from the type. The prophets, you see, were necessarily despondent in being constantly sent by God to the people, disclosing the future to them and threatening the punishments that would be inflicted. With great zeal they carried out everything designed to achieve their correction, but all to no avail, since the Israelites' wickedness worked against what was done for them by God through the prophets' efforts. Hence they naturally thought their trouble was for nothing, and they fell into utter despair of human behavior on the grounds that the nations, on the one hand, were heading in the wrong direction, while those that seemed to have been chosen for divine knowledge were no less devoted to godlessness and the depravity of their morals.[12] Wishing to console them in this condition, God, who takes great interest in all people but accords a particular care to his own, often indicated to them the transformation of human affairs that would

10. See Ex 3.11, Jer 1.6.

11. Perhaps against the grain, Theodore is having to accept a typological approach to this book as the only way to account for the "novel and extraordinary things" to be found in it, especially concerning the sea monster, which are not easily reconcilable with his habitual historical approach to Scripture. See my article, "Jonah in Antioch."

12. Jonah's displeasure in ch 4 of the book perhaps accounts for this apologia for the prophets' despondency—though in Jonah's case the author is satirizing prophetic relish for the punishment of the unrepentant. Theodore is right, though, in seeing this book as a piece of prophecy intended for the "instruction" (if not "consolation") of prophets.

occur at the manifestation of Christ the Lord, when by divine grace all were destined to turn from the worse to the better. And finally he worked this remarkable exploit affecting the prophet Jonah for the instruction and consolation of all the prophets, through whose deeds he convinced them that the events concerning Christ the Lord would be true, and that all people would at that time by divine grace undergo a change in the direction [325] of their duty. For the time being, the Jews had made a determined option for the worse, with God's permission, as a proof of human free will and weakness; but at the coming of Christ, when God chose to reveal his grace, all people, who were constantly bent on godlessness, received an impulse for the better. As blessed Paul also said, "Scripture had everything imprisoned under sin so that we might be justified on the basis of faith,"[13] emphasizing that we learnt from our forebears the human inclination in the wrong direction so that we might discover that we need divine grace to discern the right way and prefer it to everything.

As an adequate demonstration of this to the prophets he arranged for the events here described, at any rate, thinking this needed to be exemplified in the events involving Jonah in particular; in his own person he provided a kind of type of what would happen to Christ the Lord. He sent him to the city of Nineveh, remember, which was large and populous, and was the royal city of the Assyrians; everyone in it was bent on godlessness and dedicated to a depraved way of life, living in luxury and indolence, licentiousness and utter lawlessness. He bade him prophesy the city's destruction if they did not turn to their duty; then he caused them all to become immediately attentive to the voice of the prophet, even though no one knew who he was, nor had they seen him accompanied with marvels so as to be struck with admiration of him. At this point they had a change of heart merely in response to the threat so as to set their face in a new direction, pagans though they were and formerly showing no evidence of any form of knowledge in the di-

---

13. A particularly loose recall of Gal 3.22, nuanced to support Theodore's point.

rection of reverence for God. The result was that they showed from the events of that time that in this fashion at the coming of Christ the Lord he would by his grace cause all the nations to take a turn for the better, even if Jews chose not to respond to the teaching in piety.

Hence the blessed prophet realized from the events of the time that Jews would be shown to be deserving of extreme punishment for exhibiting no correction despite so much instruction, while Ninevites, who were addicted to godlessness and perversity, all of a sudden at the mere disclosure of the future proved to have a change of heart for the better. He realized also that this occurred as a sign of what would happen with Christ the Lord, and the same thing would take place to a far greater degree, when the nations were called by divine grace and moved en masse to godliness, whereas Jews remained unresponsive and resistant to Christ the Lord, despite having in their midst from the beginning prophecy and teaching about him.[14] The fact that all people dwelling everywhere would be declared heirs to the kingdom of heaven, whereas Jews would be excluded from this gift on account of their own disobedience and impiety, despite appearing to be at an advantage with such wonderful instruction, necessarily depressed him. He saw this distressing situation on all sides, and naturally grieved for the Jews' condition and the awful [328] punishments they were due to suffer; he lamented that by comparison with the Ninevites they were obviously liable to punishment in the present situation, and later would suffer complete rejection by comparison with the nations throughout the world who were destined to take advantage of religious instruction. After all, blessed Paul laments their rejection and declares himself ready to endure the ultimate retribution so that they might face up to their duty, and that the wonderful care bestowed on them by

14. Theodore naturally takes the dominical statement in Mt 12.39–41 (see Lk 11.30, 32) as a clue to the meaning of the book, namely, a reproach to the Jews for their relative hardness of heart; Paul is adduced to support this. Modern commentators would see the book rather as a satire on some aspects of prophetism and a meditation on the theme of divine compassion. See my article, "Jonah in Antioch."

God might not be rendered futile. "I am speaking the truth in Christ," he says, "I am not lying, my conscience confirms it by the Holy Spirit: my grief is extreme and the pain in my heart unceasing. In fact, I would prefer to be cut off from Christ for the sake of my brethren, my kith and kin according to the flesh; they are Israelites, theirs is the adoption, the glory, the covenant, the giving of the Law, the worship and the promises, theirs the ancestors, and from them the Christ according to the flesh, who is over all, God blessed forever. Amen."[15] If he says this, how is it not obvious that with the same attitude the prophets also lamented and bewailed the people's fate for what happened at that time and what was foretold would happen later?

On these grounds, too, the prophet opted for flight, thinking he would thus avoid prophesying to the Ninevites and prevent what would follow from it, of which the Jews' wickedness clearly gave evidence. What happened later is proof of this statement: the Ninevites, after undergoing a turn for the better with such great promptitude, not much later campaigned against the Israelites, and taking the others captive they showed great enthusiasm in sacking Jerusalem as well.[16] For this they received extreme punishment from God, which the prophet Nahum foretold and recorded in books, so that, on the one hand, the prophecy of Jonah and the events of that time affecting the Ninevites are a revelation of the divine grace by which they all underwent a prompt turn for the better, while, on the other hand, we have Nahum's account of the same people's depravity, on account of which they experienced such awful calamities and endured appropriate punishment for all their

15. Rom 9.1–5.
16. Theodore began his introduction to the book, not with precision on the time of the prophet's ministry, but with anxious efforts to account for the "novel and extraordinary things" to be found in it, especially involving the sea monster. Now he comes to the time of this ministry, reconciling it with Nahum's account of Assyria's downfall in the seventh century; he thus has to place it prior to any recidivism on the Assyrians' part after their exemplary repentance, and in doing so seems to confuse their destruction of the northern kingdom in 722 with the Babylonians' capture of Jerusalem in 586, just as he will mistakenly identify Jonah as a southerner.

crimes. One would naturally be aware of this from all that happened to blessed Jonah in the first instance and was recorded, and later occurred in the New covenant, as we demonstrated; but the happenings of that time and their record in the book, which provided to the people in those days the greatest benefit and advantage at that time, we shall come to know in detail from them. So let us proceed to commentary on them with God's grace.

Chapter One

The word of the Lord came to Jonah son of Amittai, Rise up, go to the great city of Nineveh, and [329] *preach in it, because a clamor has ascended to me from their wickedness* (vv.1–2). The prophet Jonah received a divine revelation, he is saying, to go off to the city of Nineveh and preach in it, since they were committing awful crimes of a kind sufficient to provoke God with their enormity.[17] Since it was a very big city, densely populated and more famous than all others in Assyria, it had to be known by repute throughout Judah[18]—hence his sending him to a city that was already familiar, which he knew, not by sight but only by repute. At this point, then, while he says only, *Preach in it,* he obviously sent him for the purpose of threatening the city also with destruction and obliging all the inhabitants to have an eye to repentance so as to avert in that way the city's destruction. The divine Scripture is in the habit of abbreviating things when it is possible for the readers to divine the sense, as in this case *Preach in it* did not mean God sent the prophet only with this intent without also teaching him what he had to preach, nor when he says, "Three days more, and Nineveh will be destroyed,"[19] was the prophet only ordered to say that but to make

17. Having loosely situated Jonah in history at the close of the introduction (see n. 16), Theodore is not interested in being more precise, even with the mention of Jonah's father, which recalls 2 Kgs 14.25 and thus suggests a date at the beginning of the reign of Jeroboam II (786–746).

18. In that reference to Jonah in 2 Kgs 14.25 his place of origin is said to be Gath-hepher in Galilee, which is in Israel.

19. Theodore is serving notice that he is not going to be content with the

them better by the disclosure of the destruction with the hope of averting the threat if they reformed. It would have been futile for him to threaten destruction if it absolutely had to happen, since there would have been no point in the threat; so the result was that they either reformed and averted the punishment, or they did not reform and it was justly imposed on them by God for the proof of their wickedness.

Aware also of this, the prophet *fled from the face of the Lord to Tarshish* (v.3). He would not have done this if he had been sure the destruction would definitely occur, and if he had been sent to foretell only that such a calamity would occur, with nothing better ensuing from it. Now, some commentators claim that *Tarshish* means Tarsus, deceived it would seem by the similarity in sound. Whereas Tarsus, in fact, is not a coastal city, the divine Scripture uses this name to identify coastal cities, as in the verse in blessed David, "With a violent wind you will crush ships of Tarshish,"[20] which can refer to the coastal city holding ships at anchor in port, whereas it is hardly applicable to the one established at the distance from the sea that is true of Tarsus. Other commentators by contrast claim it is Rhodes. For my part, however, I consider this entire chase after detail to be irrelevant to the subject in hand in so far as the account by the prophet is just as equally beyond question, no matter which city you think it to be.

On the other hand, the point that to a greater degree requires understanding is the fact that it said, not He fled from God, but *from the face of the Lord:* the prophet did not see himself

---

bare narrative in the text; and, as in his comment on ch 3, not grasping the author's underlying purpose, he has difficulty understanding that such a brief one-liner could achieve a people's reformation (see n. 24). The LXX of 3.4 reads "three" days, not the forty of our Heb: has the numeral been affected by the previous verse, "three days' walk"?

20. Ps 48.7. Theodore, whom we have seen imprecise (by comparison, say, with Theodoret) on geographical as on historical matters, at first notes incorrect identifications of this term by predecessors (scholars generally thinking in terms of a place in the direction opposite to Nineveh, like Spain or Sardinia— or, for Theodoret, Carthage), the phonetic confusion with Tarsus documented also from 2 Mc 3.5, incidentally. Then he reverts to type and dismisses the matter as of no consequence.

fleeing from God, [332] considering him to be Lord and maker of all things, and believing him to be present everywhere.[21] But God had commanded that all worship be offered to him on Mount Zion, thus giving the idea to the Jews that he both dwelt there and made his appearance there. For this reason the city of Jerusalem and the whole land of promise was declared God's dwelling place on the grounds that God inhabits it all and surveys it all. Hence it says that the prophet, who had left that place where God made his appearance, had fled *from the face of the Lord*, thus implying he had gone off to some other place far removed. The prophet had in fact done this: if he had been in the former place, God would have definitely appeared to him and prompted him to do his will, whereas if he was far away, he would have avoided that problem since God would not have been prepared to show himself in other places. Likewise, when the Jews were in captivity, they believed the sacrifices and the whole liturgy offered to God was pointless since he was not prepared to show himself in those places or receive worship performed in his honor there. The prophet was obviously reluctant about the matter because he recognized that he was sending him with very high hopes; he would not have sent him for destruction alone unless he intended to arrange also for some good to come of it. He thought it quite absurd if, as soon as he was seen by people who had no prior knowledge of him, he immediately gained a name as a sham and a charlatan.

He is seen suggesting as much himself in his own words in the following verses. The prophet *went down to Joppa* for this reason, and found there a ship leaving for Tarshish. He paid the price for his desperation, embarked with the others, and sailed off with the intention of avoiding the problem of God's making, since God would not show himself to him in foreign places and press him to set off for the task proposed. When he had set sail, however, God made clear to him that he had taken on a flight that was idle and futile, stirring up a violent wind

---

21. Not having accepted the book as a satire on prophet's behavior, Theodore cannot afford to see Jonah's response as flight pure and simple; so rationalizing is all that is left.

and causing such a storm at sea that the ship ran the risk of falling apart, being unable to sustain the force of the waves. Fear of it naturally seized all on board; everyone fell to calling upon anything they considered their god and normally worshiped, begging to be saved from the present danger. But as the storm intensified, they even tossed overboard the ship's contents as is usual with tempest-tossed sailors, in the hope that the ship would be lightened and escape the danger. After this he goes on, *Jonah, by contrast, had gone down into the ship's hold and was fast asleep snoring* (v.5). It was not that after this happened he went below and was sleeping: it would have been ridiculous if with such an alarm raised and everyone's life at risk he had surrendered himself to sleep; rather, [333] he did so as soon as he went on board.[22] After describing the storm, the text went on to add what was done by the prophet at that time, that the pilot went off and saw the prophet asleep in the midst of such a hubbub, and was amazed that with such trouble on hand he had no sense of the troubles affecting them, instead sleeping and snoring in utter serenity. He suggested to him to get up and call on his own god in the off-chance of their being saved by him.

The prophet, however, did no such thing, thinking it risky to offer prayers to the one from whom he was fleeing. The intensity of the storm increased; they then thought fit to discern by drawing lots the cause of the present trouble. This suggests that instead of the storm affecting the whole sea, the disturbance was caused in respect of this one ship; hence they deduced that the cause lay with those on board and wanted to discern by drawing lots the one responsible for the troubles, the Lord God as it happened imparting this insight to them so that the rest would follow logically. In fact, they drew lots, and blessed Jonah was shown to be responsible for what had happened; at this the sailors were amazed that something should in fact have been done by him of such a kind that such awful trouble should de-

---

22. Again, Theodore cannot allow this ridiculous figure to be the object of ridicule. The narrative material for its own sake is engrossing Theodore, whose paraphrase is embellishing the text, filling in any gaps a factual record would require. He is not interested in analysis of authorial purpose.

velop. With severe recriminations they then adopted a judicial attitude, as it were, so as to treat him like a man already condemned by lot, and demanded to be told what crime had been committed by him, what business was he involved in, where he came from, where he was going, what country he belonged to, and from what race of people he came. He gave them the clear reply, *I am a servant of the Lord, and I worship the Lord God of heaven, who made the sea and the dry land* (v.9). You see, since they were devoted to idols, he showed what was special in his worship by saying he was a servant of God,[23] that is, he was totally devoted to his worship; in saying *servant* he was not referring to a general devotion by which the sailors also were necessarily servants of God in being made by him. He went on to mention what was special about the God he worshiped: I worship the maker of everything, who is maker of heaven and earth and sea and all things.

On hearing this, *the men were terrified* at the thought of the maker of everything taking action against them; hence they also asked the prophet, *Why have you done this?* (v.10) When they learnt that he had fled from God and resisted an admonition from that source, and had then involved them in the present trouble so as to come to the realization that God is present everywhere and likewise works his will everywhere, and that it is not possible to flee from such a one, they then said to the prophet, *What are we to do to you so the sea will quieten down for us?* (v.11) Learning the truth about him from his own words, and that he was God's minister and prophet, [336] and realizing that the events were in agreement with his words, they wanted to find out from him what they should do to be freed from the present trouble. It goes on, *The sea was continuing to work up bigger waves,* bringing out that the storm was increasing, a fact those on board could not ignore. Then it says, *Jonah said to them, Pick me up and throw me into the sea, and the sea will quieten down for you, because I know it is on my account that these waves are so high against you* (v.12): I am responsible for all these troubles

23. In fact, the LXX has come up with this phrase by reading it for a similar form, "(I am) a Hebrew"; but Theodore is none the wiser.

of yours, and I advise you to cast me into the sea so that I may pay the penalty for my sins against God, and you for your part may gain relief from the troubles. But they thought it dangerous simply to cast out into the sea such a man who was close to God, and they strove for some way to get back to land and thus eject the prophet from the boat.

Since they could not do it, however, without the stormy sea getting worse for them, they offered excuses to God for what they were about to do, and so threw the prophet into the sea. It puts it this way, in fact, *They cried out to the Lord and said, May we not in any way perish, Lord, on account of this person's life, and do not attribute shedding innocent blood to us; because you, O Lord, have acted in the way you planned* (v.14): do not inflict punishment on us for idly throwing a righteous man into the sea, since it was a matter of great concern to us for him to be saved; but it was not to be, since you evidently did not agree, because the waves got higher and did not allow us to achieve the person's safety. With these words they made excuses to God and threw Jonah into the sea, and at once all the waves subsided, so that the men were filled with a great fear on seeing the power of the Lord of all, who both aroused the sea as he pleased, and also wished it all to be transformed into calm in a flash. It then goes on, *They sacrificed to the Lord and made vows* (v.16), not meaning that they sacrificed to the Lord on the spot, being unlikely to perform sacrifices on board boat, but in the sense that they completely gave up the idols and devoted themselves to the worship of God, promising in future to join his service and offer due sacrifice to him (the meaning of *they made vows*).[24]

24. Some commentators would see great significance in this conversion of the mariners to Yahweh through the instrumentality—albeit unwitting—of Jonah, the reluctant evangelist here, as he will be in later chapters. Theodore's interpretation of the book and the figure of the prophet does not allow him to emphasize this (see also n. 19), so in Antiochene fashion he merely raises a quibble about the accuracy of the place of sacrifice. Such literalist comment on a narrative of this kind we find also in the mouth of a modern conservative, Stuart: "This could hardly have occurred on board the ship, denuded of its cargo. The transportation of edible animals on ocean-going ships was as infrequent in ancient times as in modern. The sacrifice would have taken place on shore." Has Stuart been reading Theodore?

Chapter Two

So while Jonah was being carried for a long time on the sea, *God ordered a large monster moving on the sea to swallow Jonah, and in his belly* the prophet *passed three days and nights* quite unaffected. The result was that he marveled at being kept unharmed and quite unaffected in the sea monster, as though finding himself in some small room in complete security; and he turned to prayer, which he directed to God *from the belly of the sea monster.*[25] The words of the prayer go this way, *I cried to* [337] *the Lord my God, and he hearkened to me; you heard my cry, my voice, from the bowels of Hades* (v.2): finding myself in deep distress and being in Hades itself through despair from the troubles, I cried aloud to you and was not disappointed in my pleas. *You cast me into the depths of the heart of the sea, and rivers encircled me; all your billows and your waves passed over me* (v.3): fleeing your service, you caused me to fall into the sea and experience a mighty storm; in the course of it the sea was whipped up, and like rivers its watery billows crashed upon me. *I said, I am being driven out of your sight: shall I never again gaze upon your holy temple?* (v.4) With the ineluctable force of the calamity I thought myself rejected from your providence, he is saying, and had no hope any longer of being in your holy temple to perform the worship due to you,[26] finding myself far from it and confined by severe calamities. *Waters flooded my very soul* (v.5): the upheaval of the enveloping waters reached even to my soul. *The deepest abyss surrounded me:* I was swallowed up in the bottom of the abyss. *My head sank into mountain caverns:* I seemed no different from someone caught in the deepest mountain crevices, and then the mountains falling on him, leaving no further hope of escape. *I descended onto land, whose everlasting bars held me tight*

25. If it is not surprising that Theodore, with his historical—not say literalist—bent, does not admit to any difficulties with this picture of Jonah comfortably ensconced in his submarine room, it is less a matter of remark that he does not question the occurrence of the psalm in the text as do many moderns.

26. Not having noted the clue to Jonah's northern provenance in 2 Kgs 14.25, Theodore sees no difficulty in his attachment to Temple worship. He moves quickly through the verses of the psalm, being content to paraphrase them now that there is no narrative to embellish.

(v.6): then the sea monster took me from that place, and I seemed to inhabit some land, whence there was no possibility for the one in its grip to escape; though kept safe inside by divine providence, there was no finding any egress from there. *May my life rise up from corruption towards you, O Lord my God:* it is within your power alone to liberate my life from the corruption holding it fast there. *As my life was leaving me, I remembered the Lord* (v.7): almost despairing of my life, I begged your help. *May my prayer come to you in your holy temple:* you will personally receive my prayer from your place in your own temple, the distance in place being no obstacle to your helping me. *Those who respect vain and false things forsook their mercy* (v.8): those working as sailors, although attached to idols and devoted to that false belief, wanted to spare me; but overcome by the calamities, they abandoned that view, realizing they had no chance of life unless they were rid of my company. *For my part, with words of praise and confession I shall sacrifice to you, the vows I have taken I shall render to you the Lord for salvation* (v.9): protected on all sides by your grace alone, and receiving reprieve from death, I shall repay you with hymns of thanksgiving for being saved by your providence.

Such were the words of the prophet's prayer. For its part the sea monster under the impulse of the divine Spirit spewed *Jonah onto dry land* (v. 10), according to God's decision. It would, in fact, be a mark of extreme folly, after such [340] extraordinary things happened to him, and most of all his deliverance from the sea monster, to pry into the prophet's egress from the sea monster, and to think that one could grasp it by human reasoning and explain how it happened in our terms.[27]

---

27. The psalm perfunctorily disposed of, Theodore now addresses the issue that has been at the focus of his attention from the outset, those "novel and extraordinary things" the book recounts, taken at face value (authorial purpose escaping analysis). He can only conclude that one should not busy oneself about it: it is beyond human explanation. Fundamentalists committed to taking the Bible solely and totally as history generally stumble over parabolic or other highly figurative material, and simply throw up their hands, as Theodore does here.

Chapter Three

With the prophet now on dry land, God again bade him go off to Nineveh and preach what had formerly been told him by him. From this it emerges that it was not without purpose that he had told him to preach this message, "Three days more, and Nineveh will be destroyed,"[28] even if the divine Scripture seems to express it this way for conciseness; rather, its purpose was also to convey that he threatens this would happen unless they desisted from their bad habits and repented. Hence he says, *Preach in it the message I told you before* (v.2), suggesting to him all the instruction he had previously given him for delivery to the Ninevites. For his part the prophet, now the wiser for experience, pressed on to put God's directions into effect, though the text says, *It was, thanks to God, a very large city* (v.3), as if to say, it had grown to a great size thanks to divine providence, to teach us not to think anything in this life can achieve fame without God's providing his peculiar care. *It required a journey of three days, as it were,* meaning not that its breadth was of these dimensions, but that anyone wishing to have a clear grasp of its character would need this number of days to go right around it.[29] At any rate, the text went on, *Jonah began to go into the city on a journey of about one day, so to say* (v.4), meaning, on entering the city the prophet began to go round it part by part, and spent about a day preaching and saying, *Three days[30] more, and Nineveh will be destroyed,* and as much else as he could say to those present in each part of the city in sequence by way of instructing the listeners.

It goes on from here, *The men of Nineveh believed in God* (v.5), showing that once the prophet began to do his preaching in a part of the city, the word was passed on to everyone with great

28. Failing to plumb the author's purpose, Theodore is still concerned about the potency of this one-liner in v.4, as he was in his comments on ch 1 (see nn. 19 and 24 there). Unlike the author, he is convinced that prolixity is a virtue in a prophet.

29. Both parts of the verse in the Heb. involve the unique occurrence of phrases that Theodore likewise feels need explication; Stuart does no better than he.

30. For the occurrence of "three" for the "forty" of the Heb., see n. 19.

rapidity; everyone adopted an unquestioning response to what was said, and in the grip of deep fear they believed what was said. The verse, *The men of Nineveh believed in God,* also brings out that he did not carelessly say only, *Three days more, and Nineveh will be destroyed:* they could never have believed in God on the basis of this remark alone, from a completely unknown foreigner threatening them with destruction and adding nothing further, not even letting the listeners know by whom he was sent. Rather, it is obvious he also mentioned God, the Lord of all, and said he had been sent by him;[31] and he delivered the message of destruction, calling them to repentance. When they accepted instruction in this, then, they were naturally told to believe in God; when they accepted both the sentence and the instruction [341] from the prophet's sermon, they set their eyes on better things so as to give evidence of a decisive and serious repentance. In fact, they *proclaimed a fast* throughout the city, the text says, the mighty and the commoners all putting on sackcloth, and adopting the mien of mourners they begged God to be propitious to them. When the report got as far as the king, not even he was seen to ignore what was happening: paying scant respect to his royal dignity, he left the throne, cast off the royal vesture, actually donning sackcloth in his own case, and took to sitting *in ashes.* Orders were then given by the king and the leaders in that place, not only for human beings but also for the animals in their service, to abstain from food and drink of all kinds. Far from setting this limit to repentance, they desisted from their former evil practices and denied themselves all injustice to others in high expectation that God would repent of his decision against them and completely cancel the sentence delivered. The text says, in fact, *Who knows if God will repent, yield to supplication, and turn from his anger, and we shall not*

31. Again Theodore insists that the text is being economical with the facts: no prophet could confine himself to a one-liner and have such success (quite the author's point, of course). So, like Theodoret finding Paul's message (on the similar theme of the gratuity of divine mercy) not to his liking, he is even prepared to rewrite the biblical text—unaware that he is thus undermining the author's meaning. He could, of course, claim that Matthew and Luke present Jesus adopting a similar interpretation of the prophet's ministry.

perish? (v.9) This could not have been said by them unless they had been instructed by statements of the prophet.[32] The prophet says this actually happened: when God saw them forsaking worse things and turning to better, he even canceled the sentence he had delivered against them.

Chapter Four

At this Jonah felt a great distress and was troubled (v.1). And logically so: he was alarmed at the thought that he was likely to gain the reputation for being a sham and charlatan for threatening that destruction would occur in three days, whereas nothing happened.[33] Then, with his eyes on God, he said, *Were these not my words when I was in my own country? This was the reason I took the initiative of fleeing to Tarshish, knowing that you are merciful and compassionate, longsuffering and rich in mercy, ready to relent from imposing calamities* (v.2). In other words, he clearly indicated that this was responsible also for his flight, the realization that if in his goodness[34] he sees them repenting, he would change his own sentence, and that the upshot of it for him would be to gain a reputation with them for being a charlatan and a sham. Hence he goes on, *Now, Lord God, take my life from me, because it is better for me to die than to live* (v.3): through this I have come to the conclusion that death is preferable to living with such a reputation among people. God, who is loving towards the repentant

32. Theodore (who has not noted the similarity of this verse to Jl 2.14) will not cease insisting—quite against the author's satiric purpose—that repentance must have resulted from a prophet's verbose preaching and not a simple response to God. In this insistence, of course, there is implicit Antioch's principle of the role of human effort in the process of salvation: if people are to do their part, they need more to motivate them to this effort than a word from God. In the author's view, however, the prophets had overdone this principle.

33. Is this what the author sees as the basis of Jonah's disappointment? Or is it that people repented rather than were destroyed, a fate that prophets of the fire-and-brimstone variety being satirized by the author took relish in? Theodore has yet to grasp the author's purpose.

34. A further theme that Theodore passes over—the text's litany of God's mercy and kindness resembling those found in Jl 2.13; Na 1.3; Ex 34.6; Nm 14.18; Neh 9.17; Pss 86.15, 103.8, 145.8, which is basic to the author's purpose.

and very gentle with his own, chides the prophet in a corrective manner, *Should you be very distressed?* (v.4), as if to say, You seem disappointed that so many have been saved; you ought put the salvation of everyone ahead of your own reputation, and consider your being taken for such a person preferable to the loss of so many people.[35]

The prophet left the [344] city, sat down outside it, built himself a tent and lived in it, waiting to see what would ensue at some point for the city; he pondered the magnitude of the threat and suspected some development would occur afterwards. Next, *God ordered a gourd vine* to sprout suddenly to provide shade for the whole tent where the prophet was, so that he seemed to have the shelter of a sort of house with the vast number of its leaves, and as well the fruit hanging down suddenly on all sides provided him with considerable comfort. This naturally pleased the prophet, who was delighted with the novelty of the appearance and the usefulness of the structure. But while he was taking great pleasure in this development and seemed to be getting quite some consolation from it, all at once in turn by divine command a grub emerged from the plant, and suddenly consumed it all and completely dried it up, the phrase *early morning grub* meaning that by divine command early in the morning a grub suddenly appeared on the plant and consumed it all. The result was that when the sun rose, the harsh rays of the sun's heat fell on him. The text says, at any rate, *God gave orders to a burning hot wind, and it fell on the head of Jonah; he became depressed and renounced his life* (v.8), bringing out that, far from the heat being normal, by divine command it affected him with a very severe blast such that the prophet got a keener sense of what was happening and was even more distressed, well-nigh expiring from the effect of the heat (the meaning of *he renounced his life*). He said to God, *It would be better for me to die than to live*, meaning something like this, The plant seemed to

35. No one, not even Theodore, could escape the conclusion from ch 3 that Jonah is coming in for some criticism—though the author is probably satirizing prophetism generally rather than simply Jonah's concern over his reputation. Theodore still enters into the spirit of the narrative without any sign of realizing it should not be taken in literalistic fashion.

be some consolation for the troubles besetting me; then it suddenly disappeared, and in addition to the harm to my reputation I was affected by the severity of the heat and the troublesome impact of it. So how is dying not better than living, if I am destined to grow old through such calamities?

Hence God said to him, *Should you be very upset at the gourd vine?* (v.9) When he replied that he was upset to the point of death (so desirable had God made the plant appear to him, and had caused greater grief to develop in him at the loss of the plant such as to establish by comparison the wrongness of his greater grief at the salvation of the city), he went on, Then you so mourned the gourd plant, though you put no effort into its growth; it came suddenly in a night, and suddenly in a night it met its end. How is it not proper for me to have greater mercy on the city of Nineveh, which is so big that *a hundred and twenty thousand* inhabit it who do not know their right hand from their left? (vv.10–11), that is to say, infants, who *do not know how to distinguish right from left*, because of their infancy, not having a precise discernment of issues, nor have they been at any time in sin for the reason that age does not permit it. He mentions this, in fact, as a demonstration of the vast number of the city's inhabitants: where the number of infants was so large, how great was the number of adults? God passed over the latter [345] to cite the number of infants, who gain explicit mention for not deserving to suffer any trouble in that they had at that stage not sinned.[36] You would not claim, he is saying, that such a vast number of infants, guiltless of sin, should perish; so, even if I were not to spare the adults, at least the infants should rather get a mention in the event of the city's suffering no harm. He added the phrase *and many cattle* since they should rightly be kept unharmed for those of the citizens who were being saved.[37]

36. Not all commentators see infants referred to in the obscure phrase; but Theodore mounts a reasonable case. The puzzling mention of the cattle is also handled by him as reasonably as by his modern counterparts.

37. Theodore concludes as abruptly as the book. For all the interest of the story, its value as prophecy has had him guessing, not having quite divined the author's intentions and the nature of the composition. He will, however, sum up at length the book's contents in introducing Nahum, whom above he saw as its sequel (see n. 16).

COMMENTARY ON THE PROPHET MICAH

LESSED MICAH ALSO EMERGES prophesying things similar to what Hosea, Amos, and the rest all prophesied to these people.[1] Under the influence of spiritual grace, in fact, he did his best to foretell what would happen to the people at the hands of the Assyrians and the Babylonians, from the very outset delivering a message of general application to the whole of Israel—that is, the ten tribes, of whom Samaria happened to be head, and the two, who were led by Jerusalem.

Chapter One

It also emerges that he was prophesying at the same time as those others, that is, in the days of Jotham, Ahaz, and Hezekiah, kings of Judah: *In those days the word of the Lord came to Micah of Moresheth* (v.1)—in other words, he was the recipient of a divine activity.[2] For what purpose? *About what he saw concerning Samaria and concerning Jerusalem,* meaning the whole Israelite people, both the kingdom of the ten tribes and that of the two tribes led by Judah, over which blessed David's successors

1. We noted above on Theodore's introduction to Joel that in his text The Twelve appear in the order of the Hebrew Bible (where Micah comes sixth), not the LXX generally, which places Micah immediately after Hosea and Amos. What is said here, after a piece like Jonah that is *sui generis*, does not contradict that.

2. Typically, Theodore passes over the reference to the prophet's place of origin (which modern commentators identify with a village about twenty-five miles southwest of Jerusalem) as a troublesome detail (usually supplied in the biblical text when the individual performs his ministry elsewhere—Jerusalem in this case). He acknowledges that the text places Micah in the reign of eighth century kings, though he likes to see his baleful predictions relating to the Babylonian captivity.

reigned in accord with the promise made to him. In regard to these people and their fate Micah received a revelation of divine origin, and tells what he was taught to say by divine revelation, beginning thus, *Listen to these words, all you peoples* (v.2). The phrase *all you peoples* follows logically, as if to say, all of Israel belonging to the two kingdoms;[3] hence he went on, *and let the land and all who are in it take heed*, that is, all the Israelite region, or its inhabitants, since it was theirs by the promise made to their fathers in the beginning.

The Lord God will be a witness against you: God is addressing you through us, giving a kind of witness about the future, since [348] he had often addressed you on your duty without seeing you undergo any change for the better. So it would appear that, whereas he did everything for your benefit, you had no wish to improve in any way, simply drawing trouble down upon yourselves. *The Lord from his holy house.* The addition was necessary: he is addressing all in common, though the ten tribes practised extensive worship of the idols, even building houses for that purpose in their attempt to worship the demons as gods through the idols; so he was right to add *The Lord from his holy house* to suggest that he is addressing all in common, sent to say this by God who had his own house in Jerusalem, which he also made holy through his peculiar operation.

He then proceeds, *Because, lo, the Lord is coming out of his place, and he will descend and tread upon the heights of the earth. The mountains will be shaken under him, and the valleys will melt like wax in front of fire, and like water poured down a slope* (vv.3–4): issuing from that mountain, God showed the place of his dwelling, and, on the one hand, he will bring under his control the whole Israelite country to which the oracle referred, while, on the other, he will reduce to disorder its powerful occupants (referring to them as *mountains* on account of their eminence) and all the other occupants (calling the lowly people *valleys*), consuming them like wax placed near fire. At any rate, it is

---

3. Again we would not expect Theodore, with his limited biblical lore, to resonate with the wording of 1 Kgs 22.28 and thus detect the author's purpose to identify Micah with the prophet Micaiah in Ahab's time.

clear that he means, not that the former are being shaken and the valleys are melting; instead, in keeping with Hebrew parlance, as we have often shown, he makes a general statement by reference to one part,[4] namely, that the divine wrath will befall the powerful and the rest of the populace, shaking and obliterating them like wax placed near fire. He will bring them to face punishment like torrents of water tumbling from the heights and falling to the bottom.

What is responsible for this? *It is all due to the impiety of Jacob, and to the sin of the house of Israel* (v.5). He then goes on, *What is the impiety of Jacob? Is it not Samaria? And what is the sin of the house of Judah? Is it not Jerusalem?* There was clearly impiety on the part of those assembled in Samaria for the worship of the idols, where most of all they had temples built for that purpose. Yet no less blatant was the lawlessness of those who had Jerusalem to themselves but dishonored the Temple by not desisting from the worship of the idols.

Then he listed the punishments. *I shall turn Samaria into a fruit shed in the field, and like planting of a vineyard. I shall bring down its stones to the abyss, and lay bare its foundations* (v.6): I shall reduce Samaria to a vast ruin to be cultivated like land, and pitch tents on it as a protection for fruit, completely destroying its buildings by demolishing them from the foundations. All the rest follows from this. *They will knock down all its images* (v.7): then they will see the destruction of their futile labors, observing the destruction of the idols they made at the hands of the enemy. *All her wages will be burned with fire:* all the adornment bedecking the idols [349] and the temples, which they paid the idols as a kind of wages, they will destroy with fire. *All her idols I shall reduce to ruins, because she gathered them from a prostitute's wages, and from a prostitute's wages she collected them:* adopting the attitude of a prostitute by forsaking me and turning to the idols, they assembled, as it were, wages of their own prostitution, and devoted them to the worship of the idols, which I shall completely destroy at one fell swoop.

---

4. Theodore's familiarity with Hebrew idiom is minimal; what he classes as a Hebrew practice is no more than general literary expression.

For this reason she will mourn and lament, she will go barefoot and naked (v.8): she will be in mourning, and in her grief she will be consigned to utter captivity (the meaning of *barefoot and naked,* because this is the way a captive is taken off, completely bereft of the adornment befitting her). *She will do her lamenting like dragons, and her grief like daughters of sirens, because her affliction has overwhelmed her. Hence it has reached as far as Judah, and gone right up to my people's gate, to Jerusalem* (vv.8–9). He uses the phrase *like dragons and sirens* in terms of the fables spun by some people,[5] meaning to convey that the accounts given by many people in the form of a fable they will endure in actual fact when the severe affliction is imposed on them by me, beginning with Samaria and travelling as far as Judah and reaching even to Jerusalem, since Babylonians later took it as well.

You who are in Gath, do not magnify it, and you who are in Acim, do not rebuild mockery from the house (v.10). He directs his words to the neighboring nations, whom blessed Amos also said would suffer the same things from the Assyrians as the Israelites. You who live in those cities, he is saying, then, do not grow conceited on seeing their calamities, nor raise a loud laugh at them.[6] *Bring down earth on your mockery:* it is appropriate to scatter dust on yourselves for the laughingstock you will be to others. How and in what fashion? *Comfortably situated though she is, I shall destroy her cities* (v.11): though you think you live well in your own cities, comfortably ensconced, you will wit-

5. Without resources at hand to consult alternative translations or the Syriac version, of the kind Theodoret enjoys, Theodore opines that we must be in the field of fable for the purpose of embellishing the notion of punishment. Theodoret, on finding the term "daughters of sirens" (at least in Jer 50.49 and Is 13.21–22), goes to the trouble of consulting the Hexapla and the Peshitta to find "ostrich" as an alternative rendering, claims that demons are thus being referred to, and concludes the effect is one of general devastation; but in this case he seems content to follow Theodore. It all depends on the effort the commentator is prepared to make in following up details by way of ἀκρίβεια.

6. Vv.10–15 are a lament over the fate of twelve cities, from Gath to Jerusalem, all involving a wordplay, which is developed in the verse attached, but which is lost on the LXX in most cases, partly because of the obscurity of many of the place names. The result is quite a mish-mash, through which Theodore struggles on, probably the better off in this case for not being interested in hunting up topographical details.

ness the destruction of them all. *She who dwells in Zaanan did not come out to lament a house next to her:* on seeing Israelites as their neighbors and the victim of such awful troubles, they gave preference to their own and chose not to share their grief, instead continuing to take satisfaction in their calamities. With what result? *You will suffer the onset of pain from yourselves:* since you did not have sympathy with others' troubles, you in turn will suffer a painful attack and pay the penalty for that depraved attitude by which you took satisfaction in others' troubles. *Who began a turn for the better for the one dwelling in pain?* (v.12) It is not possible for those living in pain to have an experience of any good on account of the magnitude of the troubles besetting them. Then as proof of the statement, *Because troubles came down from the Lord upon the gates of Jerusalem, the din of chariots and cavalry* (vv.12–13): the wrath of God against them will be so great as not even to spare Jerusalem, which will be surrounded by chariots, horses, and every instrument of war.[7]

He then directs his attention to Lachish, a city of the kingdom of Judah notorious for its many crimes. *You who inhabit Lachish, which is the leader in sin for the daughter* [352] *of Zion:* for your part, too, realize the troubles that will befall you, who were the leader of wickedness for Jerusalem (the meaning of *daughter of Zion*), no different from Samaria in your attitude of impiety. *For this reason you will give envoys as far as the inheritance of Gath, futile houses; houses of futility turned into emptiness for the kings of Israel* (v.14): for this you also will suffer the same captivity (the phrase *you will give envoys* meaning, you will send some of your own number into captivity), on your own account suffering the same as the inhabitants of Gath, with the destruction of all the houses built for impious purposes, just as the houses of the idols in Samaria were also destroyed.[8] *As far as the heirs I*

7. By dividing the verses differently, Theodore (or his text) loses the sense of the wordplay on horses found in the place name Lachish.

8. Again the wordplay on the names of the towns of Moresheth-gath (Micah's hometown, in fact), sounding much like the Heb. for "dowry, gift," and Achzib, "lie," is lost on the LXX and on Theodore, resulting in nonsense that yields only to rationalizing. In the following verse Moreshah, sounding like the Heb. for "possession," suffers the same fate.

shall lead you (v.15): you suffer this when I lead the enemy, who will be heirs to your possessions. *You who inhabit Lachish, your inheritance will go as far as Adullam, the glory of the daughter of Zion:* those who will gain possession even of Lachish and extend their own inheritance even to Adullam[9]—in other words, they will occupy all the land of promise; further, even Jerusalem, which seems to be famous for the Temple within it, will be taken.

Now, some commentators claimed that the prophet says this against Lachish for doing away with King Amaziah, since killing their own king was first perpetrated by them, something that had previously happened many times in the kingdom of the ten tribes. This view can, however, be taken as an absolute fable and concoction made up by those with no understanding of the prophetic statement.[10] Amaziah, in fact, was not the first of those reigning over Judah to be treacherously assassinated: Joash, his father, was assassinated previously in the way the story of the Kings recounts in the words, "The servants of Joash rebelled, made an alliance, conspired against him, and struck him down." When his son Amaziah later came to the throne, therefore, he apprehended them, avenging the death of his father; it is of him that Scripture says, "When royal power came into the hands of Amaziah, he struck down his servants who had struck down his father." Obviously it was not the people of Lachish who assassinated Amaziah, Scripture saying, "A plot was devised against Amaziah in Jerusalem; he fled to Lachish, and they killed him there. They carried him on horseback, and he was buried in Jerusalem," clearly indicating that it was some people in Jerusalem who rebelled against him, and when he took refuge in Lachish they sent emissaries and did away with him. While, then, the view is clearly a fabrication, the prophet does direct his words to Lachish, basing his statement of what

9. Added pathos would have been gained had Theodore been able to recall David's escape to the cave of Adullam in 1 Sm 22.1 and 2 Sm 23.13.

10. There is a certain irony here, after his failure to discern the onomatopeia in the Heb. of vv.10–15, in Theodore's using a hammer to kill a gnat in disposing of an ill-considered interpretation by some predecessors by citing the evidence of 2 Kgs 12.20; 14.5, 19–20.

would happen to the kingdom of Judah on that city as part of the whole, as he had made a statement also about Samaria, having had a vision and making a statement concerning both, as the introduction clearly suggested.

Going on in the same vein regarding it, the prophet says to himself, *Shave and shear your hair for your* [353] *spoilt children; exaggerate your baldness to be like an eagle, because they have been taken off from you into captivity* (v.16): it becomes you to grieve for the captivity of your own, who previously lived amongst their own families in great luxury but are now experiencing the hardships of captivity. He uses the phrase *exaggerate your baldness to be like an eagle* since this bird is said to cast off all its feathers at a certain stage.[11]

Chapter Two

He then mentions also, as usual, the reason for the hardships. *They were planning troubles and practising wickedness in their beds; at the break of day they put them into effect* (v.1), that is, they kept forming such ideas among themselves as to give rise to troubles for themselves by sketching out on their own beds the practice of unseemly behavior, and at the break of day putting into practice their depraved intentions. *Because they did not lift their hands towards God; they had designs on property, robbed orphans, took possession of houses, cheated a man out of his house, a man out of his inheritance* (v.2): on the one hand, they had no intention of showing regard for God or setting any store by the laws laid down by him, and, on the other, they were caught up in lusting after others' property and stole the possessions of those lacking patrons and resources by embezzling them to their own advantage. *Hence the Lord says this, Lo, I am planning for this tribe troubles from which you will not extricate your necks, and you will not walk upright; all of a sudden an evil time has come* (v.3): for these designs and actions of yours I shall impose such retribution on you that

11. Theodore presumes his readers know shaving to be a mark of grief (though Smith claims that in biblical times mourning required only disheveled hair, and that shaving one's head went beyond mourning).

you will not be able to gainsay; you will stay completely bent over, facing the ground under the heavy weight of the pressing troubles.

On that day a proverb will be recited against you and a lament will be sung in the words of the singers, We have been made miserable with miseries, the lot of my people has been measured with cord. There is no one to prevent him turning away, your property has been parceled out (v.4): at that time a dolorous lament will become you (the sense of *in the words*), which you will utter in lamenting your miserable life on seeing your lot—that is, the land belonging to you—occupied by foreigners and divided up, with no one able to prevent its happening, and witnessing your property, which you acquired avariciously, now being taken from you and given to others for distribution. He then goes on, *Hence there will be no one to cast the cord by lot for you* (v.5). It was customary to mention a cord in the case of measurement on the basis of those using cords to measure, as when Scripture says, "Cords fell to my advantage,"[12] as if to say, I was given a measurement and the best portion of land fell to me by lot. So the meaning is, You will see others taking your property and dividing it up, while nothing of it all remains in your hands; so none of you will do the measuring and casting lots, since [356] everything of yours will be taken away and will belong to others; you will own nothing of your many possessions, and instead you will see them fall under the control of others, and other people dividing up your property as a matter of right.

In the assembly of the Lord do not shed tears, nor let them be shed for them; the one will not remove reproaches who says, The house of Jacob provoked the Spirit of the Lord (vv.6–7): when you congregate, therefore, you do not fall to tears in place of repentance; instead, you grieve for the magnitude of the troubles besetting you, and in some fashion also level a complaint against God in the words, We are not the only ones who have provoked God, nor have wrongful deeds been commited by us alone.[13] Why on

---

12. Ps 16.6. The term occurs frequently in the OT, but, as before, the Psalms are Theodore's immediate resource.

13. Our Heb. text of these verses, which departs from the LXX, is itself not clear. Theodore soldiers on.

earth? Is that others do what they like against us, whereas we alone suffer? There will be no benefit for you from these words, nor will you avoid experiencing the troubles on the basis of this complaint or stop being taunted for the troubles befalling you. So do not behave like this. Why? *If these are his doings, are not his words good as he speaks them, and do they not turn out right?* Consider rather this, he is saying, that in inflicting this on us, God did not omit anything necessary; rather, he employed words required in your case and taught you frequently what had to be done. By mention of the impending retribution he wanted you to desist from evildoing; but you were not willing to heed what was said and did not clearly reflect the rightness and justice of God's words, which initially were meant for your improvement. Since you did not respond, however, they were obliged to manifest their inherent truth to you in your failure to repent.

Then, to develop the accusation, *Of old my people showed hostility to his peace* (v.8): from the beginning you took a hostile and warlike attitude to me, unwilling to obey my words, and warring against your own peace rather than against anything else; so in reward for your disobedience you got the present war. *They flayed his skin to remove his hope, the damage of war:* you took from the poor all their possessions, and any sound hope of theirs you cut off; for this you brought on yourselves the damage of the present war. How and in what fashion? *Hence the leaders of my people will be cast out of their luxurious houses, for their wicked doings they will be rejected* (v.9): all those who seemed to be in charge on account of their dominance of my people in being unjust to the poor will be thrust out of the houses where they lived in luxury by collecting immense wealth from the poor. They will also pay the penalty for their vicious behavior, losing control of what they wrongly acquired. So what to do? *Approach the eternal mountain. Rise up and go, because this rest is not possible for you on account of uncleanness, you have been made rotten with corruption, you were closely pursued, though no one is following* (vv.9–11): even the pretext of fighting the enemy is not left to you, because you have been surrendered by God on account of your own depravity. Depart [357] to enemy territory, which long ago God prepared for you, so as to dwell there in captivity, for there is no chance of rest for you here, since on account of the awful impurity in which you lived in impiety and depraved behavior you have been consigned to the enemy's corruption and taken off to it, without any human being to conduct you, God himself determining this punishment for you.[14]

Citing the reason for their corruption in behavior, *Spirit established falsehood:* trusting in the deception of the false prophets proved responsible for all this for you. *It dripped wine and drunkenness for you:* she distilled this punishment for you from it, which makes you no different from an inebriate, staggering under the variety of the troubles. We have shown elsewhere that by *wine* Scripture refers to punishment.[15] *From the dripping of this people Jacob will be gathered in assembly with everyone* (vv.11–12): from this deception of the false prophets viciously affecting you, you were all associated in the present punishment, from which it is not possible for you in any way to escape. *I shall round up and gather the survivors of Israel, I shall bring together their turning away:* all of you, therefore, both those taken previously by the Assyrians and those later, I shall wait to be given over to such punishment; removed from your own places at the same time, you will return to it by being taken off into captivity. *Like sheep in distress, like flocks in the middle of their fold, they will flee from people:* such fear will fall upon them at the enemy's attack that they will be no different from sheep, which when asleep are suddenly reduced to alarm and panic at the approach of a wolf under pressure from the struggle for their own safety. *Go up with penetration before them; they penetrated and passed through the gate, and left by it, their king left before them* (v.13): since the Babylonians besieged Jerusalem for a long time, and by means of siege works they took the city by breaching the walls and thus achieving the entry into the city for themselves, they took off everyone including the king into captivity through the gate (the meaning of *Go up* and see your wall breached), which the

14. Textual problems and differences in division of verses contribute to making the sequence of thought obscure; but Theodore does his best to find meaning in it.

15. By "Scripture," of course, Theodore means the Psalms (75.8), which he cited to clarify Ob 16.

enemy cut through and rendered futile what you hitherto thought safe. Everyone in the city, in fact, after the slaughter of the fallen they took and led out as captives through the gate that you were unwilling to open up; leading out the captives was the one who was previously thought to reign over them. How will the enemy succeed in doing this? *The Lord will lead them:* since the Lord acts as general amongst the enemy in fighting against you.

Chapter Three

Then he goes on to explain what the crimes are for which they will suffer this. *He will say, Listen, you heads of Jacob and survivors of the house of Israel, are you not capable of knowing justice?* (v.1) He will give aid to the enemy against you, he is saying, citing these reasons to you, and telling all the leaders [360] among you and the others, You most of all should have discerned what was to be done, turning away from worse things and opting for the better, for the reason that this was one of all the things taught by me through the direction of the Law and all the other things I have frequently done to this end. In addition to this the rulers passed over this duty. *You who still hate good and go after evil, stealing their skins from them and the flesh from their bones* (v.2): you who do the opposite to what you were taught, avoiding the good and taking a turn for the worse, displaying complete injustice for the poor and lowly so as in various ways to rob them of all their possessions. So what will happen? *In the way they ate the flesh of my people, stripped the skins from their backs, broke their bones, chopped them up like meat in a kettle and flesh in a pot, so they will cry to the Lord, and he will not hear them, and will turn his face from them at that time because of their wicked behavior in their pursuits* (vv.3–4): since you stole all that belonged to the poor, in various ways wronging them, and being domineering, and oppressive, hence when the enemy make an attack, you will call on God under pressure of need, but you will get no help from that quarter. Rather, he will choose not even to glance your way, and will instead hand you over to the impending troubles, since he is aware of the great number of deeds marked by such awful injustice that you committed.[16]

After mentioning what they had done, and what they would suffer for it through trusting in the words of the false prophets, he directs his account again to the false prophets themselves. *The Lord says this to the prophets who lead my people astray, who grind their teeth, and proclaim a message of peace to them, but nothing was put in their mouths* (v.5): God says this of the false prophets, who in various ways distracted the people from their duty by their deception, and, as it were, devoured them with what they said and did, urging them to the things for which they were likely to suffer such awful punishment. For example, they kept on promising them peace and assuring them that they would not suffer trouble for their sins, as the prophets had claimed. Against my will they promised peace, which they had been instructed by me not to say. In response to what they did, *they declared war against them:* though promising peace, they brought war upon them, which they determined would happen to them.

Hence it will be night for you in place of vision, and it will be darkness for you in place of an oracle; the sun will set on the prophets, and the day will be darkened for them. Those having dreams will be confounded, the seers will be mocked, and everyone will berate them; hence there will be no one to heed them (vv.6–7): for pretending to see and prophesy while deceiving the people, they and their disciples will all be enveloped in darkness so that the sun will seem not even to shine on them in their gloom on account of the magnitude of the troubles, and those [361] pretending to see and declare such things will be enveloped in shame as events prove the opposite of what they claimed. Loud laughter will be directed their way from everyone, no one prepared to pay heed to what was said by them after learning by experience the extent of the troubles they brought on them by their deceit. *But as for me, I am filled with power in the spirit of the Lord, and with justice and*

---

16. Pastor though he is (or will become), Theodore is not moved by this protest against social injustice beyond paraphrase; he does not wax eloquent on the subject in the manner of a preacher like his contemporary, Chrysostom.

might to declare to Jacob his impiety and to Israel his sin (v.8): going beyond all that deception, and being filled with a holy spirit, I know how to discern what is to be done and with great power and forthrightness to proceed to charge the people with the sins they have committed and the impiety of which they are guilty, aware that this will help to bring them to their senses by the mention of their sins and the threat of what will follow, and bring the mighty to their duty.

Hear this, leaders of the house of Jacob and the rest of the house of Israel (v.9): on these matters I shall address words in common both to the leaders and to everyone else, reproaching you with your conduct. Of what kind is it? *You who abhor justice, who pervert every norm:* you who decline to distinguish in your judgments good from evil, distorting what is properly said and done by others so as not to believe our words, prophets though we be. *You who build Zion with blood and Jerusalem with iniquity* (v.10): you have filled it completely with homicide and iniquity. *Its leaders gave judgment with bribes, its priests responded for a price, its prophets delivered oracles for money, and they claimed support from the Lord in saying, Is not the Lord in us? No harm will befall us* (v.11): the rulers were not prepared to set any store by justice and sold their verdicts for money, those entrusted with priesthood made it their business to acquire money unjustly under the pretext of priestly service as though some kind of wages, and the false prophets were interested in money and delivered oracles as a favor to those supplying it. Then, after doing such evil things, they pretended to entrust themselves to God, claiming to have God within them, and saying it was impossible for people endowed with such qualities to experience the troubles foretold by us by God's will.

So what was the response? *Hence on account of you Zion will be ploughed like a field, and Jerusalem will be like a fruit shed, and the mountain of the house like a forest grove* (v.12): Since you do not believe our words delivered by God's will, then, and instead you all heed the false prophets and, day in day out, perform such acts of impiety and lawlessness, for this reason you will come to know the truth of our words, and the fact that such awful desolation will overtake Mount Zion at that time and the city on it that it will be tilled like a field and will be no different from a shelter erected for keeping a guard over fruit, with its buildings pulled down on all sides. In short, the mountain on which God's Temple is located will be no different from a sown field, with so many weeds springing up there on account of the desolation.

Chapter Four

After [364] mentioning the disasters being inflicted on them to this point, however, he then mentions also what will happen to them after its capture, and the degree of change for the better that will ensue. This custom of the other prophets and blessed David we have often demonstrated,[17] namely, the disclosure of pleasant things after the experience of harsh things and in turn mentioning baleful events in order that through both they might instruct them by the frequency of the disclosure, bringing them to their senses by the mention of baleful things and encouraging them by the brighter to hold fast to hope in God. Accordingly, he says, *In the last days the mountain of the house of the Lord will be conspicuous, established on the crests of the mountains, and will be raised up above the hills. Peoples will hasten to it, many nations will come and say, Come, let us go up to the mountain of the Lord, and to the house of the God of Jacob. They will show us his way, and we shall travel by his paths, because a law will come from Zion, and the word of the Lord from Jerusalem. He will judge between many peoples and will accuse mighty nations far away* (vv.1–3): after the experience of the troubles in which they would find themselves, made captive, first by the Assyrians, and later by the Babylonians, such a great transformation

17. This is as far as Theodore is prepared to go in the direction of literary criticism, under the pressure of possible questioning of the prophet's consistency: why the vacillation between gloom and optimism? On first principles he has to uphold the literary integrity of the book (questioned by some modern commentators, who unlike Theodore note the identity of the text of vv.1–4 to Is 2.2–5—something he does not mention, not having done a commentary on that book). He can here claim biblical precedent; and the challenge is not as great as he experienced in the "novel and extraordinary things" found in Jonah.

would occur regarding this place that the mountain on which God was reputed to dwell would become famous and would be shown to be superior to all the mountains, and far surpass all mountains and all hills on account of the glory enveloping it as a result of the divine solicitude. Large numbers from all quarters, even from foreign peoples, would hasten to assemble to reach this mountain of God, on which God is believed to dwell, and learn how they should regulate their lives and live as they ought. The result would be that the law that is in force there would be a law also for those from foreign parts, and all would seem to hear a divine voice by which they would be obliged to live in keeping with the laws of Jerusalem. They would be right to believe this on seeing the might of which God would give evidence in bringing to his own justice many of those ill-disposed to us and accusing even those with pretensions to greatness, even if they seemed to be far away, for the faults they committed against us, and actually imposing on them a punishment befitting their offences.

Now, I am amazed at those who claimed this was said by the prophet about what would happen to the Israelites when they were about to return from Babylon, and also maintained it is a kind of type of what would happen in the time of Christ the Lord. I commend them for their excellent observation that in these words there is reference to the people's return from Babylon; but I do not know how they were encouraged to make the claim that it involves a kind of type of Christ the Lord, as it is obvious that every type contains some similarity of what it is said to be a type. There is a considerable gap between the verse, *A law will come from Zion, and the word of the Lord from Jerusalem,* and the provision of Christ the Lord, who clearly said to the Samaritan woman, "Believe me, woman, the hour is coming when [365] neither in Jerusalem nor on this mountain will you worship the Father," also giving the reason, "God is spirit, and those who worship him must worship in spirit and in truth."[18]

---

18. Jn 4.21, 24. Again Theodore is scathing about his predecessors. Theodoret in commentary on the identical verses occurring in Is 2.2–5, on the other hand, under the influence of Alexandrian positions found in Cyril and Eusebius, would later take exactly the Christological position that Theodore re-

In other words, he clearly dismissed altogether specification of place and made clear there was no reason for worshiping in Jerusalem rather than in any other place, since everyone who has been taught that the divinity is incorporeal is likely to worship him with such an understanding, so that wherever they do it, they are not doing anything unacceptable. The verse, *A law will come from Zion, and the word of the Lord from Jerusalem*, would be appropriately referred to the return from Babylon, since at that time the Israelites were restored to the place of Zion so as to perform on that spot the prescribed worship according to legal prescription, having been unable to perform it when they were elsewhere—hence their saying when in Babylon, "How shall we sing the song of the Lord in a foreign land?"[19] By contrast, how would it contain a type of the situation of Christ the Lord, especially since his prescription provided for divine worship to be performed everywhere, good and bad worshipers being differentiated by their manner, not by place?

The prophet, in any case, relates this to the prophecy in what went before, saying, *They will beat their swords into ploughs, and their spears into scythes. No longer will nation lift up sword against nation, and no longer will they learn how to make war*, bringing out the fact that every war will come to an end and peace will prevail over everything, so that even the instruments of war will then be directed to use as farm implements, their military value no longer current now that war is over, and farming necessarily taking pride of place in time of peace. He next says, *Each person will rest under his vine, and each under his figtree, and there will no one to arouse fear in them* (v.4), suggesting that all will enjoy their own places, there being no one in peace time capable of arousing fear in them, or causing alarm at that time, or uprooting them from their own places. Since what was said was

---

jects and would reject the reference to the return from Babylon in similarly scathing fashion. Antiochenes were prepared to have recourse to typology if the NT encouraged it; Theodore is rejecting this NT encouragement. He is also denying, against the obvious sense of the text, that the prophecy has to do with nations other than the captive Jews, as he will also stubbornly do in the case of the similar prophecy closing Zechariah I (8.20–23).

19. Ps 137.4.

surprising, he was right to go on, *For the mouth of the Lord almighty has said this,* as if to say, God caused this to happen, and it definitely will happen. *Because all the peoples will proceed, each in their own way, but we shall proceed in the name of the Lord our God forever and a day* (v.5): now that they are enjoying peace, they will perform the works appropriate to them, some turning to farming, some to seafaring, and others to whatever trade each happens to be involved in. But all alike will have a task in keeping with God's decision for a way of life for the rest of time.

Furthermore, to confirm this, he goes on, *In those days, says the Lord, I shall assemble the oppressed, and welcome the rejected and those whom I rejected. I shall make the oppressed a remnant, and the rejected a powerful nation; and the Lord will reign over them on Mount Zion, from now and forever* (vv.6–7): at that time [368] those oppressed by the heaviest troubles and removed from my providence and their own places, I shall assemble again in their proper places; those previously oppressed, I shall so protect with my providence that the whole Israelite race will again develop from them (the meaning of *a remnant*), and I shall make those now cast out of their own place through weakness more powerful than many. God will abide on Mount Zion, giving evidence of his characteristic power through his care of the inhabitants, and intends to inflict punishment on those wanting to make war on them. The phrase *from now and forever,* in fact, clearly means for a long time: it is no secret that in turn they underwent a transformation in the time of the Maccabees, extreme and completely irreparable, when after their crimes against Christ the Lord they were altogether made to endure captivity under the Romans, expelled from their own land and reduced to a long period of servitude.[20]

Now, to this point he refers to the people's return from Babylon and the good things that would accrue to them at that

20. Though Theodore has situated Micah in the eighth century, he has identified any troubles of the people as being the effect of the Babylonian invasion in the sixth (as Theodoret seems to acknowledge). Now, he seems to see vv.6–7 as susceptible of some qualification, referring in garbled fashion to the later troubles under the Seleucids and the Romans, the crucifixion being adduced as the customary rationale for the latter punishment.

time. But from this point onwards he makes mention in turn of the harsh things, narrating the calamities that would come upon them; hence he directs his account to Jerusalem itself in the following terms, *And you, tower of the flock, squalid daughter Zion* (v.8). It is clear that he calls Jerusalem *daughter Zion*, the prophets and blessed David also referring to her constantly in those terms, as when he says, "That I may recount all your praises in the gates of the daughter Zion."[21] So it is beyond dispute that there is no reference to Zedekiah, as some commentators believed—how, I know not—but that the prophet here is directing his account to Jerusalem, which, having spoken of as *daughter Zion* in keeping with custom, he naturally calls *tower of the flock* since it is conspicuous among all the Israelite cities, and all betake themselves to it for the sake of the worship of God performed there and the help they expect from that quarter, since God was thought to live there. Now, as a reproach he calls her *squalid* for being affected by impiety like squalor and giving a lead to the whole flock in bad behavior, though supposed to be a good model. *To you it will come, and the first kingdom will come as the beginning to daughter Jerusalem:* for all your wrongful actions the mighty and most powerful king of Babylon will come upon you, and will dispose of you as a powerful king will predictably do on his arrival.

And now why are you experiencing troubles? Is there no king in you? or has your counsel perished, that your pangs have gripped you like a woman in labor? (v.9): for what cause are you in the grip of such awful troubles? You had a king capable of leading you in war; you chose the one determined by me to rule over you. You had many people eminent for wisdom, in your view; so how did you become embroiled in such troubles [369] no different from a woman in the grip of the pangs of childbirth? You would not have experienced them if you had been careful to adhere to my laws. Since you did not do so, *Suffer birth pangs, be brave, and come close, daughter Zion, like the woman in labor* (v.10): endure the pangs besetting you, put up with them like a woman in labor, coming close to the pangs of childbirth. *Because now you*

21. Ps 9.14.

will go forth from the city, erect your tent in the open country, and go as far as Babylon: your fortunes have come to an end, and you will be taken from the city into captivity; taken off into any chance place, you will live as a castaway in the usual manner of a captive until you reach Babylon itself, where you will be forced to pass your days with a calamity of your own making. Then, after mentioning the punishment, he touches in turn on the release. *From there he will rescue you, and from there the Lord your God will redeem you from the hand of your foes:* when you reach those places as a captive, from which there is no glimmer of hope of release, you will unexpectedly gain divine help—that is, by his characteristic power he will liberate you from captivity and from the power of your captors.

Many nations are now assembled against you, and peoples saying, We shall gloat, and our eyes will look upon Zion (v.11): at that time many savage Scythian nations (he is referring to those in the company of Gog),[22] who will not be responsible for your prosperity and return, will come upon you, looking forward keenly to inflicting easily upon you troubles of their pleasing. *They did not know the Lord's thinking and did not understand his plan, that he has gathered them as sheaves for the threshing floor* (v.12): they made their assault, trusting in their vast numbers and their might, and unaware of the will of our God, whose purpose in yielding to their desire to issue forth to this war was to give evidence of his care for you and prove his power against them, like sheaves harvested and gathered into the threshing floor, surrendering them all to slaughter at your hands.

And, as though completely confident that this would happen, he says to the Israelites, *Arise and thresh them, daughter Zion* (v.13): take them, subject as they are to the power of God, crush and consume them all by various forms of slaughter as though on the threshing floor. *Because I shall make your horns iron and your hooves bronze:* I have given you power no less than iron horns sufficient to take vengeance on your adversaries, and to trample them down more than you would trample them

22. Several times before in the *Commentary* we saw Theodore referring to the allegory of Gog in Ezek 38–39 as historical (see his introduction to Joel).

down using iron hooves. *With them you will melt down nations, and break many peoples into small pieces; you will dedicate their vast numbers to the Lord, and their might to the Lord of all the earth:* with this strength accorded you by God you will do away completely with them all, though they are numerous, and you will attribute the destruction of all their vast numbers [372] to God, who as Lord of all the earth will at his pleasure do away with all their strength.

Chapter Five

He next mentions the incursion of the adversaries, as a result of which they will endure the sufferings described above. *The daughter will now be walled around with a wall; he placed a restraint on you, with a rod they will strike the tribes of Israel on the jaw* (v.1): they will suffer such things for making their advance in reliance on their own numbers and power, besieging you and surrounding you with their vast numbers like a wall so as to contain and utterly destroy everyone, and inflict blows from their own power as though on your very jaws.

He then mentions also the general so as to bring out that this would happen on account of his being appointed to them for this task by God's will. *You, Bethlehem, house of Ephrathah, you are far from being among Judah's thousands. From you will come for me the one to be ruler in Israel; his origins are from ancient days* (v.2):[23] the one from Bethlehem now ruling over you, even if your numbers seem small by comparison with the enemy, will be quite sufficient, at least with my influence and power, for the attack by the enemy, numerous and powerful though they be, especially since this promotion happened by arrangement from on high at the time when God promised David that he would

23. Theodoret's text of the first clause differs (by the inclusion of the negative) from other forms of the LXX, and conversely is thus closer to the form cited in Mt 2.6—to which Theodore, perhaps for his theological purposes here, does not refer. In proceeding to identify "the ruler in Israel" as Zerubbabel (whom he describes as "reigning," going beyond the biblical text of The Chronicler), he has Micah addressing the situation of the restored community in the late sixth century.

preserve the kingdom with his successors. By that promise this person would also be promoted to the kingship and be adequate to deal with the magnitude of the present troubles. Now, he is referring to Zerubbabel: he was the one who at that time was reigning over the Israelites, a descendant of David, at the time of the return from Babylon and the attempted assault on Jerusalem by those of Gog's company.

It is also clear, admittedly, that though, consistently with what has gone before, this refers to Zerubbabel, a successor of David, yet the true fulfillment of the words is achieved in Christ the Lord. While every promise made to David about his descendants reigning seems at first flush to indicate his successors in the kingdom of Israel,[24] in reality it foretells Christ the Lord in the flesh, who as a successor of David exercises the true and abiding rule over all. You could grasp this more clearly from the Eighty-eighth Psalm, where it indicates that the promises of kingship apply to his successors, of whom it says, "If his sons forsake my Law and do not walk according to my ordinances, if they violate my judgments and do not keep my commandments, I shall punish their transgressions with a rod and their iniquities with a scourge, but I shall not disperse my mercy from them."[25] In other words, it is clear that this would apply to the future descendants of David [373] due to rule Israel, whom he promises to chastise for their sins without completely ex-

24. Whereas Theodore (though ignoring NT usage) seems to be endeavoring to recognize different levels of meaning and achieve a balance between historical and eschatological/Christological/messianic interpretations of this text, and "at first flush" (κατὰ πρῶτον λόγον) allows some place for the restoration leader, Zerubbabel, Theodoret will heatedly reject such allowance as a Judaizing one—a reversal of the narrow and broad attitudes normally predicated of them, respectively.

25. In commentary on Ps 89, of which Theodore proceeds to quote vv.30–33, 29, and 36–37, Theodoret rejects reference to Zerubbabel and prefers an exclusively Christological meaning, as he does on Pss 118.22 and 132.17 (though allowing it in some other psalms), as also in places on Isaiah (under Alexandrian influence) and Jeremiah. One argument of Theodoret (who himself is reticent about Zerubbabel's appearing in Luke's genealogy of Jesus, which Theodore cites) is that Zerubbabel was no king—just as Chrysostom disallowed reference to him in that favorite NT proof text, Ps 110.1, on the grounds that he was no priest.

pelling them from the kingship. He proceeds, however, to fore-tell Christ the Lord according to the flesh, in whose case God demonstrated the true fulfillment of his promises: "I shall establish his offspring forever and ever, and his throne as long as the heavens last. His offspring lasts forever, and his throne like the sun before me and like the moon perfected forever," words that obviously will apply in the case of none of the descendants, whereas they clearly reveal the kingdom of Christ the Lord to be enduring and unshakable, with great power and great splendor, abiding into the future. Thus you would see the present testimony applying in one case in the true and indisputable proof from experience in the case of Christ the Lord, in keeping with the statement in the Gospels, kings of Israel from David being cited on account of the divine promise.[26] Hence in this case the prophet rightly took it to apply also to Zerubbabel: since he mentioned the events after the return from Babylon, the invasion of those of Gog's company and the punishment inflicted on them by God, he logically makes mention also of the descendant of David by divine promise who was entrusted with their rule at that time so as to bring out also that what was achieved through him regarding the nation took effect as a result of God's promise previously made to David—hence the words *his origins are from ancient days,* as if to say, what was said and promised above was proposed by God; he caused him to be able to achieve such things from the beginning.

He then goes on, *For this reason he will give them up until the time the pregnant one will give birth* (v.3). The divine Scripture often refers to the unexpected appearance of divine help in the midst of disasters as birth pangs and giving birth—for example, the verse, "For fear of you, Lord, we conceived, were in labor and gave birth to a spirit of salvation that you caused to be on the earth,"[27] as if to say, For what we feared from you, we con-

26. See Lk 1.32. Repeatedly in this exercise Theodore, as if to show his Antiochene credentials as an interpreter, contrasts an initial reading of the text, "at first flush," with finding its "true" application, ἀλήθεια.

27. Is 26.17–18 LXX, neither this Isaian verse nor Micah's receiving from Theodore a Christological, let alone a Marian, interpretation. Theodoret also avoided giving the Isaian verse such an interpretation, though by taking the LXX's πνεῦμα to refer to the Holy Spirit he found himself embroiled in polemic

ceived your ineffable grace within, from which by many pangs from the magnitude of the troubles an unexpected salvation was born among us. Here, too, then, as if Jerusalem had conceived by divine grace and were giving birth to this gift, through which they for their part were saved while the enemy suffered complete ruin, it means that he will surrender the enemy to ruin when God's unexpected gift is born to Jerusalem in great pangs suffered at the enemy's attack.

The rest of his brethren will turn back to the sons of Israel: at that time all those returning from captivity will consider Zerubbabel the king of all in common, the ten tribes no longer ruled on their own, and the tribes of Judah alone along with Benjamin having kings descended from David as before; rather, all will now consider Zerubbabel to be the one king. Blessed Hosea likewise says, [376] "The sons of Judah and the sons of Israel will be assembled together, and appoint for themselves one authority"; and blessed David, "Lo, what is so fine and pleasing as brethren dwelling together!"[28] suggesting in this their harmony, which would come at the time of the return, which they afterwards preserved when put under one person reigning. Likewise here, too, then, the prophet is saying, *The rest of the brethren,* as if to say, all including those outside the tribe of Judah will be assembled together with the remaining sons of Israel, agreeing to have one and the same king.

He will stand and see, and the Lord will shepherd his flock in strength, and they will live in the glory of the name of the Lord their God. Hence now he will be glorified to the ends of the earth (v.4): it will be God who is shepherding everyone through the one ruling at the time, and he will make them famous through his name. He will continue to be celebrated with great admiration throughout the whole earth for the great and marvelous deeds he wrought for those who share his name—namely, the sons of Israel. Whereas at this point he brought them back from captivity

---

with the Pneumatomachians, who—possibly on the basis of the verse—questioned the status of the Spirit.

28. Hos 1.11, Ps 133.1. The evidence of Ezr 4.1–5, on the contrary, suggests there was no such harmony between north and south under Zerubbabel, and in fact the enmity between Samaritans and Jews stems from this period.

against all expectation, afterwards with their small numbers he achieved an actual victory in which by his characteristic power he utterly disposed of an innumerable host of strong men equipped for military engagement through these lowly men small in number.[29]

The prophet thus mentioned what would happen to them after the return to Babylon, which was due to be their lot when in accord with God's promise David's successor Zerubbabel was reigning over them. The prophet wanted to show God responding to his own promise and making a considerable contribution to events that occurred through his decision, using the history of Zerubbabel as an example. These things seemed to occur much later, however—namely, the events of the return from Babylon and what happened to those of Gog's company. So he mentions what came to fulfillment closer to his time and not long after—namely, the fate of the Assyrians in the time of Hezekiah—so that, from what happened closer to his time and not long after, he might give a guarantee of what would occur after the lapse of a long time. It is obvious, you see, that the prophet forecast these events, as the book reveals, "in the days of Jotham, Ahaz and Hezekiah,"[30] so that the prophecy was not far removed from all the events of Hezekiah's time; but they foreshadowed at that time, and shortly had their fulfillment, in the case of those who happened to receive word of the prophecy and saw the fulfillment from afar before the event, the purpose thus being to bring out the connection between the events close at hand in Hezekiah's time and what would happen much later in Zerubbabel's time, and to make clear from both cases how great was the force of the divine promise.

Hence this happened not only when Zerubbabel was in com-

29. Theodore's literalist acceptance of the apocalyptic and mythological oracles in Ezek 38–39 of God's war against Gog is affecting the manner in which he is suggesting his readers determine a timeline for Micah's prophecies. If Gog is removed from the equation, and Theodoret's objections to Zerubbabel sustained, this timeline collapses.

30. See 1.1. Theodore is sensing that his option for Zerubbabel and Gog is stretching the timeline somewhat from the textual evidence of the period of Micah's ministry. He is not likely, however, to take the option of some moderns for post-exilic interpolations in the text; literary integrity is taken for granted.

mand in Israel but also beforehand, when Hezekiah reigned over them: he also came to power in accord with the divine promise [377] when such a great army advanced on Jerusalem but was unable to achieve anything, thanks to the provision of divine influence to the one who by the promise of God exercised kingship over Israel. Although in fact they gained control of the kingdom of the ten tribes with great ease, and pressed on to Jerusalem after the victory against them, they sustained awful retribution at the hands of the angel,[31] God seeming to say in their midst, "I shall protect this city for my sake and that of my servant David,"[32] thus showing that he was mindful of the promises to him and would then personally put them into effect by cooperating with the one exercising kingship over Israel at that time, namely, Hezekiah.

Having spoken of the situation of Zerubbabel, then, which as I have said was still some time off, of necessity on account of the connection of the events, he mentions what happened to the Assyrian in the time of Hezekiah by way of confirmation of what went before. He says, *It will be peace when the Assyrian comes to your country and when he ascends to your region* (v.5): what God did at that time through Zerubbabel by bringing an end to such an awful war and giving a reliable peace to his own people he will do also in those days that will ensue not long after when the Assyrian comes against Jerusalem:[33] he will then unexpectedly dispose of such a huge multitude, and provide to his people an unexpected peace, when Hezekiah reigns as a successor of David according to the divine promise.

Then, in reference to the future, *Seven shepherds will be raised against him, and eight bites of human beings; they will shepherd the Assyrian with a sword, and the land of Nimrod with its ditch* (vv.5–6). The phrase *seven shepherds and eight bites of human beings* some commentators have understood in highly imaginative fashion,

31. See 2 Kgs 19.35, 2 Chr 32.21, Is 37.36.
32. 2 Kgs 19.34, 20.6; Is 37.35.
33. Theodore's timeline seems to take a contradictory hiccup here: are we to understand that not only is Zerubbabel Micah's primary reference, but he is even placed prior to the Sennacherib invasion of 701? Or does he mean "not long after" Micah's prophecy?

taking *seven shepherds* to imply the number of prophets was seven, and claiming *eight bites* to be Hezekiah plus those administering the kingdom for him; not being in a position to say who the eight were, they supported their view by declaration alone. If, however, you wanted to claim they were administrators of the kingdom, there could be many more than eight. The cause of the error with those of this mind, however, is the neglect of the idiom of the divine Scripture; for this reason they were compelled to come up with old wives' tales so as to appear to have something to say.[34] Now, it is idiomatic in the divine Scripture sometimes to define seven as the perfect number, and to take what surpasses it as excessive. For example, "God made heaven and earth in six days and rested on the seventh"—the reason why Jews rest on the sabbath[35]—and each number of the days is usually repeated in these seven, all beginning with the first and finishing with the seventh, and after the seventh going back to the first again. This is the reason the divine Scripture refers to seven as the perfect and complete number, whereas eight, as I said, is excessive. Likewise God says, "He will pay a sevenfold vengeance,"[36] [380] as if to say, The one doing away with him for his irreparable faults will be found to pay the maximum and complete penalty imposed on him. Such also is the saying in Ecclesiastes, "Give a portion to seven people, or even eight,"[37] as if to say, Give generously to the needy, but stop short of going to excess in this. Hence blessed Peter said, "If my brother sins against me, how many times am I to forgive him— seven times?" as sufficient, citing the perfect number; wanting him to go further in great generosity, the Lord went on, "I tell you, not as far as seven times but seventy times seven."[38]

34. Theodore, again dismissing his predecessors, launches into an excessively lengthy demonstration of the significance of the number seven in the Bible, "so as to appear to have something to say," in his own words. He might with profit have looked behind the LXX's choice of "bites" to translate the Heb. for "rulers," probably through confusion of similar forms (the LXX using its δήγμα-τα nowhere else to translate the Heb. term).

35. See Gn 2.2.

36. Gn 4.15.

37. Eccl 11.2.

38. Mt 18.21–22. Smith also cites the Eccl text to support his (unlike

Here too it means something similar: on the Assyrian advancing with his army God inflicted a severe and massive retribution through the ministry of the angel; many were killed, the rest put to flight, becoming vulnerable to people in various places, and suffering the worst possible fate in various ways from various people, who with great ease came upon them as they fled and slew those they encountered.[39] To cap it all off, their king in great disgrace made off to his own country, and was assassinated by his own sons, so that it emerges that the punishment imposed on them by God was most severe, not only for being struck by the angel in the vicinity of Jerusalem, but also in the flight of the rest from the scene in great terror and their being slain in various ways. Of them blessed David says, "You will put them to flight, in your remnants you will prepare their countenance," implying that while all will be put to flight, God will direct his anger even against the survivors.[40]

This is his meaning in this verse, then, *seven shepherds will be raised up*, suggesting the severity of the divine retribution, which God inflicted on them as perfect and complete through the angel's attack. *Eight bites of human beings* means the excess of the troubles befalling them after their flight from there, people positioned variously in different places and in their own districts, killing the fugitives and those appearing to be taking refuge in their own places, amongst whom the king also chanced to be slain by his own sons. This he well expressed in *bites of men*, dismembering them by the angel's punishing them. He then goes on, *They will shepherd the Assyrian with a sword, and the land of Nimrod with its ditch*, as if to say, The Assyrian will fall to the blade, and he will see his own land devastated, which he actually experienced later under the Babylonians. He calls it *land of Nimrod*, note, since Nimrod was in those parts, occupy-

---

Theodore's) brief comment, "This is a Hebrew literary device to indicate that an indefinite yet adequate number of leaders will arise to overthrow the Assyrians." Theodore's prolixity intends to disabuse the pervasive Christian tendency to read as a prophecy of Christ's Resurrection any mention of seven and eight in the OT.

39. We have seen Theodore before embellishing a relatively bare text.

40. The obscure Ps 21.12, the Heb. containing more than one *hapax legomenon*. Theodoret also wrestles with it to come up with a similar meaning.

ing their palaces; he was thought to be important by the people
of the time for his sense of power, the book of Creation putting
it this way, "He was a great hunter in the sight of the Lord;
hence they will say, A great hunter before God like Nimrod; the
beginning of his kingdom was Babylon."[41] Since, then, [381]
the Assyrians were descended from him and had a sense of importance from an abundance of power as being in the same
line as he, the prophet means to say something similar, that the
country of those with pretensions to bravery would all be done
away with by the enemy in their own places, gaining no advantage from their power in which they gloried, thanks to the divine wrath. The prophet, moreover, continues in the same
theme as these words and says, *He will rescue you from the Assyrian
when he advances on your land, and when he attacks your territories.*

Next, to bring the Israelites the good news that they would
suffer no harm from the Assyrians, he goes on, *Then the remnant
of Jacob will be among the nations in the midst of many peoples like dew
falling from the Lord, and like lambs on grass, so that no one may assemble or depend on human beings* (v.7): those of Israel left in Judah or Jerusalem, once this has happened, will emerge as
objects of respect to all foreigners and deserving of close attention, no less than a fall of dew at the appropriate time is much
desired by farmers; they will be no different from sheep grazing
on grass in the way that they fall upon all the spoils of both the
dead and the fugitives. The result will be that for all human beings anyone will be afraid of ever declaring war on them. *The
remnant of Jacob will be among the nations in the midst of many peoples, like a lion among the cattle of the forest, and like a cub among
flocks of sheep, in the way it passes through, dividing and seizing them,
with no one to rescue them. Your hand will be lifted up against your op-
pressors, and all your enemies will be eliminated* (vv.8–9): you will be
no different from a lion fearsome to the cattle; in similar fashion you will then be fearsome to the foreigners owing to the
blow struck against the Assyrians on your behalf: just as if a lion
(*cub* meaning the same thing, referring thus to the lion's off-

41. Genesis (referred to before by Theodore under this title Κτίσις)
10.9–10. He chooses not to investigate the sense of "ditch."

spring) were to fall suddenly upon a flock of sheep and seize as many of them as it wants in its characteristic strength, so you will be considered more powerful in the view of your foes for the ruin inflicted on those endeavoring to attack you.

After saying that these things would ensue for the Israelites from the attack of the Assyrians, the prophet proceeds to detail as well at greater length the punishment of the Assyrians themselves. At that time, he says, he will destroy all the horses and the chariots, as if to say, He will render useless all military equipment, he will destroy all your cities, even if some among them seem strong and fortified with great security. With these he will wipe out as well everything with which they took part in the worship of the demons (this being the meaning of *your charms*, implying incantations, auguries, and all such things normally used by them),[42] and so those employing oracles and divination no longer make utterances, since he will utterly consign to destruction all your idols and pillars. The result is that, despite your wishes, it is no longer possible for you to behave as before and adore the works of your hands. [384] The groves in which you performed your special worship will also be cut down, and I shall destroy all your cities. In short, venting my wrath and anger I shall inflict the maximum and most severe retribution and ruin upon you for not being prepared to spare my country, and instead expecting to consign it as well to devastation against my wishes.

Chapter Six

On bringing to a conclusion the account of the retribution imposed on the Assyrians for presuming to attack Jerusalem, he directs his discourse to the people, choosing this moment in

---

42. Unlike the trend of modern commentators (and the fairly obvious movement of the author's thought?), Theodore sees these threats delivered against Assyria's behavior, not Israel's (the use of sorcery occurring in v.12). Again, he does not bother to document divine recriminations in the Scriptures against such practices as use of horses and chariots, even in the psalms (see Ps 20.7; Is 2.7, 30.16; Hos 10.13). As he has been prolix in commentary on the chapter so far, he now contents himself with paraphrase.

particular to proceed to charge them with ingratitude. Just as though setting up a tribunal,[43] the prophet speaks in these terms: *Stand up, come to judgment before the mountains, and let hills hear your voice. Listen, hills, to the judgment of the Lord, and the valleys that are the foundations of the earth, because there is a case between the Lord and his people, and there will be a disputation with Israel* (vv.1–2): since, despite such things having been done for them by the Lord, they persist no less in their ingratitude, for which they endure also the captivity of Babylon, I would be happy to conduct a lawsuit between God and them. I shall call as judges the mountains, the hills, and the valleys, which were previously subject to that innumerable host of Assyrians advancing on Jerusalem and scattered throughout all the places beyond, fear of whom predictably beset the city's inhabitants in an extreme degree. Later, it held so many corpses all of a sudden lying in its midst of those who shortly before had high opinions of themselves; they will come to this lawsuit as reliable witnesses after observing what happened.

Then, after setting up the court and establishing the ingratitude of the Israelites from the judges and eyewitnesses of events, he then to his advantage introduces God saying to them, *My people, what have I done to you, or what trouble have I caused you?* (v.3) The fate of the Assyrian, he is saying, obviously provided a great demonstration of my care for you; and I urge you to say if you were ever harmed by me in any way, small or great, if I ever did you an injury, if I ever really distressed you, if I proved a burden to you in anything. Then, as though they had no reply to this, he goes on, *Answer me*, as if to say, Tell me if you have something to say, I shall accept it if you speak the truth. Then, as though conscience made them completely silent and they could prove nothing said by God to be false, he continues, *Because I brought you up from the land of Egypt, and redeemed you from the house of slavery, I sent before you Moses, Aaron,*

43. It is rare for Theodore (or others of his school) to take the trouble to recognize literary genres in the material, like the *rib*, or lawsuit, here. In his comment on the opening verses, he seems to position Micah's ministry after the Assyrian assault on Jerusalem in 701, and even at the time of the Babylonian captivity—despite the timing outlined in comment on the previous chapter.

and Miriam (v.4): instead, surely you do not reproach me for freeing you from such harsh slavery against all hope, and for bestowing this gift through the ministry and leadership of Moses, Aaron, and Miriam? *My people, remember what King Balak of Moab had in mind for you, and what Balaam, son of Beor, answered him from the reeds up to* [385] *Gilgal so that God's righteousness might be known* (v.5): remember also Balak, king of the Moab-ites, who sent an invitation to Balaam to be hostile to you, but by my command he first refused to go, and though later going he in no way uttered a curse, instead giving a blessing in keeping with my wishes.[44] So in all this it is obvious to you that I have al-ways upheld justice in your regard in opposition to those en-deavoring to wrong you, punishing them all without mercy.

When these words met with no rebuttal, the prophet, as though filling the role of an advocate for the people, spoke as follows from their viewpoint: *By what means am I to lay hold of the Lord? How shall I win over God most high?* (v.6) So he says, it is like the people here saying, Since I am accused on all scores of be-ing ungrateful for many benefits, what must I do to recover God's favor now at any rate, since I have set myself apart from him by my behavior, and how am I to be seen responsive to his wishes? *Shall I win him round with burnt offerings, with yearling calves? Will the Lord accept favorably thousands of rams, ten thou-sands of fat goats? Am I to give my firstborn for my impiety, the fruit of my womb for my soul's sin?* (vv.6–7) With them at a loss as to what they must do to cure such awful ingratitude, he says this, Surely I would appease him if I were to offer burnt offerings of year-ling calves, or if I were to offer him thousands and ten thou-sands of rams and sheep, or if I offer him the firstborn of my offspring so as to wipe away my soul's sin? To this uncertainty of the people the prophet says in reply, *Has it been told you, mortal that you are, what is good, and what the Lord requires of you, other*

44. See Nm 22–24, Theodore not commenting on the LXX reading "reeds" for the similar Heb. place name "Shittim." Though he is quite sensitive to the irony, if not the pathos, of the rebuke in these verses ("one of the great passages of the OT," in Smith's words, "epitomizing the message of the eighth-century prophets"), he does not betray any sense of their use in the paschal liturgy of his church.

than doing justice, loving mercy, and being ready to walk behind the Lord your God? (v.8) Forget about burnt offerings, countless sacrifices, and oblations of firstborn, he is saying:[45] if you are concerned to appease the divinity, practise what God ordered you in the beginning through Moses. What in fact is that? To deliver fair judgment and decision in all cases where you have to choose better from worse, to continue giving evidence of all possible love and fellow-feeling to your neighbor, and be ready to put into practice what is pleasing to God in every way. He means, in short, "You will love the Lord your God with all your heart, all your mind, and all your soul, and you will love your neighbor as yourself,"[46] as was said of old through Moses. Do this, he is saying, as something preferable to sacrifices in God's eyes.

The voice of the Lord will be invoked on the city, and will save those respecting his name (v.9): if you do this, the city carrying out his wishes will appear as a voice of God, giving evidence in practice of the divine law, with the result that in every danger those in it will be rendered worthy of divine care and have no experience of harm. Next, the prophet addresses them in turn by way of exhortation.[47] *Listen, tribe, who will deck out the city? Surely not fire and a house of the lawless storing up lawless treasures* [388] *and containing unjust violence as well?* (vv.9–10) Not even fire can deck out the city, he is saying, instead wiping it out, nor will a lawless man who commits lawlessness with great deliberateness and much violence and is addicted to grave iniquity escape punishment; such inhabitants, in fact, destroy the city no less effectively than fire. *Will injustice in measuring and unfair weights in a bag be condoned? From whom did they amass their wealth of impiety, its inhabitants speaking falsehood and their tongue lifted up in their mouth?* (vv.11–12) As justice cannot be seen to be done with an incor-

---

45. Again, the appearance of this principle of a hierarchy in cultic and moral obligations in the Psalms (40.6–8, 50.7–11, 51.16–17) and elsewhere in the Bible (Is 1.11–17, Am 5.21–24) is not acknowledged.

46. Theodore thinks simply in terms of Dt 6.5 and Lv 19.18—for him a Mosaic principle primarily, though cited also by Jesus (Lk 10.27, Mt 22.37–39), something Theodore does not add.

47. The Heb. of these vv.9–10 has the LXX and modern commentators struggling.

rect and unfair balance, he is saying, nor can deceitful and distorted weights be acceptable, so too will those who augment their wealth from lawless acts be unable to enjoy the proceeds: all such inhabitants of the city, addicted to falsehood and adopting a haughty mentality so as to set no store by God's punishment for it, will of necessity be subject to the divine punishment.

I shall begin to strike you, I shall do away with you in their[48] *sins* (v.13): inflicting my punishment on those committing such crimes, I shall destroy all of you in a manner commensurate with your sins. *You will eat and not be satisfied* (v.14): living off the proceeds for a while, you will not enjoy it for long, being snatched away from it by the punishment. *Darkness will come upon you, you will duck your head but not escape:* you will be enveloped in my punishment as though in darkness; and though wishing to dodge experiencing trouble, you will in no way succeed. *All who are saved will be surrendered to the sword:* even if you seem somehow to escape for a while the punishment of the enemy, you will be completely overtaken. *You will sow but not reap, you will press oil but not have oil for anointing, you will make wine but not drink wine* (v.15): a victim to the slaughter of war, you will not even enjoy the fruit of your labor, since the enemy will naturally do away with everyone (the implication of all this). *My people's rituals will be done away with, together with all the doings of the house of Ahab; you followed their advice, and so I shall consign you to destruction, and all its inhabitants to mockery, and taunting shall come upon my people* (v.16): at that time you observed all the rituals of the worship of the idols,[49] imitating the practices of Ahab and the kings of his ilk; your profits will disappear along with you, so that everyone from other places observing your ruin will fall to mocking you, marveling at the huge turn in your fortunes, and will taunt you for suffering for your misdeeds.

---

48. LXX generally and our Heb. read predictably second person.

49. Where Heb. and LXX speak of Israel observing the rituals/practices of (the kings) Omri and Ahab, Theodore—who seems to know this text—is shown citing a different text but reproducing the other text in his paraphrase.

Chapter Seven

Having thus mentioned the threat of the retribution due to fall upon them, in what follows he mentions in turn, as usual, the reasons for what is about to be inflicted on them, conducting the narration in the form of a lament, since it was very appropriate for the prophet, grieving as he was for their sufferings and relating their sins under the guise of mourners. What, then, does he say? *Woe is me for becoming like one gathering* [389] *stubble in the harvest, and like gleanings in the wine harvest with no bunches available, when my soul longed to eat firstfruits* (v.1): it falls to me to mourn as I watch such a turn for the worse in the people's attitude that no fruit of justice is to be seen among them. I am therefore obliged to suffer in their midst the kind of thing a farmer suffers when his crops fail completely at harvest time, forcing him to gather useless stubble instead of sheaves, or what falls from the sheaves at times of bumper crops, or when the wine harvest comes he finds no bunches and gathers only some little grapes.[50] At this time, despite such care and attention shown them by God, who naturally looks for the fruits of reverence and virtue, I find goodness in very short supply with them all; in fact, it is not even possible to see any firstfruits appearing among them, whereas I am gripped with a strong desire to see such a thing, it being normal for us to gather firstfruits from the ripe crop, that is, the first born. Hence Blessed David, "He struck the firstborn of Egypt, firstfruits of all their labor in the tents of Ham,"[51] meaning, On account of their extreme barrenness I was gripped with a longing to find among them something capable of playing the part of firstfruits.

Continuing the laments, *Alas, my soul, religious people have disappeared from the land, and there is no human being doing the right thing. All go to law as bloodsuckers, they each oppress their neighbor with*

---

50. At least by this stage in his commentary, Theodore is showing himself expansive (a trait Photius thought he took to extremes), and gives lengthy explication of figures the author employs, if not improving on them in the manner of Theodoret. He also recognizes the literary form of lament in which the message is couched.

51. Ps 78.51.

oppression, they set their hands to evil actions. The ruler makes demands and the judge addresses words of peace, it is what their soul wants (vv.2–3): how could a lament not be required for the absence of fear of God everywhere? This accounts for no one being found willing to give attention to duty. All their court cases involve homicide, no one stopping short at petty crimes but reaching to the extent of homicide; each of them to the degree possible tries to involve their neighbor in pain and pressing need, and are prepared for the practice of vice. Next, in addition to this the one appointed to rule neglects his duty and looks for bribes, and influenced by them he dismisses the crimes of sinners, while the one assuming the authority of judging omits to determine what is just and employs soothing words so as in this way to wangle unjust gains for himself, to which he addresses the thinking of his soul. *I shall take away their goods like a gnawing moth moving slowly on a rod at the time of your examination* (v.4): for this I shall completely reduce you to a state of need, like a moth, by means of the enemy doing away with all that is of value to you: just as a moth on a wooden rod making its way along eats and wastes it all by gradual destruction, so shall I gradually destroy all your good things; at the time when [392] I observe the magnitude of your sins, I shall impose a punishment commensurate with the deeds. *Alas, alas, vengeance has come upon you, now their weeping will occur:* the day for paying the penalty for your sins has come, on account of which you should now shed tears, realizing from the troubles affecting you how much harm you brought on yourself by your turn for the worse.

To bring out the magnitude of the troubles coming upon them, *Do not trust in friends or hope in leaders. Be careful not to entrust anything to your spouse, because son dishonors father, daughter rebels against her mother, daughter-in-law against her mother-in-law, a man's foes are all the men in his house* (v.6): at that time no help at all will come to anyone from anyone else—not to friend from friend, not to ruled from ruler, not to husband from wife, not to son from father, not to mother from daughter, not to daughter-in-law from mother-in-law.[52] The extremity of the troubles,

---

52. Again Theodore is unwilling (or unable?) to refer to Jesus' quotation of

you see, will oblige each one to strive for their own salvation and necessarily give the impression that everyone is hostile to one another, no one being in a position to consider the benefit of the neighbor through giving most thought to securing salvation for themselves.

Next, after the mention of the troubles, in turn in customary fashion he gives the good news of the change for the better. *For my part I shall look to the Lord, I shall wait upon God my savior; my God will hearken to me* (v.7): despite such troubles of so great magnitude, I shall not despair of God's care; I shall continue looking towards him, and waiting for salvation from him, which he will provide me with in those times of need, listening to the one asking his help. *Do not gloat over me, my foe; I have fallen but shall rise, because even if I walk in darkness, the Lord will enlighten me* (v.8): it will be possible for me at that time to say in response to my enemies, and most of all to the Idumeans,[53] It is futile for you to take satisfaction in my falling: I shall rise from my fall, thanks to divine grace. And so, even if I have been walking in the midst of troubles like darkness, yet God's help will come to me, brighter than light. *I shall bear the Lord's wrath because I sinned against him, until he declares my cause just and delivers a judgment in my favor. He will bring me out to the light, and I shall see his righteousness* (v.9): as a sinner I experienced his wrath and the ill-effects stemming from it; but he will provide me with a change for the better, personally judging in my favor for what I suffered from all those wrongly hostile to me, and especially according me justice in his judgment and thus investing me with the splendor of his characteristic goods. So God's verdict will be clear and beyond doubt to me, by which in his concern for justice he freed me from the troubles besetting me, and rightly punished those wronging me without cause (the meaning of *I shall see his righteousness*).

My foe will see, and shame will cover her for saying to me, Where is

---

this passage in the Gospels (see Mt 10.35–36, Lk 12.53). He is consistently anxious not to lend an NT dimension to these OT texts.

53. Theodore is not alone in taking these verses as a national (cultic) prayer; but the Idumeans have not appeared among the nation's list of current enemies since *Comm Ob*, when they figured as Babylon's henchmen in 586.

the Lord your God? (v.10) At that time, he is saying, [393] she will be ashamed for taunting me on the score that no help came from God, now that she sees the ineffable quality of his care for me. *My eyes will take note of her:* not only will he personally free me from the troubles, but as well I shall see the punishment of my adversaries. *Now she will be something trodden underfoot like mud in the streets; a day for the making of a brick, that day your destruction* (vv.10–11): she will be trampled down by the enemy like mud in the streets that is trampled by a vast number of pedestrians, and pummeled in various ways for brickwork, which is generally the custom with those engaged in that work, so that, once pounded, it becomes more suitable for the work at hand. Your destruction will be like that, too, at that time; in other words, you will be destroyed by the enemy attacking you, who will in various ways trample you down and crush you quite mercilessly.

That day will repudiate your required practices (vv.11–12): you will suffer utter devastation (suggested by the abolition of the required practices, since on the establishment of total civil and government organization the required practices, which its citizens normally follow, must hold force, whereas when devastation and captivity take over, law and order necessarily disappear). So he goes on, *Your cities will meet with termination and division by Assyrians.* He mentions the reason for the abolition of the required practices, saying Assyrians will destroy the cities and divide them up amongst themselves at will. *Your fortified cities will be subject to partition from Tyre as far as the river of Syria, from sea to sea, and from mountain to mountain,* as if to say, the Assyrians will have control of all these cities; the prophet Amos also suggests as much in mentioning the troubles from the Assyrians overtaking the neighboring peoples.[54] *A day of water and uproar; the land is set for destruction along with its inhabitants from the effects of their exploits* (vv.12–13): a vast number of foes will come upon you, like water submerging everything, as a result

---

54. See Am 8.12. The phrases "from sea to sea, and from mountain to mountain" do not appear in most forms of the LXX, which prefer the following phrase: "a day of water and uproar." Rahlfs claims both versions represent the same Heb. forms, the Antiochene text including both.

of which you yourselves will be filled with great alarm; all your possessions will disappear along with yourselves, since it is for your deeds you are undergoing a just punishment.

After thus conveying to them in many ways the punishment of those who were hostile and harmful to them, he then directs his discourse to the people. *Shepherd the people with a staff of your tribe, sheep of your inheritance, dwelling alone in a forest* (v.14): for your part, on the other hand, freed from alarm, and uproar, and foes, living in peace, make sure to conduct yourself as duty requires. Since God considered you his own possession, he rescued you from the enemy, set you apart like sheep and allowed you to graze safely in your own land. *In the midst of Carmel they will feed on Bashan and Gilead as in former days, and as in the days of your departure from Egypt I shall show them marvels* (vv.14–15): they will recover [396] their own places just as they occupied them with great power previously on leaving Egypt;[55] in fact, the deeds worked for them now by me will be no less deserving of admiration than those of that time. *Nations will see and be ashamed of all their might* (v.16): the deeds worked for them will be sufficient to cover in confusion those with the skills to make war on them previously, now that they see them the object of divine care with such great power. *They will put their hand to their mouth,* amazed at the magnitude of the deeds. *Their ears will become deaf:* their hearing will not be able to cope with the magnitude of the deeds. *Like a snake they will lick dust as they trail dirt after them* (v.17): unable to accomplish anything further in the face of the deeds done in your favor, like snakes they will fall to earth by choice. *They will be held in their own confinement:* it is no chance restraint they will endure, since the enemy confine them with slaughter in mind. *They will be aghast at the Lord our God, and will be afraid of you:* they will be stupefied, as it were, at the magnitude of the deeds done by God, and will then consider you fearsome for being accorded such great providence from God.

---

55. Taking Carmel as a proper name instead of generically as garden or orchard, Theodore is thus involved in topographical problems with the mention also of Bashan and Gilead—problems he declines to pursue.

Then, after the mention of the good things ensuing for them, in what follows he offers God a kind of thanksgiving for everything.[56] *Who is a God like you, taking away iniquities and rising above impious behavior of the remnant of his inheritance?* (v.18) Now most of all, he is saying, you have been shown in practice to be a mighty God surpassing all in power and lovingkindness, forgiving sins, dismissing impious behavior, and giving evidence to the remnant of your own people of your characteristic liberality. *He did not maintain his wrath as testimony, because his wish is for mercy:* though the wrath he bore us was just, he could not bring himself to sustain it for long, right though he was to exercise it; although he often confirmed to us what we would suffer for failing, we in no way came to our senses through the threats, yet he has overcome everything by his mercy, which he is ever concerned will overcome everything. *He will bring back and have compassion on us; he will cause our sins to sink, and all our sins will be cast into the depths of the sea* (v.19): the one who dispatched us to captivity has in turn exercised his characteristic mercy and brought us back, completely cancelling our sins and throwing them into an abyss, as it were, from which in future they will not be able to return and prevail over us. Mentioning the reason for all this, *You will give your truth to Jacob, mercy to Abraham, just as you swore to our fathers in the days of yore* (v.20): you have done all this mindful of your own promises, which with unswerving generosity you made to our fathers in earlier times, at that time making the pledges to them, and now putting them into effect for us their descendants.[57] [397]

56. Again Theodore shows some awareness of the different genre (as we might style it) employed here by the author. Predictably, he recognizes no word-play on the prophet's name in the opening clause of v.18.

57. Characteristically, Theodore does not suggest the reader look for any NT and specifically Christological realization of the ancient promise of "truth" and "mercy," such as Jn 1.14 (where, admittedly, the "mercy" of the familiar binomials becomes "grace"). For him, Micah's perspective goes no further than Zerubbabel, nor should ours in reading him. He has been distinctly more comfortable in commenting on this book by comparison with the "novel and extraordinary things" of Jonah.

COMMENTARY ON THE PROPHET NAHUM

INEVEH WAS A LARGE CITY, priding itself on its vast population, as the divine Scripture informs us, and was the most famous of all those in Assyria. In it was in fact the palace, and the king of the Assyrians made it his residence for a long period.[1] These people, however—I mean the inhabitants of Nineveh—when God wanted to give a demonstration of his characteristic grace, as we said more clearly in commenting on the prophecy of blessed Jonah, were seized with such dread at a simple threat made by an unknown man as to be converted with extreme promptitude and set their eyes on a better course.[2] But when God allowed them to show their true colors, they adopted such a depraved attitude and such ferocity and vicious behavior as to attack all the people of the ten tribes and take them captive; they laid waste their cities, robbed them of all their possessions and advanced even on Jerusalem, which they were anxious to take, showing no respect for the Temple, or the worship of God conducted there.

Something similar happened to those in Egypt at one time when Pharaoh their king and all the Egyptians showed enthusiasm for Jacob and Joseph and all those connected to them by birth as long as God caused them to maintain this attitude. But when the people's numbers increased greatly, and the time for departure became urgent, he allowed Pharaoh and the Egyptians to betray their malice towards them so as even to display complete eagerness to do away with them all on the spot; capi-

---

1. Ashur and Calah preceded Nineveh as Assyria's capital, Sennacherib, of course, choosing it for his capital only at the end of the eighth century; but for Theodore interest in τὸ ἱστορικόν does not involve researching such details.

2. One of the "novel and extraordinary things" that puzzled Theodore in the book of Jonah was the city's response to "an unknown foreigner," a phrase Theodoret borrows from him.

talizing on this opportunity, God thus led them out of Egypt.[3] This, at least, is the account given by blessed David, "The king sent and released him, the leader of the people let him go; he appointed him master of his house and ruler of all his possessions for the purpose of instructing all his rulers to be like him, and his elders to be wise." He is referring to the respect and enthusiasm for Joseph shown by the Pharaoh; he goes on, "Israel went into Egypt, and Jacob sojourned in the land of Ham. He made his people's numbers increase greatly, and gave them power over their foes." And, since he mentioned also Jacob's arrival and the vast numbers to which all of the people had grown, he went on, "He changed his heart to feel hatred for his people, to act with guile towards [400] his servants."[4] It is clear that with God's permission all the Egyptians, along with their king, changed, with the result that they felt hatred for the Israelites and wanted to annihilate them completely. After this blessed David then goes on with the events of the exodus.

In the same way in our text, too, God gave a demonstration of his peculiar grace in making a sudden change for the better occur in the king of the Assyrians and all in Nineveh. Not long after, however, he allowed them to display their natural malice and permitted such awful things to happen to the Israelites at their hands in that they devastated the ten tribes and attacked Jerusalem, advancing on it with considerable folly in that they were effectively warring against God. In fact, God immediately inflicted a severe blow on them by means of the angel, putting the rest to flight and investing them with troubles of many kinds; finally, while in his own country, Sennacherib, king of the Assyrians at the time, fell to the sword of his own sons.[5]

---

3. The "something similar" illustrated by the stories of Joseph and the people generally in Egypt is what was also one feature of the Jonah story that Theodore with his literalism had difficulty accepting—apparent contradictions in the narrative.

4. Ps 105.20–25. We have seen before Theodore's tendency to make a point twice—the tautology of which Photius found him guilty. He will now proceed, having already made his point about the relationship of Jonah and Nahum, to spell it out again at greater length.

5. See 2 Kgs 19.35, 2 Chr 32.21, Is 37.36–38. Theodore knows of Sennacherib's Jerusalem disaster in 702; his predecessors, Shalmaneser V and Sar-

Then, later, he even completely destroyed their kingdom at the hands of the Babylonians after causing Nineveh to be besieged by them, with the result that the most populous, famous, and royal city was captured and reduced to utter devastation. In other words, just as in former times God gave a demonstration of his characteristic grace in suddenly changing them all for the better, as blessed Jonah the prophet narrates, so in this case, when they gave evidence of their innate wickedness, he invested them with an extreme and fearsome retribution, teaching all people through both examples to learn the magnitude of his grace when he wishes to reveal his liberality to human beings, and also the fear of retribution when he considers deserving of it those who have an incorrigible purpose of falling.

While the prophet Jonah, then, reveals the former, Nahum does the latter, mentioning the retribution due to be inflicted in many ways on them for displaying their arrogance against both the Israelites and Jerusalem, as well as against the God of all worshiped in the city. Through this it became obvious to everyone that he would not have allowed the Israelites to suffer this fate at their hands if they themselves had not rendered themselves deserving of such sufferings through their impiety.[6] And when they had suffered what was inflicted on them by the enemy and had endured that awful captivity in payment of the penalty for their own impiety, God directs his wrath in turn to those responsible for this abuse and punishes them for what they committed and perpetrated against God and his own: the Israelites he allows to suffer as deserving of such things for their impiety and sinfulness, the others in being guilty of their actions against them from their innate depravity he was obliged to punish to exact an account of them [401] for being under the influence of a foolish and depraved mentality and rushing headlong into such a degree of impiety as to wage war also on God in them. In other words, just as Obadiah mentions the

gon II, responsible for the fall of Samaria in 722, go unnamed. He also knows of the fall of Nineveh in 612, an event beyond the period of Nahum's ministry.

6. This, in fact, is not a moral Nahum draws; his reticence on Israel's sins and need for repentance has led to his being called by some commentators a false prophet.

punishment the Idumeans suffered after the people's return from Babylon for sinning against Jerusalem and its inhabitants at that time, and makes clear in his revelation that their fate would happen by God's will at that time, so blessed Nahum in this book mentions the retribution due to befall the Assyrians from God, which they therefore suffered later through the Babylonians, and indicates in his own case that the Israelites would also be allowed to suffer these things by God's will on account of their impiety, and Assyrians would in good time for their folly pay a penalty matching their sins.

While this is the book's theme,[7] we must now proceed to its contents in detail.

Chapter One

An oracle of Nineveh, a book of the vision of Nahum the Elkoshite (v.1). While this is the customary title of the prophetical books,[8] there is need to clarify the sense of the word *oracle*. The Holy Spirit, you see, who to those thought worthy of such things provided the peculiar grace, was one; as blessed Paul says, "Having the same Spirit of faith according to the verse in Scripture, I believed and so I spoke, we also believe and hence we speak,"[9] bringing out that both those in olden times and those who served the mystery of the new covenant shared in the same grace of the Holy Spirit. On the other hand, the activities that were performed differed depending on the urgency of need; he says, "There are varieties of gifts, but the same Spirit," referring to the differences in what is given, whereas the

7. It has been a lengthy, and typically repetitious, summary of the book's ὑπόθεσις. Theodore is not consistent in the length he devotes to these introductions (dependent perhaps on the clarity of the prophet's historical setting, or the presence of worrying features of a book); Micah received only a few lines.

8. See Hab 1.1, Zec 9.1, and Mal 1.1, where for "oracle" the word λῆμμα occurs (its derivation from λαμβάνω, take hold of, leading to Theodore's theory of prophetic inspiration as possession). Semantic cross-referencing like this is a rare exercise for Theodore (see opening to *Comm Ob*).

9. 2 Cor 4.13 citing the LXX reading of Ps 116.10. The prophets, and others accorded special charisms, in Antiochene thinking, merit these gifts of the Spirit. See my article, "A pelagian commentator on the Psalms?"

Spirit giving them all is one. So, in listing the gifts, he says, "To one is given utterance of wisdom, to another an utterance of knowledge through the same Spirit," and he goes on in this vein, "It is one and the same Spirit who, in allotting different gifts to each one individually as he wishes, puts them all into operation,"[10] bringing out that all are due to the operation of the one Holy Spirit, though the activities occurring within them are manifold and in response to need, according as they received the revelation of what was required.

It was by ecstasy, therefore, that in all likelihood they all received the knowledge of things beyond description, since it was possible for them in their minds to be quite removed from their normal condition and thus capable of devoting themselves exclusively to contemplation of what was revealed.[11] After all, if it is not possible for us to gain precise learning from our mentors unless we distance ourselves from everything and with great assiduity give heed to what is said, how would it have been possible for them to be the beneficiaries of such awesome and ineffable contemplation without first being removed in their thinking from reality on that occasion?[12] This is the way Scripture says blessed Peter was in an ecstatic state and saw the cloth

10. 1 Cor 12.6, 8, 11. Theodore, influenced by the occurrence of λῆμμα for prophetic oracle, is prompted to launch into a disquisition on prophetic inspiration—a rather late decision in this study of twelve prophets, but perhaps early in his career as a whole (though, as with many of the Fathers, the opening verses of Ps 45 had prompted him to some thinking on the subject; see my article, "Psalm 45: a *locus classicus* for patristic thinking on biblical inspiration"). Such views on the nature of inspiration would, of course, affect his delineation of the canon, leading him to exclude works not betraying signs of such ecstatic possession.

11. Ecstatic possession as a mode of inspiration of the biblical authors, even the (latter) prophets, was on first principles not the prime analogue for Antiochene thinkers, with their accent on the role of human effort in biblical composition as in other areas (see n. 9). But, unlike their mentor, Diodore, both Chrysostom and Theodore in commenting on Ps 45 did allow for some element of possession by the Spirit—though Chrysostom hastens to differentiate this from the mantic possession of the pagan seers, if not always clear on the difference. Theodoret also tries to keep a balance.

12. Theodore's term for contemplation or discernment, θεωρία, is also a basic Antiochene component of the process of determining the Spirit's message. Diodore had written on this subject, too.

let down from heaven:[13] since the grace of the Spirit first distanced his mind from reality, [404] then it caused him to be devoted to the contemplation of the revelations and so, just as we are beyond our normal condition as though asleep when we receive the contemplation of what is revealed, so in some fashion they were affected by a transformation of mind from the Holy Spirit and became beneficiaries of the contemplation of the revelations.

In fact, sometimes the grace of the Holy Spirit provided them while in this condition with such a remarkable communication that they seemed to hear someone speaking, as it were, and themselves were taught, and thus received knowledge of relevant matters. Blessed Peter, for instance, at the appearance of the cloth seemed to hear a voice saying to him, "Get up, Peter, kill and eat." Hence, too, the prophet Isaiah said, "Lord, who believed our report?"[14] referring by "report" to the revelation accorded him from heaven, since he seemed to hear someone speaking, as it were. Now, it is possible that on seeing some vision or other they heard the words along with it, as in the case of blessed Peter at the one time seeing the cloth and receiving the communication of what was said to him, and in the case of blessed Isaiah saying, on the one hand, that he saw God and the seraphim,[15] and, on the other, he also heard the words addressed to him. Hence sometimes Scripture says "A word of the Lord that came" to so and so,[16] by "word" referring to the activity by which the person received some kind of communication and was instructed in what was to be done, and sometimes, "A vision that (this or that person) saw,"[17] thus referring to the rev-

---

13. See Acts 10.9–13, the text speaking of the trance, ἔκστασις, into which Peter fell, and his seeing the cloth, θεωρεῖν. Theodore proceeds to argue on this example that the prophets, too, were rapt in a trance in receiving their message. Below, he will reinforce this with the derivation of λῆμμα, from "take hold." Diodore, one feels, would not fully support this approach to biblical, even prophetic, inspiration.

14. Is 53.1, the term ἀκοή implying listening to someone speaking.

15. Is 6.1–2.

16. See the opening to Hosea, Joel, Jonah, Micah, Zephaniah, Haggai, and Zechariah.

17. See the opening to Isaiah and Obadiah.

elation by which he seemed to see something and was instructed in what to do. It means the same thing if it also says "The
hand of the Lord came upon me,"[18] in this case too giving the
activity of the Holy Spirit the name "hand of the Lord," for by
it, as though touching the prophet's mind, it provided it with
instruction in what was needed.

Something of this kind is the meaning of the word *oracle:* in
his wish to give the prophets an insight often productive of rap-
ture, he caused a sudden transformation of their mind so that
while in this condition they might receive the knowledge of the
future with deeper fear. He calls it *oracle,* then, since the grace
of the Spirit, as though suddenly taking hold of the prophet's
mind,[19] transformed it with a view to the revelation of what was
to be made clear. He is saying the same thing here, too, *An oracle of Nineveh, a book of the vision of Nahum the Elkoshite,* as if to say,
The prophet's mind was suddenly seized by the grace of the
Spirit and transformed so as to contemplate those things
through which he learnt of the fate of Nineveh and that he provided to his listeners as instruction in what was shown to him.
Hence the mention of *oracle* and *vision,* in order to indicate by
the former the manner of the activity of the Holy Spirit, and by
vision the contemplation of what was shown to him.[20]

He begins in this fashion: *A jealous and avenging God is the
Lord, the Lord is vengeful in his anger, the Lord takes vengeance
[405] on his adversaries and personally removes his foes* (v.2). By *jealousy* he refers to God's wrath, which he feels for the impious
when provoked by what is done very wrongly, the same meaning as in the verse, "The Lord saw and was moved with jealousy,
provoked by anger against his sons and daughters."[21] So here,
too, he was on the point of mentioning wrath on God's part
roused against the Ninevites (or the Assyrians: by the royal city

18. See Ezek 1.3.
19. So λῆμμα is derived, linguistically and psychologically, from λαμβάνω.
20. The prophet is able to receive revelation only when in a trance,
Theodore is saying. Having thus developed his theory of prophetic inspiration,
Theodore moves on without attention to such a mundane detail as the location
of Elkosh, Nahum's home town.
21. Dt 32.19.

he implies the whole nation) for being guilty of impiety and extreme lawlessness, and arranging for so many awful troubles for
many nations including the Israelites; they had also advanced
on Jerusalem, and were close to declaring war on God himself.
At this point, then, it was good for him to begin by saying, *a jealous God*, that is, one capable of being extremely provoked by
the acts of impiety, avenging in great wrath the acts of impiety
committed by human beings, and punishing and completely
destroying those who choose to adopt a hostile and negative attitude to him. Then, since God had given evidence of much
lovingkindness towards them when they were convinced by the
preaching of blessed Jonah and set their eyes on repentance,
he says, *The Lord is longsuffering, and his strength is great, and the
Lord will by no means absolve the guilty* (v.3): just as he knows how
to be patient and overlook a multitude of sins and impious acts
when he sees people turning towards repentance, so he gives
evidence of his own adequate power by the greatness of the
punishment when he sees them falling unrepentant and proceeding to the summit of impiety. He will not relieve them of
their crimes or the retribution for their sins, for the reason that
they are condemned by their own actions.

What is the proof of this? *His way is in consummation and in
shaking.* By *way* he refers to God's action; Scripture often uses
the same expression of human beings, as in the verse, "The
Lord knows the way of the blameless."[22] This is his meaning
here, then, He has now determined to do this, and to this end
he moves against you to shake everything of yours and inflict
utter ruin on you. *Clouds are the dust of his feet:* In keeping with
the mention of *way* he goes on, *Clouds are the dust of his feet:*
since it is normal for the person walking with great force to stir
up dust, the clouds are the dust of his feet, as if to say, Advancing on you, he directs the whole sky against you. *Threatening the
sea and drying it up, and exhausting all the rivers* (v.4): he is capable of drying up the sea by his voice alone, and with it the
rivers, he is saying, suggesting that it is no trouble to him to destroy your state and populace if he wishes. Then, to provide a

22. Ps 37.18.

demonstration also of what is happening, *Bashan and Carmel have withered, and all the bloom of Lebanon has faded; the mountains were shaken by him, and the hills tottered, all the earth buckles before him, and* [408] *all its inhabitants* (vv.4–5): everything the Israelites suffered at your hands happened by his will; in condemnation of their impiety he allowed them to suffer what you wanted to inflict on them, and so they were not effects of your power but of the divine will. Hence Bashan and Carmel and the revered places of Lebanon witnessed destruction, and mountains and hills were all close to being toppled.[23] In short, he changed all that country along with its inhabitants from their original appearance through hatred of their impiety.

Who can stand firm in the face of his wrath? and who will resist his anger? His anger wastes principalities, and rocks were broken by it (v.6): in this you have proof, therefore, that there is no one capable of resisting the divine wrath, which is quite able to smash and utterly destroy both those in positions of great influence and those invested with great power. He speaks in a similar vein to the preceding, *The Lord is good to those who submit to him on the day of tribulation, and he knows those who reverence him* (v.7): he is very loving and very practised in bestowing favors on those who look to him and are fearful of his threats. *He will prepare a crossing in the flood; darkness will pursue those who provoke him and are hostile to him* (v.8): when his move is towards wrath, and he finds some people deserving of it, he inflicts a kind of flood in his wrath, and by means of it he causes the complete annihilation of the wicked, and all those who rebel against him and presume to intend opposition to him he will envelop in darkness and great bewilderment from the magnitude of the troubles besetting them.

Why do you plot against the Lord? (v.9): so what kind of thoughts do you have of him? Surely you do not think yourself capable of warring against such a one as he? After previously advancing on Jerusalem, do you now direct blasphemous words

23. Theodore in his literalism cannot quite go along with the author's hyperbole, qualifying it slightly. He also rewrites the author's intention by supposing it is Israel's sins that have provoked this cataclysm—a feature notably lacking from Nahum's theology.

against God? *He will make an end of you, and will not twice wreak vengeance in tribulation on the same thing:* having determined to set in train your complete destruction, he achieves his will against you so suddenly as not to need a second strike, achieving your sudden ruin at the first blow. *Because they will be demolished from their very foundations* (v.10): and so everything of yours will be reduced to utter devastation. *They will be consumed like an entangled bush, and desiccated like stubble* (v.10): like the plant that clings to fences and is then consumed by all the passing cattle, you will all be wasted by the enemy; like dry stubble you will be destroyed by fire by those attacking you, utterly incapable of avoiding their assault. *Plotting against the Lord will emerge from you, intent on wicked opposition* (v.11): then you dared to devise such schemes against God and actually put them into effect, attacking the city containing the divine Temple, and considering it vulnerable to destruction as though quite beyond help by God. [409]

So what is the response? *The Lord who controls great floods says this* (v.12): listen, then, to what God, the Lord of all the nations in the land (the meaning of *great floods*) decrees for that audacity. *He will thus tear them apart:* just as if one were with great ease to separate water from water in a certain place, so God will mark you off from all the nations and consign you to destruction. *No more will a word be hearkened to:* so that there is no longer a word from you as you perish completely. *Now I shall crush his rod for you, and break your bonds* (v.13): all your sceptres and the kingdom you seem to possess I shall strike down, and all the power you have over your subjects, imposing your authority like bonds of some kinds, I shall completely sever, in that it will predictably disappear completely along with the loss you sustain of all your kingship, power, and authority you had over others.[24] *The Lord will command of you* (v.14): God has commanded this to happen to you. *There will be no further sowing of your name:* since those subject to a kingdom normally attribute everything to the

---

24. Our Heb. text of these verses is at times obscure, and the LXX departs from it somewhat. Some modern commentators see grounds for recognizing an oracle of salvation for Judah in vv.12–13; somewhat against the evidence of his text, Theodore continues to see reference to Assyria.

kings and bear their names in being subject to their authority, your name will no longer survive when you perish completely. *From the house of your god I shall destroy statues, and of the molds I shall make your tomb, because you have been dishonored:* along with you I shall destroy the idols, to which you were in the habit of according great honor, and in perishing they will become like a tomb, being destroyed and, as it were, buried in your dishonor.

As a result, behold on the mountains feet of one bringing good news and announcing peace (v.15): at that time there will be many who betake themselves up the mountains of Jerusalem and proclaim to everyone the good news of your destruction, and the peace ensuing from it for them.[25] *Celebrate your festivals, Judah, fulfil your vows to God, because in future there will be no one to consign you to oblivion any more:* now enjoy yourself and perform the prescribed festivals and vows to God with all zeal and great confidence that they will no longer attack you to destroy anything of yours, once they have perished. Hence he goes on, *They are finished, they have gone:* whoever is guilty of this has disappeared.

Chapter Two

There has ascended one who blows in his face, rescuing him from tribulation (v.1): a divine wrath resembling a blast completely snuffed out the one inflamed against you with the result that you will now not suspect any trouble from that direction.

Having addressed the above to Judah, due to celebrate a festival for the destruction of the one attempting such outrages against them, he now directs his discourse to the Ninevites. *Watch the road:* have an eye to those bent on attacking you. *Gird your loins:* be equipped against the attack if you can. *Summon up all your strength:* give evidence now of that great power of yours. *Because the Lord reversed the abuse of Jacob as also the abuse of Israel* (v.2): it is not possible for you [412] to escape the impending evils, because what you have done against Israel God directed against your own head. *For they really shook them out, and destroyed*

25. The close resemblance of this verse to Is 52.7 (cited in Rom 10.15) not surprisingly passes without comment by Theodore.

their branches, weapons of his power from human beings (vv.2–3): so
great will be the power of the enemy against you as to dislodge
you from your high station like those shaking out clothing and
to ruin everything in which you were bedecked and took pride
in being occupied in worship. In short, they will destroy all your
military skill and all your power from all people.[26]

Then he includes mention also of their former might, which
they used improperly, as being of no benefit to them at the
present time. *Men of might disporting themselves in fire:* you who
were exceptionally strong, and had no qualms about risking
even fire. *The reins of their chariots on the day of its preparation, and
the horses will be alarmed on the roads:* you who take pride in horses and in chariots, which will all prove to be useless to you, for
in the time when the imposition of punishment is effected by
God for you, alarm will seize the chariots and the horses, who
will be ineffective on account of fear of the enemy. *The chariots
will come together and collide in the streets* (v.4): all will take to
flight, with the result that from the bewilderment gripping
them they will collide with one another in the face of the enemy's assault and be lost. *Their appearance like lamps of fire, and
they dart about like lightning bolts.* He puts this ironically for purposes of ridicule, meaning, You thought yourselves no different
from lightning bolts and fire, resplendent in your weapons and
attacking the enemy with great ferocity.

*The great men will remember, they will shun days, gain control in
their bewilderment, hasten to the walls and prepare their outposts* (v.5):
on the one hand, some parts of that equipment and power of
yours will prove futile, while, on the other hand, you will stop
fighting and give thought to flight, but without having recourse
to it while running about on account of the extremity of the
dread you feel for the enemy. You will then run to the walls, forgetting about the war in your deep despair, and expecting to
gain security from them you will devote your full attention to

26. In this impressionistic description of battle (the fall of Nineveh?) the
sense, like the recipients of each part of the prophet's message, is far from clear;
unusual words abound in the Heb. In the case of this first clause of v.3, which in
our Heb. reads, "the shields of his warriors are red," clarity is further impaired
with the LXX reading a similar form, "from human beings," for "red."

the customary lookout on the walls. What is worse, *Gates of the cities were opened, the palace fell and its contents were revealed. She went up, and her maidservants were led away, like doves muttering in their heart* (vv.6–7): you gained no advantage, however, from your activity about the walls: the enemy will gain control of the city, and through the gates they will enter in complete safety. They will completely destroy the palace and make booty of all your goods and all the treasures belonging to you, exposing them to the view of all, along with what previously belonged to you and seemed to be concealed by careful protection. *She went up.* The prophet is referring to Nineveh, meaning [413] by *She went up* she will go up, by the change in tense he is accustomed to employ.[27] She will go up, he is saying, conducted to the king of the enemy as the captive she now is, and all the subject cities and regions (referring to these as *maidservants*), which had been bidden to give lengthy greetings at the approach of your former queen, will all be taken off into slavery with you, mourning and lamenting their calamities and yours, inwardly like a dove.

He next mentions their former prosperity, varying his attention from one time to another: at one time he brings out the troubles by which they will be tested, at another time he flaunts the influence formerly exercised by them, his purpose being that in this way the suffering affecting her might be increased if she was due to move from one condition to the other. *Nineveh, its waters like a pool of water; they fled and did not stop, and there was no one to gaze on them* (v.8): of old it was no different from a mighty pool, its waters overflowing in all directions, and giving nourishment of itself to many fish, so extensive was it with its own vast size, containing within itself many captives from the enemy. Now, on the contrary, it has been reduced to hardship to such an extent that they are incapable even for a moment of holding firm, let alone look to fleeing; no one is found observing such awful troubles or applying a correction to them. *They*

27. The frequent misreading of Heb. tenses by the LXX Theodore in his naïveté takes as a whim of the author. He does not specify whether he takes the description of the fall of Nineveh as eyewitness account or wishful thinking.

plundered the silver, they plundered the gold (v.9): the enemy then took spoils of all their possessions. *There was no end to its finery:* the wealth beyond counting, with which they were adorned previously, they took away. *They were weighed down with all its precious chattels:* they displayed great interest most of all in what seemed of value, and what they could take from them in their overweening lust (the term *weighed down* resembling its meaning in Kings, "The battle pressed hard upon Saul,"[28] as if to say, The enemy bore down most of all on that part; so here too *They were weighed down* means that the enemy's particular interest was directed at those things).

Concussion and flurry, stupor and heartbreak, knees gone to water and loins all tortured, their face like a white-hot vessel (v.10). He means that they are enveloped in a range of troubles from the enemy, concussed and stupefied, so as completely to snuff out their power of thinking, gone to water through fear and unable even to stand easily, all alike feeling pain—in short, in such a condition of bewilderment from the troubles as to be no different from a vessel heated by fire. He proceeds to remind them of their former power. *Where is the lions' den and the pasture for the cubs?* (v.11): not only has the lions' dwelling gone, but even their whole pasture is gone (by *cubs* referring to the same thing, namely, the lions). He means, In former times you inhabitants of Nineveh, like lions, were fearsome to everyone else, and you took from all quarters what belonged to the enemy and amassed it for yourselves, whereas now [416] even Nineveh your dwelling is gone, and along with it everything you once possessed that was amasssed for yourselves. *Where has the lion gone to gain entrance?* A very mocking remark:[29] whereas they were ever doing battle and always making an assault on someone somewhere as though on prey of some kind, he asks, Where now has your leader gone? after what prey has he gone? He means, There is an end to your fighting, your former power and might is finished. Hence he goes on, *There lie the lions' cubs,*

28. 1 Kgs 31.3.

29. Smith, in fact, classes vv.11–13 as a taunt song. Theodore shows himself not unappreciative of the author's imagery, as well as his satiric purpose.

no one afraid of them. The lion took what was sufficient for its cubs, choked prey for its lions and filled its den with it, a place for its kill (v.12): formerly like lions you attacked everyone, and fear of no one prevented your doing such things; others' possessions you made your booty, and amassed great wealth for yourselves, sufficient also for the enjoyment of your young; others you killed and strangled and gathered them like prey for your offspring, augmenting your own wealth from plunder and lawlessness.

So what is the response? *Lo, I am against you, says the Lord almighty. I shall burn your vast numbers with smoke, and a sword will consume your lions; I shall wipe your prey off the face of the earth, and your works will not be heard of again* (v.13): for all those deeds God has now given his verdict against you, that your vast numbers will be consumed by fire and extreme hardship; the enemy will destroy those who seem to be powerful among you; everything you wrongfully amassed will be done away with, so that all your power will disappear and nothing will be heard of you any longer, like someone who had done something and had utterly perished.

Chapter Three

Then, after mentioning the punishment, he goes on to reproach them for their malice. *O city of blood, completely false, full of iniquity* (v.1): you will suffer these things for all the effort you put into homicide and for your many attempts to commit irreparable crimes through the use of falsehood and deceit, such as Rabshakeh's making glowing promises to Jerusalem in his wish to make them give up.[30] *Prey will not be taken in darkness*, as if to say, you will no longer have the opportunity of snaring prey, and though trying hard you will be unable to achieve anything (using a metaphor from people trying carefully to feel about in darkness). Why? *Sound of whips, sound of rumbling wheels, pursuing horses, hurtling chariots, charging horsemen, flashing swords, gleaming weapons, numbers of wounded, heavy casualties*

30. See 2 Kgs 18.28–35.

(vv.2–3): these things will come upon you one after another—whips, crashing of wheels, charging of horses, loud din of chariots, riders' pursuit, swords, and other weapons fearsome to see in their very brightness, by which many will be smitten, and there will be widespread death of the victims.

There was no respite for its nations: far from the troubles stopping short of its subjects, one trouble will constantly succeed another. *They will be weak* [417] *in their bodies from the great degree of prostitution* (vv.3–4): with the great extent of the dead their numbers will be greatly reduced to a few (the meaning of *They will be weak in their bodies,* as if to say, few bodies will survive). He also gives the reason, *from the great degree of prostitution:* they will suffer this for the enormity of the way they forsook God, which deserved his doing what he decided. Then he continues by way of reproach: *A beautiful and charming prostitute, expert in potions:* you were delinquent in your duty, in your own view comely in the influence you wielded, charming in your zealous devotees, and you proved source of all the habits of impiety for others. *She sells nations with her prostitution, and tribes with her potions:* you do away with whole nations and whole tribes in your power, and coax them into the same impiety as yourself and complete devotion to such things.

Lo, I am against you, says the Lord God almighty. I shall expose your rear as your face, I shall reveal to the nations your shame, and to kingdoms your dishonor. I shall cast filth and your uncleannesses at you; I shall make an example of you (vv.5–6): I shall therefore inflict on you, God says, punishment commensurate with such outrageous behavior, enveloping you in manifold shame, as if a person intended to torment someone by removing their clothing and dragging them into public attention so that the sight of their nakedness would be shameful and the expectation of the torture cruel, whereas when one's features are covered in clothing, it is impossible to discern even what is in front of one. Thus, he says, by removing all your adornment in this fashion, reducing you to extreme dishonor, I shall hand you over to punishment by the enemy so that your shame and your dishonor will be notorious to everyone everywhere, and you will appear loathsome to everyone even by word of mouth alone for

being reduced to such lowliness, having proved to be everyone's doormat and been revealed as an object lesson in utter
dishonor by the extremity of the troubles. *All who see you will
back away from you and say, Wretched Nineveh, who will groan for
her? Where shall I seek comfort for her?* (v.7): those seeing this later,
and clearly aware of your former prosperity, will lose the opinion they had of you, and will change their hatred for you to pity
(the meaning of *they will back away from you*), so as to pity you
for the troubles besetting you, reasoning that no one could fittingly lament the disaster befallen you, nor could any comfort
or healing be found for such awful troubles.

*Fit a chord, prepare yourself, part of Amon, dwelling on rivers, water
around her, sea for your beginning and water for her walls* (v.8).
Some commentators claimed that there is reference here to
the city in Egypt now called Alexandria.[31] Admittedly, it is well
known that about four hundred years after this prophecy
Alexander king of Macedonia existed, who with many others
took possession of Egypt and founded Alexandria, which was
named after him. [420] If you were to claim that even before
him there was a city in the same place called Amon, and it is
about it that the prophet now speaks, I still consider attempts at
precision on such matters to be idle, as I have often said, since
they contribute nothing to clarifying the matter in hand.[32] And
so the attempts at precision on such matters are a vain display
at appearing to identify obscure places. An even wilder conjec-
ture is that put forward by them, that the prophet refers to the
fall of Alexandria to show that it was not surprising if a fate of
this kind also befell Nineveh. In fact, the prophet was not try-

31. Theodore's task is made harder by the fact that the LXX has had difficulty reading the Heb.—especially *No-Amon*, "city of Amon," for Thebes—the
Antiochene text differing again. In typical manner, he dismisses the suggestion
of Alexandria for this city by predecessors. In putting the foundation of Alexandria by Alexander (which occurred in 332) "about four hundred years" after
Nahum's time, Theodore situates the prophet in the eighth century (as he himself admitted the book's title suggests), and so no contemporary of the fall either of Thebes (to Ashurbanipal in 663) or of Nineveh (in 612).

32. We have seen Theodore often evincing an un-Antiochene impatience
with detail—especially as he is not himself inclined to investigate the matter (as
Theodoret would).

ing to console Nineveh with these words; rather, the mention of others' fate was consoling to the extent that the one suffering it was comforted. At any rate, it is always our custom to comfort sufferers with the mention of similar cases lest they be too dispirited by thinking that what is happening to them is unique.

So it is absolutely clear, on the contrary, that the prophet is relating to the mention of the impending troubles for Nineveh its former prosperity, for by this means in particular the disaster affecting her would be likely to be heightened. While this may be explained at length, the sense of the verse is, Assyria went into Egypt and caused the people there as well vast problems so as to affect even the fugitive Israelites living there with awful calamities, as the prophet Hosea declares, "For this reason, lo, they will proceed from the hardship of Egypt, Memphis will receive them, and Michmash will bury them,"[33] indicating what the Israelites taking refuge there were due to suffer from the Assyrians entering Egypt. Just as in what preceded he had mentioned the troubles that would overtake the Assyrians, therefore, and directed his words to Judah, bidding them celebrate the destruction of the enemy attacking them as though peace were then established, so too at this point he directs his discourse to Amon, a city in Egypt, and says, Pick up a harp and with great satisfaction make ready to sing on it the city's fall and your peace; though encircled on all sides by the sea and protected by rivers, you will gain nothing from these when Assyria attacks.[34] For the time being, however, you are relieved of all suspicion of its malice.

He then goes on, *Ethiopia was her strength, Egypt too, with no limit to your flight; Put and the Libyans were her helpers. She will be deported as a captive, and her infants smashed to pieces at the head of her streets* (vv.9–10): these people—Ethiopians and Libyans and all whom I have mentioned—became allies by offering support to

33. Hos 9.6.
34. His text not having identified *No-Amon* as Thebes, Theodore is no more likely to check its topographical features for accuracy (modern commentators differing as to whether Thebes is surrounded by the Nile) than its location. The mention of harps is not in our Heb.

you in all your necessities. But they would be of no benefit to you as you give yourself to flight and are led off as a captive in the hands of the enemy, who have no mercy on your infants and cast out their bodies on every street after submitting them to many forms of slaughter. Now it is obvious that by *Ethiopians* he means not those far distant [421] but those who happened to be neighbors to the Egyptians.[35] *For all her famous things they will cast lots, and all her dignitaries will be shackled in manacles:* the enemy took everything of value to them and distributed it by lot, and those thought to exercise power among them they put in chains and dragged off into captivity.

You will be intoxicated (v.11): since it is usual to understand wine as punishment, you will (he is saying) endure the severest punishment to the extent of staggering hither and yon under the troubles like a drunkard. *You will be ignored:* no one will take any notice of your situation. *You will look for respite from your foes:* you will long to gain some relief from all the troubles due to be inflicted on you by the enemy at that time. *All your fortifications like you* (v.12): everything you formerly had for your protection will be dismantled like you. *Even if they have spies, when shaken they will fall into the mouth of the eater:*[36] you will try to spy out the future with many spies when you get a report of the enemy's presence, but all to no avail: dislodged from their posts, they will be brought down by the enemy. *Lo, your people like women in your midst. The gates of your land will be opened wide to your foes, and fire will consume the bars of your gates* (v.13): all the subjects in the city will be wailing and trembling like women when they see the gates opened by the enemy and the city in their power, all the safety it formerly seemed to enjoy destroyed suddenly as though by fire.

Draw water for the siege for your own needs, and control your fortifications (v.14). It is customary for many people to dig deep

---

35. Not having identified Thebes, and thinking Nineveh is still in focus, Theodore has some difficulty accounting for mention of Ethiopia and Egypt. He would therefore not be interested in discovering that the Egyptian dynasty at the time of the fall of Thebes was composed of Ethiopian kings.

36. Where the Heb. speaks of "fig trees" here, the LXX seems to be reading "spies."

trenches in front of the walls and fill them with water to prevent mounting the walls being easy for the enemy. So this is the meaning here, too: Look to the water for help, surround your own wall with it, check everything that seems to offer you safety and give full attention to any of it that is of advantage. Now, he says this ironically for purposes of ridicule,[37] since nothing was capable of helping anyone at that stage. So he goes on, *Trample the clay, tread in the straw, lay hold of the brick; there fire will consume you, the sword destroy you, it will devour you like a locust, and weigh you down like a young locust. You increased your trading more than the stars of heaven* (vv.14–16): at that time no stratagem will result in your salvation—quite the opposite, in fact, as if you fell into some mud, the magnitude of the troubles, and were mixed up in all the troubles like chaff that is trampled down and mixed with the clay in the making of bricks. The enemy will consume you like fire, and you will be killed in many forms of slaughter. The vast numbers of the enemy will come upon you like young locust and cutting locust, wasting you and inflicting on you severe experience of the troubles. All that wealth of yours, which you amassed as though vieing with the stars of heaven, will be of no use to you. [424]

The young locust rushed forward and was airborne, your mercenary wandered off like a wingless locust, like a locust mounted on a rampart on a frosty day; when the sun rose, it took its leave, and its location was unknown (vv.16–17): all your subjects whom you herded together from all quarters to increase power for yourself, as you thought (the meaning of *mercenary*),[38] flew away from you like a young locust, and took their leave like a wingless locust; they imitated a locust in the frost, climbing up a rampart, or staying still in its own position from the cold, and when the sun rises and melts the ice, it suddenly regains its strength from its own flight and flies off, leaving behind no trace of its former position. Likewise, he is saying, these people also were subject to

37. Smith agrees with Theodore on the genre being applied, styling it "satirical warnings."

38. For a *hapax legomenon* in the Heb., the LXX's term σύμμικτος occurs elsewhere in the prophets in the sense of "merchandise." Theodore tries to find a sense that suits the image.

you through fear; but when the disaster took hold of you, as though enjoying some freedom they will all relish their separation from you.

Then as a lament for everyone the prophet says, *Alas for them! Your shepherds fell asleep; the Assyrian king put your warriors to sleep* (vv.17–18): you all deserve tears; the leaders were overtaken by punishment like a kind of sleep and have fallen. Resembling this is the verse from blessed David, "Those mounted on horse fell asleep."[39] In being consigned to destruction, your king brought down with him all those formerly influential with him. *Your people took to the mountains, and there was no one in their place:* then everyone looked to flight, since there was no one capable of relieving the current troubles. *There is no healing the crushing blow* (v.19): all treatment and correction of your troubles has disappeared. *Your wound is inflamed:* your trouble is chronic and so remains incurable. *All who hear the news of you will clap their hands at you, because on whom has your malice never fallen?* People everywhere will be pleased to get the report of the troubles affecting you, displaying by the clapping of their hands their satisfaction at your ruin. After all, since you waged war on all alike and took pains to cause all kinds of harm and abuse to the extent of your abilities, satisfaction with your destruction has accordingly affected all alike.

---

39. Ps 76.7, a citation reminding us of the paucity of scriptural documentation Theodore provides, even from the Psalms.

COMMENTARY ON THE PROPHET HABAKKUK

FTER TAKING THE TEN TRIBES off to his own country as captives, the Assyrian advanced on Jerusalem; but he [425] sustained that fearful attack by the angel, and in the great shame predictably arising from it he turned tail for his own country.[1] Then it was that blessed Habakkuk delivered this prophecy in Judah, dividing his treatment into two parts.[2] One is the censure of those among the people exercising influence and judgment, who afflicted the poor with hardships many and varied, for which above all he declares the troubles from the Babylonians would be inflicted on them. The other is the charge against the Babylonians themselves, on the one hand, of gaining control of Jerusalem and exercising this control improperly, and, on the other, of giving evidence of unrestrained severity against them, for which he says they also would be punished.

The result is that by this division, at any rate, his prophecy gives the impression of resembling the Ninth Psalm, which is a single psalm in the Greek version but two in the Hebrew, each with its own theme, so that the beginning of the first is, "I shall confess to you, O Lord, with all my heart, I shall recount all your marvels," and the end, "Appoint a lawgiver for them, Lord, let the nations know that they are human," while the beginning of the second is, "Why, O Lord, do you keep your distance? why do you look down on us in good times and in bad?"

---

1. Theodore is thus positioning Habbakuk's ministry as a sequel to the celebrated disaster suffered in 702 by Sennacherib's forces in the time of Hezekiah as recounted in 2 Kgs 19.35, 2 Chr 32.21, and Is 37.36–38. The book itself gives no clear chronological clue.

2. Implicitly, Theodore is leaving ch 3 of the text apart, as have modern critics in noting its different character (some Dead Sea mss omit it, perhaps for their own purposes). While not questioning the book's literary integrity, he is rightly noting different literary genres within it, as he had done before.

and the end, "Your ear attended to the readiness of their heart, to judge in favor of the orphaned and humbled, so that a human being may not go further in boasting on the earth."[3] Now, while in the first Psalm he censures the foreigners—I mean, the neighboring peoples—for using excessive severity against them, on account of which he says punishment was inflicted on them by God, in the second it is those among the people with wealth and influence who brought harm and abuse on the poor, who he says will also not be beyond punishment.

It is something like this, in fact, that blessed Habakkuk the prophet now also does, dividing his words against those of them using the influence they had acquired for injustice against the poor, censuring them in the first place and mentioning as well the punishment inflicted on them for it, and against the Babylonians, whose punishment he declares would be inflicted later for all the troubles they brought on the people. This being the theme of the prophet's words, the individual contents must now be considered.[4]

Chapter One

While the customary title introduces the book, then, *The oracle that the prophet Habbakuk saw* (v.1),[5] he begins as follows: *How*

3. The comparison—intrusive at this stage—tells us more about Theodore's critical acumen than about the book of Habakkuk; we hardly need such a lengthy footnote on diversity of content in a prophetic work. Theodore is aware of the discrepancy between the Heb. and the LXX in the numbering of the psalm—originally one and retained as such by the latter—which the former (and modern versions) divides into Pss 9 & 10; possibly the Hexapla contained a note to this effect, though his contemporary, Chrysostom, and later Theodoret, both of whom referred to it for the alternative versions they quote, did not advert to the fact, Chrysostom putting the relative length of LXX Ps 9 down to "the wisdom of the Spirit." Theodore, of course, is unable to claim originality for the LXX by recognizing the alphabetic nature of the Heb. text; he seems instead to give the Heb. credit for division on the grounds of difference in theme, thus supporting his observation on Habakkuk's two foci.

4. His explication of the book's ὑπόθεσις (to the exclusion of the third chapter) has been typically repetitive. Theodoret will make a point of differing from his summation of the book.

5. "Customary"? It was, in fact, not until he reached the title of Nahum that

long, O Lord, shall I cry aloud, and you will not hearken, shall I call out as one wronged, and you will not save me? (v.2) It is not as though bringing a censure against God that the prophet says this; rather, as it is the custom with people in some sort of trouble or righteously indignant with those responsible to present the injustice of what is being done under the guise of censure, so he speaks this way here, too. Blessed David also says in like manner, "Why, O Lord, do you keep your distance? Why do you look down on us in good times and in bad? When the godless act disdainfully, the poor person is inflamed," and so on, saying this not to censure God but indignant with those responsible for it, and at a loss as to how they are not quickly called to account. Likewise in another place, "Why, O God, have you rejected us forever, your anger aroused against the sheep of your pasture?"[6] Bewildered by the magnitude of what happened to the people, you see, he expresses himself here as well, and you would find many other such examples. For instance, blessed Jeremiah says, "Why does the way of the godless prosper, all lawbreakers flourish?"[7] He too speaks not to censure God, but indignant at their not being called to account for what they were doing. This was especially so since all the inspired authors were of the same mind, this being said by blessed David, "Lord, your mercy is in heaven, your faithfulness reaches to the clouds, your righteousness is like God's mountains, your judgments a deep abyss,"[8] meaning, I am struck by God's lovingkindness for being immeasurable, and his care for the righteous in that he exercises it generously in the sense that God's examination and judgment defy comprehension, even if he does not inflict pun-

---

Theodore adverted to the term λῆμμα, "oracle," which occurs elsewhere among The Twelve only here and in Malachi and in Zechariah II (9.1). So far, as well, no other has claimed the title *nabi'*, "prophet." An explanatory word about "seeing" the oracle might have been in order.

6. Pss 11.1, 74.1.

7. Jer 12.1.

8. Ps 36.5. After a paucity of scriptural documentation in the commentary on Nahum (and generally), this amount of it seems disproportionate—except that the prophet has to be defended against the charge of questioning divine justice. Theodoret is more sophisticated in seeing Habakkuk merely relaying other people's disquiet at apparent inequity.

ishment on the offenders rapidly, often delaying it, despite many people suffering abuse.

The prophet puts it the same way here, too, indignant at the injustice of the influential ones among the people who inflict much abuse in various ways upon the poor; and being keenly aware that their crimes deserve punishment, he is disappointed that with God delaying punishment some great injustice is being perpetrated against the poor.[9] Hence, like one who has often begged God fruitlessly for punishment to be imposed on those offending in this way without any further success, he says, *How long, Lord, shall I cry aloud and you will not hearken, shall I call out to you as one wronged, and you will not save me?* Taking the part of the wronged he speaks this way, To what point am I being tested by hardship, crying aloud and begging your help, but not finding it? *Why did you show me troubles and difficulties for me to look upon hardship and godlessness?* (v.3) I mean, I see nothing else each day than difficulty and oppression, which influential people with a godless attitude try to bring on the poor. *Judgment has gone against me, and the judge takes bribes; hence the law has lost its force, and justice will not reach its goal* (vv.3–4): I find fault with what I have frequently seen, that when the court is held, justice is completely bypassed, and the judge, who takes account of appearances, awards the verdict to that person and adds to the harm of the wronged. On that basis, then, attention to your laws is overlooked and no account taken of them; no trial reaches a proper outcome, and instead is clearly diverted to injustice. *Because the godless have the righteous in their control:* those addicted to godlessness and setting no store by your laws use their influence to impose every form of abuse [429] on the poor (by *righteous* here referring to the wronged poor person, because the redress he gains will be righteous). *For this reason judgment that is given is crooked:* hence you would see nothing even on the judge's part that is not crooked, since he ignores justice to give every consideration in favor of the influential.

9. As we have noted before, the unevenness in Theodore's treatment can lead to repetition of points already made, leading to that criticism by Photius of his prolixity and tautology.

Then, after thus censuring the wrongness of these doings, he next proceeds to treat of retribution as though after his dealings with God he was aware of it by divine revelation and properly disclosed it to everyone.[10] *See, you who are scornful, look on and marvel, witness marvels and disappear, because I am doing a work in your days that you would not believe if anyone described it* (v.5):[11] doing such things will be completely impossible for you who scorn the divine judgment; you will see a remarkable punishment imposed on you, one altogether sufficient for your annihilation, since it is God who will inflict such things on you (the meaning of *I am doing a work*), which would prove unbelievable from mere description prior to experience of them. He tells what it is, *Because, lo, I am stirring up the Chaldeans, that harsh nation that is fleet of foot in travelling over the stretches of the earth to take possession of dwellings not their own* (v.6): I shall inflict on you the Babylonians for your awful lawlessness, a most savage nation achieving at great speed what it wills, which will make an assault on practically the whole earth in the power it has acquired so as to take possession of it, though it in no way belongs to it. *It is fearsome and notorious* (v.7), productive of deep fear and well-known to everyone for its ability to do great things. *Its justice will be in its own estimation, and its oracle will issue from itself:* needing no help from another, it does everything from its own resources so as to judge and control whom it wishes, including a sudden decision to impose punishment on them. *Its horses will leap out more swiftly than leopards and more rapidly than the wolves of Arabia, its horses will ride out and charge from a distance, and will fly like an eagle eager to devour* (v.8): while its cavalry is ready for war, and swifter than both leopards and the wolves in Arabia,[12] the horsemen display such eagerness for fighting as to be confident

10. Theodore puts the following words in the mouth of Habbakuk, though attributing them also to God, rather in the manner of the modern commentator, Smith, "The prophet tells the people to look among the nations. They will see an incredible thing happening. God speaks through the prophet" (though for the LXX Smith's "among the nations" comes out as "you who are scornful").

11. Paul quotes these words to the Jews in Pisidian Antioch (Acts 13.41)—another NT reference omitted by Theodore.

12. The LXX comes up with "Arabia" by reading differently the form for "evening" in our Heb.

of charging to a land far distant and almost seem to those living at a distance from them to be flying, like an eagle ready for its prey. *An end will befall the impious who resist their approach* (v.9): they will completely destroy all those among the people giving evidence of sins against the poor, who dare not even for a moment to glance at them or resist. *It will gather captives like sand; it will mock at kings, and a tyrant will be its plaything; it will make fun of every fort, throw up a rampart and take control of it* (vv.9–10): it will take many captives, no less innumerable than sand; it will augment its own satisfaction by the destruction of many kingdoms, [432] easily achieving their destruction without great effort as though mocking them. With much ease it will gain control of heavily fortified cities and defences by raising a rampart with great ease and pulling down every wall or whatever else seems to offer some security.

Then he will change his spirit, pass by and be appeased (v.11): on seeing the heavy penalty imposed, inflicted as it is by men of such a kind and so disposed, God will alter his wrath against us; as though passing through our midst in his providence, he will grant pardon for the former sins and will give relief from the punishment imposed on us because of them. *This is the strength of my God. Are you not from the beginning, Lord my God, the holy one? We shall not die* (vv.11–12): this is an effect of your power, of which you gave evidence from the beginning in our regard, holy as you are and surpassing everything in existence, and on these grounds we also look forward to staying alive, once the punishment is lifted from us. *Lord, you marked it out for judgment, and formed me to censure his correction:* from the outset you personally shaped me for judgment of the sinners so that I might actually correct them by my censure and prevent their sinning with a sense of security. Then he directs his words to God himself. *Your eyes are too pure to behold evil, and you cannot gaze upon troubles* (v.13): your great concern is for righteousness; hence you cannot bear to gaze upon those committing wickedness and proving responsible for others' troubles and oppression. *Why do you gaze upon the contemptuous? Will you be silent when the godless swallow the righteous? Will you make people like fish in the sea, and like reptiles that have no leader?* (vv.13–14): you cannot bear to behold those who commit such crimes with contempt for your punishment, therefore, or to dismiss such injustice that righteous people are almost swallowed by the godless; for we shall seem to be no different from fish and from reptiles without a leader unless you make yourself known with your punishment as the one who governs us and conducts a close examination of human affairs.

After saying all this about the Babylonians, that they treated the people quite mercilessly, he then describes also his power, which he uses with ease to invest as many as he wishes with countless troubles. *He drew him to his end with a hook, pulled him in with his net, and gathered him with his haul. Hence he will rejoice and be glad, hence he will sacrifice to his haul, and make offerings to his net* (vv.15–16): as he invests them all with his own might like a kind of hook and net and consigns them to complete destruction, so he brings everyone under his power so as to take satisfaction in his own works and become so bold as to attribute to his own power as if to some god the magnitude of his achievements (the phrase *he will sacrifice to his haul and make offerings to his net* being a metaphor from those who in such matters return thanksgiving to God). So his meaning is, [433] he imagines that just like God he can do everything he pleases; and he gives the reason, *Because with them he enriched his portion, and his food is special:* he attributes to his own strength the greatness of the achievements, whence derived the increase in his wealth (the meaning of *he enriched his portion*). It is from this source he has enjoyment of all his excellent and special things (the meaning of *and his food is special*). *For this reason he will cast his net and never spare the nations from slaughter* (v.17): relying on his frequent achievements he continues to exercise his power, and involving himself in wars without end he mercilessly commits extreme slaughter of those in his path.

Chapter Two

After reciting what was done by the Babylonian, and in every way highlighting his crimes against the people, he then goes on, *I shall take my position on my lookout, and mount the rock* (v.1), a metaphor from those who in time of war and during a siege keep watch on the wall. *I shall take my position on my lookout,* as if to say, Far from abandoning my duty, I shall make a point of this, believing I find myself in complete safety if I do so. To make it clearer, he says, *I shall look hard to see what he will say to me, and what I am to reply to my charge.* He means, It is for us to look towards God, and accept what happens and emerges from that source, for from that source stems my greatest security; so I shall keep looking to see if at some time God makes a statement on events, so that on learning it I should myself relay to the people what he has revealed as a charge against them and a surety for their descendants.

Now, just as in the above he mentioned the failings of those among the people, speaking as one who knew from divine revelation the punishment from the Babylonians about to be inflicted on them, so here too, after stating the Babylonian's lawlessness, he says he is waiting to learn from God what he is declaring at some time about them as well. And he goes on in what follows to mention the revelation given to him on these matters. Hence he says, *The Lord replied to me and said, Write the vision clearly on a wooden tablet, so that the one who reads it may give chase* (v.2). In other words, after saying he was waiting to see what God would declare about these things, he said God made this reply to him: he was bidden to write on a wooden tablet what was revealed in the divine vision so that what was said and written might be clear and obvious to everyone for reading.[13]

Now, he mentions what would happen to the Babylonians, which he details in what follows, going on at that point, *Because there is yet a vision for the distant future, it will have its fulfillment and not be idle* (v.3): what has been revealed will not be realized immediately but after some time, which is yet in the future but will doubtless have its realization, since far from being an idle revelation, it will absolutely take place. *If he is delayed, wait for him, be-*

13. Theodore prefers not to enter the debate as to the meaning of the final clause of the verse: does it suggest the clarity of the reading even to a runner, or the way of observance that follows from reading?

cause the one who is coming will come and will not tarry: so even if some interval should seem to intervene after the disclosure, wait a while for it, since what has been disclosed as coming and being on the way [436] will come and take effect completely, and will not be put off forever. *If he shrinks back, my soul will not be pleased with him; but the righteous one will live from my faith* (v.4): so even if someone should be uncertain in their trust in the future and doubt if it will really happen, such a one is very much the object of dislike to me, because I define a righteous person as one who trusts in the promises and gets benefit from them.[14]

After saying this about the revelation, and exhorting them to believe in what is being revealed, he then supplies the details of the vision in these words, *But the scornful, contemptuous, and arrogant man will bring nothing to completion* (v.5): you know well, then, that this enemy of yours (meaning the Babylonian), who adopts an unrestrained attitude, scorns divine longsuffering and boasts of the misfortunes of others, will therefore not bring to completion what rests on his own powers, and instead in accordance with the divine threat will undergo a fearsome transformation. *He made his soul as wide as Hades, and like death he was unsatisfied; he will gather to him all the nations, and admit to him all the peoples:* extending himself like Hades against everyone and destroying them all, in imitation of death he will not be sated with the fallen, but will take hold of great numbers and bring them from all directions under his power, and will undergo a fearsome transformation from divine wrath.

Will they not quote all this as a proverb against him, and as a rebuttal in describing him? They will say, Woe is the one who increases for himself what is not his! How long will he load down with his collar?

14. Theodore would not seem to share the view of Smith that "there is no more important passage in Habbakuk than this one, and few in the OT more significant because of the later use of it by the apostle Paul and Martin Luther." It is not simply that Theodore, as usual, is careful to exclude an NT perspective (in this case Paul in Rom 1.17 and Gal 3.11, as well as Heb 10.37–38) from a prophet's predictions; principally, it is because the theological issue that reformist exegetes found in the verse (nuanced by Paul with the omission/displacement of "my"—an objective genitive for Theodore) on the relative place of faith in salvation is not at the heart of Theodore's thinking. He takes vv.2–4 to be parenetic—"exhorting them to believe in what is revealed," as he goes on to say.

(v.6)[15] Everyone everywhere, he is saying, will be struck by the change in him as if by a proverb, and all will say, Of all people he is the most pitiable, despite appropriating others' possessions and increasing his own wealth, and being a burden on his subjects through his excessive severity (the sense of *load down with his collar*): he will be unable to do such things completely (the force of *how long*, which is placed in the middle but refers to the whole, as if to say, He will not be like this completely, because his situation will undergo a change owing to the punishment being inflicted on him by God).

He next says how and in what manner. *Because suddenly those biting him will rise up and your conspirators will sober up, and you will be their booty* (v.7): against all expectations enemies will appear (he means the Medes and the Persians), who by their assaults that are like bites will tear down your power and influence, causing you harm with great assiduity and plundering all your possessions. *Because you despoiled many nations, all the remaining peoples will plunder you on account of people's bloodletting and crimes of country and city and all its inhabitants* (v.8): just as you attacked and robbed others of their possessions, so [437] too will your possessions be taken from you by those left behind for your punishment in repayment for your wiping out vast numbers belonging to God and for your ungodly acts against God's country and city and all its inhabitants (referring to Jerusalem and all in it).

Then, as though in mockery of him for rightly suffering this fate, he lists the crimes for which he was the object of such retribution. *Woe to the one who was guilty of such avarice in his house as to place his nest on high and keep it beyond reach of evil people! You plotted shameful things in your house, you brought many peoples to an end, and your soul has sinned* (vv.9–10): in your own person you were the one to exercise unbridled avarice in increasing your wealth from others' misfortunes and making a display of the lofty position of your kingdom. Though you kept doing this, you could

15. Modern commentators see here the beginning of five woes occupying the next fifteen verses, whereas Theodore recognizes a change in thought only after v.6.

not discern a way to succeed in finding an escape from the troubles befalling you; instead, by wronging many and offending against everyone without a qualm, you amassed in your own house, not wealth (as you thought), but shame (as the outcome revealed), paying this penalty for all the crimes of which you were seen to be guilty. *Wherefore a stone will cry out from a wall, and a beetle will give voice to it from wood* (v.11): as a result of the magnitude of the evils, therefore, even from the buildings that you unjustly erected, there will rise up voices, as it were, accusing you of avarice, as if the stones were uttering such a cry against you along with all the worms that normally lurk within stones and in the joins in the bricks, or can often be found inside the wooden planks (by *a beetle* here referring to what is found in timber and what normally lurks in walls in the middle of bricks, mentioning living creatures and worms specifically, though with this general name referring to all such creatures).

Now, you can normally find underground, especially in damp places, some creatures they call *beetles.* Certain commentators, on the other hand, claimed the Syriac says "peg." It would, however, be stupid to bypass the word in the Hebrew that the prophet used, and that the Seventy men therefore clarified for us in their translation, reliable as they were and possessed of a precise knowledge of that language, to pay attention to a Syriac translator of the Hebrew into Syriac, who furthermore in many cases was prepared to substitute his own mistake for the norm of the text, being in my view a man who did not understand at times what it is saying, and used "peg" for the *beetle* that very commonly lurks in walls so that the expression might seem to retain some sense. Actually, it does not make much sense to say a peg *gives voice from wood,* since while it is admissible to say *from a wall,* it is not admissible to say *from wood:* it is not the case that, just as a wall is made from stones, so wood is made from pegs.[16]

Furthermore, since the prophet had said the accusation was

---

16. Theodore is not the naturalist we find in Theodoret; so when we see him discoursing on the insects found in walls, we wonder if he is off the point. His purpose, however, is once again to fault his predecessors. This time the point at

being made against him both from the walls and from the things within it, he was right to proceed, *Alas for you who build a city on bloodshed, and construct a city on injustice! Is this not from the Lord almighty? A great people wasted in the flames, and many nations grew fainthearted, because* [440] *the land was filled with the knowledge of the glory of the Lord as much water covered seas* (vv.12–14): would not your building cities on homicide and injustice be lamented? You did not perceive, in fact, what would be inflicted on you by God for this; instead, you consumed, as though by fire, an unspeakable number in your savagery, and brought many to the very end of their life in unbearable calamities. For this you will now endure these things so that everyone throughout the world may acknowledge the greatness of God's plan in bringing this to be; you likewise bring on yourself for being capable and guilty of such awful crimes a fearsome punishment befitting the multitude of your sins.

Again by way of reproach he says, *Woe to the one who makes his neighbor drink a baleful overthrow, and intoxicates them so as to gaze on their caves* (v.15). I have often mentioned that wine and drinking refer to calamity; so he means, You were the one who provides all people with a turbid drink to intoxicate and overthrow completely the one capable of drinking it, in the sense of inflicting severe punishment on everyone. You did this, he is saying, in your longing for foreign possessions, searching out foreign treasures and wanting to make them your own.[17] *Drink*

---

issue is the Syriac rendering as "peg" (Grk. πάσσαλος) of a *hapax legomenon* in our Heb. (which modern versions and commentators render "plaster" or "beam") for the LXX's "beetle," κάνθαρος. Gravely, Theodore warns against preferring to the eminence of the Seventy, with their reputation and precision, a Syriac translator prone to error. In saying this, Theodore would be ignorant of the sense of the unnamed Hebrew word (the language "used by the prophet"), as of the Syriac, which he adverted to only at the instance of those predecessors. (He seems to speak of an individual Syriac translator, in the way Field and Rahlfs saw Theodoret's references to ὁ Σύρος, not of a Peshitta Bible, which we know was available by then.) His clinching argument has necessarily to be on the grounds of logic, not linguistics: wood is not made of pegs in the way walls are made of stones—so "beetle" it is.

17. Wine and drinking may be familiar figures for the commentator and his readers, but not so the "caves," arising out of the LXX's reading a similar form to the *hapax legomenon* in the Heb.

your fill of dishonor from glory; stagger in your heart and be shaken (v.16): what you did to others, therefore, it is right for you to suffer in order that you may be filled with dishonor from all that glory, and keep tottering and falling down like some drunkard from the extremity of the punishment. *A cup in the Lord's right hand surrounded you, and dishonor is piled on your glory:* God inflicted his own cup on you so as to state the punishment by his own declaration so that glory might then be converted for you into extreme dishonor heaped on you from all directions. *Because godlessness of Lebanon will cover you, and distress from wild beasts will terrify you on account of human bloodshed and godlessness of the land and all its inhabitants* (v.17): as you offended against the people, now you will justly pay the penalty from the enemy attacking you like a kind of wild beasts; you will be reduced to deep fear and misery for killing people in Jerusalem, and for offending against God's land and city without being prepared to show any mercy to the inhabitants.

Since he reproached him with the offense to the people, the city and the Temple in this, he logically goes on, *What use is their carving an idol? They made a cast image of it, a figment of their imagination, because the artisan trusted in his artefact to make idols that are speechless* (v.18): you neglected the true God, and had no qualms about sinning against what belonged to him; you thought you would gain some benefit from the idols, and by some erroneous imagining you were zealous about worshiping something made by human hands, believing you would gain some benefit from mute idols formed by human hands. He then proceeds logically, *Woe to the one who says to the wood, Wake up, arise, and to the stone, Up you get. It is a figment of your imagination, it is* [441] *gold and silver plating, and there is no breath of life in it. But the Lord is in his holy Temple, let all the earth be reverent before him* (vv.19–20): how, then, are you not the most pitiable person to be conversing with wood that has to be set upright, and looking for help from an idol lifted to its feet, made from material things and yet making an imaginary claim on the onlooker's regard, but bereft of any power of life? It would, in fact, be better for you, on the one hand, to despise such things and give them no importance, and, on the other, to ponder the greatness of

God, who has the dwelling of the heavens as an awesome and ineffable temple, and occupies a Temple also on earth with a view to the needs of human beings. On this Temple not only you but also all people throughout the world should set their eyes with great respect, and retain the thought of it within themselves.

With these words blessed Habakkuk concluded the prophecy in which, as we mentioned before, he upbraided those amongst the people who oppressed the poor and recounted the punishment imposed on them through the Babylonian invasion. After that he mentioned also the ferocity the Babylonians themselves exercised towards the others, Jerusalem and its inhabitants, and how they paid the penalty for their own crimes.

Chapter Three, Habakkuk's prayer

At this point he directs his attention to a prayer, disclosing under the form of a prayer the good things that would come to the people from God, beginning as follows. *Lord, I hearkened to your word, and I was afraid* (v.2), by *word* meaning the revelation that came to him from God, like the verse of blessed Isaiah, "Who believed our word?" and blessed David, "I shall incline my ear to a proverb," which we cited above.[18] So here too he says, Having received your revelation, in which you made known how, on the one hand, by means of the Babylonians you would punish those among the people guilty of transgressions, and how, on the other, you would in turn inflict on the Babylo-

18. See n. 14 to ch 1 of Nahum, where Theodore cited Is 53.1 to clarify ἀκοή; the citation of Ps 49.4 seems less to the point. In his introduction to Habakkuk (see n. 2 there) Theodore left the prayer aside from the work's main thrust, as has happened to it at times since its composition, though he now goes on to connect it with the foregoing chapters. He makes no mention of its title, which makes some provision for musical accompaniment (a rubric that has contributed to the notion that Habakkuk was a cultic prophet, lost on Theodore), as he does not pick up the similar conclusion to the psalm—omissions for which the LXX could be blamed; the musical notation *selah*, appearing as διάψαλμα in the LXX after vv.3a, 9, and 13 (as in some psalms), does not appear in the Antiochene text, it seems.

nians the punishment commensurate with their sins, I was right to be utterly overwhelmed with fear. *Lord, I pondered your works and was astonished:* considering all you did in various ways for human beings in exercising necessary longsuffering and in punishing on a proper basis those who fall incorrigibly, I fell into a trance in admiration of the wisdom of the plans so ineffably implemented. *In the midst of two living beings you will be made known:* lo, even now, as though in two living beings—those among the people committing sin and the Babylonians after them, on both of whom you took action—you made known your power, wisdom, and care for what is right.[19] *As the years approach you will be acknowledged, when the time arrives you will be brought to notice:* while through revelation you have now made this known to us, when the time comes for it to take effect by your decision you will make the demonstration of your characteristic power and wisdom bolder and clearer through actual events. [444] *In alarming my soul, in your wrath you will remember mercy:* at that time there will emerge also the extraordinary degree of your lovingkindness towards the Jews; when they were confused in soul and beside themselves with the wrathful imposition of punishment on them for their sins, you were mindful of your lovingkindness, you freed them from the troubles and against all human expectation led them back home.

God will come from Teman, the Holy One from a mountain under cloud (v.3). He mentions, on the one hand, Teman, the capital of Idumea, and, on the other, as *a mountain under cloud* that of Jerusalem in being accorded divine protection on all sides.[20] So he is saying, At that time you will be seen coming from Teman in Idumea, which you will punish for their sin against us, and from the holy mountain, Zion, which you will make celebrated by everyone for our return. *His excellence covered heavens, and the earth was full of his praise:* he will fill heaven and earth with the

19. Verse 2b is lengthier in the LXX, which also reads as "two (living beings)" a similar Heb. form for "years" in one phrase where it occurs.

20. Theodore makes as good a try of explaining why Teman should rate a mention as modern commentators, though he is somewhat astray in identifying it as Idumea's capital, geography not being a strength of his. The confusion of future and past tenses also escapes him, as elsewhere.

magnitude of the things done by him, so that everyone will then be brought to hymns of praise, admiring his wisdom and the greatness of what is done by him. Here too, note, he uses differentiation to imply commonality, a practice of the divine Scripture that we have illustrated on many previous occasions: he says that heaven and earth are concealed by the excellence of God, implying the totality of things, and that praise of him for his works should be recited by everyone.

His brightness will be like light (v.4): at his coming he will fill everything with light. *His horns are in his hands:* he will show he is quite capable of defending his own, while also subduing those inclined to be hostile to them (using a metaphor from animals battling with horns). *He displayed a forceful love of his strength,* as he will do with a view to exercising great love for us. *Before him will proceed a word* (v.5): before the event the future will emerge; what he always does through the prophets, therefore, he has now done no less through me as well.[21] *And it will proceed for instruction in his wake:* the realization follows, with the result that people are instructed in their duty through both, the future being forecast and its taking effect later.

He stood, and the earth shook (v.6): merely by appearing he shakes the earth, as in the statement, "God stood in the assembly of gods,"[22] as if to say, He was seen in their midst. *He gazed, and nations wasted; the mountains were broken open violently, and eternal hills wasted at his eternal procession:* simply at his glance all the nations perish, and all mountains and hills break into pieces after seeming to remain in existence for a long time by their own strength, since it falls to him to manage such things from on high, and thus to give evidence of the conduct of his personal designs. *In return for trouble I saw tents of Ethiopia; tents of Midian will be terrified* (v.7): in time long gone when we were slaves in Egypt and you chose to free us from the slavery of the Egyptians, I saw [445] the dwellings of the Ethiopians and the Midianites deserted, and all of them then showed hostility to us.

21. Theodore's interpretation of the verse is naturally affected by the LXX's reading *dabar*, "word," for the *deber*, "pestilence," of our Heb.
22. Ps 82.1.

Surely you were not angry with rivers, Lord, your wrath directed at rivers, your ire against the sea? (v.8) Is it your custom, he asks, to display your wrath against rivers and sea, as if to say, you were in the habit when angered of displaying your peculiar might against masses beyond counting? *Surely not against rivers* means, in fact, You do not intend to display your wrath and anger against rivers and sea at all times. At any rate, he goes on, *Because you rode your horses, and your riding brought salvation:* when you wish, you direct the unseen ministering powers as though riding horses of a kind; they will punish all the adversaries at once, and from this will ensue salvation for your people. *You drew your bow and aimed at the staffs, says the Lord* (v.9): with constant punishments you will cut down those who seem to be appointed to kingship and power. *The land will be split open by rivers:* and so the removal of the rivers that happens suddenly from your wrath split open the land (it being the custom for the land to suffer this effect of the dry conditions in the wake of the diminution of water). *Peoples will see and feel anguish* (v.10): most people will be in pain, unable to bear even the sight of you. *Scattering waters of passage:* if you wish, you close off every passage for the water. *The deep gave forth its voice, the height its imaginings:* at that time even the depths will release a voice, as it were, in their peculiar magnitude, moved by your bidding.[23] *The sun was lifted up, and the moon will keep its rhythm* (v.13). Since in times of difficulty the sun is said to set, here he means, The sun and the moon appear as lightsome to those established by you in prosperity. *Your javelins will travel like light:* with notoriety and great splendor you will inflict blows on the adversaries. *In the brightness of the light of your weapons:* your weapons will gleam like a light, as if to say, your power against the enemy.

With your threats you reduced the size of the earth, and in anger you will bring down nations (v.12): in your wrath you will destroy completely all the earth along with its inhabitants by your decree alone. *You issued forth for the salvation of your people, to save*

23. Theodore's efforts to enter into the mythological language of this section of the psalm are not helped by the LXX's rendering the clause in our Heb., "it lifts its hands on high," as "the height its imaginings," in which the form for "hands" has been read as a similar form for "medium, soothsaying."

your anointed ones (v.13): you do everything for the salvation of your own people, chosen as they are by you (by *anointed ones* here meaning those chosen, not those on whom oil is poured, just as blessed David says about Abraham, Isaac, and Jacob, "Lay no hand on my anointed ones, and do no wrong to my prophets,"[24] calling them "anointed," not as people on whom oil was poured, but as chosen). *You dispatched death on the heads of the lawless:* for this reason you enveloped the adversaries in death. *You raised up bonds from head to toe:* you will display the vanquished also in bondage. *You cut down heads of warriors in a stupor* (v.14): Those who were formerly men of power you [448] savagely cut down in your anger so as to bring astonishment on all. *They will be shaken by it,* staggering under the punishment. *They will relax their reins like a poor man eating furtively:* they will not dare to open their mouths in unbridled speech; like an impoverished thief eating something furtively to avoid apprehension, they will speak with bated breath.[25] *You rode your horses on the sea, and they churned up mighty waters* (v.15): you released invisible hosts on the multitude of the enemy, causing a great disturbance in them.[26]

I kept watch, and my heart was aghast at the sound of the prayer of my lips; trembling entered my bones, and my state of mind was turned upside down (v.16): often at the onset of these troubles I chose to preserve peace by falling to prayer, and from this source I received revelation of the future, my mind was gripped with fear, and trembling totally overtook me. *I shall rest on the day of tribulation so as to ascend to the people of my sojourn:* I was startled to learn of the unbelievable event about to occur through your

24. Ps 105.15. Mitchell Dahood, *Psalms III* (Garden City, NY: Doubleday, 1970), 55, observes that only in this psalm are the patriarchs so referred to, adding, "In a metaphorical sense they were 'anointed,' that is, consecrated to God, and received from him special revelations." Fortunately for Theodore, it is the Psalms with which he is at this stage particularly familiar.

25. If Theodore seems to be struggling to make sense of this verse, it should be remembered that modern commentators of the stature of William Albright simply throw up their hands before the challenge it offers.

26. As the LXX is inconsistent in its rendering of the Heb. verb tenses in these verses, so Theodore (who claims to be aware of this habit) likewise considers such differences immaterial, not even respecting the tenses of the LXX in places.

power, that, after such awful tribulation and so many troubles in which I was being tested while in captivity, I would enjoy rest and freedom from the disasters, and especially that I would reach our place of sojourn in the company of its people. *Because a fig tree will not produce, and there will be no fruit on the vines; the produce of the olive tree will disappoint, and the fields will produce no food. Flocks have lost their feed, and there are no oxen in the stalls* (v.17): I saw the fearsome anger working against the enemy, as a result of which it was not only the troubles from the enemy that overwhelmed them. Instead, they were also in the grip of total infertility, no one able to harvest anything from produce, from trees; all the cattle would also perish from lack of pasture and feed.

As for me, however, I shall rejoice in the Lord, I shall exult in God my savior (v.18): while such will be their fate, to us by your help will come satisfaction and salvation. Now, the phrase, *As for me, however,* is being spoken on his part in reference to the people as a whole, which the inspired authors are often in the habit of doing,[27] as for instance blessed David when seeming to present petitions on their behalf, as in saying, "In you, O Lord, I hoped, let me not be ashamed forever," and "Lord, hearken to my prayer, and let my cry come to you": he says this on behalf of all in captivity in such a way that each person employs this sentiment appropriately. In just the same way here, too, the prophet says this on behalf of the community, since he is also talking about the future of the community. *The Lord my God is my strength, he will place my steps like those of a deer, and makes me tread upon the heights so that I may be victorious in his song* (v.19): he it is who regales me with strength in everything, who releases us with great speed from captivity, [449] making the return from there as rapid as a deer. He makes us appear more elevated than all, with the result that nothing else so becomes us now as

27. Of the "inspired authors," προφῆται, with whom Theodore is claiming acquaintance, it is predictably David in Pss 31.2 and 102.1 he cites. The point about Scripture's use of individual expression for community sentiments Theodore has often made (see his comment on v.3); he is less forthcoming here on the reversal in the prophet's thinking that results, in Smith's words, in "one of the greatest expressions of faith in the Bible."

using songs and hymns that are due to God, in return for which he gave us victory over our foes against all human expectation.[28]

28. As observed in n. 18, the LXX does not help Theodore recognize here a rubric for the choirmaster; but he makes the best of a bad job.

COMMENTARY ON THE PROPHET ZEPHANIAH

BLESSED ZEPHANIAH delivered this prophecy at no great distance in time from blessed Habakkuk, dealing in his prophecy with the present in the time of Josiah, king of Judah, as the book indicates.[1] A short time after him the Babylonians attacked Jerusalem, and made a vast number of dispositions affecting the tribe of Judah, killing many and taking a great number off into captivity. They also plundered Jerusalem, and in particular set on fire the divine Temple and all the most beautiful of the city's buildings; they even went further and dismantled its walls to prevent the inhabitants being in a position to have any security, should some be inclined that way.

Chapter One

The following, then, is the customary title of the book. *The word of the Lord that came to Zephaniah, son of Cushi, son of Gedaliah, son of Amariah, son of Hezekiah, in the days of Josiah, son of Amon, king of Judah* (v.1), in which he indicated who the prophet is from whom he is descended and at what period he delivers the prophecy. He begins the prophecy of future events as follows. *Everything is to disappear utterly from the face of the earth, says the Lord* (v.2). The ten tribes, you see, had altogether been taken captive; the Assyrians had gained control of them and had even attacked Jerusalem with the intention of taking it as well. But after they suffered that terrible blow from the angel,

---

1. Like modern commentators, Theodore found little in the book of Habakkuk to date it precisely apart from its mention of (Chaldeans or) Babylonians. They are also the foreign villains looming here, too, in his view, though the title confines Zephaniah's ministry to Josiah's reign, 640–609.

all who survived the punishment from the angel looked to flight in deep fear.[2] The result of this was that the situation of Jerusalem was restored to complete peace. Since, then, the magnitude of the punishment of the Assyrians did not bring to their senses the inhabitants of Jerusalem from the tribe of Judah, the captivity of the ten tribes did not cause them to fear, and they also persisted in lawlessness and impiety no less than the others, of necessity for that reason he began to say this, that there was nothing for it but that the survivors would disappear, removed from the land of promise and taken off into captivity for the reason that those who remained behind also were seen to offend no less than the others.

Now, it was right for him to make his disclosure by way of a sentence[3] to bring out that [452] they had made themselves responsible for this by what they had done—hence God was obliged to deliver such a sentence on them. After saying in general terms, *Everything is to disappear,* he goes on in detail, *People are to disappear, cattle are to disappear, birds of the air and fish of the sea; the godless will become weak, and I shall remove the lawless from the face of the earth, says the Lord* (v.3). By way of hyperbole he associates people, cattle, birds, and fish, or also in figurative fashion, as is usual with him,[4] in such a way that *birds* refer to the mighty ones lording it over the others, and *fish* to those of the populace crawling on their bellies on account of the extremely abject condition. He goes on to give the reason, *The godless will become weak, and I shall remove the lawless from the face of the earth, says the Lord:* those addicted to impiety and lawlessness will fall foul of total weakness, victims of the enemy's hand; the rest will

2. See 2 Kgs 19.35, 2 Chr 32.21, Is 37.36–38. This massacre (in 702) and the Babylonian capture of Jerusalem (587) are the two key reference points for Theodore in his historical backgrounding of The Twelve.

3. Theodore, we have seen, can be sensitive to prophetic genres; his modern counterpart, Smith, puts it this way, "This pericope is in the form of a judgement oracle."

4. Again Theodore anticipates the observation of Smith, "All of Zephaniah is poetry with the exception of 1.1 and 2.10–11." He goes on to include a phrase, "and the godless will become weak," not found in all forms of the LXX, which Theodoret will read differently as "and stumbling blocks along with the godless," approximating more closely to the Heb.

be made captive and removed from the land, which they received from me and occupied with extreme lawlessness.

Then, to make it clear of whom he is speaking, *I shall stretch out my hand against Judah and against all the inhabitants of Jerusalem* (v.4). After saying he would inflict punishment on the tribe and on the city, he was obliged also to mention the reasons for such awful punishment. *I shall remove from the place the names of the Baals, the names of the priests with the priests,*[5] *those who worship on the roofs the host of heaven, those who swear by the Lord and swear by Milcom, those who turn from the Lord, who do not seek the Lord and are not attached to the Lord* (vv.4–6): I shall utterly remove them from this place, some by slaughter and some by captivity, destroying along with them all the idols, the worship given to them along with those seeming to act as their priests, and in addition to all of them those as well who were devoted to worshiping on the roofs the heavenly bodies. They in particular, after all, will receive due punishment who, though dwelling near my Temple, are not ashamed to be occupied in the worship of the idols, and instead give the impression at times of being interested in worshiping me by choosing to swear by me, while at other times swearing by the idols (referring as usual to all the idols by mention of one, Milcom).

I am, in fact, aware of bypassing the fantastic notions of those who hanker after the Syriac, lest I seem to fill up the divine Scripture with fooleries. At this point, however, I thought it opportune to raise the matter in this case as an example both of what is said inappropriately on this occasion, as also of other cases that I have, when they mentioned them, bypassed for the reason given. You see, they claim that Milcom here means the king, Milcom being the name for "king" in Syriac and Hebrew, and that the translators were in error in putting *Milcom*, which is the idol, in place of "king."[6] They ought to realize this before

5. The final phrase "with the priests" in the Heb. occurs also in the Antiochene form of the LXX alone—though said by Smith to be "not in the LXX and may be a gloss," a facile observation commonly found in commentators, who (with rare exceptions) do not trouble to check the Lucianic text.

6. We saw Theodore's disparaging comments on the Syriac version in commentary on Hab 2.11; here he dismisses it (and its supporters) again as of ques-

everything else, that whereas the contents of the divine Scripture are composed in Hebrew, they were translated into Syriac
by somebody or other (his identity is unknown to this day). The
translation into Greek, on the other hand, was done by seventy
men, elders of the people, [453] possessing a precise knowledge of their own language and a knowledge of the divine
Scriptures, approved of by the priest and all the Israelite people as particularly suited to translating. Their translation and
publication the blessed apostles clearly seem to have accepted,
and, to the believers from the nations who formerly had no access at all to the contents of the Old Testament, they passed on
the divine Scriptures written in Greek in the translation of the
Seventy. All of us, having come to faith in Christ the Lord from
the nations, received the Scriptures from them and now enjoy
them, reading them aloud in the churches and keeping them
at home.[7]

So how would it not be foolish to believe that the Seventy,
being so numerous and of such high character, and enjoying
such approval, made a mistake in a reading, despite having a
complete knowledge of the contents of the divine Scripture before any translation, including whether the meaning is "king"
or "idol"? Should some obscure individual who translated the
Hebrew text into Syriac be presumed to be more reliable than
all of those men, as these people claim?[8] Furthermore, it is also

---

tionable value, and on equally questionable grounds. His local text reads here,
as it did at Am 1.15, "Milcom (Moloch)" for "their king" (Heb. *malkam*) of other LXX forms. Not up to disputing the argument on linguistic grounds—
whether, e.g., *malkam* and not *melek* is Heb. for "king"—he indulges in some *ar-
gumentum ad hominem* to discredit the Syriac version (again suggesting it is the
work of an individual), and then falls back on the esteem enjoyed by the Seventy on the basis of the legendary account in the *Letter of Aristeas* (which refers
only to the translating of the Law, in fact, not other parts of the OT) and the use
of the LXX in the early Church.

7. The role of the Scriptures in Theodore's Gentile church is in the context
both of the liturgy and of the Christian home, the domestic church. His fellow
Antiochene, Chrysostom, can be quoted on the practice of reading the Bible in
the family circle (in his first homily on David and Saul, e.g.).

8. In Mai's text (unlike Sprenger's) this sentence appears as a statement; but
a question seems to respect Theodore's drift better. He is clearly committed *a
priori* to accepting the inerrancy of the LXX; certainly he is not in a position to
question it. We can appreciate how a native Syriac speaker like Theodoret could

clear that in this text God is blaming them through the prophet for worship of the idols; and since they did such things despite being near the divine Temple, he reproaches them with the fact that they both gave the impression of worshiping the God of the Temple—that is, the Lord of all—and also did not refrain from the worship of the idols. Blessed Amos the prophet also mentions this idol as the object of worship by the Ammonites, speaking as follows, "Milcom will go off in captivity, their very priests and leaders at the same time, says the Lord";[9] his meaning, as is frequently seen to occur in the prophets, is that the punishment being imposed in his wrath on the foreigners extended to the idols and those serving as their priests. The fact that the Israelites borrowed all the worship of the idols from the demons honored by the pagans is clear from what blessed David says, "They mixed with the nations, learnt their practices, and served their images,"[10] indicating that they borrowed the idolatry from the others. It follows that in the same way they practised worship of the idol called Milcom.

Furthermore, the prophet continues in this vein, *Those who turn from the Lord, who do not seek the Lord and are not attached to the Lord*, meaning, By this they render themselves clearly alienated from my favor, and bent on setting no store by me and my decrees, since those sincerely attached to knowledge of me would never give heed to idols. Now, after speaking of the reasons for the justice of the punishment, he goes on, *Show reverence in the presence of the Lord God, because the day of the Lord is at hand, because the Lord has prepared his sacrifice, he has sanctified* [456] *his guests* (v.7): since you had no time for the divinity, so now you will of necessity be in fear of the Lord of all when he inflicts on you punishment commensurate with your sins. In fact, that time is not far distant—it is actually very close—when

---

take umbrage at this dismissal of the utility of the Syriac, which he demonstrates frequently, if only as a tool for accessing the Hebrew text that Theodore concedes has priority.

9. Am 1.15, where again the Antiochene text alone reads "Milcom" for Heb. *malkam.*

10. Ps 106.35–36.

he will give you over as a victim to the enemy, whom he appointed by his own command and called for that purpose (the meaning of *he has sanctified his guests,* as if to say, those called to this sacrifice he has marked out, referring to the enemy), who will immolate you.[11]

On the day of the Lord's sacrifice I shall take vengeance on the rulers, on the king's household, and on all clad in foreign attire. I shall take vengeance on all brazenly in the vestibule on that day, those filling the house of their God with irreverence and deceit (vv.8–9): on that day I shall punish those among you who seem to rule; I shall completely destroy the very household of the king for the reason that the one seeming to reign over you at that time is due to be taken off into captivity; and I shall punish once and for all everyone who have given themselves in this way to imitating the pagans by way of emulating their style of clothing,[12] forbidden by the Law though acceptable to the nations. I shall impose public retribution on all those in front of the vestibule of the Temple, to which they have shown irreverence, entering to give the impression of worshiping me, but bold enough to make an entrance with hypocrisy and deceit in that, while having no intention of giving importance to religious devotion, they zealously gave their attention to the idols.

On that day, says the Lord, a sound of a cry will be heard from the gate of the slaughterers, lamentation from the second, and a great crashing from the hills (v.10): at that time a fearsome sound will arise that has its beginning in the gate on account of the enemy's entering and causing great slaughter; on that cry will follow an unspeakable lament by those being struck down and destroyed in house after house in various ways, even of those betaking themselves to the loftiest places in the hope of flight (the

11. Though sensitive to some of the prophetic genres employed by the prophets, Theodore has not resonated with the apocalyptic notion of the Day of the Lord, first encountered in Joel and Amos.

12. The reference to the wearing of foreign attire Theodore takes (on indefinite grounds) to mean aping the pagans, whereas 2 Kgs 10.22 mentions special vestments for the worshipers of Baal. Smith thinks the mention of the Temple vestibule recalls another practice of foreign religions exemplified by the priests of Dagon taking care not to step on the threshold of Dagon, cited in 1 Sm 5.5; oblivious of this, Theodore makes his own attempt at clarification.

meaning of *hills*), not only incapable of gaining any advantage from that quarter but even falling victim to the ultimate penalty.[13] He goes on in the same vein, *Lament, you who occupy the region of the stricken* (v.11): at this point all the inhabitants of Jerusalem deserve to lament, since the enemy will in various ways bring it down through those living there, dismantling its buildings and annihilating its inhabitants. *Hence all the people resembled Canaan, all those carried away with money were eliminated:* since they mimicked the way of the Canaanites, consequently they were also subjected to punishment like them in perishing completely, just as they also perished when God gave the land to the Israelites. In fact, along with the others all those who took pride in witnessing themselves as wealthy lost their lives, reaping no advantage from their prosperity, but on the contrary altogether resembling the impoverished in the loss of their possessions. [457]

On that day I shall search Jerusalem with a lamp, and I shall take vengeance on Jerusalem with a lamp (v.12): since for people looking for private things kept hidden and even in darkness it is customary to use a lamp to search for the more carefully concealed item, his meaning is, all the contents of Jerusalem will be searched for with great assiduity so that nothing will escape the notice of the marauding enemy. It was a logical sequel to the verse, *All those carried away with money will be eliminated*, bringing out that all the possessions of the affluent will be done away with, nothing able to escape the enemy's searching. *I shall take vengeance on the men who despise their precautions, those who say in their hearts, May the Lord do us neither good nor evil:* I shall punish those who absolutely scorn my commandments and my worship, by which they could have been protected and preserved from all abuse,[14] holding the view that it is impossible for any evil to befall those guilty of such crimes (the phrase *May the*

13. The references to quarters and occupations in the city in the Heb.—fish gate, second (new) quarter, quarry, (Canaanite) traders—are lost on the LXX, and naturally Theodore is none the wiser.

14. Theodore does his best with the LXX's reading "precautions, protections" where our Heb. speaks of men musing over the "dregs" of their wine, the forms being not dissimilar.

Lord not do us good to be read as a pretense in the sense "He will do us good"). *Their power will become booty, and their houses disappear; they will build houses and not live in them, they will plant vineyards and not drink wine from them, because the mighty day of the Lord is near, near and exceedingly swift* (vv.13–14): all their might will be done away with, and all their houses destroyed; they will not enjoy the houses they built with great care, nor gather the fruit of their own farms, since God's day[15] is coming and is very close, on which everything will turn out that God decrees against them.

The sound of the day of the Lord has been arranged to be harsh and dire: the moment of the divine sentence has been revealed, marked by great bitterness and harshness. *A powerful day of wrath is that day* (v.15): that day's extremely virulent anger. *That awful day, a day of distress and anguish, an untimely day of destruction, a day of darkness and gloom, a day of cloud and fog, a day of trumpet blast and battle cry against fortified cities and against lofty turrets* (vv.15–16): at that time anguish and distress will be extreme, and untimely death for those slain in their infancy; such great slaughter of people that consequently everyone will seem to be enveloped in darkness, gloom or a kind of cloud and fog; or a trumpet call to arms, and with it the sound of the enemy will produce a mighty sound to forecast the devastation of strong cities and the biggest buildings.

I shall bring distress on people, and they will move about like the blind, because they sinned against the Lord; I shall pour out their blood like dust, and their flesh like dung (v.17): through the excess of the tribulation they will be no different from blind people, not being able to see a foot in front of them. In short, they will be subjected to it all for offending gravely against God, for which there will be shedding of blood as if from general slaughter; and the bodies of the dead, since the fallen remain unburied, will be tossed all round the place like a kind of manure. [460]

15. Not a biblical phrase, suggesting again that "the Day of the Lord" has not registered with Theodore as a traditional formula. In the following verses the language, found also in Amos, becomes typically apocalyptic; but Theodore does not advert to the development of a new form of biblical expression, apocalyptic, though some moderns attribute Zephaniah with its beginnings.

Their silver and gold will not succeed in rescuing them from the day of the Lord's wrath, and in the fire of his jealousy all the land will be consumed. Hence he will bring a hasty end upon all the inhabitants of the earth (v.18): no benefit will come to them from the wealth they wrongly amassed, since all this will follow at that time of divine wrath, which will consume the whole earth like fire, and will destroy all its inhabitants with great rapidity.

Chapter Two

Then, after disclosing the troubles, as usual the prophet gives them hope, proceeding in this way, *Assemble and pray together, incorrigible nation that you are, before becoming like a bloom withering in a day, before the wrath of the Lord's anger comes upon you* (vv.1–2): all you who to this point have not accepted instruction in your duty, now at any rate assemble and offer to God prayer in common lest you suffer absolute ruin like a flower suddenly blown away when the divine wrath is inflicted on you overwhelmingly.[16] *Seek the Lord, all you lowly ones of the land* (v.3): you who were humbled by the disasters inflicted on you beyond all the inhabitants of the land, give attention to reverence and beg for divine mercy. *Exercise justice and seek righteousness:* at this time become upright judges of what is your duty, and by distinguishing between better and worse give your attention to what is right. *Seek gentleness and make it your choice so as to feel secure on the day of the Lord's wrath:* choose fairness and tolerance instead of pursuing injustice against poorer people as you formerly did, and be concerned to show interest in these things (the phrase *make it your choice* having this meaning), so that in the time of retribution it will be your good fortune to attain some help from God.

Next, he mentions the punishments against the Philistines

16. Theodore's text has obviously incorporated a copyist's error, found also in some other forms of the LXX, whereby the similar Grk. forms for "gather together" and "pray together" have been confused. As usual, he can rationalize the false reading, none the wiser. Theodoret by contrast knows of the two forms, and rejects Theodore's reading—though only on numerical grounds.

due to be inflicted for their wrongs against them so as to give a greater demonstration of God's care for them. *Because Gaza will be plundered, Ashkelon destroyed, Ashdod cast out at midday, and Ekron uprooted* (v.4): for what they did against us all the Philistines will receive no light punishment (the word *midday* intended generally in the sense of "patently, lest it escape anyone's attention"; what he says of each of the cities—Gaza, Ashkelon, and the rest—he applies to all in common, though making distinctions in his expression, as usual). His meaning is, in fact, All the cities of the Philistines will be plundered and destroyed, they will be cut off from their former prosperity and suffer complete destruction. *Woe to those who occupy the cord of the sea, Cretan sojourners; the word of the Lord is against you, Canaan, land of the Philistines, I shall destroy your habitation. Crete will be pasture for flocks and a fold for sheep* (vv.5–6). Since it happened that the cities were coastal, he called them *cord of the sea,* [461] just as blessed David does in saying, "I shall give you the land of Canaan, cord of your inheritance,"[17] as if to say, I shall assign the land of the Canaanites to your possession, the metaphor being taken from those measuring the land with cord and dividing it. So here, too, he speaks in the same terms of *the cord of the sea* in the sense of the inhabitants of the coastal part. He uses the phrase *Cretan sojourners* since some people from Crete arrived there for commerce since they were coastal cities and chose to dwell among them; as it says also in Amos, "I shall cut down the tribe from the men of Haran,"[18] referring to those sojourning in Damascus from there, so here too he refers to *Cretan sojourners* to mean those from Crete dwelling among them. His meaning is, then, You who occupy the coastal area, including the Cretans sojourning with you, are the most miserable people of all: our God has passed this sentence on all the foreigners dwelling in the land of Canaan, that he will destroy you

17. Ps 105.11, on which Theodoret comments in similar terms.
18. Am 1.5; see n. 14 there for Theodore's not grasping the full force of the reference to Haran, as here he does not mention that the Philistines on the sea coast were partly Cretan (the Cherethites of the Heb.). As this is the only occasion where Canaan is identified with "land of the Philistines" alone, he might also have seen synecdoche, his favorite biblical expression, at work.

completely, and he will reduce to utter desolation the region occupied by the Cretans in your midst, which will become pasture for flocks and a dwelling for sheep. *The cord of the sea will belong to the remnants of the house of Judah, on them they will graze in the houses of Ashkelon, in the evening they will rest before the sons of Judah, because the Lord their God has watched over them and reversed their captivity* (v.7): those from the tribe of Judah who are saved will occupy all the coastal area and will possess it all as their own country as far as Ashkelon. Following his custom of referring to the whole through a part, he takes one city to mean all the cities of the Philistines, who were suspicious of the strength of the sons of Judah and lived in their own land in great fear (the sense of *in the evening they will rest:* since he had used *midday* to mean "patently," he used *in the evening* to mean "fearfully" for the reason that, since those lying low shun the daytime, they are normally out and about in the evening in the hope of escaping detection). This will happen, he is saying, since God would watch over those of the tribe of the Judah, free them from captivity, and bring them back to their own country again with his peculiar assistance.

He next shifts his attention from the Philistines to others. *I heard taunts of Moab and insults of the sons of Moab, with which they taunted my people and made boasts against its frontiers. Therefore as I live, says the Lord of hosts, the God of Israel, Moab will be like Sodom, and the sons of Ammon like Gomorrah* (vv.8–9): I saw what was done by Moabites and Ammonites against my own in claiming by way of a taunt that they gained nothing from worship of me, and in inflicting all possible troubles on them; the result was that with extreme boasting they made free with my frontiers so that in future they would belong to them, and for this they would come to resemble the devastation of Sodom and Gomorrah. *Damascus deserted like a salt heap and destroyed forever;* [464] *the remnant of my people will plunder them, and the remnant of my nation will possess them:* like a heap left on the threshing floor that will disappear, so Damascus will become invisible,[19] dragged

19. Damascus, evidently a rogue element in an oracle directed at Moab and Ammon, seems to have entered the LXX from a misreading of the rare Heb. term for "pile (of nettles)."

down from its great importance and extreme arrogance to utter lowliness, so that those of my people who chance to return will put them all to plunder and take possession of their lands.

This will be their fate in return for their abuse, because they leveled taunts and boasting against the people of the Lord almighty (v.10): they will suffer this for their presumption against God, and abusing and taunting my people, and on my account mocking them for finding themselves in extreme calamities. *The Lord will be clearly their adversary, and will annihilate all the gods of the nations of the earth; all the islands of the nations will bow down to him, each from their own place* (v.11): God will therefore make his vengeance known, so that all the foreigners along with the gods worshiped by them will perish; all people everywhere, both in cities and on islands, will be greatly astonished at what is done by God and will render universal adoration to him, each one confessing in their own places the extraordinary degree of his power.[20]

Ethiopians, you are wounded by my sword (v.12): you yourselves will be punished with the sword at the hands of my people for your sins against them. Now, he mentions Ethiopians at this point as being on the borders of Egypt; so he says this in a way that resembles blessed Amos the prophet, who in mentioning what would happen both to Israel and to Jerusalem touches also on everything they would suffer—I mean, people of Damascus and Tyre, Idumeans and Ammonites, and everyone else he mentions—from the foreigners.[21] In the same way blessed Zephaniah also, in fact, in mentioning in this what would happen to Jerusalem from the Babylonians, touches also on all that was due to happen to the foreigners at that time.

After the aforegoing, from here he shifts his attention to the Assyrians and Nineveh, since at that time Babylonians also de-

20. Modern commentators point out that vv.10–11 in the Heb. are the only verses in prose form in the book; but the LXX makes no differentiation in this case, nor does Theodore, predictably—though we have seen him sensitive to aspects of poetic expression.

21. See Am 1–2. Theodore makes no mention of the Ethiopian dynasty in Egypt that came to an end some decades before Josiah's and Zephaniah's time, as he had difficulty also accounting for its inclusion in Na 3.9, where he offered the same explanation.

stroyed the Assyrians' rule, sacking their royal city—Nineveh—
and reducing it to ruins.[22] Hence he goes on, *He will stretch out
his hand against the north, destroy the Assyrian, and make Nineveh a
waterless ruin like a desert; flocks will graze in the midst of it along
with all the earth's wild beasts, chameleons and hedgehogs will sleep in
its mangers, wild beasts will cry out in its canals, and ravens in its
gateways, because a cedar is its summit* (vv.13–14): at that time I
shall also call the Assyrians to account, attempting as they did
to attack Jerusalem with such awful intent; I shall also destroy
their royal city so that it will be turned into absolute desert, and
in its midst flocks will be pastured [465] and wild beasts will
live, as well as all other animals that normally lurk in the most
deserted places. I shall, in fact, exact this as a just penalty for
their arrogance against all cities, like a cedar that in relation to
the other plants is judged to be loftier than all.

*This city is full of contempt, living in hope, saying in its heart, I ex-
ist and there is no one else after me* (v.15). Now, it is obvious that he
is referring to the conceitedness of the city's inhabitants: he is
not speaking of inanimate stones. So it is contemptuous of
everything else, he is saying, confident that there are no others
beyond it, convinced it is capable of everything (the meaning
of *living in hope*, that is, entertaining the hope of itself that it
would never suffer any trouble from anyone else), standing
alone, the other cities not worth comparing with it as far its existence goes. Then, after saying this by way of a taunt, reproaching it for its arrogance towards all others, he does well to continue, *What a pasture for wild beasts it has become in its destruction!
Every passerby will whistle at it, and shake their fists:* what transformation have you undergone in being reduced to desolation
and turned into a pasture for wild beasts, so that all passersby
whistle at you and shake their fists, marveling at such a huge
change in you?

---

22. The fall of Nineveh in 612, another reference point in Theodore's
chronology, still lies ahead for the Zephaniah of Josiah's reign: is that
Theodore's understanding?

Chapter Three

What have you to say for yourself? *O the famous and redeemed city! The dove did not hearken to a voice or accept correction, it did not trust in the Lord or draw near to its God* (vv.1–2): they will say, How great its fame, how removed it was from all the troubles (the meaning of *redeemed*), how great its charm (calling it a *dove* since the creature seems to be a delightful bird and dignified in its movement, as blessed David also says, "If you sleep among the lots, where wings of a dove are covered in silver and its pinions with the gleam of gold"),[23] meaning that on acquisition of the land of promise, the Israelites resemble a dove in being more delightful than all the others. Likewise, he means here "beautiful" or "comely," as blessed Nahum also says to it by way of a taunt, "A beautiful and charming prostitute."[24] Such she was for refusing to the end to hear the word of the prophet sent to her, and not accepting in any way the instruction from that source. Though seeming to undergo a change for a while, once more she betook herself back to her characteristic wickedness; at any rate, she took no account of God's sending the prophet nor did she make the decision to pay attention to him later, despite having such a remarkable experience. On the contrary, she forsook him completely and declared war on him, attacking Jerusalem after the annihilation of the ten tribes, the city in which the Temple of God was to be found.

At this point once again the remarkable Syriac storytellers [468] claim that in Syriac Jonah means "dove"; and so whereas the prophet wanted it to refer to the city of Jonah the prophet on account of his preaching there, the translator mistakenly

23. Ps 68.13, an obscure and textually difficult verse (to which Theodoret will apply an eschatological interpretation after seeking help from alternative versions). Theodore, at the mercy of his text, is getting into a tangle here: the LXX reads "redeemed" for a difficult Heb. term "impure," and sees in the adjective "oppressive," *hayonah*, reference to "Jonah/dove," this leading him into a digression.

24. 3.4, in an oracle against Nineveh, the city to which Theodore sees this "woe oracle of judgement" (Smith) by Zephaniah against Jerusalem referring (though Smith admits that "the epithets fit both cities").

called it "dove."[25] About the inerrancy of the Seventy, on the one hand, and the far greater plausibility of errors happening to the translator of Scripture into Syriac, on the other, enough has been said by us above. Now, the remarkable storytellers did not understand that he says this as a taunt to the city, *O the famous and redeemed city, the dove.* In fact, such things and the following can be found also in Nahum, "Beautiful and charming prostitute"; here as well he taunts her similarly after her formerly being celebrated for her comeliness; he would never have called her as a taunt the city of Jonah the prophet on the grounds of her being saved by him. Failing to understand the reference, however, they turned to the Syriac and old wives tales.

The prophet goes on in the same vein with what follows, mentioning by way of both irony and taunt at the same time its former prosperity. *Its rulers roaring within it like lions* (v.3), so powerful and bold in their attitude to everyone else. *Its judges like wolves of Arabia, leaving nothing for the morning:* quick to bring their business to an end so as to conclude everything within the day and leave nothing incomplete till later.[26] *Its prophets, though moved by the spirit, are contemptuous men* (v.4): those of its inhabitants claiming to be seers used to utter their pronouncements with extreme conceitedness. *Its priests profane holy things, and have no respect for the Law:* those who claim to serve as priests among them show no respect for either my Law or Temple, giving all their attention to urging their devotees to these practices. He went on in the same vein, *But the Lord is in their midst, and will do nothing unjust; in the morning he will bring his judgment to light* (v.5): they gained no benefit from that lawless behavior;

25. The LXX's solecism in rendering Heb. "oppressive" as "dove" (the meaning of the name Jonah) gets Theodore into deeper water. He blames commentators with a penchant for citing the Syriac version for the problem, unaware of the misreading of one Heb. term by the LXX and the double meaning in Heb. of the other; being thus on shaky ground, he does what he did in his similar tirade on 1.5, fall back on an *a priori* defence of the LXX's inerrancy. In these circumstances, he has no chance of considering the possibility that it is Jerusalem, not Nineveh, that Zephaniah is addressing.

26. As in the case of Hab 1.8, the LXX reads a different form to come up with "Arabia" for "evening."

God was in their midst, resistant though they were, and despite their refusing to give him any importance. He has intense interest in what is right, and now will not allow the injustice performed by them to exercise influence any longer; believing it unfair to let such people go unpunished, he will deliver a swift judgment against them, and for their failings he will inflict the punishment that is clear to them (the phrase *morning by morning* referring to its great rapidity).[27]

He next mentions what comes of it. *I brought down the arrogant in corruption, their turrets disappeared; I shall devastate their roads to prevent their ever being traveled. Their cities failed to be ever again in existence or in occupation* (v.6): on account of their arrogance[28] I consigned them to corruption, and I shall make all their cities disappear; to such desolation shall I bring their condition that even their roads shall be unknown through lack of travelers, and to this fate I shall consign all their cities as well so that no one will be found living in them.

Having indicated in this, however, [469] both the desolation of Nineveh and the abolition of the Assyrians' rule, he turns his discourse to the people of Judah in the following words. *I said, Only fear me and accept correction, and you will not disappear from her sight as a result of everything for which I took vengeance against her* (v.7): I have already in anticipation given evidence to you through the prophets so that you would be in fear of me for being able to punish you easily should you fall, and have required you to accept the instruction provided you; and so that I would not remove you from my sight in places where arrangements were made for you to attend to my worship, and do away with you; nor would I any longer carry out what I did to you to avenge your frequent faults. *Get ready, rise early, all your gleanings are ruined:* since at that time you forsook your duty and suffered such a fate, however, prepare yourselves for what is required to

27. The doubling of "morning" Theodore has not, in fact, included above. The final clause of the verse, obscure in the Heb. and omitted in some modern versions, is missing in some forms of the LXX, including Theodore's (but not Theodoret's) text.

28. By reading a different if similar form, the LXX sees this verse directed against the "arrogant" instead of the "nations."

attend with all care and enthusiasm to what has been commanded by me for the reason that you have the complete destruction of all the enemy's might as a demonstration of my care for you. *For this reason wait for me, says the Lord, until the day of my resurrection in testimony* (v.9): continue looking to me, expecting from me the help I shall provide you with in good time in raising you from the dead, freeing you from slavery, and bringing you all back to your own places. I promised to provide this, in fact, of old through the prophets and now to you, so that you may have the outcome of events as testimony to the truth of what was foretold by me.

Because my judgment is for assemblies of nations with a view to receiving kings so as to pour out on them my wrath, all the wrath of my anger, for in the fire of my jealousy all the earth will be consumed: at that time I shall give particularly clear evidence of my judgment that I shall pass on you, submitting to punishment those assembled from the nations from all quarters. I shall admit—that is, allow to approach—many kings and viceroys along with their armies moving on Jerusalem so as to make clear my care for you through the events themselves, on the one hand, and, on the other, to pour out extreme wrath on them and bring it all to bear on them, since in the grip of jealousy of some kind I shall consume them all as though by fire because of their enormous crimes against my own people. Now, he is referring to those in Gog's company, who made their attack on them after the return, and whom he destroyed despite their innumerable forces.[29] *Because at that time I shall change peoples' language for generations of them with a view to all calling upon the name of the Lord and serving him under one yoke* (v.9): a general astonishment will seize all people everywhere at the novelty of what happens, in that those settled in different places and behaving as different nations will use one language, as it were, and with one accord confess the God of the Israelites to be God; and all established under one yoke, as it were, they will believe service under him

29. The focus of these verses not being clear, and their apocalyptic character becoming more pronounced, it is not surprising that the character of Gog is again introduced by Theodore from the similar material in Ezek 38–39.

to be a blessed thing [472] on the basis of what you are due to be granted by me. *From the limits of rivers of Ethiopia I shall welcome the suppliants, with those scattered they will offer sacrifices to me* (v.10): they will come in haste to my service from the parts of Ethiopia, and with you, who are now scattered in slavery but by that time will be returned, they will offer to me sacrifices in common.

On that day you will not be put to shame for your exploits by which you offended against me, because at that time I shall remove from you the vile elements of your insolence, and you will no longer be boastful on my holy mountain (v.11): at that time you will not endure anything of the great shame in which you are now enveloped because of your irreverence; all you did in treating my name with dishonor and being the source of such insolence to me through the worship of the idols I shall remove from you all by lifting the penalties imposed on you for them. No longer will you live with such arrogance on the mountain appointed for my worship, neglecting my service while devoting complete worship to the idols. *I shall leave in you a people gentle and lowly* (v.12): I shall bring you back chastened by captivity, so that you will live a life of gentleness and lowliness, and in reverence you will enjoy my favor.[30] Hence he goes on, *The remnant of Israel will have reverence for the name of the Lord, they will not commit iniquity and not say idle things, nor will a deceitful tongue be found in their mouths. Hence they will pasture, and there will be no one to cause them fear* (vv.12–13): on your return from captivity you will continue to hold my name in honor, desist from all iniquity, and keep clear of all the improper practices in which you engaged before; at that time you will also take care to avoid making pretense of worshiping me with deceitful purpose while being devoted to the idols. So from now on you will be enabled to pasture in complete security and enjoy your own property, and to live in utter peace, with no one in a position to alarm you or remove you from your own place.

---

30. One can hardly read this verse without evangelical echoes of the Beatitudes ringing loudly (see Mt 5.5); but Theodore persists in suppressing any eschatological sense.

Having promised that this would be their lot after the return, he then goes on, *Rejoice exceedingly, daughter Zion, proclaim, daughter Jerusalem, rejoice and be glad with all your heart, daughter Jerusalem. The Lord has removed your crimes, the Lord has redeemd you from the hand of your foes, the Lord will reign in your midst, you will witness troubles no longer* (vv.14–15): live now in utter delight, O Jerusalem, living in complete happiness and satisfaction; for God has removed all your lawless deeds, and of necessity has rescued you from the power of the foe, to whom you were subjected in paying the penalty of punishment. The Lord will now be in your midst, showing his kingship by his care for you, so that trouble will no longer be able to approach you. *On that day the Lord will say to Jerusalem, Have confidence, Zion, your hands will not lose strength. The Lord your God is in you, in his might he will save you, he will bring happiness upon you, he will renew you in his love, he will rejoice in you in satisfaction as on a feastday, and will bring together* [473] *the downtrodden* (vv.16–18): God will rid Jerusalem of all weakness, saving her personally with his own might, and by establishing her in great joy he will renew his love for you, performing such deeds and, for the sake of your salvation, demonstrating what he demonstrated at a time when he led you out of Egypt with great signs and wonders. This, in fact, is the way he will now free you, crushed by captivity, from the troubles besetting you, and return you once more to your own country.

Alas, who has brought reproach upon her? Lo, it is I who am doing it in you for my sake, says the Lord (vv.18–19): they are most to be pitied who committed some crime against her, for God has demonstrated his power against them for your sake, with the result that your name is on everyone's lips for what was done for you. *At that time I shall save the oppressed, and welcome back the rejected:* while punishing the others, I shall save those crushed by such troubles, and bring back once more to their own place those rejected from their own place. *I shall bring notoriety and fame to them in all the land* so that they will be the object of wonder and commendation by everyone for what was done for them by me. *They will be put to shame at the time when I act in your favor, and at the time when I welcome you back* (v.20): your enemies will be completely covered in confusion when I perform wonderful things for you and lead you back again to your own land. *Because I shall make you famous, celebrated by all the peoples of the earth for my reversing your captivity in your sight, says the Lord:* so many wonderful deeds in your regard I shall work on your behalf against your foes that everyone everywhere will keep remembering and praising you, marveling at the way I freed you from such awful captivity and led you back to your own land.

COMMENTARY ON THE PROPHET HAGGAI

HE BLESSED PROPHETS Hosea, Joel, Amos, and Micah directed their discourse in general to all the Israelite people, both those of the ten tribes ruled by Samaria and especially those of the tribe of Judah, who dwelt in Jerusalem.[1] They accused both in similar fashion of acts of impiety and [476] lawlessness, which they committed in various ways, and went on to mention also the troubles that would thus befall them for sinning without repentance, namely, the fate of the ten tribes, first at the hands of the Assyrians, and later what happened to those of the tribe of Judah under the Babylonians. To these predictions of theirs they attached also the change in their fortunes of the latter, namely, leaving captivity and returning to their own land. Blessed Obadiah mentioned the punishment that would be imposed on the Idumeans at the time of the return. Blessed Jonah threatened the Ninevites with overthrow if they did not change their evil ways. Blessed Nahum clearly disclosed both the siege of Nineveh and the destruction of the whole kingdom of the Assyrians, which they were due to undergo at the hands of the Babylonians. After those in the ten tribes had already been deported by the Assyrians and had suffered total captivity and removal from their own place, the blessed prophets, Habakkuk and Zephaniah, charge those left behind, who were from the tribe of Judah and living in Jerusalem, with their acts of impiety and lawlessness,[2] citing the punishment due to be inflicted on

1. As has become clear, it is not the order of The Twelve in the LXX generally, where Amos precedes Hosea, and Micah Joel, that Theodore finds in his Antiochene text, but the order in the Hebrew Bible.

2. After the four eighth-century prophets, there succeed in Theodore's reckoning three others still prior to the fall of Samaria, and two prior to the fall of Jerusalem in the early sixth century. When cutting to the basics in such an historical summary, he leaves the mythical Gog out of calculation.

them for this by God through the Babylonians, and saying that, far from its being long in coming, all the foretold troubles would come on them suddenly and right away. The prophet, Zephaniah, foretold that the realization of the coming troubles would be close at hand.

The blessed prophet, Haggai, on the other hand, to whom it falls to us now by the grace of God to bring clarity,[3] delivers his prophecy not only after the captivity inflicted on Jerusalem by the Babylonians had happened but when the Israelites were already released from captivity and by divine grace had returned to their own country in defiance of all human expectation. He directs his words to those who had returned and were living in their own country, thanks to such an unexpected favor, and accuses them of indifference to the rebuilding of the Temple. In its rebuilding God had clearly taken great interest, though not for his own sake, as he says of himself, "Heaven is my throne and earth a footstool under my feet: what house is this you are building for me, says the Lord, or what is my resting place?"[4] Admittedly, this too is insignificant if words are compared with the divine magnitude, which clearly surpasses everything in existence, to a degree beyond anyone's capacity to grasp. For the sake of the Israelites, however, the one who has care for human beings sets much store by the rebuilding of the Temple: he provided for them to assemble in that place and Temple, and to render worship of a kind suited to him in accord with the legal provisions, and he wanted the people to adhere to religious practice in all these ways so that appropriately from there at the right moment Christ the Lord according to the flesh might appear for the salvation of all.[5] Of necessity, then, he devoted at-

3. Theodore sees his task to bring "clarity," σαφήνεια, to the often obscure text of the prophets—a goal similar to the one espoused by Theodoret, who in speaking of his work on the Song of Songs, saw it as his role to "bring clarity to obscurity."

4. Is 66.1.

5. The building of a temple for God's habitation poses something of a theological problem for eastern theologians committed to upholding divine transcendence. And if it enjoyed the status of divine prescription, this too had to be justified—hence a rare eschatological glimpse by Theodore ahead to the Incarnation, where material realities take on a (more eminent) salvific value for all people.

tention to the construction of the Temple so that the people [477] through assembling in it might undergo reformation, such great attention having been accorded in this way for the sake of all people, as I have said. You see, just as God allows sacrifices and other such things, not through need of them but for our benefit, so too he was concerned for the Temple, not for his own sake but for those whom it behoved to assemble in that place and render to God the worship due to him on behalf of all humankind, as I said previously.

Now, the book also contains some disclosure of the future— I refer to those of Gog's company—as you would see better from the text itself. While this is the book's purpose,[6] however, let us now concentrate on it in detail.

Chapter One

In the second year of King Darius, in the sixth month, on the first of the month, the word of the Lord came by means of Haggai the prophet as follows (v.1). In the second year of Darius, the fourth to reign over the Persians after Cyrus, who was the first to reign over the Medes and Persians together, when those of the tribe of Judah and as many of the rest as were interested in accompanying them had already returned to their homes and especially occupied their homes in Jerusalem, it says Haggai the blessed prophet was granted a divine revelation.[7] It was to do with his giving those returned an address on their duty, and before everything else to accuse them of neglecting the rebuilding of the Temple, which especially those returned from captivity

---

6. While Theodore has not summarized the book's theme, ὑπόθεσις, in the way he often has with other books, he has shown its σκοπός, its purpose—a challenge to the population to get to work.

7. The chronological reference—unusually precise, as he will proceed to remark—Theodore feels the need to improve upon with the inclusion of Cyrus, but in the process places Darius (Darius I Hystaspes, 522–486) at four removes from Cyrus, not two (Cambyses intervening). Could he have been thinking of Darius II a century later, 423–404 (he rethinks the matter in introducing Zechariah), or allowing for unnamed pretenders who followed Cambyses? The author is thus speaking of 520.

were supposed to erect with great enthusiasm. Now, there is an indication of both the month and the day when on the basis of the revelation the prophet used these words, the purpose being that he might bring out in orderly fashion their situation when they were neglectful of the rebuilding of the Temple, and the great change for the better when they began to take the proper interest in the rebuilding of the Temple.[8]

Now, what the prophet was bidden by God to tell them the following verses explain. *Tell Zerubbabel son of Shealtiel, of the tribe of Judah, and Joshua son of Jehozadak, the high priest, Thus says the Lord almighty: This people say the time has not yet come to rebuild the house of the Lord* (vv. 1–2). To Zerubbabel, who was of the tribe of Judah,[9] and who as a descendant of blessed David according to the divine promises reigned over the people at that time, and indeed also to Jehozadak's son, Joshua, who as a descendant of Aaron was entrusted in the Mosaic provisions with discharging the role of chief priest by his lineage, he bids him convey the instructions that should be given by way of reproof of the people's neglect of the Temple. These were, in fact, rightly given to them in particular as leaders in that it was their duty to stir the others on to the task. It was not them, however, he was seen to be blaming with his words, but the people; so it emerges that while they had the necessary enthusiasm for the task, they were unable to accomplish what they wanted, the people being un-

8. Though he can be impatient of those, especially his predecessors, who get involved in what he regards as a pointless exercise in ἀκριβολογία (being embarrassed by his own inadequacies), and though he can get details wrong when he himself supplies them, as an Antiochene he appreciates the ἀκρίβεια of an author in supplying them for a particular purpose.

9. The LXX version here leads Theodore into a critical misunderstanding with considerable consequences. Our Heb., employing a term thought to be originally Akkadian, speaks of Zerubbabel as "governor of Judah." Smith therefore remarks, "The local authority and leadership seems to have been shared by the Jewish governor and the high priest, but both of them were under the authority of the Persian king." The LXX, however, perhaps unfamiliar with the Akkadian term, describes him rather as "of the tribe of Judah." This allows Theodore to see him as king in the commentary (right from Hos 3.5)—another of his errors in historical detail—and thus a successor to David in messianic promises, much to Theodoret's irritation when wanting to give such promises a Christological realization.

willing to cooperate with them in it. Hence he told them what
was relevant to reproving the people with a view to their stirring them further to the task and the people's [480] acceptance of the due correction, so as to carry out with all enthusiasm what was required for the rebuilding of the Temple and
with great readiness to obey the leaders in matters on which
they gave orders in carrying out the command in accord with
the divine will.

Addressing himself to reproving the people, he makes a
good start with the excuse that they concocted and that they
thought they could speciously use to neglect the work. They
claimed, you see, that the time had not yet come to rebuild the
Temple, and so they seemed to have right on their side in neglecting the work. He then charges them with concocting an
excuse stemming from malice as a cover for their laziness, and
proceeds, *The word of the Lord came by means of the prophet Haggai
as follows, Is it time for you to live in your paneled houses while this
house is in ruins?* (v.3) He then says, You are so concerned with
your own buildings, not only erecting them with great enthusiasm but also decorating them at great expense: is it my house
alone for which the time has not come? Are you not even
ashamed to leave in such devastation the one who is in fact
completely responsible for your salvation, with the result that
your houses have been built and also decorated with extreme
care, whereas the place of the Temple is still given over to ruins
because you are utterly unwilling to take on its rebuilding?

*The Lord almighty now says this, Bring your hearts into keeping
with your ways* (v.5): ponder within yourselves and make a judgment of what you have done in neglecting the divine Temple,
and of what has come to you from it (by their *ways* clearly referring to their behavior, as usual). He then says, *You sowed much,
but harvested little; you ate, but not to satiety; you drank, but not to
inebriation; you had clothes to put on, but did not warm yourself; the
one collecting a wage collected it in a bag full of holes* (v.6): consider
to what a state of need and lack of necessities you reduced yourself through that laziness, reaping a meager crop from many
seeds, enjoying neither food, nor drink, nor clothing to meet
pressing need owing to your lack of all necessities. As a result of

this, all the earnings you made from selling properties and suchlike proved to be of no benefit, since with the crops failing not even your earnings sufficed to satisfy your creditors. Just as in a pouch, or a purse, or some bag full of holes, money can in no way be collected without falling out and being completely lost, so by the failure of the crops even your savings must be disbursed.

Thus says the Lord almighty, Bring your hearts into keeping with your ways. Climb the mountain, cut wood, bring it, and rebuild the house, and I shall take pleasure in it and be glorified, said the Lord (v.7): ponder this, put to rights what has so far been neglected by you, and set your mind on the rebuilding of the Temple; chop wood, and contribute with great enthusiasm whatever else [481] is needed for rebuilding. For my part I shall be pleased with your rebuilding of the Temple, and shall perform for your benefit the kinds of things that will make me known to everyone as capable of greatly benefiting those prepared to obey me with good grace. He next reminds them again of what they formerly endured as a result of their laziness, saying, *You looked for much, and little happened, it was brought into your home and I blew it away* (v.9), as if to say, I did not even allow the crops to give you a yield from the ground, and what seemed to come I destroyed. He goes on differently, *Hence the Lord almighty says this, Because my house is in ruins while each of you hastens to your own house, the sky will therefore withhold dew, and the land withdraw its yield from you. I shall bring a sword on the land, on the mountains, on the grain, on the wine, on the oil, on all that the land produces, on the people, on the cattle, and on all the labors of their hands* (vv.9–11). He intends by this to remind them of what they have suffered by neglecting the Temple. When you overlooked my house lying in ruins and took an interest in rebuilding your own houses, he is saying, then the rain stopped, the land did not yield its crops, and I destroyed all the crops on the ground as though with a sword,[10] striking many times both people and cattle, and

10. Theodore rightly, if only intuitively, thinks there is some need of qualification of the use of "sword," arising from the LXX's reading a form similar to our Heb. for "drought."

in short ruining the fruit of your labors. In fact, to this exhortation to climb up, cut wood, bring it, and give thought to rebuilding, he added these things to cause them fear by the reminder of what had happened lest they receive the command listlessly.

He goes on, therefore, *Zerubbabel, son of Shealtiel, of the tribe of Judah,*[11] *and Joshua, son of Jehozadak, the high priest, and all the remnant of the people listened to the voice of the Lord their God and the words of Haggai the prophet as the Lord their God had sent him to them, and the people felt fear from the presence of the Lord* (v.12), bringing out that his words to them had not proved fruitless, but that all were frightened by the threat in his words and turned to their duty. The result was that the prophet sent by God said to them, *I am with you, says the Lord* (v.13),[12] to emphasize that as soon as they changed their behavior and showed enthusiasm for the rebuilding of the Temple, God for his part immediately promised to provide them with his care in all circumstances (the sense of *I am with you, says the Lord*, meaning, to accompany and care for you and meet all your needs). *The Lord stirred up the spirit of Zerubbabel, son of Shealtiel, of the tribe of Judah, and the spirit of Joshua, son of Jehozadak, the high priest, and the spirit of the remnant of all the people. They went in and began work on the house of the Lord almighty their God* (v.14): God for his part did not simply promise his care: [484] he strengthened the resolve of the leaders and all the people at the same time so that they set everything else aside and occupied themselves with the building of the Temple in order that the work might be brought to a conclusion by them.

---

11. This time the phrase (see n. 9) is not in our Heb. at all, but does recur in v.14.

12. Theodore omits the term used of the speaker of these words in the text of the LXX for Heb. "Haggai, the Lord's messenger/angel," where confusion has occurred between the similar words ἄγγαιος, ἄγγειος, ἄγγελος. Smith tells us that Jerome says some people in his day thought that Haggai and Malachi were really angels and possessed bodies in appearance only; Theodore is perhaps ensuring his readers entertain no such ideas.

Chapter Two

Then, having strengthened their resolve considerably, God appears once more to the prophet with these words,[13] *Speak to Zerubbabel, son of Shealtiel, of the tribe of Judah, and to Joshua, son of Jehozadak, the high priest, and to all the remnant of the people in these words, Who is there among you who saw this house in its former glory? And how does it look to you now—like nothing on earth in your sight? Be strong now, Zerubbabel, says the Lord, and be strong, Joshua, son of Jehozadak, the high priest, and be strong, all you people of the land, says the Lord almighty. My spirit has taken a position in your midst* (vv.2–5): if any of you was familiar with the former glory of this house and what was often done by me in its regard or for the people on account of devotion exhibited in it, they would realize how great the change is from that situation and this. At this time, you see, the majority of you are ignorant of the former,[14] having regard only for the present situation, and you have the impression of something nonexistent, as it were, on account of the desolation affecting it. But persevere in your enthusiasm for the rebuilding and with due zeal do everything for the completion of the Temple, for you will then sense my care, and by offering to God all that is required in the Temple you will be granted the remainder. I shall actually be in your midst to demonstrate it through the events themselves, and you will be accorded the effects of my grace as though I had taken my position in your midst, planning and administering your affairs (the phrase *my spirit* meaning the grace coming from him).[15]

The people of the Old Testament were unaware of a distinct hypostasis of a Holy Spirit identified as a person in its own right in God, since everyone before the coming of Christ the Lord

13. Both the closing verse of ch 1 and the opening verse of ch 2 contain chronological references in respect of the reign of Darius, which are difficult to separate and assign to one verse or the other. Theodore, typically impatient with ἀκριβολογία, cuts the Gordian knot by omitting both.

14. A reasonable deduction by Theodore, the destruction of the Temple being sixty-six years before.

15. In both Heb. and LXX the words, "Get to work, because I am with you," precede the mention of the spirit; Theodore (unlike Theodoret) has omitted them.

knew of God and creation but nothing further.[16] The divine Scripture taught this to its readers at that time without having an insight into anything in invisible creation consisting of separate kinds, referring to all the invisible and ministering beings in general as angels and powers, which according to its teaching carried out the divine decisions. Consequently, they were not in a position to know of a Holy Spirit as a distinct hypostasis in God, being unable even to list separate kinds among the ministering beings, or to associate with God what could be described as a distinct person, since they understood nothing of this sort. Christ the Lord, on the other hand, taught us this in giving his apostles the command, "Go, make disciples [485] of all the nations, baptizing them in the name of the Father and of the Son and of the Holy Spirit,"[17] from which we learn of a distinct person of a Father, a distinct person of a Son, and a distinct person of a Holy Spirit, believing each of them in similar fashion to be of the divine and eternal substance, this being a single doctrine in which we have been thoroughly versed through instruction in the knowledge of God, and there being one single baptism performed in their name.

Now, the Old Testament, as I said, by way of distinction in God did not come to knowledge of a Holy Spirit as a distinct person and distinct hypostasis;[18] by holy spirit, or spirit of God,

16. Theodore does not seem to be aware of any of his predecessors upholding evidence for an OT belief in the Holy Spirit (else he would have disparaged it—as he will disparage any OT evidence for the Trinity in comment on Zec 1.9). His terminology here for "hypostasis" and "person" is ὑπόστασις and πρόσωπον, and he proceeds to use the two terms interchangeably, though repeating them together again later. His point is that only the NT (and later catechesis and liturgical practice) makes the necessary distinctions, in regard both to the Trinity and to invisible beings like the angelic choirs (the angels ranking high in Antiochene thinking, we learn from Theodoret).

17. Mt 28.19.

18. The phrase "distinct person and distinct hypostasis," applied here to Father and to Son as well as to Holy Spirit, Kelly (*Early Christian Doctrines*, 5th ed., [San Francisco: Harper and Row, 1978], 306) claims is not found in any of Theodore's undisputed works, though at that point he is discussing Theodore's Christology specifically. Theodore has immediately above insisted on the *homoousion* of each divine person, "each of them being of the divine and eternal substance, οὐσία." He clearly subscribes to what Kelly (254) terms "the badge of orthodoxy" in the fourth century, namely, "one *ousia*, three *hypostases*"; and his trinitarian terminology is all of a piece with that of the Cappadocians.

it refers to his grace, his care, his attitude to something, or some such: "Where am I to go from your spirit? or where am I to flee from your presence?" meaning, It is impossible for me to be beyond your knowledge, since it is present to everything; so he moves on to God, making no further mention of a spirit, "If I should ascend to heaven, you would be there," meaning, Wherever I am, I am subject to your authority, by which you are present to everything and arrange my affairs in whatever manner you wish. "Your good spirit will guide me on a straight path," meaning, You always managed my affairs in your goodness, and will now also bring me back in accord with it. "Do not take your holy spirit from me," meaning, Do not remove your special and particular care from me.[19] Likewise here, too, when he says, *My spirit has taken a position in your midst,* he means, My grace and my disposition towards you accompanies you, taking a position and providing you with its benefit. In other words, just as he speaks of a soul in reference to God, thus implying not some hypostasis but his attitude to something—as when he says, "My soul hates your new moons and sabbaths" to refer to the attitude by which he hated what was done by them in their depraved behavior[20]—so too is his mention of the *spirit.*

Enough said, however, by way of excessive chase after precision. God had in the aforementioned words stirred up the people sufficiently through the prophet to the work of rebuilding and had made them more enthusiastic, and saw them wondering from what source would they, still suffering the effects of captivity, acquire all that was needed for them to be able to complete the Temple and bring to it all due decor such as the former one had in its structure, its holy vessels and the rest. So he goes on, *Have confidence, do not fear:* have no fear about how this will be possible. *Because the Lord almighty says this, Once and for all I shall shake heaven and earth, sea, and dry land; at the same time I shall shake all the nations, and the chosen of the nations will come. I shall fill this house with glory, says the Lord almighty. Mine is the silver and mine the gold, says the Lord almighty, because great is the glory of this house, the latter beyond the former, says the Lord almighty,*

19. Pss 139.7–8, 143.10, 51.11.
20. Is 1.14.

and in this place I shall give peace, says the Lord [488] *almighty, and*
to every builder peace of soul as a possession for erecting this Temple
(vv.5–9): do not be concerned about the lack of necessities; by
shaking almost all the nations, numerous as they are and laden
with great wealth, I shall allow them to come to you (speaking
of those in the company of Gog).[21] Once they have come, I
shall at that time make the magnitude of the glory of this house
conspicuous through my care; after all, the silver and gold belonging to them and, in short, all their possessions are mine for
the reason that all things in existence are mine, since the whole
of creation is also my work. So what I take I shall pass on to you,
doing no wrong to the owners, who owned what was not theirs,
but in all justice giving to my people what is mine, so that the
former glory of this house may be revealed by what I do, accepting your prayers in it and providing you with power against
the enemy, despite their being so numerous and strong, the result being that you will surpass them in number and be invincible in strength and martial arts. Its glory will seem to be greater
than at any time before, because the task is greater than before
at the time of the Assyrians and some others, the reason being
that not only in numbers but also in strength and martial arts
the present enemy surpass those of former times. By my power
you will against all odds prevail over them all and enjoy complete peace, continuing to have tranquillity of soul through being rid of every enemy and amassing as booty all the enemy's
possessions. By acquiring that for yourselves, you will easily
have the capacity to construct and erect this Temple, if you
wish, so that it will have its characteristic beauty for those assembling in it for prayer and worship.

He exhorted them sufficiently through all the aforesaid and
prompted them to the work of rebuilding, and in particular he
aroused strong hope in them by the promise that they would
share in great affluence by gaining control of the enemy, and
so would have in abundance all they wanted for the rebuilding
of the Temple. For the future he rightly believed they could

21. Modern commentators are uncertain as to the upheaval suggested here.
Theodore predictably invokes Gog.

also develop in themselves an improvement in other matters in which they had offended. He speaks in these terms, *On the twenty-fourth day of the ninth month, in the second year of Darius, the word of the Lord came to the prophet Haggai in these terms: The Lord almighty says this, Ask the priests a ruling in these words, If someone takes consecrated meat in the fold of their garment, and the fold of their garment touches bread, or stew, or wine, or oil, or any other food, will it become holy? In reply the priests said, No. Haggai said, If someone defiled from any of these things touches someone, will they be defiled? In reply the priests said, They will be defiled. Haggai replied, It is like that with this people, and like that with this nation in my sight, says the Lord, and it is like that with all the works of its hands: whoever approaches there will be defiled* (vv.10–14). It means [489] he is charging them with handling the priestly vessels and the other things devoted to the worship of the divinity carelessly, and casually, and without due deference, and it was on this that he ordered the prophet ask the priests for a ruling, they being the ones to declare such things performed carelessly or with due deference. It was also most appropriate that he addressed his question on lowly items so as to highlight the fault against the sacred vessels.

So he says, If meat that is holy from a sacrifice or some offering comes into contact with some part of one's garment, and this fold later touches something else—wine, or oil, or some other kind of food—does such a thing as a result become holy through the fold of the garment in which the meat was placed? They logically said such a thing does not become holy, since the fold of the garment is not sufficient to transfer its holiness to some foodstuff on the score of the meat contained therein. He then asks again, If someone defiled in some way or other touches any such thing, do they altogether defile it or not? They said it is defiled. His meaning in this was, Just as the fold of the garment was unable to sanctify what was brought close as a result of the holy contents, whereas the defiled person by touching any of these things does defile it, so you too ought believe that by touching carelessly, and without due reverence, the sacred vessels or things belonging in some fashion or other to God their holiness does not sanctify you, whereas your defiled behavior commits an outrage on holy things if it proves you touch them without due respect.[22] Hence the prophet also replies, as though it were God speaking, Your behavior is like this when you touch any of the things properly sacred to me: you ought to know that everyone approaching me (*approaching* me meaning touching what is proper and dedicated to me), if doing it casually, and carelessly, and with contempt, not only gains no benefit from the touch but is actually defiled by wrongful and harmful behavior in touching holy things casually. *On account of their morning duties they will grieve when confronted by their wickedness, and you hated their reproof in the doorways* (by *their duties* meaning that they attempted to behave improperly).[23] For the wrongful actions you engaged in, he is saying, rising early for them and performing improper rites with utter enthusiasm, you were overwhelmed by the gravity of the troubles besetting you, the more so since you did not accept the reproof of the prophets and resented them standing up to you in the doorways so as by their words to propose reform to everyone entering and leaving.

Now ponder in your hearts from this day forth: before the laying stone upon stone in the Temple of the Lord what condition were you in when you put twenty measures into a chest and there were ten measures of barley, and you went into the winevat to draw fifty measures and there were twenty. I struck you with sterility and all the works of your hands with [492] *windblast and with hail, and you did not turn to me, says the Lord almighty. Get your hearts in order from this day forth, from the twenty-fourth day of the ninth month, and from the day the foundation stone of the Temple of the Lord was laid. Ponder in your hearts whether it will be recognized on the threshing floor, and whether the vine, figtree, pomegranate, and olive trees are bearing no fruit. From this day I shall bless them* (vv.16–19). Once more by a comparison between the past, when they neglected the building of the Temple, and the present, when they began to show some enthusiasm for the work, he wanted to bring out the difference in their

22. Again the lengthy paraphrase of verses that are self-explanatory gives grounds for the criticism of Theodore for being tautological and prolix.

23. The sentence does not occur in our Heb.

fortune, and the extent of the sterility they felt through their neglect, and the degree of good things they experienced when they showed great zeal in attending to the rebuilding of the Temple. So consider, he is saying, the previous times when you were still not interested in the rebuilding of the Temple, and the condition you were in when you gathered sheaves sufficient to produce twenty measures of the crop, but scarcely ten remained from the spoiling of the crops. You harvested a yield sufficient for fifty measures, and finished up with scarcely twenty on account of their being dried by the heat. Whereas I inflicted on you the disasters of sterility and windblast, and frustrated all your labors with hail, you remained incorrigible even after that.[24] That was before this, however. Consider the benefits that came your way from that day when you showed enthusiasm for the Temple: you will find no comparison between the yield of the threshing floor or the trees and what could be recognized at that time. I mean, whereas no crop was produced from them before, from the time you showed enthusiasm for my Temple I bestowed every blessing on your fortunes and made you enjoy an abundance of crops.

After thus exhorting and prompting them to the task by mention of the past and by comparison with what came later, he next in turn consoles the city, uncertain as they were on account of their poverty. He speaks as follows, *The word of the Lord came a second time to Haggai the prophet on the twenty-fourth day of the month in these terms, Speak to Zerubbabel, son of Shealtiel, of the tribe of Judah, thus: I shall once and for all shake heaven and earth, sea and dry land. I shall overthrow thrones of kings, and shall destroy the power of the king of the nations and overthrow chariots and riders; horses and riders will fall, each of them with the sword against their brother* (vv.21–22). He had said the same thing before, as is suggested by the phrase, *The word of the Lord came a second time to Haggai,* though it seems in the former case the prophet received the divine revelation many times and conveyed it to the

24. The close similarity of this verse to Am 4.9 escapes Theodore's notice. Again he is simply giving a generous paraphrase of material neither cryptic nor elliptic.

people. He says *a second time*, however, because now for a further time he makes the promise in reference to Gog's situation[25] lest on account of its magnitude they might not believe
what was said, and instead be in two minds from God's promising the same thing [493] not once but also a second time. Tell
him, he says, As if by shaking I shall cause total overthrow of
many kings possessing royal thrones, destroying all their power
and overturning the chariots along with those riding in them
so that they will collapse on one another, horses and riders becoming killers of one another, causing wide slaughter and being done away with by one another. I shall do this, accordingly,
so that it should be obvious from everything that the change in
the course of the war and the victory are not the work of your
hand, but are achieved totally by my power.

*On that day, says the Lord almighty, I shall take you, Zerubbabel,
son of Shealtiel, my servant, says the Lord, and make you a seal, because I have chosen you, says the Lord almighty* (v.23): at that time,
O Zerubbabel, having found you worthy to be leader of the Israelite people, I shall cause you to have control over all, so that
it will be clear from the events themselves that by my decision
you have been firmly established as king and appointed to this
office to my satisfaction. Everyone will be readily aware that this
would have been quite impossible for you unless you held the
kingship by my decision and achieved such a great victory by
my influence. Since, you see, the conferral of a seal is seen to
provide security to those on whom it is conferred, he says, *I
shall make you a seal*, that is, I shall present you as the security
and strength of the whole people in being entrusted with the
leadership of so many, since you were chosen for this by my decree. It says likewise in the Gospels, "It is on him that God the
Father has set his seal,"[26] that is, he presented him indisputably
as the source of the highest goods for all people; and blessed

25. Theodore's text alone of v.22 (unlike Theodoret's) seems to speak of a
single "king of the nations," allowing him to see Gog referred to.
26. Jn 6.27. Finally, and atypically, Theodore brings Jesus into focus as another person realizing messianic promises—but only as a second string to
Zerubbabel, for the reason of his taking a misreading by the LXX of Zerubbabel's role (see n. 9) to mean royal status.

Paul, "You are the seal of my apostolate,"[27] that is, you confirm my apostolate by believing. So here, too, he is to be taken the same way, *I shall make you my seal,* that is to say, I shall present your kingdom as firm, proposed as it is for security of all its members to my satisfaction. It follows that, while in all cases speaking in common both to Zerubbabel and to Jesus, at this point he addressed his words to Zerubbabel alone, especially since it was particularly necessary for the king to attend to his leadership in time of war.

27. 1 Cor 9.2. Theodore makes no mention of the seal or signet ring that the Lord threatened to take from King Jehoiachin and give to Nebuchadnezzar (Jer 22.24–25), and that is now restored to Zerubbabel. The reference would have deepened the significance of the figure given here, and could have been used by Theodore to strengthen his case.

COMMENTARY ON THE PROPHET ZECHARIAH

T IS CLEAR THAT, AT THE SAME TIME as the prophet Haggai, blessed Zechariah was also prophesying: *in the* [496] *second year of Darius,* as you can learn from the divine Scripture itself,[1] the former says he began his prophecy according to a divine revelation, and similarly the latter. So it becomes clear that each was delivering his prophecy after the return of the Israelite people when brought back from Babylon to Judea. When Cyrus, you see, who was the first to rule over Persians and Medes at the same time, gave instructions for them to return to their own country, a considerable number returned to Jerusalem and Judea with Zerubbabel in charge; they laid the foundations of the Temple and erected the altar in it. But as the work was prevented from reaching a conclusion, at one time through the malice of those obstructing them and at another through their own indolence, the blessed prophet Haggai as a result of divine revelation blamed them for their indolence and charged them with a depraved attitude in neglecting the work when they had shown such enthusiasm for their own houses as not only to build them but also to decorate them considerably. The divine house, on the other hand, had been neglected; so he roused them all to the work, as the prophet's book itself discloses.

Now, blessed Zechariah by divine revelation in his case as well confirms in similar terms the people's return in his own prophecies, while verifying also that Jerusalem would achieve its own restoration, a king being appointed in it by divine decree,[2] elevated from that source, managing its affairs and fight-

---

1. See Hg 1.1, Zec 1.1.
2. This conclusion of Zerubbabel's kingship, encouraged in Theodore by the LXX's evident misreading of an unfamiliar term employed by Haggai (1.1) for his role in the restored community, has had a marked effect on Theodore's

ing for everyone in the wars against the foreigners, while the priesthood recovered its status again with its former splendor. The result was that through this he convinced those who had returned to accept that their occupation of the site was secure, something that those who had come back were naturally in two minds about, as to whether their residence was permanent, either through the severity of the captivity that they had not anticipated enduring, or also through the unexpectedness of the return. In particular, the secure return of those repatriated proved a guarantee that would convince others of those still in captivity that they would return to Judea.

Now, it seems he had many different revelations, and he describes the gist of each: he discloses the attack of those in the company of Gog and their total ruin that ensued, and the fact that unexpectedly and against all human hope Jews under the reign and generalship of Zerubbabel would gain control of them. He mentions also the distress besetting them after that, which happened to them at the time of the Maccabees from the successors of the Macedonian kingdom.[3] Now, there is no cause for surprise if what happened previously he presents through revelation as future events, as when he says that he saw four horns being struck down that had scattered Israel: it is quite clear that this was not due to happen, but had happened. I mean, if he suggests through the four horns the Assyrians, Babylonians, Medes, and Persians, as some people's opinion holds, [497] it is obvious that both Assyrians and Babylonians had already paid the penalty by that time. Cyrus wiped out the Medes,[4] and after him was Darius, the fourth horn, while from

treatment of him throughout these commentaries, and especially his ability to fulfil (in preference to Jesus) messianic prophecies.

3. The unity of the book—something Theodore could not question—has been the subject of discussion since the seventeenth century, some scholars placing chs 9–14 later than Zechariah's ministry in the late sixth century (as Theodore accepts it above), even relating them to Alexander the Great's invasion of Palestine in the late fourth century. Theodore here, implicitly, admits grounds for a late date.

4. See Theodore's comment on the relevant verse, 1.18. The ascent of Cyrus the Persian to power in the mid-sixth century was rather by way of amalgamation with the Medes and the joint empire's defeat of Babylon under Nabonidus in 539, his decree of release of the Jews coming in the next year. Theodore no

the Persians nothing by way of harm befell the Israelites—on the contrary, they had good experiences of that kingdom, first from Cyrus, the first ruler, who released them from captivity, and after that Darius, who provided the rest of the Jews with the certainty of returning to their own homes. If, on the other hand, you also wanted the four horns to suggest other things inimical to the Israelites at the time of the captivity, clearly those things also were fulfilled. It is likely, however, that the prophet mentioned such things for this purpose (divine grace also in this case revealing it to him for this purpose), namely, that from the divine revelation he personally might have an un-wavering faith in what had happened and might teach the lis-teners to believe precisely that, whereas punishment awaited those causing them distress, the effects of the kindness be-stowed on them awaited them without doubt.

Now, it is not without purpose that this is told us: it is for us, on seeing some things in the commentary mentioned in detail as future though already past, not to be surprised or bewil-dered by the form of expression.[5] So much for the theme; we must now proceed to details, according as divine grace allows.[6]

Chapter One

In the eighth month of the second year of Darius the word of the Lord came to Zechariah son of Berachiah, son of Iddo, the prophet, in these words (v.1).[7] By this he indicated the time at which he was ac-

---

longer thinks of Darius as "fourth after Cyrus" to rule the empire, as he re-marked on Hg 1.1, even Cambyses going without a mention. He is right, of course, in identifying the prophetic procedure of citing past events as guaran-tees of the future.

5. Theodore, whom we have seen identifying different forms of prophetic utterance, does well in the case of this book, which Jerome about this time called "the longest and most obscure of the twelve prophets," to urge his read-ers not to be put off by the puzzling utterances.

6. An Antiochene commentator, while acknowledging divine help in his task, might also credit himself with his own effort, as Theodoret is wont to do.

7. Modern commentators on the Heb. text of Zec 1.1, 7, where Zechariah is said to be "son of Berechiah, son of Iddo" (as though father and grandfather), are much exercized by the fact that in Ezra 5.1 and 6.14 Zechariah is called only

corded the divine revelation, and thereupon proceeded to say what he was bidden to tell the people. *The Lord was very angry with your fathers* (v.2). The prophet's opening was suited to the occasion:[8] since their memory of the troubles of the captivity was keen and fresh, only lately being freed from it and in a position to return home, he was right to remind them of the recent calamity before any other remark so that they might be preserved by mention of what had happened from being forced to have the same experience again. You are aware, the implication is, of the awful punishment that in my anger I inflicted on your fathers, and the extent of the troubles I forced them to experience as a result of disobedience, removing them from their own country and taking them off as captives to a foreign land that they had never seen before. The consequence? *You will say to them, The Lord almighty says this: Turn to me, says the Lord of hosts, and I shall turn to you, says the Lord of hosts. Do not behave like your fathers, whom the prophets in the past upbraided in the words, The Lord almighty says this, Turn away from your evil ways and from your evil pursuits. They did not listen, and did not give themselves to hearkening to me, says the Lord almighty* (vv.3–5): now at any rate stop [500] imitating your ancestors, set your eyes on me and keep your gaze directed at the words spoken and the advice given to you by me so that I may choose to watch over you and keep your affairs in my care. Avoid all imitation of your ancestors, who were the recipients of much constant advice and exhortation from the prophets of former times to abstain from their wickedness and avoid the punishment for their evil actions, but they refused to heed or set any store by their teachers.

Where are your fathers? Surely the prophets will not live forever? Only accept my words and my laws such as I command in my spirit to

---

"son of Iddo"—so who was his father, Berechiah or Iddo? Theodore's LXX text has Zechariah as son of Berechiah *and* son of Iddo—an anomaly he prefers to let pass without comment.

8. Theodore anticipates the question of a modern commentator like Smith, "Why did Zechariah or an editor begin his book with a call to repentance?" He was unlikely to give Smith's response, "Repentance was a prominent theme in Jeremiah and Ezekiel, who were Zechariah's models," preferring logic to scriptural cross-referencing.

my servants the prophets, who restrained your fathers (vv.5–6): admittedly you might well reckon that neither your fathers nor the prophets are still alive, the common lot of death overtaking the one group and the other, not allowing their life to be extended any further. But whereas the former suffered the penalty for disobedience and departed, the prophets, though leaving this life, showed by their deeds the truth of their words, since even after their death what they said had no less effect, being spoken in accord with my will. It would have been proper for you not to ignore this or to regard as idle what was said by me through the prophets, and rather to accept everything they say to you through spiritual grace, since nothing of what is said by them could be false, nor is it without risk for you to choose to ignore what is said by them.

Since the facts adequately confirmed the truth of what was said, pricked by these words the people were right to reply by giving a clear manifestation of their responsiveness. For it says, *They replied in these words, As the Lord almighty has ordained to treat us according to our ways and according to our behavior, so has he treated us* (the word *has ordained* meaning "had ordained": he was referring not to the present but to the past): we admit that whatever God decreed should happen to us, delivering a decree in keeping with our actions, we did experience so as to be convinced that the truth of what is said by God is irrefutable, and it is not without risk for us to want to ignore what is said by him.

After these words were said in this manner, the prophet then recounts a revelation given him by God, from which he for his part acquired firm confidence in the good things pertaining to the people and also confidently passed on the good news of the visions to the listeners. He spoke as follows. *On the twenty-fourth day of the eleventh month, which is Shebat, in the second year of Darius, the word of the Lord came to Zechariah, son of Berechiah, son of Iddo, the prophet, in these words* (v.7). The phrase *The word of the Lord came* means, I was accorded a divine revelation.[9] From this point he goes on to mention the revelation, *I saw in the night*

9. Theodore is not going to go to the trouble of ferreting out the significance of Shevat, which occurs only here in the OT as the Babylonian name for the eleventh month.

(v.8). It was not [501] the word of the Lord, nor did the Lord intend to say *I saw in the night:* obviously it is the prophet speaking.[10] By these words, then, he indicated that a divine revelation had come to him, and in them he describes what the revelation was—hence the statement, *I saw in the night,* meaning, I had such and such a revelation. Then he also says what it was like: *Lo, a man riding a red horse, and he stopped in the middle of the shady mountains, and behind him horses red, piebald, and white. I asked, What are they, Lord? The angel who was talking with me said to me, I shall show you what they are. The man standing amidst the mountains replied, saying to me, They are those whom the Lord sent to roam the earth. They replied to the angel of the Lord standing amidst the mountains, saying, We roamed all the earth, and lo, all the earth is inhabited and is at peace* (vv.8–11). It is quite clear that all the things shown to the prophet were tokens of certain realities, just as Joseph saw sheaves, sun, moon, and stars, each of which carried a clue to some coming event, and the Pharaoh saw ears of corn and oxen, some fat and some skinny,[11] and by these as well other events were signified from what was shown. In exactly the same way the prophet also sees these things by divine revelation, and each of the things shown him contained some sign or indication of a reality. Likewise blessed Peter also saw a cloth let down from heaven, full of various living creatures clean and unclean, and the vision contained a clue to some other things.[12] In the same way blessed Zechariah also in describing the revelation mentions before anything else that that he saw a man riding a red horse, and he stopped in the middle of the shady mountains.

10. If not prepared to engage in ἀκριβολογία to the extent of hunting up details like Shevat, Theodore is at least prepared to comment on the inconsistency in details of expression involving the giver and the recipient of the words/visions. He did not think it worth pursuing in the more obvious case of Jonah, where comment on the distinction between author and central character would have been in order.

11. See Gn 37.7, 9; 41.17–24. Some forms of the LXX (Theodoret's text among them) include a fourth horse here, dappled in color, probably influenced by the four horses in ch 6.

12. See Acts 10.11–12. Theodore could be less repetitive in making these comparisons.

Now, the statement of certain commentators, characterized by extreme error and stupidity, and not innocent of impiety, is to the effect that he saw the Son of God here, it being obvious that none of those who lived before the coming of Christ the Lord knew of Father and Son, none knew that God the Father is the father of God the Son, that God the Son is the son of God the Father, being what the Father is, in that he draws existence from him.[13] While terminology for father and son [504] is to be found in the Old Testament, since God is commonly called father for his care when people are shown attention from that source, and they are called sons in having something more on the basis of relationship with God, yet absolutely no one of those living at that time understood God the Father to be father of God the Son, as I said before, or God the Son to be son of God the Father. You see, the people before the coming of Christ the Lord in their religious knowledge were aware only of God and creation, identifying God as eternal in being and as cause of everything, and creation (to put it in a nutshell) as what was brought by him from nonbeing to being.

A sufficient demonstration of this could be gained from the blessed apostles, who at the coming of Christ the Lord were in his company for a long time, but while confessing him to be Christ, which they knew through much instruction, did not understand him to be Son of God, for the reason I have given, except to the extent that they called the Christ God's son in a special way in the manner of the holy and righteous people in olden times. Hence Philip says to the Lord, "Show us your Father, and it is enough for us," which he would not have said if he had understood who the Son is and who the Father is, fully realizing that the divine nature is invisible. Hence the Lord says

13. Theodore felt it necessary in comment on the term "spirit" in Hg 2.5 to reject the idea that people in OT times knew of a Holy Spirit; his relatively irenic approach to the idea suggested he knew of no predecessors who expounded it. Here, by contrast, where the Son is involved, and also the Father, he is aware—and typically intolerant—of people holding the view that the OT knew of the Trinity, a view for which editor Mai cites Hippolytus, Apollinaris, and Eusebius, and thinks Theodore may have had specifically in mind the reference to Christ appearing in Jerome's *Comm Zec* 1.9, under the influence of Didymus. Smith cites more recent interpreters following Jerome's view.

to him, "So much time have I been with you, and you do not know me, Philip?" proving that he did not know him whom he thought he knew. This was the reason he asks also to see the Father, hankering after something impossible. So he goes on, "Whoever has seen me has seen the Father,"[14] bringing out that in his divinity he is what the Father is, invisible like him, and sight of one is also sight of the other. Elsewhere the Lord says more clearly to them, "I have told you this in parables, but the time is coming when I shall no longer speak to you in parables, but shall openly report to you on the Father," bringing out that they had heard word of the Father obscurely, taking it in human fashion, but they would truly know the Son when they knew him to be God in his being, coming from him, and one in being with him.[15] If, on the other hand, the prophets and [505] all those in olden times understood Father and Son, and learnt it from the divine Scriptures, the apostles would have learnt it before the others; it is clear, however, that they did not understand it, but came to know of it when they received the grace of the Spirit coming upon them after the ascension of Christ the Lord into heaven. Hence also the Lord says to them, "I have many things yet to say, but you cannot bear them now; when that Spirit of truth comes, however, he will guide you in all truth."[16] But if they understood the divinity of the Only-begotten, and especially a Father who is God the Father of God, what more than this would there have been that they were due to learn later? Consequently, neither did anyone of the people before the coming of Christ the Lord understand the divinity of Christ the Lord, nor does any of the prophets speak about it.

That claim is also characterized by utter stupidity, or more truthfully insanity, that when the Old Testament mentions an angel of the Lord, it refers by this to the Son of God. We should

14. Jn 14.8–9. Editor Mai refutes Theodore's position about the apostles' lack of understanding of Jesus' divinity by reference to Peter's confession in Mt 16.16 including the phrase "the Son of the living God" (a phrase not found in the parallel passages in Mark and Luke—a fact known to Theodore?), and cites many Fathers in support.

15. Jn 16.25. Theodore is insisting on the ὁμοούσιον of the Son without citing that term or the language of Nicea or Constantinople generally.

16. Jn 16.12–13.

therefore also respect the statement of blessed Paul distinguishing the Son from the angels and showing that the difference between one and the other is as great as between master and servant. So he puts it this way, "While of the angels he says, 'He makes his angels winds, and his servants flames of fire,' of the Son, 'Your throne, O God, is for ages of ages, a rod of righteousness is the rod of your kingship,'"[17] bringing out the degree of difference between the Son and the angels, and the fact that even these words cannot be compared with one another. That is, while the invisible powers that are given the role of service are rightly called angels and servants for the reason of their service, and on this basis they are comparable, the Son does not admit of such terms, properly accepting only this sentiment, "Your throne, O God, is for ages of ages, a rod of righteousness is the rod of your kingship," which has the sense of Eternal king, Lord of all, governing everything with utter righteousness. How, then, would it not be stupid and insane, when such a great difference is illustrated to us by blessed Paul, to presume to combine what cannot be combined, and to claim that both angel and Lord can be called Son?

It is quite clear, however, that whenever such a matter is dealt with in the divine Scripture, there is mention of an angel being assigned for the service of those in question, since "they are all ministering spirits sent for service for the benefit of those due to inherit salvation," as blessed Paul says.[18] Now, he calls it *Lord*, not referring to the angels in this way, but attributing the effect of what happens to God, just as the prophets also frequently mention things appropriate to God, not claiming for themselves what is said but attributing their cause to God. You could see this in the very same text in the case of the present prophet: after saying, *A word of the Lord came to Zechariah in the words,* he went on, *The Lord was very angry with your fathers.* Admittedly, it would have been logical for him to say, *A word of the Lord came to Zechariah saying, I am angry with your fathers,* so that the word of the Lord that came to the prophet should not

17. Heb 1.7–8, citing Pss 104.4, 45.6.
18. Heb 1.14.

appear to refer to some other lord as angry. It is quite clear, however, that after mentioning the one revealing by the phrase *A word of the Lord came,* the prophet then adds the words that God himself said, not using his own but inserting those spoken by God. In just the same way, when he mentions the *angel* and then uses the name *Lord,* he points to the minister by the word *angel,* and by the word *Lord* to the one directing those things to be done through the angels. It is quite clear, in fact, however, in appearing to people when God wishes, angels normally take the form of human beings, this being suited to the witnesses and those receiving instruction. You could find this happening no less in the New Testament as well: in describing the events of the resurrection of Christ the Lord, the divine Scripture says an angel was seen rolling back the stone, and then describes what it was like and how it appeared. "Its form was like lightning and its clothes white as snow,"[19] it says. And after the ascension of the Lord into heaven, when the disciples were gaping at the novelty of what happened, "Lo," it says, "two men stood by in white clothing": they were angels instructing them in how they should interpret the events.[20] In exactly the same way here, too, he beholds an angel in the form of a human being sent by grace for service in those things to do with human salvation.

Appearances suggested an angel, therefore, whereas what accompanied him was indicative of realities: he was *mounted on a horse* as a sign of the speed that is a characteristic of the invisible powers that God commands; it was *red* to bring out the anger he felt on their behalf against the foreigners. He stopped *in the middle of shady mountains*—*mountains* declaring the loftiness and solidity of the ministering power,[21] *shady* conveying an indication of the shade God promised to provide his own people. The prophet asks, then, *What are these?* when the revelation encourages the question so that the instruction might lead somewhere. *The angel speaking within me replied, I shall show you what they are,* meaning the same man he saw mounted on the

19. Mt 28.2–3.
20. Acts 1.10–11.
21. The LXX arrives at "mountains" by reading a form similar to Heb. "myrtles"; but Theodore can still rationalize it.

red horse—hence his saying *who was talking with me*, since he heard a voice not coming from outside but impressed on his mind by revelation, just as blessed Peter heard the words, "Get up, Peter, kill and eat":[22] obviously such a voice did not come to him from the sky, or knowledge of what was said would have filled the whole world, the voice rather being impressed on him as if it had come to him from heaven.

Now, the fact that by the angel speaking to him he refers to the one mounted on the red horse is clear: after saying, *I shall show you what they are*, he goes on, *The man standing amidst the mountains replied, saying to me, They are those whom the Lord sent to roam the earth*, clearly indicating that the man who appeared to him amidst the shady mountains was the same as the one talking to him, who promised to teach him what the horses had to do with it. He actually went on to teach him that they are the ones normally sent by God to patrol the whole earth and perform a service appropriate to each place according to God's decision. It is quite clear, then, that he is talking about angels, this being a task for angels, and by this he does not mean horses, since the vision of the angels was not changed into an apparition of brute beasts. Instead, when he says *horses red, piebald, and white* he mentions the horses to highlight their being seen with some riders. Hence the interpreter also, in saying they were *sent to roam the earth*, means not the horses but the riders. Also, in being angels, they were necessarily seen on horseback, like the one mounted on the red horse, *horses* suggesting the rapidity of the service. Now, some were *red* for the anger they felt against the foreigners, and some were *white* as a reminder of the splendor that would invest the Israelites as a result of their service, while others were *piebald*, a reference to the diversity of the action and ministry that the angels perform in inflicting punishment on those liable and providing gifts to such people as God wishes to reward.[23]

---

22. Acts 10.13.

23. Despite admissions by commentators from Jerome to the present day of the obscurity of the prophecy, Theodore is typically definite in assigning meanings to all the realities, πράγματα, mentioned, even if we have seen that he can be equally definite in dismissing those too much bent on ἀκριβολογία.

The proof of what we said is given in what follows. *They replied to the angel of the Lord standing in the midst of the mountains, saying, We roamed the whole earth and, lo, the whole earth is inhabited and is at peace.* He did not say the horses replied: how could a voice come from horses? Instead, it is clear that he is referring to the riders of the horses, who appeared in the form of a human being, like the one appearing amidst the shady mountains on the red horse, and were about to hold a conversation with him related to the vision; the prophet by revelation heard what was said and received instruction from it. It is obvious, you see, that the whole revelation and what was seen in it as well as question, answer, and suchlike were all products of the imagination in the revelation, the result being that the prophet received instruction from it all, and he both personally gained a firm trust in the future events and also imparted the benefit to others.[24]

Now, it is likely that the rider on the horse between the mountains refers to the angel presiding over the nation of the Israelites, according to the statement, "He set up boundaries [512] of nations according to the number of the angels of God."[25] The other angels, who presumably shared the responsibility, spoke of the aforegoing matters, and also mentioned to him that the whole earth was in a state of peace at that time. The angel in question, who was seen amidst the shady mountains, in being entrusted with the care of the people and being somewhat troubled by the fact that with everything else at peace Jerusalem's affairs alone were disturbed, took occasion to offer to God prayer and supplication for the whole nation. *The angel of the Lord*—the one who was standing amidst the mountains, while the others said the whole earth was inhabited

24. Theodore has no difficulty with the prophets receiving oracles from the Lord and transmitting them; his notion of prophetic inspiration we have seen approximating even that of pagan seers (as in explicating the sense of λῆμμα as ecstatic trance in the case of Nahum). Zechariah's visions represent a different charism from mere oracle, and closer to ecstasy; and, literalist that he is, and feeling something of the unease he experienced in dealing with the "novel and extraordinary things" in the book of Jonah, he feels the need to justify the process of ἀποκάλυψις in which πράγματα are conveyed through visions and tokens, γνωρίσματα.

25. Dt 32.8 LXX.

and at peace—*replied saying, Lord almighty, how long will you re-frain from showing mercy to Jerusalem and the cities of Judah, which you have scorned for seventy years?* (v.12) as if to say, you provided secure habitation and peace to all other nations throughout the earth and arranged for them to live in that condition, whereas it appears that your Jerusalem alone and the other cities of Judah do not enjoy this common gift. But since their sins were the cause of this for them, their devotion to impiety and their disobedience, heal their condition with mercy, have regard for the number of years in which they suffered these calamities, and consider as sufficient punishment for their sins the troubles besetting them in that period. Cancel their sins with your characteristic mercy and restore to them their former prosperity so that Jerusalem may be inhabited as before and the other cities of Judah may come into existence again.[26]

He continues in the same vein, *The Lord almighty replied in kind words and consoling expressions to the angel who was talking to me* (v.13). He brings out also through this that such was the prayer of the one amidst the shady mountains who was talking to him; he says God replied to him in words full of great good-ness, containing the promise of many good things, sufficient to provide every comfort to those in so many extreme necessities. Gaining confidence from them, the angel discloses to the prophet all that had been said by God that contained promise of wonderful goods, which he would later demonstrate in re-gard to Jerusalem. He says this, *The angel speaking within me said to me, Shout aloud these words, Thus says the Lord almighty: I am jeal-ous for Zion and Jerusalem with a great jealousy, I am angry with a great anger against the nations who attack her. In response to my being a little angry, they joined in creating troubles. Hence the Lord says this, I shall return to Jerusalem in compassion, and my house will be rebuilt in it, says the Lord almighty, and a measure shall be extended again over Jerusalem. The angel who was talking to me said to me, Shout aloud these words, Thus says the Lord almighty: Cities will again over-flow with good things, and the Lord will again have mercy on Zion,*

---

26. His readers might have expected Theodore to comment on the signifi-cance of seventy years, a figure found also in other prophets.

and will again choose Jerusalem (vv.14–17). Receiving such a reply from God, he is saying, the angel was personally [515] over-joyed at the words and bade me take heart for the future so as to be emboldened to disclose to everyone that he was very an-gry over Jerusalem with those who gave evidence of such feroci-ty to them. In their malice, he is saying, they inflicted a punish-ment on them more severe than my anger; so for the sake of all I shall show great mercy to Jerusalem so that my house that is in it may provide the customary benefit to those assembling in it, Jerusalem may be extended beyond its present limits, and in short all the cities belonging to it may attain abundance of many goods. At that time, you see, I shall show it great mercy; I have decided for the future to do what is of benefit to it and those belonging to it.

Now, it is obvious that when he says, *I am angry against the na-tions who attack her, in return for my being a little angry they joined in creating troubles,* he is referring to the Babylonians sacking her and those who joined with them in that exploit at the time, and thus suggests the punishment to befall them. The Babylonians, in fact, had already paid the penalty and their kingdom had been overturned, the city had been completely taken over by Cyrus king of the Persians, while the Idumeans and all the oth-ers who were their allies had been punished.[27] So it is clear, as was said by us on the theme, that God mentions many things that had already happened and thus confirms them with his promises. The Israelites at that time needed them, being uncer-tain of their salvation even after the return, the result being that having begun the divine Temple they could not bring it to completion, either through the hindrance from the adversaries or also through their own indolence, which probably was aug-mented by the enemies' malice.

He said he had learnt two things from the revelation, that God would punish those wronging the people, and that he would restore Jerusalem to its former prosperity. In confirma-

27. Theodore is thinking of the overthrow of Idumea as having by 520 already occurred, though the Nabateans only completed this in the fourth cen-tury.

tion of both, however, he unfolds other revelations; having seen them personally, he had unshakable confidence in what was said, and convinced all the people to believe likewise. He describes the former, which is to do with the punishment of the adversaries, having mentioned it first in the preceding revelation. *I raised my eyes, and behold, I saw four horns. I said to the angel speaking within me, What are these, Lord? He said to me, They are the horns that scattered Judah, Israel, and Jerusalem.*[28] *The Lord showed me four smiths. I said, What are they coming to do, Lord? He said, They are the horns that scattered Judah and Israel, and they shattered them, and no one can raise their head; they went out to sharpen them in their hands. The four horns are the nations lifting up a horn against the land of the Lord to scatter it* (vv.18–21). Some commentators who indulge in fairy tales claim the *four horns* are the Assyrians, Babylonians, Medes, and Persians, [516] unprepared as they are to heed the fact that often the divine Scripture cites a number not to be precise about number but as a symbol of something else, and they try to fit names to the number. They are probably forced to spin fairy tales in composing their fictions, something they often fall victim to elsewhere, and especially in the case of the prophecy of blessed Micah that says, "Seven shepherds will be raised against him, and eight bites of human beings":[29] they strive to list seven people as the shepherds and eight people as the bites, forced on this account to utter a great deal that is deserving of ridicule. In the same way here, too, they claim the four horns to be what we mentioned before, not giving due thought to the fact that Assyrians and Babylonians had paid the penalty in the past, Medes had been destroyed by Cyrus, while Persians are found to have done them no harm at all, but on the contrary had released them from captivity.

28. There are some discrepancies in these vv. between the Heb., the LXX, and Theodore's text. In v.19 not all LXX forms contain "Jerusalem"; Smith strangely comments, "'Israel' is not in the LXX . . . many scholars take it as a gloss." In v.21 LXX adds "Israel" to "Judah," unlike the Heb., and its version reads differently from Heb.

29. Mi 5.5 (where, in fact, the LXX has evidently misread "rulers" as "bites"), an instance already cited also with some heat in the introduction to the book. As mentioned before, the fate of the Medes under Cyrus has been misrepresented.

Now, by *four horns* the divine Scripture is not referring to specific people; instead, since we say the world is divided into four quarters, east and west, north and south, it often mentions these regions to suggest what is happening in many places, as when blessed David says of the Israelites, "Let them say, those redeemed by the Lord, whom he redeemed from the hand of the foe, and assembled them from their hands, from east and west, from the north and from the sea."[30] It is obvious, you see, that God did not assemble the Israelites who were scattered to the four quarters of the world, and returned them to their own land when held captive by Babylonians and Assyrians alone; instead, Scripture means by the phrase, "from east and west, from north and from the sea," that he gathered together those scattered in many directions and brought them back home. Likewise, then, in this case, too, he mentions *four horns* in the sense of those who had attacked from many directions and intended to harm them in many ways, whether Assyrians, Babylonians, Idumeans, Moabites, even the other neighbors or anybody else whatsoever. For this reason he gazes also at *four smiths* in the sense of the ministering powers for the reason that they inflict punishment on them from many sources, each exacting vengeance of them in accordance with the divine decree. He speaks of *sharpening* the horns in the sense of reducing them and doing away with all their importance, meaning to remove the power accompanying the attackers.[31]

Chapter Two

Having confirmed by the revelation the punishment of those who wronged the Israelites, the prophet cites a different revelation given him that suggests the restoration of Jerusalem. He speaks in the following terms, *I lifted my eyes and saw and, lo,*

---

30. Ps 107.2. Theodoret—perhaps influenced by Theodore—will simply state the conclusion the latter reaches on the four horns, without any of the satire of alternative views. He deserves Bardy's epithet "modéré."

31. Again the LXX is reading a different form from our Heb. "terrify." Reference to the smith at work in Is 54.16–17 would have illuminated the text here.

a man, and in his hand a surveyor's cord. I said to him, Where are you
going? He replied to me, To measure Jerusalem so as to see the extent of
its breadth and length. [517] *And, lo, the angel speaking within me*
stood by, and a different angel came out to meet him, and said to him,
Run and tell that young man, Jerusalem will be inhabited prolifically
with crowds of people and cattle in its midst. I shall be for it a wall of
fire all around, says the Lord, I shall be its glory in its midst (vv.1–5).
Since those working on buildings normally use a cord to measure the breadth and length of the land and the outlines of the
building, he necessarily sees the angel, who as usual is once
more in human form, holding such a cord. When asked in the
revelation happening to the prophet where he was going, he
said he was going to measure the building of Jerusalem, and
the kind and extent it should be. He next says to the angel
speaking within him, whom above he saw seated in human
form on a red horse amidst the shady mountains (it was clear to
us in the preceding section that it was the same angel he saw
standing amidst the mountains and also speaking within him)
—this one he now says he saw standing by as though pleased
with what was happening and that his prayer to God had been
answered (the prayer he had offered to God for Jerusalem and
the nation), not only by the proof that punishment had been
imposed on those who had wronged them, but also by the apparition of the surveyor's cord as a sign of the rebuilding of the
city now being in operation. He next says that a different angel
was sent and told him to speak to the young man—obviously
the one holding the surveyor's cord:[32] he referred to him this
way because by revelation the prophet saw the young man revealed in a vision as an indication that what was proposed
would be brought to fulfillment in its entirety. So the angel who
was sent, the text says, told the angel who was speaking within
me to run at speed and tell the young man that with very great
affluence Jerusalem would be inhabited and crowded with both

32. We have observed before that, as Theodore can be impatient with search
after detail, so he is anything but tentative in his interpretation of the visions.
This contrasts with the approach of modern commentators, Smith remarking,
"Ambiguity still prevails in this vision. The identity of the man with the measuring line is not clear."

people and the cattle serving them, so that with this knowledge
he would extend the breadth and length of the city that was required for the great number of its inhabitants. We shall provide
it, the text says, with greater security than would be provided by
a wall of fire that is capable of incinerating the attackers. I shall
reveal myself in the events themselves through my care for
them so as to enjoy the praise and commendation of everyone
for the magnitude of favors conferred on them.

Now, the meaning of that phrase *in the midst* also needs looking to, namely, where it says that the angel who was sent to the
angel that was speaking within him, that is, to the one mounted
on the red horse in the midst of the mountains, said, *Run and
tell that young man.* If according to those intent on spinning
fairy stories the one that appeared in the midst of the shady
mountains was the Son of God, how could the angel presume
to tell him, *Run and tell that young man, Jerusalem will be inhabited
prolifically?* It would, after all, [520] be out of the question for
an angel to give orders to the Son of God, and to believe it
would be the mark of extreme impiety.[33] Nothing remarkable,
on the other hand, for an angel to indicate to an angel what
has to be done, since it is normal for servants to tell one another of the master's wishes, and much more so for those sent for
that purpose by the Lord of all, as happens in this case as well.
That is to say, with the angel that talked to him offering prayer
for the city, it was right for the angel sent by God's will to run to
him and bid him tell the young man what was required, like
bringing the good news that his prayer had been answered and
God's will for Jerusalem had taken a turn for the better, and
that he should carry out with pleasure what was bidden him
now that he was strengthened by what he had begged from
God, and with great haste inform the one sent on the rebuilding of God's decisions about it.

The prophet, in fact, was necessarily filled with confidence
on the basis of what had been revealed, and he cried aloud in

33. Is the phrase "in the midst" critical to his argument, or simply the notion
that commands could be issued by an angel to Christ masquerading as an angel,
an identification made by Jerome, as observed in n. 13?

the words, *O, O flee from the land of the North, says the Lord, because I shall assemble you from the four winds of heaven, says the Lord; save yourselves in Zion, you who dwell in daughter of Babylon* (vv.6–7). He bids the rest of those still in captivity to set out from there with great haste to Mount Zion, trusting in what was promised concerning Jerusalem by God, who pledged to assemble them from all directions to Zion. Here, of course, once again the phrase *from the four winds* suggests not a particular number but from all directions, to the effect that those of the Jews still living in the country of the Babylonians might all head for Jerusalem, where as residents they will have a firm hope of salvation for the future, with God protecting them in accord with his promises, because at that time—namely, the time when Darius was king—Babylon had been destroyed and all the power of the Babylonians had come to an end. Nevertheless, his prophecy concerns those who at that time would return: not a few did return under Darius, but he bids them return home from Babylon, that is, the captivity they suffered at the hands of the Babylonians. Now, it is obvious that he delivers his prophecy of the future as a command.

Because the Lord almighty says this, In the wake of glory he sent me to the nations despoiling you, because the one touching you touches the apple of his eye. Hence I lift my hand against them, and they will be plunder even for the slaves, and you will know that the Lord almighty sent me (vv.8–9): I tell you what has been said since I am bidden by the words of God, who sent me to inform you of the glory and the magnitude of his power, of which he will give evidence against those who wrong you.[34] He is as angry with those who wish to harm you as he would be if anyone were to harm the apple of his eye (obviously meaning in human fashion the special object of his care). I shall inflict on your foes such severe punishment that they will be captured [521] and plundered by those whom previously they held in the condition of slaves. The result is that is that from the events themselves it is clear

---

34. "In the wake of glory he sent me" Smith classes "the most puzzling clause in the book," but again Theodore shows no hesitancy in coming up wih a paraphrase. He does well in explaining the rare phrase "apple of his eye," without documenting it even from Ps 17.8.

that by the will of God the Lord of all I bring you this good news.

Next, he directs his discourse also to the city, calling Jerusalem *daughter Zion* as usual. *Rejoice and be glad, daughter Zion, because, Lo, I am coming, and I shall dwell in your midst, says the Lord* (v.10): Be pleased from now on, for you will have my care as a sign of me in your midst. *Many nations will have recourse to the Lord on that day, they will be a people to me, and they will dwell in your midst, and you will know that the Lord almighty has sent me to you. The Lord will inherit Judah as his portion in the holy land, and will still choose Jerusalem* (vv.11–12): I shall give evidence of such great care for you that even many of the foreigners will have recourse to you, confessing me as their own God once I have been made known by you; they will leave their own places and choose a dwelling for themselves among you on account of my care. At that time most of all you will know me as I bring you this good news by the will of God the Lord of all, who will restore to Judah its former portion of the land, and make all of Jerusalem splendid in the eyes of everyone.[35]

He then goes on in the same vein, *Let all flesh show reverence before the Lord, because he has roused himself from his holy clouds* (v.13): and so it is fitting for everyone, both his own people and foreigners, now to be in dread of God, who from the places on high, in which he normally dwells and which he renders holy from his dwelling there, is active in coming to your help. It behoves all his own people to fear him lest they sin, and the foreigners lest in the future they make any attempt against those belonging to him.

---

35. Theodore, like some modern commentators, could clarify for his readers who it is that is speaking in these verses. The term "holy land," a unique occurrence in the OT, could also come in for comment. If he seems to adopt an unusually parenetic tone in commenting on the following verse, it may be that the LXX's finding "clouds" in a similar Heb. form for "habitation" has misled him.

Chapter Three

Having with these revelations thus confirmed what was disclosed in the former revelation, namely, that he would punish the adversaries and would bring prosperity on Jerusalem and all the Jews belonging to her, he turns to other revelations required by the present situation. Being in captivity, you see, they were deprived of both king and priest, who were needed for the constitution of the nation—the king meeting their needs in wartime and the conduct of other affairs, and the priest to preside over prayer and supplication and the whole of worship due to God. This is what the prophet Hosea also predicted, "Because for many days the sons of Israel will stay without a ruler, without sacrifice, without altar, without priesthood, without insignia."[36] God shows the prophet through the present revelation as instruction for the whole people that these things that are needed first and foremost for the constitution of the community, and of which they were naturally deprived in captivity, will now be restored to them by God in that the city together with the nation is due to recover its distinctive decor.

He speaks thus, [524] *The Lord showed me Joshua the high priest standing before the angel of the Lord, and the devil stood at his right hand to oppose him. The Lord said to the devil, May the Lord rebuke you, devil, may the Lord who has chosen Jerusalem rebuke you. Lo, is not this like a brand plucked from a fire? Joshua was clad in soiled garments, and stood before the angel. He said in reply to those standing before him, Take the soiled garments off him, and to him he said, Lo, I have removed your offenses from you. Clothe him in a frock, and put a headband and a clean turban on his head. They clothed him in garments, and put a headband and a clean turban on his head* (vv.1–5).[37] He necessarily sees in the person of the priest the restoration of the priesthood for the reason that priesthood is not visible in itself but in those assigned to participate in it. So he sees Joshua the high priest (calling him *high* because per-

36. Hos 3.4. Theodore anticipates the objections of some modern scholars to the placement of this fourth vision, predictably justifying its occurrence here.

37. The Antiochene text includes mention of a headband as well as the clean turban in v.5.

forming worship is proper to Aaron by right of succession) standing near the angel because angels are entrusted with authority over all human beings, as the Lord says in the Gospels, "Their angels gaze constantly on the face of my Father in heaven," and in the Acts of the blessed apostles, "It is his angel" in reference to blessed Peter.[38] Of necessity also he appears *before the angel*, that is, the one entrusted by divine decree with his care. The devil also stands there to oppose him, his role being to act in opposition to the good of human beings; he made every effort at that time (it is saying) to abuse him, to expel him from the duties assigned him, which he was unable to perform in captivity. It says that God, who had chosen Jerusalem, rebuked him, to bring out that all the devilish opposition had been brought to an end by God's care, who chose Jerusalem and necessarily thus restores also the dignity of the priesthood.

The phrase *Lo, is not this like a firebrand plucked from the fire?* means, just as if someone plucked out and kept unharmed a piece of wood on the point of being consumed by fire, so this man, put in dire straits by captivity as though in a fire and almost at risk of being set alight by it, he plucked out and freed from the troubles besetting him. Now, Joshua was clad in soiled garments, meaning, overwhelmed as he was by grief at their captivity, in which he passed his days kept from the divine liturgy, reduced to oppressive slavery, God ordered him to be relieved of it by the bystanders, that is, by the powers involved in liturgical ministry, in that [525] they ministered to the divine commands and removed the clothing of his captivity and all that grief, and brought him back to his own city. Then, when this happened, he said to him, *I have removed all your offenses*, implying that the troubles of the captivity have been canceled, since he annuled the memory of the sins. He then goes on to bid him be clad in the frock and have the headband and mitre

38. Mt 18.10, Acts 12.15. We saw in Theodore's lengthy disquisition on "spirit" on Hg 2.5 the Antiochenes' interest in and regard for angels, something Theodoret also concedes. This is a factor in his taking the διάβολος, with which the LXX renders "the Satan" of the Heb. (a member of the heavenly council we find also in Job), not strictly as "the false accuser" (Smith) but simply as one of the devils who act as negative counterparts of the angels.

put on him as a sign of the return of the authority of the priesthood to him for the future, and this happened to him by divine
agreement.[39]

After saying this, the prophet adds the following words as a
sign of the restoration of the priesthood to them and of the
priest's being presented once more in the customary liturgy
with necessary confidence and authority for the task. *The angel
of the Lord said to Joshua, The Lord almighty says this: If you walk in
my ways and keep my commandments, you will also have the power to
make decisions in my house. If you guard my court, I shall give you
those dwelling in the midst of these attendants* (vv.6–7). Logically he
mentions this being addressed to the one who had assumed the
authority of priesthood so that he might know how to participate in worship. If you persevere in paying attention to what is
commanded by me, he is saying, you will continue to judge
everyone with the authority of a priest; and by providing due
custody of my court with your characteristic diligence, you will
hand on the office to your successors, who in the midst of all
the people will be performing the due rites for them. Then,
suggesting also the restoration of the king,[40] he says, *Listen,
Joshua the high priest, you and those close to you seated before you, for
they are seers* (v.8), meaning, My words are for you and all those
with you who are entrusted with ruling the people by instruction and explanation of laws and other forms of ministry in
matters pertaining to cult. He refers to them as *seers* for being
capable of discerning and understanding the causes of what is
done in puzzling fashion by God.

*Because, lo, I bring my servant Dawn. Hence a stone that I have set
before Joshua, and on the one stone are seven eyes* (vv.8–9): I bring my
servant—namely, Zerubbabel—and I reinstate him to the kingship, presenting him as no less splendid than the dawn in its au-

39. Theodore has done his best to comment on the features of the vision,
perhaps only losing the sense of any guilt involved by reducing the Satan to a
mere devil.

40. For better or worse, Theodoret is bent on finding in the following verses
evidence for the restoration of the monarchy under Zerubbabel (as the LXX's
misreading in Haggai so encouraged him). Finding such evidence in v.8 is surely a case of drawing the long bow.

thority.[41] I set him like some stone before your eyes, and on him you must be fastened, providing him the help from prayers and from priesthood, on the one hand, and, on the other, acquiring from him the zeal that he displays against the adversaries so that you may properly discharge the priesthood by living in peace. You ought have confidence in this stone, thinking it has seven eyes. Now, in this case too he does not intend a chase for precision about numbers;[42] instead, he means, Appointed by me to the kingship, Zerubbabel will manage this because I shall provide him in large measure with my ineffable providence and attention. What more will come of it? [528] *Lo, I dig a ditch, says the Lord almighty, and I shall feel about for all that iniquity in that day:* this is the way I shall make him capable of turning back all the enemy with his skill, and enveloping them in destruction as though in some ditch through my punishment of the wrong they chose to commit against the land belonging to me, over which I appointed him to preside as king.

Then, to bring out as well the extent of the assistance they will enjoy as a result of Zerubbabel's leadership, he says, *On that day, says the Lord almighty, each will invite their neighbor under their vine and their figtree* (v.10): whereas the enemy will suffer that fate when he is commander, those belonging to my people will with great satisfaction so enjoy their crops as to invite one another even habitually to a feast.

41. Theodore finds in this passage further evidence for seeing a reference to Zerubbabel, as also in 6.12, in both vv. the LXX reading Ἀνατολή, "Dawn," for Heb. "Branch, Shoot" (as a proper name, Zerubbabel meaning "Shoot of Babylon"). The same difference in readings occurs at Jer 23.5; in his commentary on that place Theodoret, after citing Symmachus's more accurate version βλάστημα, "shoot," expostulates against the Jewish interpretation in favor of Zerubbabel despite his not being a king. Theodoret, probably aware that Luke at 1.78 (probably with Zec in mind) has used ἀνατολή in a messianic sense of Jesus, does not want Zerubbabel in that role. We have seen Theodore reluctant to accept such Christological interpretations. Perhaps also the use of "my servant" of Zerubbabel in Hg 2.23 was a further factor for him.

42. The "seven eyes" puzzle all commentators. Theodore has no difficulty discounting seven with his habitual dismissal of ἀκριβολογία, an idle "chase for precision," and then simply omits the eyes as well to reinforce the Zerubbabel interpretation. He is forced to change his mind about the number in the next chapter.

Chapter Four

Having indicated in this the restoration of the monarchy and the priesthood, he goes on to cite a revelation that was quite necessarily given him on these words. He speaks as follows, *The angel who talked to me came back, woke me up as someone would be woken from sleep, and said to me, What do you see?* (vv.1–2) indicating once again that angel appearing in the form of a human being who talked to him on a red horse amidst the shady mountains. We learnt precisely, in fact, from the above that he is the one he mentions talking to him in every case, and in this case also he woke him up as though fallen asleep with the sight of what was revealed. Again in the case of what was revealed this time he asks what he sees, so that he might describe the vision and the other might bring out the meaning of what was revealed. So he continues, *I said, I see something and, lo, a lampstand all of gold, and a lamp on it, with seven lights on it and seven spouts below its lights; there are two olive trees above it, one on the right of the lamp and one on the left* (vv.2–3). The lampstand is a symbol of divine grace, burning on earth but extending to realities beyond earth in that everything is affected by it; because it is wonderful and illustrious, he saw it as all gold, gold being the most precious of all earthly materials. The lamp on it suggests the light from divine grace shining from on high on everyone on earth. He sees seven lights, indicating the perfection and wealth of grace, as it says above, *On the stone are seven eyes*, referring to the greatness of his special care.[43] Next, olive trees on different sides of the lamp, one on the right, and one on the left, indicating the monarchy and the priesthood, which God set as the highest offices among human beings, in one case for managing what is necessary for the condition of human existence, the other being required for leading people to God.[44]

After telling the angel he had seen these things, the prophet

---

43. Theodore's previous dismissal of a search for the significance of the number seven as an idle exercise of precision he cannot now sustain, and he briefly and appositely settles for the traditional denotation of completeness and perfection (as he does again on v.10).

44. This succinct statement of his belief in the appropriateness and necessity

proceeds, *I put a question to the angel who talked to me in these terms, What are these things, Lord?* [529] *The angel who talked to me replied to me, Do you not know what they are? I said, No, Lord. He replied to me, This is the word of the Lord to Zerubbabel, Not by great might, nor by strength, but by my spirit, says the Lord almighty* (vv.4–6). This angel, whom the prophet says was talking to him, is the one who was also seen making supplication for Jerusalem as being entrusted with authority over all in Judea and necessarily offering prayers to God for them. Hence he is also the one the prophet asks, and gets an answer in each case: since everything revealed contained a sign of God's prodigality regarding both the city and the nation, consequently it was fitting for him to learn from him what each of the things revealed meant. Briefly, therefore, he explained to him the gist of the things revealed, that they were a sign of divine grace, which had made provision for the kingship of Zerubbabel, who could not hold power of his own accord, being appointed by divine grace and holding power through it. Hence to demonstrate the greatness of the gift given to him by grace, since he could achieve nothing by way of the monarchy or governance of the people, *Who are you, great mountain, what can you achieve in the face of Zerubbabel? I shall bring forth the stone of inheritance, equality of its grace* (v.7). Since he called Zerubbabel *stone*, by *great mountain* he refers to those who are most eminent for kingship and the number of soldiers and subjects. Who are you, he asks, who are so great or so very powerful in the number of your subjects and military equipment as to be able to prevail in opposition to Zerubbabel? I appointed him as successor to the royal inheritance, which was the object of the promises I made to the ancestor of the race— namely, David—and I shall fulfil them completely with my grace (the meaning of *equality of its grace,* from which will necessarily accrue to him the ability to achieve great things as general against the adversaries in favor of his own).[45]

---

of spiritual and temporal governance, for Theodore's own community as for the restored community of Judah, may account for his insistence on finding in the text a role for monarch as well as priest.

45. The text hardly supports this consolidation of Zerubbabel as successor to David by divine promise. Admittedly, modern commentators are likewise forced to adopt creative interpretations of the obscure references.

Then in confirmation of the promises about him, *The word of the Lord came to me saying, The hands of Zerubbabel laid the foundations of this house, and his hands will complete it. You will acknowledge that the Lord almighty has sent me to you. Who then has been scornful for a long time?* (vv.8–10) He it is who personally put down the foundations of my house, and he it is who will also bring it to completion, so that it may be clear to everyone also from this that by God's will I came to foretell this to you. Do not, therefore, lose faith in these words even if this is not due to happen for a long time: foolish would be the person who believes my decrees would fail through the passage of time (the meaning of *scornful for a long time*), since I am easily able to do whatever I wish and to bring to completion with great rapidity [532] what requires length of time. In confirmation of his statement, *They will rejoice and will see the tin stone in the hand of Zerubbabel:* do not lose faith in the words, since you will see their fulfillment and rejoice to behold Zerubbabel's great capacity for every task (the meaning of *tin stone*, indicating the power from God that would surround him). Hence he proceeded to give also the reason, *These seven are the eyes of the Lord, which look upon the whole earth:* he who surveys, governs and saves in a rich and diverse manner is the one who both makes these promises regarding Zerubbabel and brings them to completion (*seven* here too denoting perfection).

In reply I asked him, What are these two olive trees on the right of the lampstand and on its left? I asked a second time and said to him, What are the two branches of the olive trees in the hands of the two golden pipes that pour out and bring back the golden cups? He said to me, Do you not know what they are? I said, No, Lord. And he replied, These are the two sons of plenty, who stand in attendance on the Lord of all the earth (vv.11–14). He asks what is meant by the two olive trees, one of which was on the right and one on the left of the lampstand, or the lamp on it, and what is meant by the two branches growing from the olive trees. He was told about them, *These are the two sons of plenty, who stand in attendance on the Lord of all the earth.* Since, you see, the olive trees were tokens of the monarchy and the priesthood, which God had put in charge of the earth, by the two branches of the olive trees he refers to Zerubbabel and Joshua: the former by divine grace succeeded to the kingship, the latter was appointed to divine worship by virtue of the priesthood. Hence he also calls them *sons of plenty*, meaning those who have sprung from the greatest and most honorable ranks of men, monarchy and priesthood, who have all been assigned by the Lord of all to serve God.[46]

In all this the prophet indicated that the situation both of Jerusalem and of the nation of the Jews would take a decisive turn for the better, with their foes being punished and their being accorded great care from God in every event in that others almost beyond counting were on the point of returning from captivity who were to that point still in that condition. As well, the royal and priestly office had been restored to them in the person of those appointed by divine grace to those positions.

Chapter Five

Lest, however, the surpassing disclosure of the good things should result in their becoming more indifferent, trusting in the divine promises while neglecting their duty, he now has a revelation in which fear is instilled into them with a view to shunning the worse way and following in the better. He speaks as follows. *I turned around, lifted up my eyes and looked and, lo, a scythe flying. He said to me, What do you see? I replied, I see a scythe flying,* [533] *twenty cubits in length and ten cubits in breadth. He said to me, This is the curse that issues forth on the face of all the earth, because every thief will be punished from this point to the moment of death, and every perjurer will be punished from this point to the moment of death. I shall bring it forth, says the Lord almighty, and it will enter the house of the thief and the house of the one swearing falsely in my name; it will cause destruction in the middle of his house and topple it, its timbers and its stones* (vv.1–4). He sees a *scythe* capable of cutting from top to bottom whatever it encounters,[47] and *flying*

46. Theodore is typically categorical in his interpretation of a vision generally conceded to be most obscure. His dogmatism might be more specious if he looked for some scriptural support—e.g., the lampstands and olive trees standing before the Lord of all the earth in Rv 11.4.

47. The LXX, in fact, is reading a form for "scythe" similar to our Heb. for

as an indication of the speed of inflicting the divine punishment on those deserving it, and of such breadth and length as also to terrify the listeners by its size.

He says this punishment is directed against thieves and perjurers, though it is obvious that these are not the only transgressions found among human beings, but as well murder, adultery, and others that would not easily be numbered. What, then, does he mean? The divine commandments happen to be divided into these two particular parts, the attitude towards God and the love for the neighbor, as the Lord also said, "You will love the Lord your God with your whole heart, your whole mind, and your whole strength, and you will love your neighbor as yourself," and then added, "On these two commandments depend the whole Law and the Prophets,"[48] thus referring in short to what concerns God and what concerns the neighbor. By perjury as affecting God he refers in brief to all acts of impiety—that is, faults against God—and by theft to that affecting the neighbor: since theft is taking what does not belong to one, he referred in general to all taking of others' property as theft. His purpose was to say in short that this curse is the greatest, most fearsome and threatening thing to anyone, both in offending God or in being a fault against the neighbor. He says also that *it will cause destruction in the middle of his house and will topple it, its timbers and its stones*, meaning, with such a person failing unrepentantly, divine punishment will endure to the point of destroying him along with his possessions.

After terrifying them sufficiently by these words, he brings out in what follows the remission of their sin and the punishment for transgressions so that they may be in a position to know better that, having attained grace for the past, they should more earnestly adhere to God's decisions. Hence he

---

"scroll"; none the wiser (despite Ezekiel's scroll), Theodore can handle the notion of a flying scythe, though without following Didymus into flights of spiritual fancy.

48. Mt 22.37–40. Theodore, like the Lord himself and a myriad pedagogues since, thus presents revealed morality under two heads. He also puts the same question to the text as Smith, "Do these two groups represent offenses against the two parts of the Decalogue?"

proceeds, *The angel speaking within me went out and said to me, Look up with your eyes and see what is this that is coming out. I asked, What is it? He replied, It is the measure that is coming out. He said, This is their iniquity in all the land. And, lo, a leaden weight being lifted up and, lo, one woman was seated in the middle of the measure. He said, She is Lawlessness. He pushed her into the middle of the measure, and pushed the leaden weight on her mouth* (vv.5–8). Once again he sees the same [536] angel bidding him fix his eyes on what seems to be transpiring in the vision. On seeing it the prophet then asked, What is it? He replied that this was the measure of punishment that the Israelites had to endure for their exploits. Next he espies a leaden weight, which is heavy by nature and involves a great weight, and so it thus demonstrates the severity of the punishment. There was a woman sitting on the measure, who he said was *Lawlessness,* the severity of the punishment probably deriving from the lawlessness. He then pushed her into the middle of the measure and put the leaden weight on her mouth to emphasize that he did away with both the sin and the punishment of it at the same time. He put all the severity of the wickedness into her mouth as if to shut it and keep her from plundering, a sign that all faculties had been taken from her and she had not even the power of speech, and such a power of speech had been completely taken from those previously mocking them for what they suffered in being abandoned by God, as blessed David says, "May silence fall on deceitful lips that speak lawlessly against the righteous."[49]

While he saw this, however, as a sign of the total removal of the Israelites' lawless deeds and the punishment for them, he goes on to show that whereas their punishment was removed, it had been transferred to their enemies. *I lifted up my eyes and saw and, lo, two women issuing forth, and a breath in their wings. They*

---

49. Ps 31.18, Theodore tending to accentuate Israel's punishment more than its lawlessness. But he does his best to explain this phantasmagoric vision: without identifying the book as apocalyptic and enumerating its features, he consistently uses ἀποκάλυψις for the visions the prophet receives, realizing the kaleidoscopic scenario presented is not to be taken as factual. He is thus not phased in the way he was affected by the Jonah story, where he felt unable to make the same concession.

had wings like a stork's wings. They lifted up the measure between earth and heaven. I said to the angel who talked to me, Where are they taking the measure? He replied to me, To build a house for it in the land of Babylon and furnish it; they will set it down there on its furnishings (vv.9–11). He then sees in addition two women who flew at great speed (the meaning of *a breath in their wings*, being lifted up by it and making a more rapid journey). The reason he says that their wings were like a stork's wings is because the bird's flight is swift. These women, he says, snatched up that measure of punishment, took it up high, and with great determination took it away as they flew. He said *between earth and heaven* for the reason that for birds flight is easier and faster from on high downwards. I asked, then, he says, where they were going and where they taking the measure, and I learnt from the angel that they were taking it to the land of Babylon, and would build a house for it there, and decide all its location would be there, meaning that he would inflict all the punishment on Babylon, which would remain with them and never be remitted in the way yours gained remission.

Chapter Six

In confirmation of these words, in fact, he proceeds once more, *I turned around, lifted up my eyes, and saw four chariots coming out between two mountains, and the mountains were mountains of bronze. In the first chariot were red horses, in the second chariot black horses, in the third chariot white horses, and in the fourth chariot dappled horses. I asked in reply to the angel speaking within me, What are they, Lord? In reply the angel who talked to me said to me, They are the four winds of heaven issuing forth to attend on the Lord of all the earth. The chariot with the black horses issued forth to the north country, the white issued forth after them, the red issued forth to the south country, the dappled issued forth searching and gazing and roaming the earth. He said, Go and roam the earth, and they roamed the earth. He cried out and called aloud to me, and spoke to me thus, Lo, those issuing forth to the north country have set at rest my anger with the north country* (vv.1–8). He mentions four chariots to suggest the invis-

ible powers stationed in the four regions of the world performing everything to do with the divine will.[50] Hence when the angel was asked by the prophet what they were, he said they were
the four winds of heaven attending on the Lord of all the earth.
That is to say, since we normally refer also to the four quarters
in terms of the winds, he spoke of the powers in the four quarters as the four winds of heaven, describing these heavenly beings as attending on God, that is, engaged in constant worship
of him. He refers to them as coming from heaven in the sense
of being above us, as in our speaking of the birds of heaven,
since none of the invisible and worshiping powers are above
heaven. He was also right to refer to them as winds as an indication of their being everywhere present so as to minister with
great promptness to the divine decrees.

While he saw them issuing forth from the mountains, then,
suggesting their natural loftiness and power, he also said the
mountains were of bronze so as to imply the firmness and vigor
of their service. He dispatched the black ones to the north,
then, suggesting by the color the dejection to which they were
about to reduce everyone there through the punishment they
inflicted on them, the angel also saying of them, *issuing forth to
the north country, they have set at rest my anger with the north country*,
as if to say, In keeping with my anger they went off to that place
and did everything to invest them with the most severe punishment that was their due. Behind them the white ones, who in
the wake of the defeat of the Babylonians and their being overcome with severe punishments assisted in the release of those
who were due to return from captivity, thus bringing out by

50. Logically, and following his text, Theodore presumes four horses proceed on four errands. Our Heb. text, however, has only three lots of horses going on errands, while the LXX in vv.6–7 loses sight of the errand of the red
horses from v.2 and instead divides the dappled ones into two. Against modern
versions like the New English Bible and Jerusalem Bible, which presume that a
mention of the red horses' errand has been lost, Smith claims that all four
points of the compass have still been included—not quite the evidence of the
text. In short, the Antiochene text makes most sense of all—and its commentator is unaware of any variants to it, nor is he inclined to mention the four horses
of Rv 6.1–8 arising from this passage.

their particular color the splendor that would in future envelop them. *The red ones* [540] *issued forth to the south country* as though breathing anger against those hostile to the Israelites there.[51] After them the dappled ones were seen to be searching out where they should go on the earth; the implication is that the responsibility of the remaining ones was a variety of service, designated as they were by color to see where anything else had to be done by them in God's will regarding punishment of the adversaries and support for the nation of the Jews, since it was said to them, *Go and roam the earth,* to which was added, *And they roamed the earth,* showing that they were entrusted with the task of bringing things to fulfillment, and being so commissioned they persisted in it.

A word of the Lord came to me saying, Take from the rulers, from the affluent of the earth and those familiar with it, from Heldai, from Tobijah and from Jedaiah what is the result of captivity. On that day enter the house of Josiah, son of Zephaniah, who comes from Babylon. Take silver and gold, make a crown, put it on the head of Joshua, son of Jehozadak, and say to him, Thus says the Lord almighty, Here is a man, Dawn is his name, and it will dawn beneath him, and he will rebuild the house of the Lord; he will receive virtue, he will be seated and rule on his throne. A priest will be at his right hand, and a counsel of peace will be between them both. The crown will be for those who wait, its men of affluence and those who know it, as a gift for the son of Zephaniah and as a psalm to the house of the Lord. Those that are at a distance from them will come, and will rebuild in the house of the Lord. And you will know that the Lord almighty has sent me to you, and it will happen if you listen and hearken to the voice of the Lord your God (vv.9–15). In the same way that blessed Moses left Egypt and according to a divine command took from the people what contributed to the building and adornment of the tabernacle, blessed Zechariah requires it of those returning from captivity, be they leaders or anyone else capable of it on the grounds of affluence, and in fact everyone repossessing their property. In fact, by *affluent of*

51. Theodore is being typically categorical in assigning each of the groups of horses to a task, though unable to be specific about the enemy in the south. No point, he feels, in being too fastidious about details in such a fanciful narrative, which he is now content to take in large gobbets, not verse by verse.

the earth he refers to those in a position because of affluence to contribute something to meeting the need, and by *those familiar with it* those who had repossessed it in receiving contrary to hope what they had previously lost.[52] So he took from each one of these, who contributed at the rate possible, for the building and adornment of the house of God, as was required.

After mentioning the names of some, probably those most suited, to this end he bids him enter the house of Josiah, son of Zephaniah, who had returned from captivity in Babylon and who surpassed the others both in wealth and in zeal for the task. With as much silver and gold collected as he could give, he was to fashion a crown out of it that was to be placed on the priest's head as an ornament and embellishment of priesthood. Once it was made, he was to place it on the priest's head, [541] and tell him to be confident about the task in hand, which was of great importance, and that by God's will a man had appeared whose name in the circumstances was Dawn.[53] This refers to Zerubbabel for the reason that he emerged in a position of royal authority through the events themselves: *It will dawn in his wake,* that is, all fame will come to the Jewish populace from him, for he will rebuild the Temple, and he will be invested with every virtue by divine grace and remain securely on the royal seat. This is a basis of your confidence for the task in hand, he is saying: you will be associated with him in great honor (the meaning of *he will be at his right hand*), harmony prevailing between you both, so that your affairs will proceed more easily under the royal authority while he will enjoy divine help abundantly through your priestly offices.[54]

52. Where our Heb. uses the proper names Heldai, Tobijah, and Jedaiah, and the LXX instead renders them as occupational skills, the Antiochene text alone (aware of what has happened, or just for completeness?) includes both, a tendency it reveals especially in the text of Ezek. Theodore opts to comment only on the skills, though admitting names also are supplied.

53. As observed in n. 41, the LXX renders Heb. for "shoot" as "dawn," the suitability of which Theodore—unaware that Zerubabel means "Shoot of Babylon"—rationalizes here. Once again, despite Luke's acknowledgement of this passage, he allows no messianic—let alone Christological—sense here.

54. For all his enthusiastic endorsement of Zerubbabel, Theodore the cleric does not let Joshua, the high priest, slip from sight. Our Heb. text, in fact, speaks of "crowns" in the plural, the oracle dealing with both men; the fact that

The adornment of coronation will not be for him alone: it will be commendation for the whole community of those with their eyes on hope in God and now contributing their assets to the construction of the house, Zephaniah before all exemplifying such generosity. Everything has been done in the past and in the present so that there will be continual service by the priests and that the hymns of praise to God will be able to be performed by the congregation; you will even see vast numbers hastening hither from afar, contributing from their resources to the rebuilding of the house, so that it will be obvious to all through the facts themselves that by God's will I have come to announce to you this good news, which will therefore actually come to pass if you continue being zealous in obeying my laws.

Chapter Seven

After this he says that *in the fourth year of the reign of Darius* some of those who were reigning over the Israelite people amongst the foreigners were sent to the priests and prophets in Jerusalem to propitiate God with sacrifices for the sins for which they felt guilty.[55] They were to enquire and find out if God's Temple had regained its proper condition so that they might practise the fasts required by the worship of the divinity. They did what they had done in many years past, and this task was performed by them; and when the ambassadors present discharged the business on which they had been sent, the prophet was bidden by a revelation to convey this to the whole people of the land and the priests; those who had arrived needed to know it for the reason that what was said contained in-

---

the LXX sees only one crown, indicative of royalty, is another factor in Theodore's taking Zerubbabel as a royal figure.

55. Theodore thus cuts through a lot of detail, some of it ambiguous, that is found in the text: precise details of dating are omitted, such as the name of the ninth month, Chislev, and the names of the ambassadors, some transposed into roles by the LXX, resulting in a general summary "reigning among the foreigners" and thus obviating the need for precision as to origin of the ambassadors, whether Bethel or Babylon. Ἀκριβολογία should not get in the way of meaning, he feels.

structions not only for the local people but also for the visitors. This was the directive: I am not interested in seeing you fasting and lamenting, for I do not find worship in this. You practised no fasting for the seventy years you were in captivity; I returned you to your homes without requiring anything of the kind of you, seeing only your changed ways. Whether you eat and drink, or do not, it is your pleasure to indulge in eating, and it is your loss to go without eating: it is of no account to me.

To bring out that this was not the first time he had said this to them, he says, *Are not these the words the Lord spoke by means of the prophets of old when Jerusalem was inhabited and prospering along with the cities round about, and the mountain country and the plains were inhabited?* (v.7) I said this to you through the prophets also in olden times, he is saying, when Jerusalem enjoyed its prosperity, and all the cities under it likewise, filled as it was with the inhabitants of the mountain country and the plains belonging to it. I told you at that time that I set no store by your fast when you did not fast with the right attitude; what I do set store by, to which you should most of all have given attention, I taught through the prophets. *Deliver a fair judgment, have mercy and compassion each one for their neighbor, do not oppress widow and orphan, sojourner and poor person, and do not harbor grudges in your heart against your brethren* (vv.9–10): I advised you in every case to show particular care for justice, to have sympathy with the neighbor, to avoid harming the poor and isolated, and to refrain from wrath and anger against one another by dismissing the memory of the grievances developing between you.[56] On the contrary, in giving you this advice, I set fasting aside.

The result? *They refused to give heed, they turned their backs in irritation, they blocked their ears against hearing, and made their hearts resistant to hearkening to my Law and the words the Lord almighty issued in his spirit by means of the prophets of old* (vv.11–12): far from

56. Theodore is content to give a brief paraphrase of this summary of the Lord's requirements in personal converse and social justice, which Smith classes "one of the finest summaries of the former prophets. It has a strong emphasis on social justice," comparing it with Hos 4.1, Am 5.24, and Mi 6.8; on these, in fact Theodore likewise did not expatiate, let alone moralize. He could not be accused of trespassing on the role of a preacher.

agreeing to set any store by this, with utter irritation you completely turned away from what I said (the sense of *they turned their backs in irritation*), you refused to heed my words, choosing to be absolutely resistant to my laws, which I had explained to you through the prophets of old.

The response to this? *Awful wrath arose in the Lord almighty:* for this you suffered such terrible punishment, since I set aside your fasting and gave you the advice to adhere to the laws as was required of you; but you set no store by my laws. *It will happen that as he spoke and they did not hearken to him, so they will cry aloud and I shall not hearken, says the Lord almighty* (v.13): just as they refused to listen to what was said by me, so too I did not heed them when they were in such awful difficulties.[57] What did I do? *I shall banish them as in a storm to all the nations they do not know, and the land will be devastated behind them, with no one to cross it or return to it; they turned a special land into devastation* (v.14): I threatened to scatter you all as though enveloping you in a tempest, and by consigning you to captivity to drive you off to a land that you did not know before; [545] and I decreed your land would be enveloped in devastation, no one ever returning to it, no one passing through the unparalleled wilderness. What I threatened, he is saying, I actually did: the land I previously chose for your possession I have consigned to devastation (the words *they will cry aloud* and *it will be devastated* implying the future but meaning past, with his usual change in tense, as often happens in the divine Scripture, as we have shown in many cases previously from blessed David and the other inspired authors. His meaning in the words *they turned a special land into devastation* in fact showed that he was referring not to a future event but to one already over and done with). His general meaning is, On the one hand, I declined your fasting that was wrongly performed, while, on the other, I advised what should be done by you; since you paid no heed to it, I inflicted awful punishment on you.

57. Theodore is doing his best to rationalize the inconsistency of tenses in the LXX, which commonly confuses the Heb. usage. He eventually comments on the inconsistency, though attributing it rather to scriptural idiom than to the limitations of his version (being unable to do otherwise), as he has done in the past.

Chapter Eight

So much for that time: what of this? *The Lord almighty says this, I am jealous for Jerusalem and Zion with a deep jealousy, and with a deep anger I am jealous for it* (v.2):[58] I have changed my attitude to it so as even to be very angry for what it suffered at the hands of those who wronged it. He continues with these words: *The Lord says this, I shall turn back to Zion and dwell in the midst of Jerusalem; Jerusalem will be called a true city, and the mountain of the Lord almighty a holy mountain* (v.3): I shall revive in me my favorable disposition to Mount Zion, and shall give evidence once again of my characteristic care for Jerusalem; I shall present it as a city of real value,[59] established in great prosperity, and the mountain on which the city is built I shall present as holy in that it is vouchsafed my presence. He goes on in the same vein, *The Lord almighty says this, Old men and old women will again sit in the streets of Jerusalem, each with their staff in their hand on account of great age. The city streets will be filled with boys and girls playing in its streets* (vv.4–5): in this way I shall keep the city and all its inhabitants safe from meeting an untimely death like those before from the troubles besetting them; the city will enjoy great prosperity, and inevitably its inhabitants' life will be extended, so that even the infirm on account of the length of their life will have recourse to a stick for help in walking. The city will also be full of boys and girls playing, a sign of the city's prosperity and large population.

Then, since this seemed to be impossible in the light of the present situation, *The Lord almighty says this, If it will be impossible in the view of the remnant of this people in those days, says the Lord almighty, surely it will not be impossible also in my view?* (v.6) Even if, he is saying, it is impossible for you [548] in the light of the small number of those now assembled in the city, it is not im-

---

58. The customary opening to these oracles, found in Heb. and LXX, "The word of the Lord almighty came to me, saying" (merely an "editorial comment" for Smith), Theodore does not include (but Theodoret does).

59. While modern versions and commentaries tend to see reference to Jerusalem as a "faithful city," Theodore takes the ἀληθινή of the LXX to mean "true" in the sense of a city of real significance.

possible for me to achieve such a great change in the situation so as to transform the city and its whole condition from the present hardships to great prosperity. And to confirm by this the possibility of the promises, he goes further, saying, I shall gather to this city from all directions many other Israelites still in captivity, and restore them to possession of their own land; I shall be known to them through my care, so that they will be shown to be my people by the events through which they are accorded such providence by me, and I shall be manifested as their true God by the characteristic grace I unfailingly give them. And by exercizing my characteristic righteousness I shall punish all those endeavoring in any way to harm them at any time.[60]

With these promises he associates this statement, *Thus says the Lord almighty, Let your hands be strengthened, you who in these days hear these words from the mouth of the prophets, from the day when the foundations of the house of the Lord almighty are laid and the Temple is being built* (v.9): so come now, give heed to these promises of mine, which I often made you through the prophets, and with great diligence be zealous for the completion of my house, recalling how great a change for the better your fortunes have undergone from the time you have been engaged in this and in the construction of my house. Then, to bring out the change by comparison with the previous situation, *Because before those days people had no wages to their credit, there was no payment for the animals, and there was no relief from distress for the one leaving or the one arriving; I dispatched everyone against their neighbor* (v.10): in former times before the rebuilding of the Temple you were reduced to great hardship, and you got no reward for all your labors when laboring and engaged in work with your cattle. In fact, all you did was of no avail for enjoying any peace, and instead everyone entering the city or leaving your midst—that is, the city residents—were forever caught up in various tribulations. The insurrection of great numbers against you from

60. Theodore's recourse to mere paraphrase of vv.7–8 in place of textual citation may be due to the mention there of the return of people "from the east and from the west," a phrase that may have required some awkward explication and would thus be best avoided.

abroad as a result of my aversion to you added to your tribulation and prevented your being in peace. It resembled the drift
of the words of blessed Haggai the prophet in clearly reproaching them for their indolence: while he reminded them of the
troubles besetting them when they neglected the rebuilding,
he indicated how much their situation changed for the better
when they opted to take an interest in the rebuilding of the divine Temple. This is what blessed Zechariah says here, too: you
were in great hardship when you neglected the house, whereas
now that you have changed your attitude and show the proper
enthuasiasm for the house, what happened?

*At this time I shall not deal with the remnant of this people as in for-
mer days, says the Lord almighty. Instead, I shall let peace emerge: the
vine will yield its fruit, the land will yield its produce, and heaven will
give its dew. I shall give* [549] *all this as an inheritance to the remnants of my people. As you have been a curse to the nations, house of Judah and house of Israel, so I shall save you, and you will enjoy blessing*
(vv.12–13): the present lot of those who have returned will not
be like those in the past; though few have survived when many
perished, I shall in turn increase their numbers and bring them
to be a multitude, causing them to enjoy complete peace, providing them with prosperity from their crops, and in short regaling them with enjoyment of good things so that, just as in the
past you seemed to everyone to be deserving of punishment on
account of my wrath, so you will seem to all people fortunate in
my care. To encourage them further, *Have confidence and be
strengthened in your hands. Because the Lord almighty says this, As I
planned to cause you troubles in my wrath against your fathers, says the
Lord almighty, and I did not relent, so I have disposed and planned in
these days to act kindly to Jerusalem and the house of Judah* (vv.13–
15): putting aside all fear and all despair, you will enjoy good
spirits and deep confidence, and you will take to the rebuilding
of the Temple with great enthusiasm, well aware that, as in the
past I decreed punishment of you for the sins your fathers did
against me and put it into effect without altering my decision,
so now I shall completely put into effect the promises I uttered
about Jerusalem and the whole tribe of Judah. So prosperity will
return, and they will share in a good season.

To bring out what they had to do in trusting in the reliability of the promises, *Have confidence. These are the directions you will carry out: speak the truth each of you to your neighbor, deliver a peaceable judgment in your gates, do not ponder evil in your hearts each of you to your neighbor, and do not entertain a false oath, because I loath all this, says the Lord almighty* (vv.15–17): have confidence in my promises; if you give considerable attention to what I advise, dealing with one another guilelessly, preserving friendship with one another in a sincere attitude, and if you take care to dissolve all quarrels that arise and be joined in a seemly friendship that contributes to peace by achieving the solution of disputes, and pass over offences that occur, and if you make sure not to swear false oaths (these being very hateful to me), and if you obey the rest of my commands and agree to carry them out zealously, you will surely attain the good things I once promised.

A word of the Lord almighty came to me, saying, The Lord almighty says this: The fast of the fourth, the fast of the fifth, the fast of the seventh, and the fast of the tenth will be occasions of joy for the house of Judah and of happiness and good festivals, and you will rejoice. Love truth and peace (vv.18–19). Since in the above, when there were foreigners present whom the kings of the nations sent,[61] [552] he deprecated fasting and substituted what he believed had to be performed by way of instructing both the local people and the foreigners at the same time, after the instruction in what followed he necessarily adds this in his wish to bring out that it was not indiscriminately that he deprecates fasting but only when done improperly; if on the contrary it is done properly, he gladly accepts its performance. His meaning, therefore, is, Previously in fasting you grieved for your own sins, being beset with such awful calamities for them, whereas now that you have returned, it would not be fitting for you to practise fasting with grief, but gladly and with joy in the thought that fasting is suited to festivity in being capable of relating you to God. It will in

61. As observed in n. 55, Theodore arrives at this idea of kings dispatching ambassadors to Jerusalem to look for a ruling on fasting in the fifth month from the LXX's muddled interpretation of their names, such as Regem-melech.

fact be appropriate for you to fast gladly if you give priority to truth and peace.

To bring out the magnitude of the good things for which they should practise fasting with celebration and joy, he goes on, *The Lord almighty says this, Many peoples will still come, the inhabitants of many cities, and inhabitants of one city will assemble in another, saying, Let us go and make our way to plead our cause before the Lord and seek the face of the Lord almighty: I shall go, too* (vv.20–21): it is not surprising if this were to happen among you, many foreigners dwelling in different cities coming together from each city (the meaning of *inhabitants of one city will assemble in another*).[62] They will prompt and urge one another to be present here so as to persevere in pleading with God and awaiting from him any good whatsoever. They urge one another in the words, *I shall go, too,* as if to say, each person displays enthusiasm for the event and stirs up the others also to do likewise. He next says that a great number will come to Jerusalem from many and varied nations to appease the divinity for their own sins and seek whatever they need from him. From there he goes on, *The Lord almighty says this, In those days ten men of all the languages of the nations will lay hold of the hem of a garment of a Jewish man, saying, We shall go with you, because we have heard that God is with you* (v.23): God will make the return of the remainder[63] so conspicuous that many people who are from different nations and have shared that calamity will perceive God's care for the people, and will lay hold of anyone of them and use him as a guide for a return to Jerusalem, since everyone is sufficiently stirred up to that end from the clear realization that God is with them on the basis of the incredible deeds done for them. The phrase *ten men,* note, here too refers not to number, but has the meaning of many.

---

62. Most forms of the LXX, unlike our Heb., read "of *five* cities will assemble in one."

63. As he did in comment on a similarly obvious prophecy of "the coming in of the Gentiles" (Smith) in Mi 4.1–5, Theodore—again against the evidence of the text—insists that only Jews are referred to here, just as he again acknowledges no eschatological dimension to the text. What he will say later in comment on Is 2.1–4, verses identical to the Micah passage, and 60.1–3, is not extant.

Chapter Nine

He then mentions those people among the nations who acted this way through fear of God, on the one hand, and, on the
other, those who through a sense of superiority set no store by
it. Hence he says, [553] *An oracle of the word of the Lord in the land
of Hadrach. Damascus is his sacrifice, because the Lord surveys human
beings and all the tribes of Israel, and Hamath on its boundaries*
(vv. 1–2):[64] the people of Damascus, those both of Hadrach and
of Hamath, will with great enthusiasm offer sacrifices to God as
Lord of all, surveying humankind as his own works and servants, while assigning his special care to Israel.[65] *Tyre and Sidon,
because they were very conceited, Tyre built its fortification, and stored
silver like dust and gold as dirt of the street. Hence God will take possession of them, and will strike its power into the sea, and it will be consumed by fire* (vv. 2–4): since Tyre and Sidon adopted a lofty attitude, of course, and scorned my worship, and were interested
in the security that comes from walls in the belief they were sufficient to themselves, heaping up gold and silver like dirt, they
will receive punishment commensurate with their folly. God
will, in fact, take possession of them and humble them all, consigning all their might to the sea nearby. It will be food for fire
from the enemy attacking it.

After saying this of Tyre and Sidon, he goes on, *Ashkelon will
see and be afraid; Gaza too, and will feel severe pangs; Ekron too, because she is ashamed of her fall. A king will perish from Gaza, and
Ashkelon will be uninhabited; foreigners will inhabit Ashdod. I shall*

64. Unlike many scholars since Joseph Mede in 1653, Theodore would like
to see ch 9 following on sequentially from the preceding chapter. Though he
had commented on the unusual word for "oracle," λῆμμα, at the beginning of
commentary on Nahum as a "customary" introduction to a prophetic work (see
Hab 1.1, Mal 1.1), he does not think this worth raising here as a clue to the beginning of a new work.

65. Though no geographer, Theodore might have helped his readers trace
the movement of the author's thought in listing the cities of Syria (Damascus,
Hadrach, and Hamath), the Phoenician coast (Tyre and Sidon), and then
Philistia—had he been aware of this sequence. Admittedly, the text offers difficulty even to modern commentators, and the Antiochene form differs in some
respects from the LXX, itself diverging from our Heb. Theodore, however, typically shows no signs of hesitancy in interpreting the author's purpose.

destroy the insolence of the Philistines, and take away their bloodshed
and their abominations from the midst of their teeth; they too will be a
remnant to our God, they will be like an officer in Judah, and Ekron
like a Jebusite (vv.5–7). He means that awful punishment will befall the Philistines for abandoning the worship of God, describing it in various ways in listing off the cities: Ashkelon will be
gripped with fear, Gaza will feel pangs, Ekron along with them
will be ashamed of the sins committed for which she paid the
penalty, the king of Gaza also will be done away with, Ashkelon
no longer inhabited and foreigners occupying Ashdod. Now,
he went on to include these, not meaning one fate would ensue
and another would not, as if to say this would befall Gaza and
this Ashkelon; rather, by his characteristic practice of speaking
in general by particular reference he means that this fate would
befall all the Philistines—hence his proceeding after the listing, *I shall destroy the insolence of the Philistines,* as if to say, I shall
punish them for all their violent behavior, I shall punish them
in a way commensurate with the blood of the Israelites they
shed, destroying in one fell swoop all their idols that they
thought to worship, with the result that from the punishment
inflicted on them many will be seized with dread at what is happening and will have recourse to the worship of God, and
though holding the rank of some sort of officer they will join
our ranks. By throwing in their lot with us in this way, even such
people from Ekron will be saved no less than a Jebusite.[66] Here
too, note, by mention of Ekron [556] he means that the people
of the five districts were converted to their duty, the sense being, They will be numbered with the Israelite people and be
saved by being plucked from the punishment befalling them,
whoever of them came to their senses and were converted to
their duty.

   I shall provide my house with an elevation to prevent going and

___

66. The fate of the Philistine cities had been treated of in Am 1.6–8, the significant difference here being the prospect of the Philistines being converted
"no less than a Jebusite"—a reference to 2 Sm 5.6–9, where the possibility occurs of David having spared some Jebusites from massacre. The commentator,
however, once more does not go to the trouble of chasing up the reference to
enlighten the reader.

coming; no one will invade them any longer to drive them off, because now I have seen with my eyes (v.8): I shall raise up for those belonging to me some kind of strong support that will keep at a distance all the foreigners, not allowing them to enter the boundaries of those belonging to me, so that no one will any longer dare to invade or strike the land belonging to me, since I thought fit to survey them, according them my care (by *my house* meaning all the country of Israel in that it belongs to him).

Then, to bring out even more clearly who it is through whom this will happen, and who has been appointed by God for this purpose, *Rejoice exceedingly, daughter Zion, proclaim, daughter Jerusalem! Lo, your king comes to you, righteous and saving, humble and riding on a beast of burden, a colt. I shall wipe out chariots from Ephraim and a horse from Jerusalem, and a battle bow will be destroyed, a multitude and peace from nations* (vv.9–10): be glad, therefore, O Jerusalem, since of such a kind is a king appointed for you by God, and he has come to you, capable of saving his own on account of the divine influence accruing to him, and justly inflicting total punishment on the adversaries. While he is riding a lowly animal for the reason that he has just arrived back from captivity, he assumes great power through divine help, and so from Ephraim and from Jerusalem he will remove all the chariots of the adversaries,[67] every war horse and every battle bow—that is to say, he will drive off all enemies so that there will be no longer any adversary against the country of Judah. He will also wipe out a great multitude of the adversaries, and completely deprive them of peace, crushed and destroyed in a war waged by him.

While, then, it is clear that here this refers to Zerubbabel, I am amazed at those adopting farfetched ideas, applying part to Zerubbabel and part to Christ the Lord, which results in nothing else than their dividing the prophecy between Zerubbabel

---

67. Like the Heb., the Antiochene text has the verb beginning v.10 in the first person, "I shall wipe out chariots," whereas other forms of the LXX and some modern versions—and Theodore in his commentary—see fit to read third person. As emerges below, the latter usage is important for Theodore's application of the verse to Zerubbabel.

and Christ the Lord. Now, this is the height of folly; the true sense of such an expression, on the contrary, as I am aware I have stated before as well, is that the Law contained an outline of everything to do with Christ the Lord. Many things that happen in unlikely fashion, therefore, affecting either the people or the individuals chosen for some tasks, Scripture expresses in a rather hyperbolic manner in these same cases, the expression at face value not doing justice to the reality. Such things are found to achieve reality, however, when looked at in reference to the person of Christ the Lord, who in every case brings the outline of the Law to a close and ushers in the reality in its place, rightly demonstrating the reality of such statements.[68] Such a statement is the one made to Abraham, [557] "All nations will be blessed in you and in your offspring":[69] while at face value it indicates those descended from him, the reality of the expression is achieved in Christ the Lord, in whom it really happened that the nations were blessed. Such also is the statement of blessed David, "His throne like the sun in my sight, and like the moon perfected forever; I shall make his offspring last for ages of ages, and his throne like the days of heaven":[70] while at face value it seems to refer to his successors, in whom the kingdom was due to continue, the reality of the matter is brought out in the case of Christ the Lord, whose kingdom has been made to be truly more splendid than any sun and more permanent than any heaven. Such is the statement, "His soul was not abandoned into Hades, nor did his flesh see corruption,"[71] which is expressed hyperbolically by blessed David of the people of the Israelites, but is seen in the true reality of the

68. Though he does not acknowledge it, Theodore would be aware that in the NT (Mt 21.5, Jn 12.15) v.9 is applied to Jesus in his entry into Jerusalem on Palm Sunday. While he admits that the prophecy is more fully realized in the case of Jesus, he insists—still under the misapprehension of Zerubbabel's royal status—that it is at one level applicable also to him (at face value, κατὰ τὸ πρόχειρον), protesting only at distribution of verses or words to one figure or the other. His terminology for distinguishing between the different senses of a text is typical of the Antiochenes—outline, shadow, σκιά, and reality, ἀλήθεια. His rebuttal of opposing views is done in his customary manner.

69. Gn 26.4.   70. Ps 89.36–37.

71. Ps 16.10.

matter to have been realized in the case of Christ the Lord; hence blessed Peter, too, applied the verse appropriately, "His soul was not abandoned into Hades, nor did his flesh see corruption."[72]

You would find many such statements—it would take too long to list them at present—that were expressed hyperbolically in the first place, not doing justice to the precise reality of the meaning, but which are found to contain it, as has been said, in reference to Christ the Lord. Of such a kind is this one, too: while he referred to Zerubbabel as leader of the Jews by right of succession to David by God's will, the contents were seen to contain their irrefutable reality in the case of Christ the Lord. To the former, you see, belonged the brief punishment of the nations and the paltry saving of his own people—hence the logical comment in addition, *He will wipe out chariots from Ephraim and a horse from Jerusalem,* revealing that he would contribute to their being rid of war. The true expression emerged, however, in Christ the Lord, in whom there is the real possibility for lasting and enduring joy, since he is really righteous in that he judges the whole world and transfers everyone to a salvation that is lasting and secure. In this case, then, there is reference to Zerubbabel when the expression is assessed by that to which the text immediately refers, whereas in the Gospels the sense has moved on to Christ the Lord, who is seen in every way to be mighty, lofty, and righteous, to save and to provide his own abiding beneficence, which is utterly irreversible and incapable of undergoing any change.[73]

This position, therefore, it is most logical and appropriate to state and to hold. On the other hand, to say part of it refers to Christ, and then to turn around and transfer it to Zerubbabel, then to Christ from him, and then to Zerubbabel from Christ the Lord is nothing short of proving the prophecy to be far-

---

72. Acts 2.31.

73. In the light of this strong admission of a fuller sense in the text of Zechariah, Theodore could not be accused of denying a Christological sense to OT texts ("The Law contained an outline of everything to do with Christ the Lord," he concedes), even if he is reluctant—except when under pressure from his peers—to advert to it. He proceeds to pillory the opposite procedure, the irregular oscillation from literal to eschatological sense of a text.

fetched in the first place, and then dividing the written words up equally between the servant and the master. To claim by way of proof of the inapplicability of the verses to Zerubbabel that the prophet said *he comes*, whereas it was in the past that Zerubbabel had come back from captivity with the others, is a mark of idle pedantry and unfamiliarity with the divine Scriptures. The verse, "He was led like a sheep to slaughter,"[74] for example, is expressed not as though in the future but as already happened: it says not "will be led" but "was led." So it would not apply to Christ the Lord in the view of those savants, who ought be aware of various changes in tense occurring in the divine Scripture, which in many cases we demonstrated in the *Commentary on the Psalms* and sufficiently in the case of the prophets. Here, moreover, the use of the word, if you were to judge it on the basis of tense, would not be applicable to the coming of Christ, either: while that was due to occur a long time later, it did not say "he will come," which would be appropriate to say in the case of the future, but *he comes*, which normally refers to what is happening here and now.

By this reasoning of theirs many other details occurring in the prophet are found to be irrelevant; it says in one case that Joshua's soiled clothes are removed, a sign of captivity, in another he is garbed in priestly vesture, although it is clear that he also had returned with Zerubbabel, freed from captivity and established in the condition of priesthood.[75] Hence also blessed Haggai the prophet seems to address both Zerubbabel and himself on the need to attend to the rebuilding of the Temple, and says the measure of the punishment has now been removed along with the sin of Israel and has been taken off to Babylon. In fact, it was Cyrus king of the Persians who terminated the people's captivity and destroyed Babylon, but the prophet seems to say this in the time of Darius, who was the fourth king after Cyrus;[76] so it would be inopportune, in the

---

74. Is 53.7. While Theodore is making a valid point here, his further argument that Scripture often interchanges tenses is undermined by his failure to recognize in such cases the limitations of the LXX, not an idiom of "Scripture."

75. See Zec 3.3–5.

76. Theodore made this mistake about Darius, who was in fact second in

view of those who lay down the law in these matters, to claim
that what happened long before in the past was happening
then. Yet it is very clear that though the events had happened,
the prophet by revelation sees them happening at that time so
that all the members of the people should also learn that instead of anything happening by chance, everything of good in
their regard is worked out by divine will and determination. So
it was not inappropriate in this case, too, in connection with
what would happen to the people through the kingship of Zerubabel, who was appointed for that purpose by God's will, for
the prophet to say that *he comes righteous and saving* so as to suggest that he is present in that situation and has been chosen for
the kingship by God for doing what in the following verses it
says was done for the people by him.

So much for rather precise instruction. Speaking in reference to Zerubbabel, however, and prophesying present events
in his regard, [561] if also as prophet having some vision of the
future, the prophet goes on, *He will control waters from sea to sea,
from rivers to ends of the earth,* saying this also in hyperbolic fashion as usual, that he will prevail over the many adversaries and
take possession of much land, giving it to Jews for occupation.
Such also is the statement of blessed David in the Seventy-first
Psalm containing in the form of a prayer an indication of the
prosperity of Solomon, where it says, "His name will abide before the sun, and before the moon for generations of generations, he will have dominion from sea to sea, from rivers to further limits of the world."[77] Is not this, too, after all, clearly said
in hyperbolic fashion?

---

succession to Cyrus, in commenting on the opening verse of Haggai. It may be,
however, he is allowing for unnamed pretenders to the throne at the death of
Cambyses.

77. Ps 72.5, 8. The hyperbole Theodore remarks on encouraged early commentators (other than him) to take the psalm messianically; Theodoret, perhaps aware of his Antiochene predecessor's being the odd man out, exclaims,
"The fact that the present psalm in no way applies to Solomon I believe even
Jews would admit if they were willing to tell the truth." Modern commentators
also note the resemblance of the passages in prophet and psalmist, and debate
which depends on which. The location of the seas and river in question
Theodore predictably ignores, unlike the geographer, Theodoret.

He then goes on, *And you by the blood of your covenant des-patched your captives from a waterless pit; you will take your place in a fort as prisoners of the assembly, and for one day of your sojourn I shall repay you double* (vv.11–12). In all this he mentions what is going to happen to Gog in the days of Zerubbabel; in reference to him he says that after slaying many, shedding the blood of great numbers and confirming his kingship of the people by the slaughter of the adversaries as though by some covenant,[78] he will free everyone from great perils in which they live as though in some waterless pit, as if to say, they have no relief from implacable troubles. You who were formerly captives of the synagogue of the Jews will continue living in great safety in your own homes thanks to the security of your ruler, so that for what you suffered when you were living in captivity your reward will be much greater than the present goods. He continues in the same vein, *Hence I have bent you to me, Judah, like a bow, I have filled it with Ephraim. I shall stir up the children of Zion against the children of the Greeks, and stroke you like a warrior's sword* (v.13). He mentions Judah and Ephraim to suggest the whole community of the Jews by reference to the principal part. So he is saying, Like a bow drawn against the enemy I shall make you strong so that you may advance with great enthusiasm against the foreigners invading you and wreak much slaughter on them, and be like a man who ever unsheathes his sword in battle, and war, and killing.

To suggest from which quarter this help will come to them, *The Lord will appear over them, and his javelin will go forth like lightning. The Lord God almighty will sound the trumpet, and will issue forth brandishing his threat. The Lord almighty will protect them; they will consume them, overwhelm them with slingshot, drink their blood like wine and fill their bowls with oil like an altar* (vv.14–15): this will happen since God as your leader directs his fearsome eye against your adversaries, drawing his sword against them like lightning; [564] rousing you all to war with his might as though

---

78. If the Heb. of these verses is obscure, the LXX version confounds the confusion; but Theodore shows no signs of being tentative in his interpretation. The phrase "blood of the covenant," celebrated for its occurrence in the paschal passages of Ex 24.8 and Mk 14.24, is passed over without comment.

with a trumpet, he will be your leader, shaking all the adversaries with his peculiar threat. He will also provide you with such assistance through his support that you will remain unharmed, consume all your adversaries, overwhelm them with bolts of stone, and almost drink their blood through the extreme amount shed in showing great enthusiasm in their slaughter. The result will be that after the victory you will fill your bowls with oil and offer them like sacrifices to God as an acknowledgement of the lovingkindness by which you were the beneficiaries of such great power. He goes on in the same vein to say that God will save all his people, keeping them unharmed like sheep. He also gives the reason: *Because holy stones roll on his ground, because if there is anything good, it is his, and if there is anything beautiful, it is his* (vv.16–17): many among you have proved to be devoted to virtue; though they seem to crawl on the ground with the rest of humankind, invisible to the general run of people, it is thanks to them that God does not despise the others. Since everything that is good and beautiful is due to him, he makes his own the sufferings of holy people and those whose eyes are fixed on virtue, and is ready for their sake to be beneficent also to others.[79]

Chapter Ten

Next, by way of promising them prosperity after the slaughter of the enemy, he goes on, *Ask of the Lord rain at the right time, early and late. The Lord made visions, and he will give winter rain to them, to each one vegetation in the field* (v.1): ask him also for rains suited to the bearing of the crops, accustomed as he is to disturb the sky and impress everyone on earth with the magnitude of what is happening,[80] and capable of providing us with suitable rain for everything necessary for us to grow in the ground (by *vegetation* referring to crops in general, as in the phrase,

79. Theodore gives the impression of confidence in interpreting the obscure LXX text, though omitting the second half of v.17.

80. The LXX is reading a form for "visions" similar to the Heb. for "(thunder) clouds."

"Let the earth produce vegetation for food,"[81] where it clearly refers to everything that comes from seeds growing in the ground). Then, to bring them to their senses by reminding them of past exploits, he goes on in turn, *Because in their utterances they spoke of troubles, and the seers narrated false visions and false dreams, they gave idle consolation. Hence they were dried up like sheep and abused, because there was no healing. My anger was aroused against the shepherds, and I shall call my lambs to account* (vv.2–3): when in olden times you heeded the seers communicating everything to you in utter falsity, ignored my prophets and put your faith rather in what was said by the former, then I found your condition beyond healing and correction and consigned you to punishment like sheep,[82] venting my anger alike on the leaders and the subjects, and in that spirit I destroyed the one and the other alike.

While at that time you suffered such punishment for those sins, what now? *The Lord almighty will call his flock to account,* [565] *the house of Judah,* and so on, the full text of which I shall for the sake of brevity decline to quote, and shall give the sense, please God, by accommodating it to the inspired text for the readers' understanding.[83] He means, in fact, I shall take care of the house of Judah, whom I regard as my own flock; they will become strong against their adversaries in war more than a strong horse ridden by a warrior against the enemy. From him—Judah, that is—I foresaw that Zerubbabel should be appointed, I took him from there and made him king,[84] I caused

81. Gn 1.11.

82. In arriving at the meaning "were dried up" and "healing," the LXX is reading different if similar forms for Heb. "wandered" and "shepherd." None the wiser, Theodore comes up with the gist of the thought.

83. There were times earlier in his commentaries on The Twelve where Theodore settled for paraphrase of the text (e.g., Am 8.7–10, 9.13–15): why should he pointedly admit he is resorting to it now (vv.3–11)? Possibly because, for one thing, he senses the LXX is having difficulty with the Heb., and in particular in v.4 with the three images of the ruler emerging from Judah, viz., cornerstone, tent peg, and battle bow, only the last of these emerging intact from the translation (and in fact omitted from the paraphrase). Typically, he does not invoke the abundant documentation from the psalms and prophets of the theme of the Lord as shepherd.

84. Again the text is forced so as to allow Theodore to find Zerubbabel referred to, and particularly his appointment as king.

him to be strong and breathe anger against the adversaries, since I also once and for all marked out the leaders to come from the tribe of Judah who were to lead the people always in war. They will gain such control over the adversaries in wars as to trample them underfoot like mud trampled in the streets by the passersby; in like manner will the enemy suffer, he is saying, and be affected, and be in no condition to resist. In confidence they will be deployed against all the adversaries, believing divine help is with them; whereas at that time those of the enemy who boast of their horses will be confounded, they will emerge as mighty and powerful thanks to my help (calling them *house of Judah* and *Joseph,* note, meaning the people, naming the whole from the part). I shall provide them with secure habitation amongst their own, since through love for them I saw fit not to reject them from my care; I shall be always with them, and when they beg my help in times of need I shall hearken, and they will prevail over their adversaries in battle (referring to the people by mention of one part, *those of Ephraim*),[85] so that they will rejoice in victory against the adversaries more than people full of wine.

Their descendants also will see this and rejoice at the help coming to them from God. Giving a signal as with a trumpet, then (he says), I shall assemble them and welcome them, freeing them from every need, so that they will live in safety among their own and grow to large numbers as in days of yore. Pressed for room in their own land through their growing numbers, they will be scattered among many foreign countries, which they will control, occupy, and settle. Remembering me for the magnitude of what occurred, they will not only come to no harm but will also pay full attention to it (the meaning of *they will raise their children and turn back* (v.9), that is, they will do it by turning to me and to knowledge of me). After their descendants are later scattered, whether in Egypt or in the land of the Assyrians, I shall have a change of heart and bring them back

85. Twice in this paraphrase Theodore adverts to the mention by the author of northern tribes, but sees no significance in this reference to a new relationship of the Lord with the north, a development Zechariah II shares with the major prophets. He sees only further examples of synecdoche.

from all directions to their own country to occupy their own places, none of them living beyond them any longer. They will pass through in great numbers, under pressure from the multitude of the adversaries but prevailing over them by my power so as to destroy all their might, punish them all for raging against you like a surging sea, and by punishing and slaughtering them [568] reduce such people to nothing (the sense of *all the depths of rivers will be dried up* [v.11], meaning that so many will be destroyed). Not even the Assyrians will have left to them the power to prevail over them, nor the Egyptians, though the latter once enslaved them and the former later took them off as captives: they will be freed from both. In what manner? *I shall make them strong through the Lord God, and they will boast in his name, says the Lord* (v.12): because I shall make them strong and invincible to all the adversaries so they will boast in my name and my help.

Chapter Eleven

After saying this, he proceeds, *Open your doors, O Lebanon, and let fire devour your cedars; let a pine wail because a cedar has fallen, for the mighty ones have met great hardship. Wail, oaks of Bashan, because the dense forest has been felled. A sound of shepherds lamenting the magnitude of their hardship, a sound of lions roaring for the hardship befallen Jordan's insolence* (vv.1–3). Since he had said, remember, From all directions I shall bring them, from Egypt and from the land of the Assyrians, and they would never again experience anything of the kind, logically he now turns his attention to the captors, saying, You mighty ones who boast of your greatness like the cedars of Lebanon in giving evidence of your own strength, desist from any further fighting against those belonging to me and open up your frontiers like doors, allowing everyone safe passage from you and return to their own country before my power like fire destroys all the mighty ones among you and the weaker ones wail at the sight of the fall of the mighty (the meaning of *Let a pine wail because a cedar has fallen:* at the sight of the destruction of the mighty, they will naturally despair of their own safety). All who take pride in some power will wail at the sight of their vast numbers wiped out like some dense forest when divine punishment falls upon them like fire, for their princes will be in mourning for having presumed to oppose further those belonging to me, and now seeing all their might gone; those trusting in their own might will also grieve like lions at the sight of all those showing arrogance to the Jordan now in difficulties. Since the Jordan river, you see, is part of Judah, the prophet by mention of the river wished to indicate the land of the Israelites.[86] To this point the prophet has conveyed the Israelites' change in fortunes in that Jerusalem would be restored to its former prosperity with the restoration of the priesthood and the monarchy to the nation, and with the people reassembled from all directions, and because God would punish their enemies, on the one hand, and, on the other, bring them to an abundance of many good things. But he also conveyed that he would provide marvelous support to Zerubbabel, who was appointed to the kingship, and on the basis of this they would be strong against their adversaries and prevail also over Gog's forces, innumerable and invincible though they were. In short, in all the aforesaid he declared the extent of the development for the better that their fortunes would experience. [569]

Since, however, Jews did not make proper use of the prosperity and peace they enjoyed for a lengthy period, and were changed by it and took a turn for the worse, everything went in the opposite direction for them. A kind of disorderliness and confusion overtook their nation through neglect by them of the divine laws. Some of the lower classes, in fact, were by evil inclination naturally opposed to the chief priests and leaders of the whole people, who were governing it with great diligence. Unable to prevail against them on account of their popularity with the people, they went to the kings who succeeded the

86. The text suggests that the Jordan valley, like Lebanon and Bashan (and like the three groups of hostile places in 9.1–6), is about to be punished for its insolence and provide room for those returning. Theodore for his part finds synecdoche operating again and reference being made to the restored community, and in particular Zerubbabel.

Macedonian and were in control of the provinces of Syria, and put at risk their leaders and the men who acted as priests lawfully and properly. The office of chief priest was transferred to others in defiance of the ordinance of the divine laws at the will of those kings; they effectively sold the nation to the kings, and improperly paid money for the presidency of the people and committed as much evil as possible, reducing the whole people to disorderliness and confusion: observance of the laws was completely undermined, criminality took over as everything was done in opposition to the divine laws.[87]

While Jews were involved in countless troubles as a result of all this, the Maccabees could not tolerate the offence against the divine order or consider acceptable such transgression of the divine laws and the introduction and operation of such awful impiety, and so of themselves they declared war on the kings who succeeded the Macedonian. Not a few of those with the nation's interests at heart emulated their attitude and took part in the war that was foretold. Countless troubles difficult to describe befell the city, the Temple of God, and in short the whole people at the hands of the Macedonians. This situation was ameliorated when God, pleased with those in the company of Maccabeus, provided them with his support, with the result that against all hope they prevailed over the kings, despite their being low in number and doing battle with a great power, and they succeeded in restoring to the nation the due good order.

The prophet by divine revelation received knowledge of the essential elements of these events, and disclosed to the people what was to happen; and to their descendants he transmitted an account of them in writing, employing the following words.[88] He begins this way, *The Lord almighty says this, Shepherd the sheep of slaughter* (v.4). It is customary with the divine Scrip-

87. Unable to recognize an apocalyptic landscape in this part of the book (or elsewhere), Theodore is committed to finding an historical basis for the following chapters, which are clearly not related to Zerubbabel's time, and even outside the scope of the mythical Gog. So it has to be the conflict between the Diadochoi and the Maccabees.

88. The prophet's ministry, then, is twofold: preaching to his contemporaries, and leaving his visions in writing for later ages.

ture frequently to present the future in the imperative, as in
the verse, "Rejoice exceedingly, daughter Zion,"[89] though rejoicing does not respond to a command, since while it is impossible not to rejoice when pleasant things are at hand, we cannot
rejoice when pleasant things are absent. Rather, intending to
mention the satisfaction arising in them from Zerubbabel's
leadership, it made a beginning to its treatment in the imperative mood. Shortly after, *Ask of the Lord rain at the right time, early
and late,*[90] though it is obvious that no one in need would neglect to ask if aware that the request would definitely be met;
[572] the meaning is, however, God will provide you with rain
abundantly and in due season (making mention of the future
in the form of an imperative). In the same way here, too, he
foretells what is going to happen to the people in the form of a
command, meaning something like this, This will happen to
the people at my hands, as I have said before, the nation will
enjoy such good things and Jerusalem will have such prosperity,
and they will gain control of the enemy, from whom they will
amass great wealth. But because they will use the prosperity improperly and set their eyes on evil ways, they will fall under the
control of such shepherds as to be led by them like sheep set
for slaughter, as in the verse from blessed David, "We were reck-
oned as sheep for slaughter,"[91] which was said of the same people. Now, his meaning is, They will be vouchsafed no care, and
instead will suffer everything as though handed over to slaughter, as it were. And to tell how, *Those who acquired them slaughtered
them, and were not sorry* (v.5): the kings in power over them did
not look after them as their own possessions, but did away with
them as though enemies, heedlessly (the meaning of *they were
not sorry*). *Those who bought them said, Thank God, we have made
money:* those who handed over the nation to the kings and got a

---

89. Zep 3.14. Theodore is coming to grips with a prophecy that has been
styled the most enigmatic in the OT. The imperatives he takes note of suggest to
some modern commentators a commissioning narrative, which is also in the
form of allegory, not an Antiochene's favorite genre; but as he can find the
psalmist speaking in similar terms, he is not deterred.

90. Zec 10.1.

91. Ps 44.22.

return for it were so far from being ashamed of it as to consider such exchange a matter for gratitude. *Their shepherds had no feelings for them:* government of them was entrusted to men who were not interested in feeling pity for them.

Hence I shall no longer spare the inhabitants of the earth, says the Lord (v.6): for these crimes I shall desert them, according them none of my care. *Lo, I am giving these people up, each into the hand of their neighbor, and into the hands of their king. They will devastate the earth, and I shall deliver no one from their hand. I shall shepherd the flocks meant for slaughter into the land of Canaan.* (vv.6–7): I am leaving them to suffer a deadly fate at the hands of depraved people in their own country, and at the hands of the kings warring on them, since they bring it on themselves; in this way almost all the inhabitants of Judah will disappear (the meaning of *they will kill the land*), no help being supplied them by me to be freed from the control of the adversaries. On the contrary, I shall lead to slaughter those who are victims of their own actions, as probably happens to such people in the eyes of the Canaanites. The verse *I shall shepherd the flocks meant for slaughter* means, I shall lead them to slaughter, not doing it myself but allowing it. For it is also a custom in the divine Scripture to speak of divine permission as a fact, as in the verse, "You turned our paths from your way,"[92] not that God turned them, but that he permitted them to suffer what was appropriate for forsaking their duty. The phrase *in the land of Canaan* [573] means in the eyes of foreigners: it was harder for those who were aware of their former prosperity to see them all of a sudden caught up in these troubles.[93]

I shall take two staffs for myself; one I called Beauty, the other I called Cord. I shall shepherd the sheep: what I gave them by way of government for leadership, namely, monarchy and priesthood, which were particularly necessary for their good order and con-

92. Ps 44.19 LXX. Theodore might also have remarked on the confusion of tenses by the LXX in these verses in his text, only obscuring an already obscure text.

93. Smith remarks that most modern commentators accept this final phrase from the LXX in the sense of "to the Canaanites" (the Canaanites being traders—a reference lost on Theodore here and in v.11).

trol, these I shall take from them, since they adopted depraved ways, and I shall now bring them to punishment; what he said above, *I shall shepherd the flocks meant for slaughter,* he repeated here, *I shall shepherd the flocks, and I shall remove the three shepherds in one month* (vv.7–8). By *three* he does not refer to number in this case, either:[94] since from Joshua, son of Jehozadak, up to those times they were shepherded by upright chief priests, I shall bring to an end (he is saying) all those upright priests in one fell swoop, because they took a turn for the worse compared with the better priesthood that was law-abiding, and chose for themselves the worse one that was lawless. In customary fashion, you see, he associates the troubles that befell them with the person of God so that everything bad happening to them might appear as punishment. In similar fashion blessed Paul also says in one place, "God gave them up to shameful passions," and in another place, "God gave them up to a reprobate attitude,"[95]—not that it was God who gave them up to it, but that he considered it a form of punishment for their making a bad choice in that direction, as if such people were alienated from divine care and so took a turn in the wrong direction unrepentantly. So in this case, too, it means, It will come to an end in one fell swoop—that is, the government by those formerly shepherding well will come to an end *in one month*—and they will fall under the control of some depraved people exercising this government lawlessly. *My soul was impatient with them:* hence I took a real dislike to them at the sight of their choosing the latter in place of the former, thus rejecting the good in favor of the bad. And to bring out that it was a just penalty he imposed on them for becoming evil through their own perversity, *for their hearts were hardened against me:* I adopted such an attitude to

94. Admittedly, it is an enigmatic prophecy, and allegory is also involved in the two staffs and three shepherds; so Theodore would not want to follow modern commentators in a game of hunt-the-slipper to identify the three as Moses, Aaron, and Miriam; three kings of Israel; three world empires; three high priests; kings, prophets, and priests; or Pharisees, Sadducess, and Essenes. He therefore resorts to his frequent disclaimer about indefinite numerals in the Bible, agreeing with Smith that "no precise meaning should be given to the expression."

95. Rom 1.26, 28.

them because they intensified their anger against me like wild beasts in that what they did to the upright priests they obviously committed against me. As was said to Samuel, "It was not you they scorned but me."[96]

I said, I shall not shepherd you (v.9). At this point he withdrew from shepherding them and taking proper care of them as his own sheep. He showed that above *I shall shepherd* means, I shall hand over to punishment. Here he used the phrase *I shall not shepherd* to suggest shepherding attentively and the fact that he will not exercise such care of them. At any rate, he goes on, [576] *What is to die, let it die; what is to fail, let it fail; and let each of the survivors eat the flesh of their neighbor:* I shall let each person undergo their own punishment, wearing one another out with disputes, and fights, and attention to scheming. *I shall take the beautiful staff and cast it out so as to cancel my covenant I made with all the peoples of the land* (v.10): I shall remove the upright and noble priesthood that has been brought down by those assailing it, and I shall direct the outsiders away from it in the opposite direction; though those from foreign nations had previously made their way with great enthusiasm to my Temple when lawful rites were performed reverently, they also will desist from doing these same things in conditions of confusion and disorder obtaining there, prevented from assembling in the Temple in the usual fashion. Such is the meaning of *so as to cancel my covenant I made with all the peoples of the land,* as if to say, I shall stop happening what has been happening before with the foreigners (once again applying to his own person what occurred as a result of the malice of others); so in short they gave every indication of wrath.

It will be canceled on that day, and the Canaanites will know the sheep that observe me, because it is the word of the Lord (v.11): while at that time the attention given to the Temple by the adversaries will cease, naturally with the dissolution of the covenant I made with them, those who are really mine and give great attention to the observance of my decisions will be known even to the foreigners. A divine decree consigns the wicked to mis-

96. 1 Sm 8.7.

fortune, on the one hand, and, on the other, it brings to light
the value of my relationship with those attending to duty, few
though they be, such that they are accorded so much care from
me as to prevail easily over the adversaries, many and powerful
though they be. Then, in his wish to emphasize the probity of
the ways of his own—that is, those in the company of the Maccabees, who waged war against the Macedonian kings in the
cause of the nation and the divine laws—he goes on, *I shall say
to them, If it is good in your sight, give me my wages, or refuse* (v.12):
they will be so upright and reliable in my regard that I shall
confidently say to them, If you are pleased to be subject to me
and accept my government, give me the reward of your good
will and obedience; but if it is a problem for you to experience
all such troubles in being subject to me as you are forced to endure now at the hands of the enemy, make your abandonment
of my government clear. It is, in fact, like what was said by the
Lord to the disciples, "Surely you also want to go away?"[97] which
he said not to discourage them from being with him, but [577]
by the remark to bring out their greater commitment. He
means the same thing here, too: I am confident in proposing
this to them, knowing that they will agree to suffer abuse for my
sake rather than be in a more favorable situation by being outside my government. He therefore goes on, *They set my wages as
thirty pieces of silver,* not referring by *thirty* to number here, either, but to imply, They gave me much good will on their part
and continued to give evidence of their gratitude.

*The Lord said to me, Put it into the melting pot, and examine
whether it is true in the way I was tested for their sakes. I took the thirty
pieces of silver and threw them into the house of the Lord in the melting
pot* (v.13). He means, As I enclosed their choice of me in the
experience of troubles as in a kind of mold to see if they would
this be proved true in my regard as I was in their regard—that
is, to see if their good will to me is reliable as I provide them
with my reliable government. *So I put them into the melting pot in
the house of the Lord,* rightly saying *in the house,* since for its sake
they put up with all the struggle when it was violated by the en-

97. Jn 6.67.

emy. The meaning is that they were found to be true in the mold of the troubles.[98] Then, after mentioning the good will of his own, he returns in the remainder to the former ones; and since he had said above, *I took my beautiful staff and cast it forth,* he goes on, *I cast out the second staff, Cord, and canceled the covenant between Judah and Israel* (v.14), as if to say, I stripped them also of the monarchy and the good things coming from it on account of the wickedness of their behavior; as he called the priesthood *Beauty* for making them comely and true to God, he called the monarchy *Cord* for measuring and correcting the proper behavior of the subjects, as in the saying, "I shall give you the land of Canaan as a cord of your inheritance,"[99] meaning, By alloting to you the land of Canaan and marking off all the land, I have given it as an inheritance.

Next, to bring out that for a long period they would be embroiled in these troubles, he goes on, *The Lord said to me, For a further time get yourself shepherd's equipment of an unskilled shepherd. Because, lo, I am raising up an unskilled shepherd over the land; he will not have an eye to the abandoned and search out the dispersed, and will not put to rights the crushed. He will eat the flesh of the elect, and root up their ankles* (vv.15–16). Here again he speaks of the future through the imperative. The hardship of the people, he is saying, which stems from whose who shepherd badly, those who practise the priesthood badly, will continue (*shepherd's equipment* referring to the tasks of the office of priesthood, through which this ministry is normally performed). Men will take on the priesthood, then, with no experience of the job, unaware of what should be done, and they will have no eye to the infirm, make no enquiry for the missing nor apply any treatment to the injured; [580] yet their attention will not go to the healthy, either, to ensure they continue in their good health. Instead, it will go to those with their eyes on better things, and they will as much as possible eat the meat and ankles,[100] being hostile to

98. Again Theodore studiously avoids Matthew's use of vv.12–13 as a *testimonium* of Jesus in his passion narrative, 27.9, lest a Christological dimension enter the interpretation of the text.

99. Ps 105.11.

100. The phrase in the text is obscure, and Theodore does not trouble to clarify it.

them in every way, harming them at one time and what belongs to them at another, since with their own inclination to evil they are hostile to the servants of duty. They vent their spleen on them, betraying their extreme indignation at God's doings.

O those who shepherd futile things and desert the sheep: may a sword strike his arm and his right eye. His arm will completely wither, and his right eye be completely blinded (v.17): this will not go unpunished for you who practise the role of shepherd badly and surrender the people of God to slaughter; you will pay the penalty with your arms and eyes, the former withering completely and the latter blinded. He means that all their strength will disappear in punishment, along with the authority of seeming to oversee others.

Chapter Twelve

From here he continues, *An oracle of the word of the Lord to Israel. Thus says the Lord, who stretches out heaven and lays the foundation of earth, forming in him a human being's spirit* (v.1): I tell of what was revealed to me in revelation by God, who is maker of all that is and also made the human being, conferring on him a soul and a faculty of reason. That is to say, God as he wished permitted this to happen, he who as Lord of all allows also human beings to do whatever they decide when he wishes it. So who is he? what does he say? *Lo, I am making Jerusalem like a shaken threshhold for all the peoples round about, and in Judah there will be a siege against Jerusalem* (v.2): I therefore, on account of the wickedness of the inhabitants, have surrendered Jerusalem to extreme weakness with the result that it will be possible for anyone interested to assault and shake it as they wish, whence even war has been stirred up by the kings of Macedonia against them.[101] *On that day I shall make Jerusalem a stone trampled on by all*

101. The sweeping scenario and the doxology of the Lord as cosmic creator are so suggestive of apocalyptic that Smith gasps, "This is Armageddon, the last great battle of earth"; and the picture of Armageddon in Rv 16.16 will evoke v.11 of this chapter (but see n. 104 below). Theodore, however, wants as ever to root the prophecy in historical events. He is not in the mood to develop the notion of a shaken threshhold, or "cup of staggering" in modern versions.

the nations; everyone trampling on it in jest will jest, and all the nations of the earth will come together against it (v.3): from this point foreigners will advance on it, and all the attackers will enjoy security in doing to it what they want for the reason that many will be assembled against it for this reason.

Then, having mentioned the disasters occurring as though with God's permission, he goes on to refer also to the change for the better they will experience when God wills. *On that day, says the Lord almighty, I shall strike every horse with stupor, and its rider with madness. But on the house of Judah I shall open my eyes, and I shall strike all the horses of the peoples with blindness. All Judah's commanders will say in their hearts, We shall find for ourselves the inhabitants of Jerusalem in the Lord almighty their God* (vv.4–5): I shall not allow their experience of the troubles to be taken to extremes, but shall suddenly [581] provide them with help, and through those who witness my help (meaning the Maccabees) I shall smite the equestrian might of the adversaries so that even their riders will be driven to utter madness with the magnitude of the troubles. While I shall do this to the adversaries, to those of the tribe of Judah, including also the generals the Maccabees, I shall provide my providence and care, enveloping all the adversaries' cavalry in blindness, as it were, and thus rendering them useless against those belonging to me. Then the leaders of Judah will be satisfied that they have been given by God security to go up once more to Jerusalem with confidence and occupy it with the former prosperity, observing everything that inhabitants there should observe if they want to please God.

He goes on in the same vein, *On that day I shall make the commanders of Judah like a firebrand in wood and a blazing lamp in straw; they will devour all the peoples round about on right and left, and Jerusalem will have Jerusalem to itself to inhabit. The Lord will save the tents of Judah as in the beginning lest the boasting of the house of David be magnified and the pride of the inhabitants of Jerusalem over Judah* (vv.6–7): at that time I shall make the leaders of the tribe of Judah so strong against the enemy that they will affect them all with blows and slaughter like fire falling upon wood or straw, so great will be the slaughter of the adversaries they cause from one direction and another. Jerusalem will then be left to live in peace, suffering no problem from the adversaries, for the reason that I am looking after the tribe of Judah and those belonging to them and restoring the former prosperity. At that time the descendants of David and all the Jews inhabiting Jerusalem will cease taking pride in their good things, and will come to the realization from the events themselves that it was through my willing it that they formerly enjoyed prosperity, being in no position to acquire anything by their own power, and were excluded from my care, proved to be utterly weak as a result of their depravity and incapable of being of any assistance to themselves. To explain how this will happen, *On that day the Lord will be a protection for the inhabitants of Jerusalem. The weak among them will be like David on that day, and the house of David like the house of God, like an angel of the Lord before him* (v.8): at that time they will come to realize that with my help they are all so powerful against the adversaries that those who shortly before were weak will emerge with such power against the enemy as David was seen to enjoy in his time through divine influence. The house of David will again be the object of envy and admiration; the leaders of the people descended from that house and tribe were seen to be so strong against the foreigners that all took refuge in them as in the house of God, which supplied great help to the fugitives, or in some angel sent to strike the adversaries, as was the case when the Assyrians [584] advanced on Jerusalem and all fled to the house of God, and from that quarter came the help from the angel annihilating such vast numbers of the enemy in attack.[102]

He explains the way this will happen. *On that day I shall seek to do away with all the nations coming against Jerusalem, and shall pour out on the house of David and the inhabitants of Jerusalem a spirit of grace and compassion* (vv.9–10): while at that time I shall destroy all those attacking Jerusalem, on *the house of David*—that is, all the leaders of the people from there and those belonging to Jerusalem—I shall give evidence of my grace and lovingkindness in abundance, and provide them with every form of care.

102. See 2 Kgs 19.35.

What will the result of this be? *They will look upon me whom they have pierced, and will mourn for him with mourning as for a loved one, and will suffer pangs for him as for a firstborn:* at that time those who formerly opted to oppose my decisions and showed such audacity against me will sense their ill-considered lawlessness, with the result that they will repent and engage in deep mourning like someone feeling the pangs of grief on the death of a firstborn.[103] He then mentions that many of those in Jerusalem who formerly had chosen the opposite of their duty will repent and be caught up in mourning; at the sight of the nation's change for the better they intended to repent of their own transgressions, as was appropriate.[104] He goes on to mention the tribes, indicating that each one will fall to grieving in its own case, with the result that—to put it in a nutshell[105]—repentance will seize all those who had opted for evil: as the nation had taken a turn for the worse in the past, later there was a change for the better due to the leadership of the Maccabees, who were the recipients of divine grace. The result was that the adversaries were destroyed by them, good order was restored to the city, and the Temple of God, and the divine laws and the practice of the priesthood once again received due attention; so they necessarily had recourse to repentance for the awful acts of impiety and lawlessness into which they had fallen.

Chapter Thirteen

Having conveyed the grief and the repentance, he mentions the turn for the better that most of all was responsible for pro-

103. With almost indecent haste Theodore dismisses this familiar *testimonium* to the suffering Jesus (see Jn 19.37, Rv 1.7), not even enquiring as to the identity of a possible OT figure. Even the Talmuds take the reference to be messianic.

104. Theodore is content to paraphrase the remaining verses of the chapter. This v.11 sounds like a repetition of v.10, and bears little resemblance to our Heb. mentioning "the mourning of Hadad-rimmon in the plain of Megiddo," the latter Heb. term the basis of the Grk. Armageddon appearing in Rv 16.16 as the site of the cosmic battle. Theodore could be excused for not seeing the connection.

105. Theodore sees no value in detailing the families named in vv.12–14, or searching for significance in the groupings included.

ducing the effects of such repentance in everyone. *On that day every place will be opened to the house of David* (v.1),[106] as if to say, all will gladly welcome them as leaders, making their way in all eagerness to them, who give the appearance of being pious and strong against the enemy by the help of God. Then to bring out how the religious attitude will change in the direction of duty through the influence of the Maccabees, who caused all signs of deterioration to disappear and God's will to prevail, *On that day, says the Lord Sabaoth, I shall eliminate the names of the idols from the land, and there will be no further remembrance of them; the false prophets and the unclean spirit I shall remove from the land* (v.2): at that time under their command all the cult of the idols will be removed, [585] and all the error of the false prophets dissipated, with no one daring to commit any such abuse.

To bring out how far the dominance of virtue will extend, he says that if anyone dared to come forward at that time and pretend to disclose anything of the future by the operation of an alien spirit, he would no longer meet with any pardon or mercy for this outrage and lawlessness even from his parents: they would practically tie him up for daring to practise falsehood and deceitful prophecy, and hand him over for punishment. They will all be so ashamed, on the one hand, of attempting such things in this way, and, on the other, they will give themselves to repentance and grief for the troubles befalling them (the meaning of *They will put on a leather covering* (v.4), as in the saying of blessed David, "You tore my sackcloth and clad me in joy,"[107] as if to say, you took away grief and filled me with joy). Such people, after turning to repentance and divesting themselves of the vesture of grief, will abjure their error and say that, far from knowing anything or practising any such thing, they will be occupied in future in working the land, an occupation

106. Where our Heb. speaks of a fountain, the LXX reads a similar form for "place." Theodore's text omits the second half of the verse.

107. Ps 30.11. Ancient and modern commentators, whether reading a text that includes a negative (our Heb.) or not (LXX), hazard an interpretation of this style of attire. Likewise with the wounds borne by the reformed seers; Theodore's opinion seems as valid as Smith's, who recalls the wounds made in an ecstatic orgy by the prophets of Baal (1 Kgs 18.28). Recourse to paraphrase, in any case, suggests the content is of a lesser importance.

they learnt from the very first day from their parents. Even if people should ask them about the recent scars they carry from the assailants as to how they came by them, they would announce clearly without equivocation that, instead of being involved in anything they should not, they got the wounds in their own house from people by whom they thought they were particularly loved, such as sons by parents, who showed no mercy for their sins, since they set devotion to religion ahead of natural sympathy.

The prophet had thus mentioned the change in the situation for the better, how the adversaries were wiped out through the leadership of the Maccabees, on the one hand, and, on the other, how the nation came to live in good order so as to rid themselves of their impiety and lawlessness, and everything that proved to be in keeping with the divine laws took over. He was then inspired in such a revelation, which he was granted from the operation of the Holy Spirit,[108] and saw clearly the future, namely, the fate of the Jews, the reform of their condition due to the leadership of the Maccabees, and the extent of the disorder that ensured from the malice of those who in defiance of propriety and obedience to the divine laws took over from the kings both the priesthood and the leadership of the people and filled everything with extreme confusion. The prophet, therefore, felt great indignation for those responsible for such trouble, and spoke as follows, *Sword, rise up against the shepherd and against a man who is his fellow citizen, says the Lord almighty* (v.7). Again in this case, too, he discloses the future in an imperative; directing his words to him like a sword, he says, Be brandished, O sword, against those who exercise leadership so badly, and [588] against all those who zealously tried to involve the nation in wrongdoing.[109] *Strike the shepherd, and the sheep will*

108. Though Theodore has spoken of Zechariah receiving visions or revelations, *apokalypseis*, only at this point does he speak of him as being inspired, *enthous*, by the Holy Spirit—perhaps because a particularly comprehensive grasp of the future is involved, though not so comprehensive as to include the NT realization of the figure of the Martyred Shepherd.

109. Commentators have differed as to the probity or malice of this shepherd, some transposing vv.7–9 to follow the treatment of the evil shepherds in 11.4–17—an option not open to Theodore. Despite Jesus' application of this

be scattered: with a blow of yours inflict death on those who so abuse the leadership of the people, and at one blow for their punishment scatter the whole group of those involving them. After expressing this in the imperative mood as a disclosure of the future, he goes on in the same vein, clothing his words in a form suited to the contents: *I shall turn my hand against the little shepherds:* if some are subject to the leaders, prepared to cooperate with them in their depraved leadership and be entrusted themselves with some role given to them in their zeal for bad government, I shall punish them as well (referring to such people as *little shepherds*).

Next, to bring out the justice of the punishment, *On that day in all the land, says the Lord, two-thirds of it will be destroyed and will disappear, and one-third of it will be left. I shall pass the third through fire and heat them as silver is heated, and I shall test them as gold is tested. He will invoke my name, and I shall hearken to him; I shall say, He is my people, and he will say, The Lord is my God* (vv.8–9): the fact that such people suffered due punishment was proved in the event, since they were responsible for such deterioration in the people that the two-thirds of the people who took a turn for the worse were consigned to punishment, meaning by *two-thirds* the majority. Still, the lovers of duty that would be left were not so few, even if fewer than the others (the meaning of *one-third*); they were tested by the magnitude of the troubles befalling them as if by fire and provided a greater proof of their virtue by putting up with so many troubles, on the one hand, and on no occasion failing in good will towards me, on the other. They witnessed my help and benefited from it, while I made them my own, promising my care, while they entrusted everything to me, putting everything under my lordship and governance.

---

verse to himself (Mk 14.27), an application on which Theodore is predictably silent, he sees the bad leaders referred to. The "little shepherds" of v.7 are thus unlikely to remind him of Jesus' "little flock" (Lk 12.32).

Chapter Fourteen

Having once again mentioned the prevalence of evil stemming from the malice of those giving bad leadership and the punishment imposed on them for that reason, he contrasts it with the care he provided to those holding firm. *Lo, a day of the Lord is coming, and the spoils will be divided among you. I shall gather all the nations against Jerusalem to do battle, the city will be taken, the houses plundered, the women defiled. Half the city will go off into captivity, but the rest of my people will not be wiped out from the city* (vv.1–2): a time has come when great numbers of the foreigners will attack Jerusalem and plunder all its contents; some of it will taken by the enemy, all of the contents of the houses will be plundered, those attacking the city employing such violence as not even [589] to refrain from indignity to the women's bodies, and taking captive as many residents as possible. Yet despite these things happening this way owing to the malice of the others, those who cling to my favor were kept unharmed in the city through my care.

He then goes on to mention the divine help, thanks to which everything took a turn for the better for them through the leadership of the Maccabees.[110] God will go at the head of his own, he is saying, as though in battle array, acting as their general and deploying them against the adversaries; taking his position *on the Mount of Olives opposite Jerusalem,* he will shake the mountain and make everything before the city tremble, and the city, too, so that the mountain will seem to be split in two with fear at the movement, and the events of that time will seem to resemble what happened in the earthquake that happened in the time of King Uzziah through divine wrath. As usual, he is thus telling everything in hyperbolic fashion, including the fact that by the magnitude of the help provided to his own and by his indignation against the adversaries everything will seem as it were to totter. Now, he used the comparison with

110. With Zechariah 14 we come, in the view of Paul Hanson, to "full-blown" apocalyptic. But despite showing appreciation of the author's panoramic—even cosmic and cataclysmic—scenario, which he classes again as merely hyperbolic, Theodore insists on finding an historical reference.

Uzziah since he, too, though having no right to the priesthood attempted to usurp it, at which God also betrayed his indignation by the magnitude of the earthquake.[111] In the same way in this case, too, on account of those who with impious aspirations set aside the order of law and made an attempt on the priesthood in defiance of propriety, God betrays his peculiar indignation by shaking everything as a means of punishing the adversaries, on the one hand, and, on the other, saving his own.

He goes on: *The Lord my God will come, and all his holy ones with him* (v.5): from the very magnitude of the events God seems to come to our help as if from a distance, bringing his own army with him. Now, he is referring to the invisible powers, referring to them as *holy ones* in that they are accustomed to serve all his wishes in what concerns human beings.[112] *On that day there will be no light; instead, there will be cold and ice on one day* (v.6). He means, not that there is real light and cold and ice, but that just as people normally say that the sun will be darkened, or will set on them, or something similar, as people in times of calamity have no sense of light, seeming instead at that time to be in some kind of darkness, as it were, so too here. Affected by the magnitude of the events, people seem not even to see light, and alarmed as if by cold and ice they will keep shaking and trembling, grinding their teeth at the magnitude of the troubles about to happen at the divine coming, like the saying of the Lord, "There will be gnashing of teeth there."[113]

111. Again to demythologize and historicize the description of events, Theodore cites the earthquake mentioned in the opening verse of Amos as belonging to Uzziah's time, where in fact he passed over it without comment. The incident of Uzziah's effrontery he is referring to (see 2 Chr 16.16–21) has, predictably, no mention of such an earthquake, though archeologists claim there is evidence at ancient Hazor of such a quake in his reign—hence perhaps Amos's remark. In Theodore's view, τὸ ἱστορικόν requires insistence on historicity, not evidence of it. On similar grounds, geographical details in v.5 are passed over.

112. Martin Noth, who is unaware of Theodore's interpretation, concurs with him in seeing the holy ones here as "the heavenly companions of the coming God" (in an essay, "The holy ones of the Most High," trans. D. R. Ap-Thomas, in *The Laws in the Pentateuch, and Other Studies* [Edinburgh: Oliver and Boyd, 1966], 215–28). But for Theodore even such a heavenly army does not remove the scene from the realm of history.

113. Mt 8.12, a detail from the eschatological account of the just dining with the patriarchs while the damned are in exterior darkness—a reference hardly

That day is known to the Lord (v.7), as if to say that these things will happen by God's will, since it was his pleasure that they should occur this way at that time, as it says, "The Lord knows those who are his,"[114] meaning, He related them to himself and considered them his friends. In the same way also he says the day is known [592] to the Lord as being pleasing to him in that such things happen on it by his will—for punishment of the adversaries, for salvation of his own. Hence he proceeds, *Not day and not night, and at evening there will be light:* since the troubles prevail, such awful darkness will envelop everyone that there will be no difference between night and day, so great a darkness will overtake everything. On this will follow (the sense of *at evening*) light, that is, divine support, since all this is done for punishment of the adversaries so that he may preserve his own for himself.

He thus goes on this way, *On that day living water will flow out from Jerusalem* (v.8), as if to say, At that time an undefiled and lawful priesthood will be practised, a leadership pleasing to God and a teaching in accord with the divine laws, which will be suitable not only for the members of the nation at that time but also for those coming later.[115] In fact, while he calls the people of that time a first sea, it is those after them he calls the last one. To this he added, *It will be like this in summer and in spring,* as if to say that in every season good will prevail through divine care; in this way throughout all the earth God the creator and Lord of all will be known and acknowledged as king. Through what he does, in fact, he gives evidence of his care and his power, and everyone throughout the earth (that is, the members of the nation) continue in the future to be free of every error and refer to God by his name alone.

Next, he mentions also different places,[116] meaning to imply of all of them, In every part belonging to our land God will con-

---

calculated to reinforce the historical character of Zechariah's scene. (Other forms of the LXX read "no light, or cold, or ice.")

114. 2 Tm 2.19; see Nm 16.5.

115. Theodore declines to pick up eschatological and specifically Christological echoes of this living water, as in Jn 4.10, Rv 22.1–2.

116. The topographical details in v.10 are typically omitted, Theodore preferring to take v.11 as the intention behind them.

tinue to be known and adored, now that all error and impiety
has been expelled from us. With this knowledge all who belong
to our nation will dwell securely in Jerusalem, and no one in
the nation will then take pleasure in impiety or be alienated
from God, as he says, *No one any longer will be accursed*. As blessed
Paul in fact says, "If anyone does not love Jesus Christ the Lord,
let him be accursed."[117] This will no longer be the case, then,
since no one will any longer be alienated from God; Jerusalem
will then continue to be inhabited by all in complete security,
which thanks to divine care it will enjoy on account of attention
to virtue.

With this he concluded the prophecy of the Maccabees,
what would happen at that time, what offences would be committed by them, what would be done to them by the enemy,
and all the care God would show them in providing his aid to
the champions of virtue. At this point he resumes what was said
by him before the reference to the Maccabees, in which he
mentions the good things that would come to the nation
through Zerubbabel and went on to include the destruction of
those in Gog's company. Reference to these he makes at this
point as being in the near future so that what happened in the
short term would encourage acceptance of what was to happen
much later, namely, to the Maccabees, and so that it might be
possible for the prophet to conclude his prophecy with a more
salutary account.[118]

Accordingly he says, *This will be the fate with which the Lord will
strike all the peoples that attacked Jerusalem* (v.12): with divine
might they will prevail over that mighty and invincible nation,
as if the flesh of those standing around rotted, nor will they be
allowed to advance into battle, God anticipating their attack
with the punishment inflicted on them. The faculty of sight will
fail before the magnitude of the troubles gripping them, and
they will remain speechless with bewilderment at what occurs.

117. 1 Cor 16.22.
118. The prophet's material cannot be simply apocalyptic (in Theodore's
view); it must have an historical reference of one kind or another, earlier or later—despite the character of the ghoulish description that follows in vv.12–13
(losing nothing in paraphrase).

In short, such a sudden shock from divine wrath will seize them that each man will turn his hand against his fellow, all unawares, thinking he is striking foreigners, with the result that they suffer the worst impact from one another and most of them fall to the blows of their own men rather than of the Jews. While they are caught up in such awful troubles, he is saying, *even Judah is deployed in Jerusalem* (v.14), as if to say, They will confidently issue forth to war against them under the generalship of Zerubbabel, who being from the tribe of Judah succeeded as their king by divine decision.[119] They will so prevail over the enemy that all their possessions—gold, silver, apparel, and anything else of worth they own—they will completely steal to add to their own wealth (the sense of *they will amass the might of all the peoples round about,* meaning their possessions on which they depended for their power—hence his adding by way of clarification *gold and silver and clothing in great abundance*). He follows this by saying that some awful ruin will befall horses, mules, camels, donkeys, and all the animals belonging to them that they thought useful for war and brought with them.

While their death and ruin will be so terrible and extensive, all of them that survive will acknowledge God's power in their sufferings and accept the Law for themselves, regularly going up to Jerusalem to pay the appropriate worship to God and observe the feast of tabernacles, summer being a suitable time for those coming from a distance. On many of those who out of arrogance do not observe these rituals I shall, on the contrary, inflict punishment, condemning them to drought and the ensuing infertility so that they may perceive their neglect of respect for the Lord of all. If some of the Egyptians do not at any time adopt this attitude, they will pay the same penalty (meaning that many of the foreign nations will be terrified at the magnitude of what happened and will come flooding to Jerusalem from all directions, paying the appropriate worship to God, and meeting with punishment if they do not do it).[120]

---

119. Zechariah's text in this unequivocally apocalyptic canvas, of course, makes no reference to Zerubbabel, let alone his royal status on the grounds of Davidic descent.

120. Vv. 16–19 are thus reduced to a paraphrase.

On that day there will be inscribed on the horse's rein, Holy to the Lord almighty. There will be cooking pots in the house of the Lord like bowls before the altar (v.20). He means that many things will be dedicated to God by the Israelites that are taken from the enemy, [596] these being innumerable, just as blessed David did in dedicating Goliath's sword to God after slaying him.[121] His meaning is the same here, too, they will also offer to God at that time the reins of the horses they took from the slain, implying by mention of the rein the rest of the accoutrement and spoils they intended to dedicate, each offering what he chose from the spoils according to his own preference. Hence he goes on to say that a great number of cooking pots as well that the enemy brought with them they thought useful for themselves for cooking meat, which owing to their great number would be exposed like spoils in the divine house. Now, by mention of the rein he meant the dedication of accoutrement, and by the cooking pots the possessions, in the way the divine Scripture normally implies whole from part whenever it considers chasing detail superfluous.[122] In this case, too, it was superfluous to itemize shields, swords, breastplates, cooking pots, and whatever serves people's needs, such as writing tablets, goblets, and the like; instead, as I have said before and often observed, by mention of the part he meant the whole.

To bring out the purpose of the cooking pots that were dedicated, he goes on, *Every cooking pot in Jerusalem and in Judah will be holy to the Lord almighty; all who sacrifice will come and take some of them and cook in them* (v.21): all the cooking pots that are presented will be holy in being dedicated to God from then on; as a result there will be an abundance for the offerers to have in cases where it is necessary to cook and perform the sacrificial

---

121. We have no record of David's doing so. Theodore is reading to this effect the incident of David's being given the sword by the priest, Ahimelech (1 Sm 21.8–9), the implication being that it had earlier been dedicated as a religious offering, though not so mentioned at the killing of Goliath.

122. Theodore flatters himself that his dislike for ἀκριβολογία is shared by the biblical authors, whom he sees settling here again for synecdoche, whereas in fact Zechariah's apocalyptic message is that in the endtime "every distinction between the holy and the profane will be eliminated . . . all of life will be sacralized" (Smith).

ritual properly. After all, does not the divine Scripture say as much in the first book of Kings in describing the lawlessness of the sons of Eli, that "when the meat was cooked, the priest's servant came in with a three-pronged hook in his hand and lowered it into the pot, or cauldron, or copper vessel, and all that came out on the hook the priest took for himself"?[123] So this is what he meant, that for those congregating in Jerusalem for worship of God there would in future be an abundance of cooking pots, which were required for use when performing their sacrifices.

To this he adds, *There is no longer any Canaanite in the house of the Lord almighty on that day.* Since Canaanites were inveterate practitioners of impiety and depravity, this means that in the future everyone from Israel in the habit of adopting impiety and depravity would learn from the events themselves how great the value of piety and the practice of virtue. This is what blessed Hosea also says, "Canaan, in his hands scales of injustice, he loved to oppress; Ephraim said, But I have become wealthy, I have found relief for myself,"[124] by the name *Canaan* referring to the Israelites' wrongdoing in imitating their behavior. [597]

123. 1 Sm 2.13–14. Theodore is still trying to historicize the prophet's message, the universalism characterizing the world after Armageddon.

124. Hos 12.7, where as here Theodore misses the Canaanites' reputation for (shady) commerce suggested in passages like Prv 31.24 and Ezek 17.4. He is missing more than that, however, in the case of Deutero-Zechariah.

COMMENTARY ON THE PROPHET MALACHI

HE BLESSED PROPHETS Haggai and Zechariah prophesied through divine influence after the return of the people from Babylon. While blessed Haggai addressed the people on the rebuilding of the Temple and in particular disclosed the destruction of those in the company of Gog, blessed Zechariah mentioned those things as well as the doings of the Maccabees much later,[1] setting out as well many and varied revelations in which he indicated the variety of God's beneficence towards them and provided instruction sufficient to bring them to the practice of religion and a devout life. Since Jews, however, though vouchsafed divine providence and the return from Babylon, and though being in receipt of countless good things and enjoying great prosperity, did not use the respite properly, the priests sinning in some matters and the whole people in others, of necessity the present prophet under divine influence was appointed to this task, accusing the priests and the people of the sins, the nature of which you could learn better from the text itself, and disclosing also some future events.

Now, the prophet's name in Greek is Messenger, and in Hebrew Malachi, the Hebrews' normal term for messenger; hence in translation into Greek he is called Messenger in place of Malachi.[2]

---

1. As we have noted in connection with Zechariah in particular, Theodore tries to see the prophets treating of historical situations, unwilling as he is to recognize nonhistorical material like apocalyptic (even though unwittingly incorporating an apocalyptic figure like Gog). Yet we shall see him typically unwilling to investigate some of the historical details of Malachi's ministry. His customary statement of the book's ὑπόθεσις, however, would be helpful for his readers.

2. It may be that Theodore's lack of Hebrew does not allow him to appreciate the fact that, whereas the Greek speaks of "his messenger," the Hebrew title

Chapter One

He begins this way, *An oracle of the word of the Lord to Israel by means of his messenger* (v.1), as if to say, By divine influence the messenger was entrusted with the task of prophecy by way of an accusation against Israel, since he was on the point of indicating by this general term both the priests and the people, all the Israelites being referred to in common.[3] Then, after this title customary in the prophetic books,[4] the prophet begins his own address thus: *Take it to heart*, words most apposite for those who had neglected hitherto to do as they ought.[5] He now bids them give careful thought to their duty, realize what they have been guilty of, estimate how far they have strayed from the right path, and thus also apply some correction to their failings.

Next, after the exhortation and encouragement by which he made them more solicitious for their duty, he goes on, *I loved you, says the Lord* (v.2). It was right that to the ingrates, accused as they were of the depravity of their behavior, he should mention his love above all, as though they were judged against that. [600] *You replied, In what way did you love us?* It is not a statement he cites, since there were no grounds for them in reply to ask, *In what way did you love us?* as it was clear to everyone how many good things he had brought them, whether what had happened in the past or occurring frequently afterwards and happening just lately. It is normal for the divine Scripture, remember, to use the word for the event, and to indicate by a word the disposition of those doing something, as for example, "They said, Who will see them?"[6] meaning, Their attitude was

---

reads *malachi*, "my messenger." Or it may be, on the other hand, that the LXX represents the original Heb. reading.

3. One of the historical issues calling for comment, referred to in n. 1, is this mention of "Israel" as the recipient of the prophet's message at a time when the northern kingdom had long disappeared, Judah and Jerusalem receiving less attention in the book. A comment to the effect that the title had been taken over by Judah as a "dignified religious name" (W. Rudolph) might have been helpful.

4. Theodore made the same observation at the beginning of Habakkuk, where this word for "oracle," λῆμμα, is used, even though it occurs elsewhere in the titles only to Nahum and Zechariah II.

5. The words are not in our Heb. text.

6. Ps 64.5.

that no one was observing what was happening, something they would not have put into words like this; and, "For he said in his heart, I shall not be moved, and shall last from generation to generation without problems,"[7] meaning, they felt as though they would never have a problem; and you could quote many similar cases that it is not the time to assemble at present. So this is what is meant here, too, *In what way did you love us?* meaning, Though loved by me and frequently treated well, you adopted a depraved and ungrateful attitude as though not loved by me or ever having received any good.

He then mentions the things from which it was possible to discern the extent of the goods they had received beyond other people. *Was not Esau Jacob's brother? the Lord asks. I loved Jacob, but hated Esau. I reduced his boundaries to a desolation, and his inheritance to a desert house. Hence if he says, Idumea has been overthrown, and we shall recover and rebuild its desolate parts, the Lord almighty says this, Let them build and I shall overthrow. They will be called Frontiers of Iniquity, and a people against whom the Lord is forever set in battle array. Your eyes will see and you will say, The Lord has been magnified beyond the frontiers of Israel* (vv.2–5). The Idumeans had lately been punished and were suffering innumerable troubles for being hostile to the Israelites at the time when first Assyrians and later Babylonians attacked them. This had been foretold by blessed David in the Psalms; he says, "Remember, Lord, the sons of Edom on the day of Jerusalem who said, Raze it, raze it, down to its foundations, wretched daughter of Babylon,"[8] in which he brought out that Babylonians also would pay the penalty for the troubles brought on them, and Idumeans would be punished for conspiring with them in the troubles against the Israelites. Blessed Obadiah, the prophet, also made

7. Ps 10.6. Theodore is identifying a feature of the text that has struck modern commentators who, calling it a prophetic dispute, like Joyce Baldwin believe that it is "extremely unlikely that the words he puts into the mouth of his opponents were in fact voiced . . . Malachi reads the attitudes of his people and intuitively puts their thoughts into words."

8. Ps 137.7–8. Theodore sees Edom's punishment as due to their assistance to Nebuchadnezzar against Judah, but is imprecise about the time and occasion of its misfortunes ("lately, fresh in everyone's mind"), as are modern commentators.

this prediction later; but since it had now been fulfilled, and the memory of the punishment from God befalling the Idumeans was fresh in everyone's mind, it was right for him to give evidence of his love for them by a comparison with the others, beginning with the ancestors of themselves and the Idumeans: while Jacob was their ancestor, Esau was the Idumeans'.

So he says, Whereas they were both brothers, and the law of nature meant they had everything in common, I loved [601] your ancestor, but I hated theirs, Esau; and to this day I have continued giving proof of love for you and hatred for them. In fact, I devastated the whole of their country for your sake, calling them to account for their crimes against you; I transformed all their land into wilderness, which I left in such a bad condition for them that even should they ever wish to change and restore it as their own, and rebuild their devastated cities and regions, it would be impossible to do. For I sentenced them to devastation, and in no way would it be possible for their fortunes to be reconstituted; even if they were to try to rebuild, I would overturn it again, the result being they will be given the name *Frontiers of Iniquity* for being devastated by lawlessness. In your regard, on the contrary, I determined that everything should be done so well that you would actually be witnesses of the good things bestowed on you and come to a knowledge of the power of God who brightens up your prospects with so many good things.

Next, to extend the accusation, *A son honors a father, and a servant will fear his master. If I am a father, where is my honor? if I am the Lord, says the Lord almighty, where is fear of me?* (v.6) It belongs to sons, he is saying, to do the kinds of things from which esteem and respect will accrue to fathers, and ministering to masters' commands in fear belongs to servants. I am your Lord in bringing you into existence from nothing, and with surpassing love and goodness I made you my own, and agreed to your being called my sons, and I imparted to you the confidence to refer to me as your father. But I see you are grateful to me for nothing, not anxious to show me respect as father by the practice of your good works, nor in fear of me as Lord to keep in mind my commands.

So in directing this general accusation against them all, he distinguishes both persons and actions, and in addressing the priests he speaks as follows, *You priests, a disgrace to my name:* you who are entrusted with divine worship, and ought be guides for the others to better things, you are guilty of such awful crimes as to present me as worthy of no regard to those witnessing your behavior. *You said, How are we a disgrace to your name?* likewise here, too, meaning by *You said,* From your extreme inattentiveness you show no sense of your awful failings, and instead have the impression of doing nothing wrong, though committing such awful evil. He then mentions also what has been done. *Bringing to the altar bread that is polluted* (v.7): you do not take care to make the offering of loaves in accord with the teaching of the Law or in accord with the Mosaic provisions; instead, in defiance of regulations you take ordinary ones that come by chance and put them on the table (*polluted* meaning leavened ones, something opposed to the Law's requirement that unleavened loaves be brought to the altar, never leavened ones). "You shall make [604] an offering of nothing leavened to the Lord,"[9] Scripture says, remember, an ordinance clearly opposed to offering leavened loaves, and on these grounds they were rightly condemned for clearly doing the opposite to the Law. *You said, How did we pollute them?* In doing this, he is saying, you did not want to consider the inappropriateness of the action (the term *You said* here again expressing their disposition, as if to say, You were disposed to do nothing, by insensitivity and laziness committing this awful fault). *By your saying, The Lord's table is despicable, and you despised what was on it.* Here again the phrase *By your saying* has the effect of suggesting disposition in place of action, the meaning being, Your doing this shows you have no other intention and no other disposition than for my table to meet with no due attention and consequently for no due respect to be shown to what is placed on it; it betrays your carelessness in making the offering of the loaves, unconcerned as to whether it be performed according to the

---

9. Lv 2.11. The clerical commentator warms to the condemnation of priestly indifference, even tracking down details of Mosaic legislation.

provision of the Law. He first made mention of the loaves as though the preeminent sin, since it was required of them that in particular the loaves placed on the table meet with care as in some way being offered for the whole people. God had ordered that they be six in number, two tribes identified with each one, so that by the six the twelve tribes be represented, on behalf of whom he bade the offering of the loaves be made.[10]

He proceeds to mention also another failing of theirs. *Hence if you offer a blind creature as a victim, is it not wrong; and if you offer one that is lame or sick, is it not wrong?* (v.8): by offering such things to God by way of sacrifice, do you think you commit no sin? To bring out the inappropriateness of what is done, *Offer that to your leader, and see if he will accept it, if he will welcome your visit, says the Lord almighty:* if you give no heed to the inappropriateness of what is done, try offering it to the person entrusted with your leadership, and see if he accepts it, if out of regard for you he overlooks the insult. Will he not, on the contrary, be insulted by you rather than honored, and with injured pride give you short shrift along with the offering, such as it is? Having brought out their inappropriate behavior in both cases, in regard to the loaves and the victims, he goes on, *And now be conciliatory to the presence of your God, and implore him to have mercy on you* (v.9): amend your former sinful ways by your later behavior, stop committing such faults, and even ask to gain pardon from God for your past. He rightfully instilled fear, *It is on your hands:* you have recent experience of the troubles, of which you fell foul not long ago on account of your neglect of duty; mindful of them you should pay every attention to good behavior. *Am I to accept any of your appeals? says the Lord almighty:* from this you ought know that not even now shall I have any respect for you, sinners that you are, unless by repentance you make some amendment for the faults committed by you. [605]

Because even among you doors will be closed, and you will not kindle fire on my altar freely (v.10): it is not difficult for me even now[11] to make my Temple inaccessible to you and stop you serv-

---

10. Lv 24.5–6 speaks of twelve loaves being baked, and laid out in two rows of six on the golden table.

11. In opening his commentary, Theodore implied Malachi is engaged in

ing at my altar, since you have committed such sins. I actually did this, consigning the Temple to flames, since I saw you guilty of intolerable behavior, and consigning you to captivity in which you found yourself, unable to perform anything required for priestly ministry. *My good pleasure is not found among you, says the Lord almighty, and I shall not accept an offering from your hands:* you are well aware that as long as you commit such sins, I shall turn away from what is done by you and not accept your sacrifices, so that you do not gain the benefit you hope to achieve by offering these sacrifices. *Because from the rising of the sun to its setting may my name be glorified by the nations, and in every place incense is offered to my name and a pure offering, because my name is great among the nations, says the Lord almighty* (v.11): everywhere on earth all people wherever they may be found seek after my name, each of them anxious to reverence God and honor his name as master and Lord, as in fact I am, so that even if they are deceived in applying my name to what they should not, all still honor it as mine and in my name they perform their sacrifices, believing the divinity excels and surpasses everything. You, on the contrary, are seen to insult what is believed by everyone to be so mighty and venerable, since by treating my table as common and lacking anything beyond the ordinary, by believing what is placed on it to be worthy of no attention, and by offering such things to me you clearly insult my name and appear to set at nought the divinity, who is rightly regarded by everyone as so mighty, fearsome, august, and surpassing everything.[12]

You said, This involves distress. I blew it away, says the Lord almighty (v.13): you pride yourself on making your offering with

---

his ministry after the return from Babylon. Here he also implies the Temple has been rebuilt, and in fact there has been time for Temple liturgy to lapse into mediocrity. A key chronological clue in the Heb. text, the Persian word for "governor" in v.8, a clue to its provenance and late date, is lost in Theodore's text.

12. This v.11 has been taken in various ways over the ages, from messianic and even eucharistic interpretation to an endorsement of other religious traditions. On first principles Theodore shows no interest in the former, and in a guarded fashion sees value in the latter, though principally seeing the words directed at the restored community's indifference.

your own sweat, and tears, and distress, but I rejected it, observing the great contempt in your offering. *You bring stolen goods, lame and handicapped things, and present them as offerings: am I to accept them from your hands? says the Lord almighty:* since you even bring such things as your offerings, I would all the more discard them as worthless things offered with a worthless intention. Then to lay down the law, *Cursed be a man of means who had a male in his flock, and his vow involved it, and he sacrifices spoilt things to the Lord. Because I am a great king, says the Lord almighty, and my name is illustrious among the nations* (v.14): everyone who makes a vow to sacrifice and then, though affluent and in a position to bring from the flocks in his possession a male that is reputable [608] and fitting to be offered to God, does not offer it, and instead sacrifices to God something worthless and spoilt, is liable to the worst punishment, because to God who rules over all and is acknowledged by all people alike for the greatness of his nature he does not offer what is required, though well able to do so.

Chapter Two

And now this command is for you, you priests: If you do not listen and if you do not set your heart on giving glory to my name, says the Lord almighty, I shall send out the curse on you, and I shall curse your blessing and curse it, and I shall annul your blessing. It will not remain with you, because you do not take it to heart (vv.1–2): lo, this is my decree concerning you who have been appointed to priestly worship: if you are now not prepared earnestly to heed what is said by me, and to accord God the due and obligatory glory by attention to worship, I shall inflict extreme punishment on you and change the honor you now enjoy into dishonor and experience of troubles. I shall completely remove from you the priestly office so that none of you will hold this rank (by *curse* obviously referring to punishment, and by *blessing* to the enjoyment of good things). Hence his nominating priesthood, in that it is the source of many good things both for those enjoying them and for those to whom it fell to exercise it.

Then, as a stronger indication of his indignation, *Lo, I reject your upper arm, and shall scatter offal in your faces, the offal of your festivals, and treat you the same way* (v.3). Assigning the upper arm to God as a special part of the offerings was commanded in the Law.[13] No longer shall I accept this from you, he is saying, since I am in need of nothing, and have directed this to be done for your benefit. Since you show your neglect of me in such things and think you honor me in this way by dedicating the upper arm to me, I revoke this so as to provide proof of my indignation; I shall allow you to take this for yourself as well along with animals' dung, since it is appropriate for it to be offered by you on the festivals, which you have defiled with the wickedness of your practices, and I shall impose on all of you in common the penalty for your practices (the meaning of *I shall treat you the same way*).

You will know that I the Lord have issued this command to you as my covenant with the Levites, says the Lord almighty (v.4): from the ignominy and punishment befalling you at that time you will precisely perceive my power and might, and that, in my wish to be beneficent to you from the beginning, I promoted you to the priestly office, making some such agreements with you[14] so that you might enjoy the honor bestowed by me and do everything for the benefit of those for whose sake you exercise priesthood. You, for your part, however, set no store by them, [609] and instead scorned the honor bestowed on you and treated my service with such neglect. Then, since the practice of priesthood took its beginning from Aaron,[15] who emerged as

13. The LXX comes up with "I shall reject your upper arm" for our Heb.'s "I shall rebuke your offspring" by reading similar but not identical forms. Undeterred, Theodore rationalizes the text before him, finding evidence for his position in scriptural loci like Ex 29.27, a provision that seems to be reversed in Lv 7.34, as he goes on to say.

14. Was there a covenant "with the Levites" as a whole (as distinct from the "covenant of peace" with Phinehas in Nm 25.12)? Modern commentators find no trace (beyond Moses' blessing of Levi in Dt 33.8–11); Theodore again prefers not to investigate.

15. Theodore therefore, since the LXX has in v.4 spoken not of Levi but of "the Levites," now sees the original priest as Aaron. The bishop warmly endorses this encomium of priesthood as he had in ch 1 warmed to the condemnation of priestly shortcomings (see n. 9 there).

the first high priest by divine appointment, he goes on, *My covenant of life and peace was with him, and I gave him fear to fear me and shrink before my name. A norm of truth was in his mouth, and iniquity was not found on his lips; proceeding in peace, he walked with me and turned many away from iniquity; because a priest's lips will preserve knowledge, and they will look for a norm from his mouth, for he is a messenger of the Lord almighty* (vv.5–7): him I chose first, and made a covenant with him, promising him enjoyment of long life and peace, on the one hand, while, on the other, bidding him have fear of me in mind and with deep reverence preserve my memory. He, for his part, adopted the things befitting the office I gave him, setting himself the norm of living with truth and rejecting all falsehood, and never uttering anything that was unjust or that proved a source of harm to those subject to the priesthood. For their sake in keeping with my promises he lived in peace himself and was never at odds with me, doing nothing in opposition to me (the meaning of *proceeding in peace, he walked with me*) and leading as many as possible from bad ways to good. In short, he did what was particularly appropriate for a priest, teaching the knowledge of truth, leading to the divine Law everyone subject to him, and teaching how they might always be devoted to it, this being the task of a priest, appointed to have the role of a kind of messenger to other people, leading everyone to virtue, which it is the function also of angels to perform.

While I made this treaty with Aaron, who did what was in keeping with my laws, you, on the contrary, who succeeded to the priesthood from him, have cut yourself off completely from them. How and in what way? *You, on the contrary, turned aside from the way, and undermined the attachment of many to the Law; you corrupted the covenant of Levi, says the Lord almighty* (v.8): you abandoned zeal for these things, with the result that you rendered the others indifferent about the Law; thus, in short, by your malice you corrupted the whole agreement I made with him in my wish for it to remain in force even under his successors. *I allowed you to be scorned and humiliated before all the nations in return for your not observing my ways and instead showing partiality in matters of law* (v.9). He was right to bring them to their

senses by reference to what had recently happened. Finding
you guilty of such crimes, he is saying, I handed you over to
captivity so as to show your nothingness and deprive you completely of the priestly office in return for your refusing to set
any store by my commands and instead assisting the others to
neglect my laws, when by rights they should have been brought
to their senses [612] by you (the meaning of *showing partiality
in matters of law*, meaning, You were unwilling to rebuke those
sinning in defiance of the Law).

*Did not one God create you? Have you not all one father? Why have
you each abandoned your brother so as to profane the covenant of your
ancestors?* (v.10): you and he (he means Aaron) were made by
the one God, and accorded the same care and rank, his words
being addressed to you both in common, "I said, You are gods,
and all sons of the Most High," which is relevant in particular
to those raised to the priestly office and thereby exercising
leadership of the people.[16] Hence you caused such corruption
in morals, with the result that, whereas he in his case reformed
them and led them zealously to their duty, you neglected those
subject to the priesthood, though your own brethren and so
sinful and effectively trampling on exact observance of my laws.
So what happened? *Judah has been abandoned and, an abomination has been committed in Israel and in Jerusalem, because Judah profaned the sanctuary of the Lord of which he was fond, and has gone after foreign gods* (v.11): since the people did what they should not,
therefore, and no word of correction came to them from you
priests, they were deprived of my providence and taken off into
captivity for neglecting the worship of God, which you in particular should have performed wih great zeal, and for turning
to the worship of idols.

He thus switches his discourse from the priests to everyone,
as though such things had occurred through the malice of the
former and of the rest, and proceeds to speak for the common
correction of all. *The Lord will destroy the person who does such*

16. Ps 82.6. Unlike modern commentators, who see heathen gods referred
to, Theodoret will also see leaders of the Jewish people in focus in this psalm,
though not priests, to whom Theodore wants to apply it. The next verse of the
psalm, of course, proceeds, "But you shall die like mortals."

things until Jacob is brought down from its tents and from those offer-
ing sacrifice to the Lord almighty (v.12): unless you refrain from
this, destruction will completely overtake you all, so that the
others will be brought to extreme humiliation, and you who
pretend to act as priests and the sacrifices for others will fail to
benefit you or them by the offering of sacrifices.

From this point he moves to a different transgression of
theirs: on return from captivity, when they shared in the prosperity provided them by God, they turned to an indulgent life,
overlooked their former wives to direct their gaze at other
women, and those who had lived with them for a long time and
had actually shared with them the troubles and hardships in
captivity in the same place they had no qualms in dismissing,
and turned to others out of licentiousness.[17] Since no help was
forthcoming from them for the women suffering this injury,
and no one reproached them for what happened, the women
naturally could not bear the outrage and dishonor, and thus
betook themselves to God with much weeping and wailing,
pleading to be granted providence from God on the score of
their being helpless. On their behalf he replies, [613] *You did
what I hated: you covered the altar of the Lord with tears, with weeping
and wailing from hardship. Is it still worth having regard to your sacrifice, or taking it as acceptable from your hands?* (v.13) You covered
the altar of the Lord with tears, weeping and wailing. He says
this in reference, not to the grief-stricken but to those responsible for it: he was not about to blame the women for doing so,
forced by such necessity and abuse to run to him, and bewail-
ing the troubles befallen them. Instead, it is very clear that he
rightly blames the wrongdoers responsible for such laments
and tears. So *you covered* means, you caused it to be covered: you
did what most of all is outlawed by me and is obviously very
hateful. And so he rightly proceeded, *Is it still worth having regard to your sacrifice, or taking it as acceptable from your hands?* How

17. Theodore recognizes that with vv.13–16 the prophet addresses another
topic, whether to do with marital infidelity and divorce or, in the view of some
modern commentators, cultic syncretism. Presuming the accent falls on the former, he adopts a strongly parenetic tone that—perhaps for the first time in
these commentaries—shows him trespassing on the role of a preacher.

could I accept a sacrifice or anything else offered by you when your wives bring to me such weeping and wailing for the awful wrongs and abuses they suffer at your hands? It would be so wrong for me to ignore it that, even if I were to ignore your sins committed against me, I shall not ignore the wrongs done to your partners. It is a similar ruling to the one given by the Lord in the Gospels, "If you offer your gift on the altar, and there you remember that your brother has something against you, leave there your gift on the altar, and first go, be reconciled with your brother, and then return and offer your gift."[18] In other words, as he says the offering was pointless in that case without the wronged person being first attended to, so too in this case he says, It is impossible for me to accept anything offered by you when I see those suffering such wrongs at your hands.

You asked, Why? (v.14), in this case also saying *You asked* in similar fashion to mean, You perpetrate such wickedness as though guilty of nothing, adopting such an attitude in the course of committing it. Then, to bring out the wrong in such behavior, he goes on, *Because the Lord was a witness between you and the wife of your youth, whom you have abandoned, though she is your partner and your wife by covenant. No one else did so, and a remnant of your spirit* (vv.14–15): while it was my ordinance from the beginning and at the outset of creation that they should leave father and mother and be joined to their wife so that the two should be one flesh,[19] you neglected these laws of mine so as to set aside the woman who was linked to you in marriage from your youth and was your partner in life, banishing her from your house without any reason, despite your contract with her in the marriage laws that you would be one [616] flesh and hold everything in common. Then, after putting aside the woman joined to you on such a basis, you involved yourself with another woman in incontinence, without considering that marriage was established for the continuance of the race so that the race, although under threat from death, might be preserved by

18. Mt 5.23–24. To some extent the woman's situation in marital difficulties is being upheld by Theodore.
19. Gn 2.24.

having children. So marriage is a means devised by God for propagation (the meaning of *a remnant of your spirit*, that is, since you are destined to discontinue the living of the present life, as in the saying, "Their spirit will depart and they will return to their dust")[20] so that, in case you should seem to perish without trace, God left you successors as a memorial and a kind of relic of your existence. The upshot is that, when you have regard for the reason for marriage, you should be in dread of such a development and not sin against the laws on this matter laid down by God from the beginning, but keep them unimpaired by adhering to your former commitment not to dismiss out of incontinence your first wives, whom you married for those reasons, and change to others.[21]

What is most remarkable, he went on to say, *You asked, What does God look for other than offspring?* Since they seemed to have children even by the wives with whom they were unlawfully living, he says, You do this, not because you respect the divine laws about marriage given by God, but because like brute beasts you are bent only on intercourse and childbearing; and as though made by God for this purpose, you thus dismiss your former wives and move on to others, thinking there is no difference between having children with the latter and with the former. You ought to realize that heedless propagation is typical of brute beasts, whereas the characteristic of those given a share in reason is married life in accordance with the divine laws and raising children in that context. Here too, of course, *You asked* does not imply words, because it would not have been possible for them to say this, that God looks for nothing other than offspring; rather, it was to imply their attitude of mind was depraved, and that they did this not as rational people obliged to live by the divine laws, but as interested like brute beasts only in copulating and propagating.

20. See Eccl 12.7, Ps 104.29. Of the text of v.15, R. C. Dentan claims, "In the Hebrew this is one of the most obscure verses in the entire Old Testament." Joyce Baldwin thinks scribes may have taken exception to its teaching and tampered with it.

21. Theodore gives the impression here of delivering a well-rehearsed homily on the ends of marriage and its inviolability, complete with proof texts.

He then imposes a law, *Be on the lookout in your spirit, and do not abandon the wife of your youth:* make every effort in future, then, to live with your wives you took originally in the proper disposition and not dismiss them. Since he had given directions through Moses for a bill of divorce to be given to wives,[22] he proceeds to bring out the extent of the difference. *But if you hate her, send her away, says the Lord God of Israel* (v.16): whenever on the grounds of a wife's unpleasantness, or some depravity, or any other factor that proves her to be deserving of hatred, you are forced into having such an attitude towards her, I bade you at that time to release her, not for the purpose of dissolving the marriage law but on account of circumstances, permitting you to dismiss her not so much for your fault [617] as for being reduced to daily skirmishes with her, in case length of time might result in something worse and somehow you are brought to the point of murdering your wife. After all, the Lord in the Gospels in similar fashion also asked the Pharisees, "Why, then, did Moses permit a bill of divorce?" and went on, "Moses gave such permission in light of your hardness of heart, but it was not like that from the beginning: from the beginning the creator made them male and female, and said, For this reason a person will leave his father and his mother, and will be joined to his wife, and the two will become one flesh."[23] This means that, while the best thing in the beginning was for man and wife to continue living together as was proper, he realized your impulses to be unchecked and gave orders that, if faults developed between you and seemed to provoke some exasperation, it would be better to dismiss your wife than to be driven by hatred to plotting her murder. Then, since it was possible that, without the wife supplying any cause, under the influence of another woman he might of himself manufacture an unjusti-

22. See Dt 24.1–2. Theodore's text of v.16, incorporating an imperative, differs from the LXX, which itself differs from our Heb.

23. Mk 10.2–9. Malachi's text has been left behind in this marshalling of Deuteronomic and evangelical testimonies on divorce—obviously part of the traditional treatment of the subject at the time. Does Theodore's omission of Mk 10.10, "What God has joined together, let no one put asunder," imply that the possibility of divorce (or separation) in desperate situations was allowed for in his church?

fied dislike, *Impiety will unmask your desires, says the Lord almighty:* in case this is not the situation, and you manufacture the cause and dismiss the wives you have been living with from the beginning, God exists as the examiner of your impieties. He does well to proceed in this vein, *Be on the watch in your spirit, and do not renege on your agreement,* so that with your whole mind and disposition you observe the marriage law with the required good will, and keep the contract inviolate with those with whom you entered into the marriage partnership.

Rounding off the treatment of wives in these words, he mentions also a further fault of theirs, no mere sin but impiety. Many people, you see, far from wanting to recognize the sins committed by them, think there are no consequences of these sins; on the contrary, they take it hard when reduced to experiencing distress, even if in many cases they suffer less than they deserve, though quick to blame God for others when they sin gravely without paying the penalty. At that time this happened also with some of the Israelites, and to upbraid them the prophet speaks this way: *You who provoke God in your words, and say, In what have we provoked you? By your saying, Everyone doing evil is good in the sight of the Lord, and he was pleased with them, and, Where is the God of justice?* (v.17) I shall not pass over that impiety of yours, by which you move God to indignation against you without sensing it. The phrase *You say, In what have we provoked God?* he uses here, too, to upbraid them for their attitude in having no sense of being impious in such matters. Now, to indicate what the impious action was, he says, You claim that God gives the impression of being satisfied with your doing evil, and that this emerges from people's not paying the penalty for such sins, even though God would properly inflict extreme punishment on them if there were any element of justice in him. So what about it?[24]

24. This question of theodicy Theodore realizes is a separate issue that will receive treatment in what follows (our chapter division not respecting the movement of thought). The notion of an interventionist God held by "some Israelites at that time" he must feel is not unlike the picture his own morality likes to convey.

Chapter Three

Lo, I shall send my messenger, and he will survey the way before me.
The Lord whom you seek will come suddenly into his Temple, and the
messenger of the covenant whom you wish (v.1): since you make
these claims, then, and look to find attention to justice in punishment from me, I shall send my messenger to minister to my
wishes (the phrase *he will survey the way before me* meaning, He
will go to the trouble like some forerunner of carrying out my
wishes); through him I too shall be present to reveal myself in
action in the Temple, since, on the one hand, in all that happens by God's decree the ministry of angels is understood, and,
on the other, it is God working in them in what he bids be
done. Likewise Scripture also calls the manna the food of angels in their role as ministers, "Human beings ate the bread of
angels," and it was God's bidding for it to be given, "He commanded clouds from on high, opened the doors of heaven,
and rained down on them manna to eat."[25] The term *will come*
normally refers to what happens by the ministry of the angel
when God emerges as the cause of something being achieved,
as in the saying also of blessed David, "He bent the heavens and
came down, and darkness was under his feet,"[26] as if to say,
When he came to our assistance, we got a sense of it from the
effects. Hence, after saying, *The Lord whom you seek will come into*
his Temple, he went on, *and the angel of the covenant whom you*
wish, bringing out that through what happens by the ministry
of the angel God will give evidence of his presence. I for my
part shall come, he is saying, then, whom you look to as punisher of sins; and there will be present also the angel who ministers to the agreements I have often made with you; when you
seek him, you will find him punishing the transgression of your
agreements with me.

While the prophet said this as a consequence of what preceded, it is not surprising that the same verse was cited at the

25. Ps 78.23–25.
26. Ps 18.9. For Theodore ἄγγελος denotes what we think of both as messenger (or forerunner, πρόδρομος) and as heavenly being. Theodoret also testi-
fies to the esteem—even cult—accorded angels in churches in his time.

coming of blessed John the Baptist,[27] the statement being fulfilled in actual fact by the coming of blessed John as predetermined forerunner and minister, and by the emergence of
Christ the Lord, who came at the same time as he, and was testified to by him, and in whom the salvation of all people was
destined to be achieved.

In consequence, at any rate, the prophet went on, *Lo, he is
coming, says the Lord almighty. Who will withstand the day of his entry? or who will endure sight of him?* (vv.1–2) Since God comes, he
says, emerging as punisher of what is done improperly, none of
you who now presume to say this will withstand the magnitude
of the punishment. Now, it is clear that in this he discloses to
them the troubles at the time of the Maccabees that they endured on account of their wickedness. So, whoever thinks this
applies to Christ the Lord, referring to him and to no one else,
[621] is probably ignoring the difference between what is written here and the events that unfolded at the coming of Christ
the Lord. Even if, like a judge, he separated the worthless from
the better people among the Jews, bringing those who believed
in him to better things and consigning the unbelievers to punishment, it is nevertheless obvious that by common consent the
purpose in his coming was what blessed John indicated in saying, "Behold the lamb of God, who takes away the sin of the
world."[28]

The sequel brings out even further the purpose in the
words, proceeding thus, *Because he will come like a fire in a melting
pot and like fullers' grass, he will sit refining and purifying like silver
and gold, he will purify the sons of Levi, and pour them out like silver
and gold. They will present an offering to the Lord in righteousness,
and an offering of Judah in Jerusalem will be pleasing to the Lord, like*

27. Matthew (11.10), Mark (1.2), and Luke (7.27) all apply the verse to the
Baptist, though as editor Mai notes, other patristic commentators associate it
also with the coming of Jesus. Theodore, while also noting this, proceeds to dis-
qualify Jesus, thus earning the sobriquet *Ioudaiophron* from Mai (but see n. 30
below).

28. Jn 1.29. Apart from wanting, as usual, to relate prophetical statements to
historical events and thus exclude an eschatological sense, Theodore can claim
that Jesus is disqualified from fulfilling the prophecy on the grounds of the
σκοπός of his coming—redemptive, not punitive.

the days of yore and the years past (vv.2–4): there will be some benefit from the punishment imposed on you at that time; like fire in a furnace that purifies silver and gold, and grass purifying clothing through the fullers, through the calamities then befalling you he will purify all those guilty of exercising the priesthood improperly. So he will then present as offerings to God those brought to their senses by the occurrence of the troubles, as it was in accordance with law to make an offering to God as champion of justice, to whom they were obliged to celebrate worship in deep reverence, capable as he was of punishing those prepared to pay him no heed. At that time, he is saying, Jews in Jerusalem will offer sacrifices pleasing to God as in the former time, when for the righteous people living at that time who were duly observant it was in accordance with law to offer their sacrifices.

Now, neither the phrase *he will purify the sons of Levi* nor the phrase *an offering of Judah in Jerusalem will be pleasing to the Lord* would be applicable if you were to think the words refer to Christ the Lord: at that time it was not sons of Levi alone who were the object of cleansing, but all people, to whom is therefore applicable the statement of blessed Paul, "Clean out the old leaven so as to be new dough, as you are unleavened."[29] Neither at that time did an offering of Judah in Jerusalem prove acceptable to God; on the contrary, when all sacrifice performed in Jerusalem in accordance with law came to an end for the reason that occupation of the site was terminated, a sacrifice both ineffable and rational emerged, which believers, not in Jerusalem, but everywhere in the world performed equally in memory of the passion [624] of the Lord and his resurrection from there. "Believe me, woman," he said, remember, "the hour is coming when neither in Jerusalem nor in this place will you worship the Father," and giving the reason, "God is a spirit, and those who worship him must worship in spirit and in truth, the Father seeking such as adore him,"[30] clearly showing that

29. 1 Cor 5.7.
30. See Jn 4.21–24, somewhat muddled. In view of arguments like these, it would be difficult to sustain a charge against Theodore of being *Ioudaiophron.* He comes through as no more partial to Jews and Jewish ways than he is inimi-

he repudiated those who confined divine worship to Jerusalem and Samaria, whereas he gave priority to the lovers of truth who equally throughout the world offer the sacrifice to God, who is the creator of everything and is equally present everywhere.

On the other hand, this refers appropriately to the time of the Maccabees, when, with the extreme prevalence of sin on the part of those who were thought to be exercising priesthood and also the people, God consigned them to the war of the kings of the Macedonian line, in the course of which they were enveloped in numerous troubles. When those of the company of Judas Maccabeus championed the divine Law, and on its behalf declared war on the Macedonian kings, a kind of massive reform happened to the whole race. In fact, in receipt of divine grace the Maccabees fought the kings, punished their depraved supporters, and brought the whole nation to a state of stability and good order, so that the divine laws were in force amongst them, all lawlessness previously in force was expelled from them, and the priesthood performed appropriately all the liturgy required of them. What blessed Zechariah had indicated in his words, therefore, he says here, too, Since you seek a just judgment, the time will come when I shall punish your sins, making your attitude sounder through the troubles inflicted, and, to rid you of the impurities of your former sins as in a furnace, I shall make you attentive to all God's decrees and especially to perform the offering of sacrifices to God in a pleasing way.

As a consequence of this, since he had mentioned the benefit of the punishment to be inflicted on them at that time, he goes on to provide the listeners with a more complete correction. So he says, *I shall draw near to you in judgment* (v.5), that is, I shall appear among you at that time judging what is done by you, *and shall be quick to be a witness against the sorcerers, against the adulterers, against those who swear falsely in my name, against those*

_____

cal to the person of Jesus; it is just that he is unwilling to wait for the NT for immediate application of OT texts, though admitting the οἰκονομία extends beyond that immediate application to where final and complete fulfillment is achieved.

*who deprive a worker of his wage, oppress widows, thrash orphans, per-
vert a judgment given in favor of a sojourner, and do not fear me, says
the Lord almighty,* bringing out in this all the evils they committed and for which they will pay the penalty. The phrase *quick to
be a witness* means, inflicting a rapid punishment from my precise knowledge of your record. On all these, he is saying, and
on absolutely all who are negligent in fearing me and have no
qualms about upholding evil ways I shall inflict such punishment. He then proceeds, *Because I am the Lord your God* [625]
*and do not change. You sons of Jacob do not desist from the sins of your
fathers, you turned away from my laws and did not observe them*
(vv.6–7): I am always the same, I know when to be tolerant and
I understand the time for punishment, whereas you are dili-
gent imitators of your fathers' sins, deviating from my laws like
them, and giving no importance to their observance, and for
this you will receive just punishment.

The prophet switches in turn to a different sin, which they
committed in connection with the firstfruits and the tithes in
their unwillingness to pay them in accord with the provision of
the Law. *Turn back to me, and I shall turn back to you, says the Lord
almighty:* incline towards me so that what comes from me may
also be agreeable to you. *You said, In what way shall we return?*
You think you do not need a return; thus you made any reversal
on my part imperceptible. *Does a human being cheat God? Because
you cheat me* (v.8): you believe this, thinking to deceive me; for
human beings to attempt this in regard to God is a mark of extreme naivety and madness. *You said, In what way did we cheat
you?* Without even doing it, you have a sense of the inappropriateness of what is being done. Then to specify the sin, *Because
the tithes and the firstfruits are with you; in your gazing you gaze at the
same thing, and you cheat me* (vv.8–9): you do not offer the tithes
and firstfruits to the priests in accordance with regulations, but
keep them for yourself; then, with the intention of procuring
some advantage for yourselves from this, and with a view to
some special benefit, you cannot sincerely do what you should,
namely, give what should be given by you. Instead, you pretend
to give what the law required by offering a few little baubles,
which is nothing other than a sign of your intending to deceive

me, for it would be a mark of deception not to repay sincerely a legitimate debt, but to attempt chicanery in repaying him.[31]

He then goes on, *The year is finished; you put the whole crop into the storehouses, and robbery of the poor is in your homes* (v.10): the year has reached its end, and the seasons of the year according to my arrangement have completed their course, and the produce of the crop was due to them. You then gathered the ripe crops from the ground and, though obliged to repay God for them with the offering of the firstfruits and tithes by way of thanksgiving, you did not do so, in effect casting only a few items at the priests and storing everything in your own storehouses. You do not even consider that this is no different from stealing food from the poor, the purpose for which this has been ordered by you to be provided, that those serving at the altar and those coming as suppliants to my Temple out of need may have their needs met.

He goes on in the same vein, [628] *Turn back with this, says the Lord almighty, unless I open to you the gates of heaven and pour out on you my blessing to the point of sufficiency, I shall distribute food among you, and not destroy the crops of the earth, and your vine will not wither in the field, says the Lord almighty. All the nations will count you happy, for you will be a chosen land, says the Lord almighty* (vv.10–12): reform yourselves and put a stop to all this; you will see how I shall provide you with abundant moisture, and how I shall provide you with an abundance of crops for satiety (the meaning of *my blessing to the point of sufficiency*) so that you will have a rich enjoyment of them (the meaning of *I shall distribute food among you*). All your crops will be kept unspoilt, the vine also providing you with its enjoyment in abundance, with the result that from your life of prosperity everyone living elsewhere will bless you because God has really decreed the best of good fortune for you so as to regale you with an abundance of crops from the soil far beyond the others.

Next, he returns to the former sentiments as though accord-

31. If the thinking is a little convoluted here, it may be because the LXX has seen in v.9 the notion of "gazing" by reading a similar form to the "cursing" of our Heb.

ing impious and vicious people a second admonition, saying, *You have burdened me with your words, says the Lord almighty* (v.13): you have directed harsh abuse at me. *You said, In what way have we reviled you?* Even then you have no awareness of such awful infamy (the prophet employing the term *You said* as if to reproach them with great insensitivity in being guilty of inappropriate behavior without having any awareness of it, and, instead, having such an attitude to their own sins as to think they had not even sinned). He then specifies the sin, *You said it is useless serving God* (v.14): no good comes to us from paying attention to the observance of what is commanded by him; instead, frequently nothing more comes to those appealing to him. Things reach the point where we are in need and distress, and we declare blessed others who set no store by his decrees, and for whom things turn out better, though always being hostile to him without suffering any harm from it. *Those fearing the Lord contested this, each one to their neighbor* (v.16): those who pretended in the face of all the foreigners to be in fear of me did not hesitate to say this to one another. God gave heed to them and left in writing a memorial of them for those coming later as to when those who used such words and were addicted to every form of lawlessness would pay the penalty.[32] On the other hand, every good thing would accrue to those really attentive to my laws, and I shall vouchsafe them my care at the time I punish the scoundrels, thus choosing to have them among my special friends and seeing fit to confer every highest favor on them in the manner of someone [629] well disposed to his son and always giving evidence of his benevolence towards him.

He then goes on, *You will be converted and see the difference between the righteous and the lawless, between the one serving God and the one not serving him* (v.18): at that time the difference will be made clear between the righteous and the lawless, between those zealous in serving God and those unwilling to give it any

---

32. Theodore's readers might have been interested in knowing if this record resembled the book in which the Lord enters the names of his people, as in Ex 32.32–33; Pss 69.28, 87.6; Dn 12.1. But this would be too much like ἀκριβολογία, and at this stage of the commentary when he is obviously hurrying (unlike his interest in matters of priesthood) he cannot be bothered.

importance, between the penalty for wickedness and the good things accruing to the upright; those who are evil make the distinction clear between the good and the evil. What he says is consistent with his former treatment of what would happen at the time of the Maccabees, when most of all the evil members of the people were the object of the severest punishment, and the lovers of the good were the beneficiaries of divine aid in everything.[33]

Chapter Four

Hence he goes on in confirmation of these words, *Because, lo, a day is coming, burning like a pan, and it will ignite them, and all the foreigners and all those committing crimes will be like straw, and the day that is coming will burn them, says the Lord almighty, and no root or branch of them will be left* (v.1): on that day all the foreigners will be set alight like fire, and the workers of iniquity will like straw be done away with by the punishment falling upon them. While he says this, then, of the wicked, what does he say to those who fear him? *For you who fear my name, a sun of righteousness will arise, and healing will be in its wings* (v.2): on you great distinction will rightly fall, supplied by God for your good will towards him; he will rid you of every trouble, sheltering you with his care as though by wings of a kind. You will be no different from calves released from bonds and leaping about with great joy; for you will have control over the lawless, who will be like ashes under your feet, at that time accorded no attention or further correction. Now, in this he refers, as I have often said, to events at the time of the Maccabees, when God provided his aid and punished the evil, while establishing in respite and prosperity those adhering to his laws, who punished and had complete control over the adversaries, not only those from the foreigners but also from their own people.[34] From that

33. It is an unconvincing recourse to historicizing the prophecy, no mention of the Maccabees having been made since his equally gratuitous preference of them to Jesus as the subject earlier.

34. Again, where there is question of an expression, "sun of righteousness," which the NT (see Lk 1.78, Jn 8.12) and the Christian liturgy seem to apply to

event it was obvious to all how great the difference between those serving God and those of the opposite mind, who were the object of severe punishment, whereas the former were established in extreme satisfaction and prosperity.

Now, this was the purpose of the prophecy of the blessed Messenger,[35] which he delivered to the people concerning matters affecting them, both at that time and at the time of the Maccabees. Yet since he was thus the last prophet of all those who consigned their prophecies to writing,[36] he was right in considering he could then show the end of the Law, on the one hand, and, on the other, show what would come after it. [632] Hence he says, *Remember the Law of Moses my servant, as I gave directions at Horeb as commands and ordinances for all Israel. Lo, I shall send you Elijah the Tishbite before the great and illustrious day of the Lord comes, which will reconcile a heart of a father to a son, and a person's heart to their neighbor, lest I come and strike the earth from on high* (vv.4–6): in addition to all that has been said I transmit this final command to you so that you may keep in mind my Law that I gave to the whole of Israel through Moses, having clearly stated that they must observe it in detail. The first token of obedience you will provide, then, will be acceptance of the coming of Christ the Lord, who comes for the salvation of all people: he will bring the Law to an end and make clear his own way of perfection. It would therefore be good for you immediately and at the outset to believe in him at his appearance, and acknowledge him to be the one whom Moses and all the prophets predicted as bringing an end to the Law and revealing the salvation of all in common. So it is also obvious to all that this is the summit and highest good of the whole economy of the Law,

---

Jesus, Theodore is in haste to head off any such application by rooting it in an historical situation.

35. That is, Malachi. See Theodore's opening comment on the prophet's name.

36. We have seen Theodore speaking variously of a prophet's ministry as preaching and as writing. Here also he anticipates a modern commentator like Rudolph in seeing the closing verses as the conclusion to the entire prophetic canon. But he is not likely to join the moderns in seeing the verses as two appendices by a later editor, partly on the grounds of the use of "day of the Lord" in place of Malachi's "coming day."

bringing all people to Christ the Lord, who appeared at that time for such wonderful benefits. Since, however, even at his revealing you will give evidence of your typical lack of responsiveness, blessed Elijah will be sent to you before the second coming of Christ the Lord, which he will make from heaven, so as to unite people divided over religion, and especially through the knowledge of religion to bring parents into harmony with their children who were formerly divided on the score of religion. In short, to reduce all people to the one and the same unity, so that those formerly in the grip of impiety may receive the knowledge of the truth through him and thus enjoy fellowship with religious people. God will do this in his concern for the salvation of all people, lest they persist in impiety and experience his fearsome coming, which will mean the utter annihilation of the wicked.[37]

37. After a ringing endorsement of the saving work of Jesus in his first and second comings—an encomium that doubtless helped ensure the work's survival—Theodore closes abruptly on the low note the prophet (or editor) sounds. Not surprisingly, he does not cite the NT citations of v.5 (Mt 17.11, Mk 9.12) and v.6 (Lk 1.17) lest these lend the text an eschatological dimension.

INDICES

GENERAL INDEX

INDEX OF HOLY SCRIPTURE

Old Testament

New Testament